AF725557

CHILD PERPETRATORS ON TRIAL

Following a devastating genocide in 1994, the Rwandan government elected to hold all perpetrators accountable – including children. Thousands of children were held in prisons while awaiting charges; some were later convicted. This book is about these children. Drawing on interviews and extensive archival research in Rwanda, it documents their journey through prisons, formal courts, *gacaca* proceedings or re-education centres. Its insights extend beyond Rwanda, looking at how international law protects children accused of even the most serious atrocities. The book is about law in action, and how states, and international organisations, operationalise international standards on child perpetrators in challenging post-conflict conditions. Engaging with theories from international law, international relations and anthropology, it illuminates strategies utilised by UNICEF to promote the rights of alleged child *génocidaires* and traces UNICEF's positive influence on their protection. It makes the case for principled pragmatism as an approach to human rights promotion in post-conflict societies.

JASTINE C. BARRETT is a UK-qualified lawyer and independent human rights consultant. She is currently an Honorary Researcher at Kent Law School, the University of Kent. Jastine completed her PhD at the University of Cambridge and also holds an LLM in International Law and International Relations and a BA(Hons) in Languages. She has served as Editor and Managing Editor for CJICL and on the management committee of the UK's Solicitors' International Human Rights Group. She is the author of several peer-reviewed articles and book chapters on international human rights law and transitional justice and has co-edited the *Research Handbook on Child Soldiers* with Mark Drumbl. Her research interests include international human rights and child rights law and transitional justice.

CHILD PERPETRATORS ON TRIAL

Insights from Post-Genocide Rwanda

JASTINE C. BARRETT

CAMBRIDGE
UNIVERSITY PRESS

CAMBRIDGE
UNIVERSITY PRESS

University Printing House, Cambridge CB2 8BS, United Kingdom

One Liberty Plaza, 20th Floor, New York, NY 10006, USA

477 Williamstown Road, Port Melbourne, VIC 3207, Australia

314–321, 3rd Floor, Plot 3, Splendor Forum, Jasola District Centre, New Delhi – 110025, India

79 Anson Road, #06-04/06, Singapore 079906

Cambridge University Press is part of the University of Cambridge.

It furthers the University's mission by disseminating knowledge in the pursuit of education, learning, and research at the highest international levels of excellence.

www.cambridge.org
Information on this title: www.cambridge.org/9781108496551
DOI: 10.1017/9781108678186

© Jastine C. Barrett 2019

This publication is in copyright. Subject to statutory exception and to the provisions of relevant collective licensing agreements, no reproduction of any part may take place without the written permission of Cambridge University Press.

First published 2019

A catalogue record for this publication is available from the British Library.

Library of Congress Cataloging-in-Publication Data
Names: Barrett, Jastine C., author.
Title: Child perpetrators on trial : insights from post-genocide Rwanda / Jastine C. Barrett, Independent Human Rights Consultant.
Description: New York: Cambridge University Press, 2019. | Includes bibliographical references and index.
Identifiers: LCCN 2019000711 | ISBN 9781108496551 (hardback) | ISBN 9781108733939 (paperback)
Subjects: LCSH: Juvenile delinquents – Rwanda. | Trials (Genocide) – Rwanda. | Rwanda – History – Civil War, 1994 – Atrocities.
Classification: LCC KTD472.2.B37 2019 | DDC 345.67271/0251–dc23
LC record available at https://lccn.loc.gov/2019000711

ISBN 978-1-108-49655-1 Hardback

Cambridge University Press has no responsibility for the persistence or accuracy of URLs for external or third-party internet websites referred to in this publication and does not guarantee that any content on such websites is, or will remain, accurate or appropriate.

The dilemma of dealing with children who are accused of committing acts of genocide illustrates the complexity of balancing culpability, a community's sense of justice and the 'best interests of the child'. [...] The severity of the crime involved, however, provides no justification to suspend or to abridge the fundamental rights and legal safeguards accorded to children under the Convention on the Rights of the Child.

– Graça Machel, *Impact of Armed Conflict on Children*, 1996

CONTENTS

FOREWORD

I remember them even though they were few in number and middling in stature. I remember them well, the children detained in the Kigali prison. I crossed their paths on my first journey to Rwanda – on my initial encounter with international criminal law, with mass atrocity and with law in the context of transition from collective violence. The year was 1998 and the moment was a haphazard, and altogether too brief, chance to work as a public defender representing individuals accused of genocide and crimes against humanity in regard to the violence that had metastasised throughout Rwanda in the spring and summer of 1994.

Despite their small numbers and modest size, these accused children left a mark on me. I am hopeful that I did the same, for them, in our interactions: a positive mark I might further hope. Yet I have lost track of them and their meanderings through the sinews of the Rwandan penal system. I know not how that system may have treated them, tried them, released them, acquitted them or left them. I hope their journey has been one of closure, rehabilitation and reintegration and that, in the event their hands had hurt others in that painful spring/summer of 1994, that those others – and all who loved those others – too have found a measure of peace and serenity over the course of the nearly 25 years that have since passed.

These children, together with all children accused of atrocity crimes in Rwanda – and, what is more, all children implicated in the commission of such crimes everywhere and anywhere in the world – are the protagonists of this stunning book, *Child Perpetrators on Trial: Insights from Post-Genocide Rwanda,* adroitly authored by Dr Jastine Barrett. Very little has been written about children who perpetrate atrocity crimes. Barrett's erudite and comprehensive book has the muster and muscularity to help fill many of these gaps.

Barrett writes deftly. She eschews the politics and posturing that plagues much of anything scholarly or journalistic penned about Rwanda today. Her book is about international law as it pertains to the child, what that law requires, including in the post-conflict, and how actors (states, international organisations and implicated individuals) contribute to the push-and-pull of actually operationalising it. Barrett's research methods are rich, ranging from first-person interviews to careful compilation of secondary sources with a fascinating perusal of internal grey material along the way. Her goal is to examine whether young age was a factor the Rwandan government took into account in its policies of maximal accountability and, concomitantly, whether these policies respected child rights standards. The verdict is mixed. Barrett concludes that '[w]hilst child perpetrators were, to some degree, given preferential treatment on account of their age and some progress was made in implementing international standards, on the whole, child perpetrators were not granted the full protection provided by international law.'

Barrett escorts her readers from room to room through doors carefully connected. Each room to and through which she leads her readers is a room brightened with windows whose views lead onto other new vistas.

One such vista is the role of the international organisation in lives lived locally. Barrett takes up UNICEF as a case study. Through its interventions and intercessions, she asks, did UNICEF as interlocutor make a difference? Devastated by genocide, with its infrastructure eviscerated, Rwanda nonetheless elected to proceed through a policy of maximal accountability. The Rwandan government initiated thousands of criminal prosecutions in Specialised Chambers of National Courts and then many hundreds of thousands of proceedings in *gacaca* tribunals. Throughout, UNICEF strove to advocate for international standards, best practices and commitments to juvenile justice to infuse and suffuse these proceedings. Infusion and suffusion, of course, were lofty goals, not realisable in light of time, resource and logistical constraints. But UNICEF did nudge the needle and move the bar some. Through what Barrett astutely describes as 'principled pragmatism', UNICEF made some difference. Barrett leverages her analysis into a broader rebuke of critical scholarship that portrays international organisations as painfully starry-eyed and myopically fixated on mandates rather than missions. She demonstrates, again through the work of UNICEF, that international organisations, even in the passionate area of children's rights, can act in measured fashion and achieve goals while compromising on what otherwise would be seen as sacrosanct, namely, the avoidance of incarceration for minors.

Another vista that Barrett opens is that of how the rights of the child still ought to be respected within the context of overall criminal proceedings that, as a whole, may fall short of the strictures of international human rights law generally as applicable to all who are accused. On this note, without explicitly saying so, Barrett's research reveals a continuum. Advocacy strategies adopted by UNICEF for minors largely resembled those adopted by other actors, whether domestic or transnational, for the overall treatment of the great number of people – children and adults, men and women – alleged to have contributed to the industrialisation of genocide. Children's rights are human rights; the rights of victims of atrocity to justice, as well, are human rights that ought to be articulable regardless of the characteristics of the harm-doer – whether child or adult, powerful or weak, convinced or confused, man or woman.

It is a great privilege to draft some prefatory words for a book of this stature. Lucid, compelling, comprehensive – Barrett delivers the signature volume on the intersection between children and transitional justice in Rwanda. Her advocacy for the application of international standards to such children is measured and meaningful. Her understanding of the need for social and moral justice, and her differentiation of these justice(s) from criminal justice is a brilliant insight. This insight, in turn, leads to yet another vista: the invocation of methods other than criminal trials to promote transitional and reconstructive goals in the wake of mass atrocity. In my own work I have argued in favour of such interventions generally in cases of children associated with armed groups or armed forces suspected of having been embroiled in the commission of international crimes. Barrett's leveraging of the Rwandan experience illustrates the need for such modalities – traditional ceremonies, truth-seeking initiatives, reciprocal obligations between youth and society – to fill the space between impunity and penalisation. If left unfilled, this space becomes a void. Several of Barrett's interlocutors underscore community scepticism of the victimhood and innocence of the juvenile *génocidaires*, findings which map onto what other researchers have identified elsewhere in regions unsettled by crimes committed by child soldiers. It is in the interests of former child soldiers, and all those committed to thinning gerontocracy, to meaningfully fill this space. This is because the emptiness of that space, paradoxically, accelerates the pull towards one of the two extremes, thereby encouraging the indulgence of 'it's not their fault' excuses (leading to the perfunctory return of the children to their communities) or the harshness of 'it's all their fault' condemnations (leading to indefinite detention or application of criminal law coercive even for adults). Each extreme is a poor result for children. Neither promotes or even comes remotely close to addressing their best interests.

The Rwandan genocide is a generation old. *Gacaca* trials have long ceased; criminal proceedings largely are no more; even the ICTR, directed by the Security Council to prosecute those most responsible, has shuttered after having completed its work. Rwanda is far more concerned with tech than with trials. But concerns over child soldiers persist globally. Tough questions now emerge.

Children in Rwanda committed crimes as part of governmental forces and related militia at the behest of the state. So, too, did children in Sierra Leone, for example, but in Sierra Leone many children also became implicated in the activities of armed groups and rebel factions – as has been the case elsewhere in Africa and throughout the world in dozens of jurisdictions as diverse as Nepal, Colombia, Sri Lanka, Uganda and the DRC. Today, non-state actors are the principal recruiters of children. Hotspots shift: now, to Iraq, Yemen and Syria. The role of ISIS and 'violent extremist' and 'terrorist' groups in deploying children, including as executioners and suicide bombers, has attracted considerable (and sensationalist) media attention but has elicited little in the way of thoughtful (and reflective) policymaking. Barrett's work is a wise antidote, and gentle civilising corrective, to contemporary discourse, often fuelled by security concerns, that may tend not to see the 'baleful child terrorist' as a 'protected child soldier' and, hence, to eschew the legal guarantees that would otherwise apply to the child soldier. On this note, Barrett's comprehensive documentation and exposition of the content of the law is an invaluable resource to international organisations and activists in their efforts to urge states to treat children captured in counter-terrorist actions in a manner that comports with the law and with sound reintegration policies that, in turn, can help decelerate new cycles of recruitment and recidivism. Advocates, in turn, perhaps might learn from the small moves that UNICEF had made in Rwanda in the past. And 'advocacy' today is different from advocacy in the 1990s. Rwanda's atrocities took place before the ubiquity of social media. Today anyone and everyone with an iPhone can be an activist, a compiler of evidence, a 'source'.

Child Perpetrators on Trial is never didactic. Barrett recounts. She neither tutors nor schools. Yet her book is wonderfully pedagogic. Rwanda's experiences become insights for tomorrow.

Mark A. Drumbl
Class of 1975 Alumni Professor of Law
Director, Transnational Law Institute
Washington and Lee University
Author of *Reimagining Child Soldiers in International Law and Policy* (OUP 2012)

PREFACE AND ACKNOWLEDGEMENTS

The idea for this book stemmed from a brief spell of volunteering at the Genocide Memorial Centre in Rwanda back in 2011. Walking around the exhibits and witnessing first-hand accounts from survivors, rescuers and perpetrators on my very first day in the 'office', I was struck not only by the vast numbers of victims killed during the 1994 Rwandan genocide, but also by the involvement of ordinary men and women – and children – as perpetrators.

My stay in Rwanda was just before I was to return to the UK to start a PhD at the University of Cambridge. Initially, I had planned to work on an entirely different research project (albeit also focused on perpetrators), but the memories from Rwanda stayed with me and, as a new project began to take shape, the child perpetrators of Rwanda occupied an increasingly dominant position in my research reflections. I wanted to know more about them – more about what happened to them after the genocide and what the Rwandan authorities had done with them. The international lawyer in me wanted to learn more about their rights under international law and how these rights played out in practice. I also wanted to know how international actors, in particular UNICEF – the lead UN agency for children – approached the issue of children accused of one of the gravest international crimes; what had it done to promote and protect their rights? This is not to say that I was more concerned about the rights of these children than the rights of victims and survivors – far from it. My experiences in Rwanda, which included assisting with the Genocide Memorial Centre's Social Programme and thus gave me the humbling opportunity to meet beneficiaries who had suffered horrific events, will always be with me. But my interest in human rights, child rights law and transitional justice, as well as my previous work on child soldiers, steered me down this research route.

The book is the culmination of a long and winding seven-year research, writing and editing journey, and it is only due to the help and support of numerous people and institutions along the way that this project has come to fruition. From my time at the University of Cambridge, I remain grateful for the advice, patience and encouragement from my PhD supervisor, Antje du Bois-Pedain, and for the guidance and, in particular, tips for conducting fieldwork from my adviser, Sarah Nouwen. I would also like to thank my PhD examiners, Nigel White and Stephanie Palmer, for their valuable comments and encouragement to take the PhD forward into a book. A postdoctoral position at Kent Law School gave me the time, space and financial support to continue working on this project and I would like to acknowledge and thank my colleagues at Kent, in particular Emily Grabham, Emily Haslam, Sara Kendall and Toni Williams for their words of encouragement and for help, in particular with some of the trickier aspects of writing up empirical research. I am also deeply grateful to Mark Drumbl, who has so generously provided time, advice and – not least – a fabulous foreword to this book. He has been a tremendous support and source of inspiration and humour over the last few years. I would also like to thank Phil Clark, Barbora Holà, Nicola Palmer and William Schabas for insights and information on Rwanda. Thanks are also due to Finola O'Sullivan, Marianne Nield and the rest of the team at Cambridge University Press (CUP) as well as to the two anonymous reviewers, whose instructive comments and suggestions have greatly improved this book.

This research benefited from generous financial assistance from The Modern Law Review Scholarship, as well as several funds in Cambridge whose contributions assisted fieldwork in Rwanda: The Smuts Memorial Fund, managed by the University of Cambridge in memory of Jan Christiaan Smuts, the UAC of Nigeria Travel Fund, the Yorke Fund, Cambridge University Fieldwork Funds and Magdalene College.

For assistance in Rwanda, my thanks go to the National University of Rwanda for sponsoring my project and assisting with the research authorisation process, and to the Ministry of Education for granting authorisation (clearance permit MINEDUC/S&T/0120/2013) for the research conducted in Rwanda as part of the PhD project on which this book builds.

Countless individuals from the Rwandan government and various institutions, in particular UNICEF (and its Innocenti Research Centre) and international and Rwandan NGOs, have shared with me valuable sources as well as their knowledge and expertise. In many cases, they also kindly agreed to be formally interviewed for this research, and I was also fortunate enough to be able to speak with a number of Rwandan judges, lawyers, prosecutors, judicial defenders and former detainees. These interviewees shared their personal experiences of encounters with the law, in practice, as it pertained to child perpetrators: experiences that were sometimes painful, often inspirational and always meaningful. This book would not have been possible without their contribution. My gratitude goes to all of my interviewees and informants who generously gave time and effort (extending, in one case, to driving from one country and across another solely to meet with me for an hour!) to assist with this research. Some participants are expressly mentioned in the book, but for those who are not listed for reasons of confidentiality or who did not formally participate, I hope that my acknowledgement of their contribution reaches them. A number of other individuals went out of their way to assist me in making contacts, procured documents and/or provided crucial information. In this regard, I am indebted to Nigel Cantwell and some dear friends in Rwanda – you know who you are – who graciously responded to my endless requests for information and assistance. I should also add that I bear sole responsibility for any errors or misinterpretations, and that the evaluations and conclusions are purely my own.

For moral support, advice, motivation and good company, I thank all those friends I made over the years at Cambridge (in particular Emma Bickerstaffe, Nora Ni Loideain, Jasmine Moussa and Shona Wilson Stark) as well as 'old' friends who have continued to provide their support. They are too many to mention all by name, but I am particularly grateful to Amanda Summerscales who was kind enough to read through the various iterations of the manuscript. I also thank my parents for their love, encouragement and support.

Moving closer to home, and although they will never read this book, special thanks go to Giuseppe and Huxley, for keeping me sane and never failing to amuse me. And last, but certainly not least, a final word of thanks to Paul, who endured this long and sometimes arduous book-writing journey with me. Without his belief in me and his support – moral, emotional and in the form of wine and good holidays – this book could not have been completed.

Parts of Chapters 6–8 are reproduced from Jastine C. Barrett, 'Balancing Pragmatism and Principle: UNICEF, Child Rights and Child *Genocidaires*', *Human Rights Law Review* 2018, Volume 18, Issue 1, 31–59, by permission of Oxford University Press.

ABBREVIATIONS

ACRWC	African Charter on the Rights and Welfare of the Child
ASF	Avocats Sans Frontières (Lawyers Without Borders)
ASOFERWA	Association de Solidarité des Femmes Rwandaises (Association for Solidarity of Rwandan Women)
CEDC	Children in especially difficult circumstances
CLADHO	Collectif des Ligues et Associations de Défense des Droits de l'Homme au Rwanda (Rwandan Collective of Leagues and Associations for the Defence of Human Rights)
CNLG	Commission Nationale de Lutte contre le Génocide (National Commission for the Fight against Genocide)
CRC	Convention on the Rights of the Child
CRC Committee	Committee on the Rights of the Child
DCHR	Danish Centre for Human Rights
EU	European Union
FAR	Forces Armées Rwandaises (Rwandan Armed Forces)
HRC	Human Rights Committee
HRW	Human Rights Watch
ICC	International Criminal Court
ICCPR	International Covenant on Civil and Political Rights
ICESCR	International Covenant on Economic, Social and Cultural Rights
ICRC	International Committee of the Red Cross
ICTR	International Criminal Tribunal of Rwanda
ILC	International Law Commission
IPJ	Inspecteur de police judiciaire (judicial police inspector)
IRIN	Integrated Regional Information Networks
LDGL	La Ligue des Droits de la Personne dans la Région des Grands Lacs (Great Lakes Human Rights League)
LIPRODHOR	Ligue Rwandaise pour la Promotion et la Défense des Droits de l'Homme (Rwandan League for the Promotion and Defence of Human Rights)
MIFAPROFE	Ministry of the Family and Women's Promotion
MIGEFASO	Ministry of Gender, Family and Social Affairs
MINALOC	Ministry of Local Government and Social Affairs

MINIJUST	Ministry of Justice
MINITRASO	Ministry of Labour and Social Affairs
MSF	Médecins Sans Frontières (Doctors Without Borders)
NGO	Non-governmental organisation
NHRC	National Human Rights Commission (Commission Nationale des Droits de l'Homme)
NPPA	National Public Prosecution Authority
NSGC	National Service of Gacaca Courts
NUR	National University of Rwanda
NURC	National Unity and Reconciliation Commission
OHCHR	Office of the United Nations High Commissioner for Human Rights
OPJ	Officier de police judiciaire (judicial police officer)
OSRSG-CAAC	Office of the Special Representative of the Secretary-General for Children and Armed Conflict
PAPG	Projet d'Appui de la Société Civile au Processus Gacaca au Rwanda (Civil Society Project in Support of the Gacaca Process in Rwanda)
PRI	Prison Reform International
RCN	Réseau de Citoyens (Citizen's Network)
RDRC	Rwandan Demobilisation and Reintegration Commission
RPA	Rwandan Patriotic Army
RPF	Rwandan Patriotic Front
SCF	Save the Children Fund
SCSL	Special Court for Sierra Leone
TIG	Travail d'intérêt général (community service)
TRC	Truth and Reconciliation Commission
UDHR	Universal Declaration of Human Rights
UN	United Nations
UNAMIR	United Nations Assistance Mission for Rwanda
UNDG	United Nations Development Group
UNDP	United Nations Development Programme
UNESCO	United Nations Educational, Scientific and Cultural Organization
UNGA	United Nations General Assembly
UNHCR	United Nations High Commissioner for Refugees
UNHRFOR	United Nations Human Rights Field Operation in Rwanda
UNICEF	United Nations Children's Fund
UNSC	United Nations Security Council
UNSG	United Nations Secretary-General

1

Introduction

'I went to prison when I was 17. When I came out, I was 28: it is the whole era that has been killed.' These compelling words of lost youth were recounted to me by Lucien,* arrested in January 1995 and released from prison in August 2005.

One of five children, Lucien was attending high school in April 1994, when one of the most horrific and brutal killing sprees of the twentieth century unfolded. Over the next few weeks, Lucien joined his neighbours on the roadblock – 'everyone was there' – but he denies killing anyone: 'Our area was quiet; no-one was killed at our roadblock. In our village, almost everybody I know was killed by people from the next village to us.'

Yet, in January 1995, a neighbour accused Lucien of killing three people. Picked up off the street, Lucien was taken by soldiers to a local prison, where he was placed in a holding cell with around 65 other people: 'It was horrible – the soldiers would come during the night and call people out and you would never see them again. Everyone was waiting for his time to come.' One day, Lucien was called into the office, where he was interrogated by judicial police about the killings. Denying any involvement, he was beaten with large branches and glass bottles, before being sent back to the holding cell.

Lucien was transferred to a central prison about a week after his (informal) arrest. From then until 2001, he was never called to appear before a judge, never spoke to anyone from the prosecutor's office, never saw a lawyer, and he had no official case file: all he recalled seeing was a scrap of paper from a notebook that the judicial police had referred to when initially questioning him.

Life in prison was 'painful, disrespectful': Lucien struggled to put into words just how difficult he found it. When he first arrived in 1995, people were dying every day from dysentery and cholera, prisoners were

* Not his real name.

tortured, and they would never know when the next meal was coming. Things on that front improved once the International Committee of the Red Cross got involved. Yet life in prison was also 'good': 'it was good because of all the knowledge I acquired, all the people I met – I had a new family I met in there. I had experience of being a leader of a lot of people from all walks of life. That's the good side.' Although only 17 when first imprisoned, Lucien was incarcerated with adults. There was a specific quarter for minors in his prison, but only 'small children' stayed there.

On New Year's Day in 2003, Lucien was listening to the radio. He heard President Kagame announce the decision to release certain categories of detainees – including minors. Initially hopeful that he, along with others under 18 at the time of the genocide, would be released, his hopes were dashed when the Chief Prosecutor came to the prison later that month and told them that only those minors who had admitted to their participation in the genocide would be liberated. As a result, only a couple of minors were released from his prison: one who had admitted to killing more than ten people; a second who had confessed to being part of a 'killing group' but claimed that he himself had not killed anyone. Those who proclaimed their innocence remained in prison. Two years later, he heard again that the same categories would be released – this time, it included all minors: not just those who had confessed. Whilst Lucien was released at this time, the release was conditional. Lucien first had to spend one month at a solidarity camp before he was formally released to go home. And, once back in his village, he was summoned to a local *gacaca* court, which was collating information on genocide crimes committed in the area. One of the *gacaca* judges – the same neighbour who had accused him in 1995 of committing the killings – stood up during the meeting and accused him of wanting to kill her during the genocide. Lucien denied the allegations; the meeting was adjourned. After the meeting, neighbours told Lucien that the woman was looking for people to kill him. With these threats, and 'not having any faith in the *gacaca* courts … in that kind of justice', Lucien decided to leave Rwanda: his intention was to return if things got back to normal. He left Rwanda in October 2005. His case is still pending. He has been told that it would be heard by the formal courts if he were to return, now that the *gacaca* courts have concluded their proceedings. But Lucien stays where he is: 'If I have faith in justice, I could go back, but the way it is now, I don't think so.'

Lucien's story is just one of many. Over 4,500 'children' – a term I use throughout this book to refer to persons below the age of 18 in accordance with Article 1 of the Convention on the Rights of the Child[1] – were held in Rwandan prisons in 1998, most accused of participating in the genocide. Some denied any wrongdoing; others admitted to committing crimes, including the most heinous of crimes, often under duress but sometimes seemingly with zeal. This book is about them. It is about their journey from the genocide through prisons, formal courts, *gacaca* proceedings or re-education centres – a journey that in many cases took years. Whilst they were under 18 and thus 'minors'[2] at the time of their alleged crime, often by the time their cases were processed, they were well into adulthood. Nonetheless, for the purposes of their penal accountability, certain sanctions, and also arguably for their procedural rights under international law, they remain 'minors' or 'juveniles'.[3] I therefore use these (and related) terms throughout this book to refer to individuals who were under the age of 18 at the time of the genocide, but the reader should remain aware that these 'minors' or 'juveniles' may have been in their mid-20s or early 30s when the relevant judicial or administrative measure was taken (a point to which I return at various stages in the book). This time lag between the alleged acts and the accountability measure, uncommon perhaps in 'normal' circumstances, was particularly notable in Rwanda, but may also arise in other post-conflict states,[4] and illustrates the complexities of holding minors accountable for atrocities where trials (and other responses) occur many years after the fact.

The book not only documents the journey of these children however; it is also about international law. It is about how international law protects children like Lucien as well as those who committed the most serious

[1] Note that, where this term (and other similar terms) is used in this book in the context of juvenile justice, the age refers to age at the time of the alleged commission of the act, unless otherwise stated.

[2] 'Minor(s)' is used interchangeably with – and in the same sense as – child(ren) in this book. Additionally, for the purposes of this book: 'juveniles' are those above the age of criminal responsibility (the lowest age at which persons can be held criminally responsible) but below 18 (the age of penal majority in many states, which is the lowest age at which persons can be held responsible in adult criminal courts) (except in the phrase 'juvenile justice' which may include children below the minimum age); and 'non-responsible children' are those below the age of criminal responsibility.

[3] Additionally, Rwandan legislation and official documents, as well as reports by international agencies and civil society frequently use these terms to refer to those under 18 at the time of their alleged participation in the genocide, even where these individuals were (often significantly) over 18 at the time the relevant document was issued.

[4] The term 'post-conflict state' is used to describe states emerging from conflicts, genocide and other widespread violence.

atrocities. It is about international law in action. It is about how states, but also international organisations – with a particular emphasis on UNICEF (United Nations Children's Fund) – operationalise international standards on child perpetrators in the very challenging conditions of post-conflict societies.

The book centres on children accused of genocide in Rwanda. But its insights extend well beyond Rwanda. Whilst Rwanda may have been the first country to try children, on a large scale, for atrocities, it is far from being the only country in which atrocities have been committed by minors. Of course, it is important to emphasise that children are very frequently the *victims* of international crimes – the core crimes being war crimes, crimes against humanity and genocide.[5] And it is equally important to recall that, whilst children may be associated with armed groups, not all such children commit atrocities: indeed, only a small minority become involved in their perpetration, and very often under coercion or manipulation. But there are reports of children committing such acts throughout the world: in the last three decades, 'Small Boys Units', which counted children as young as seven or eight amongst their members, wielded grenades, knives and machetes in Sierra Leone, amputating limbs, raping and burning people alive; troops of 'little boys' attacked civilians in Mozambique; and 13-year-olds summarily executed prisoners and civilians in Colombia.[6] In ongoing conflicts[7] that frequently hit the headlines today, girls commit suicide attacks in the Lake Chad Basin, 12- and 13-year-olds execute and behead prisoners in Syria, and children as young as seven are trained as suicide bombers in Iraq, Pakistan and the Sudan.[8] Distinctions are often drawn between children involved in these ongoing conflicts and the child soldier of yesteryear, yet how to deal with these children presents similar challenges, and their protection under international law is the same.

[5] For the purposes of this book, 'international crimes' is used to refer to offences over which international courts and tribunals have jurisdiction pursuant to international law.

[6] See e.g. Amnesty International 2000b; Drumbl 2012 (in particular chapter 3); Fisher 2013 (in particular chapter 1); HRW 1996, 1999 and 2003c; Oosterveld 2019. See also references in section 4.1.2 for literature relating to Rwanda.

[7] 'Conflict' is used here not solely in the legal sense of an 'armed conflict' (for which a certain threshold of confrontation must be met) but also to cover widespread violence which may give rise to crimes against humanity or genocide crimes.

[8] See e.g. Bloom 2019; Casey-Maslen 2019. See also various reports by UNSG referencing the use of children by armed groups as suicide bombers and executioners.

Countries that are emerging from conflict and that are attempting to address large-scale human rights violations have to grapple with the question: what to do with these children? The way countries deal with the legacy of past violations differs: some take a minimal, or even zero, approach to accountability, offering amnesty to perpetrators; some use a truth-seeking mechanism that explores the crimes committed and that may be accompanied by amnesty or by restorative justice that holds perpetrators accountable through non-judicial processes; and others decide to hold perpetrators individually accountable through criminal prosecutions.[9] Where a country opts for the judicial trial-based approach, they most often pursue those most responsible for the most serious crimes. However, what happens where a country resolves to try all those responsible and thus adopts a maximalist approach to accountability? What happens to child perpetrators then?

International law does not preclude the prosecution of children for atrocities although the enforcement of criminal responsibility in respect of child perpetrators has effectively been left to the discretion of individual states. When states pursue domestic prosecutions of minors, customary and conventional human rights law prescribe a number of minimum standards that must be respected. In addition to customary rules, the International Covenant on Civil and Political Rights (ICCPR) contains due process guarantees in respect of all persons who come into conflict with the law and has some juvenile-specific provisions. The Convention on the Rights of the Child (CRC) (which has achieved almost universal ratification – the United States being the only country not to have ratified it), however, is the most significant human rights treaty in this regard with a number of juvenile justice standards. The CRC is supplemented by non-binding instruments that expand on the rights of child offenders.[10]

None of these instruments (binding or non-binding) specifically address crimes that are committed in the context of a conflict or genocide. However, the applicability of juvenile justice standards to children accused of atrocities has been affirmed by the United Nations (UN), most notably by a 1996 report on the 'Impact of Armed Conflict on Children'

[9] These are not the only ways states may deal with the past: there are also other mechanisms including lustration or vetting, institutional reform, reparations and traditional forms of justice or reconciliation, all of which come under the umbrella of 'transitional justice'. See UNSG 2004: [8].

[10] 'Offender' and 'perpetrator' are used for ease to refer to alleged or convicted individuals (unless specified).

by Graça Machel.[11] The standards in the CRC are binding in respect of all children in states that have ratified the treaty. Thus, all children who come into conflict with the law – be it as ordinary citizens in a non-conflict situation, as part of an armed militia group involved in a civil war or as a member of a group designated as 'terrorist' – are entitled to child rights protections. Child rights law does not differentiate.

Yet in the aftermath of an armed conflict, genocide or other widespread violence, a state faces multiple challenges which may include dealing with the past, reconstructing state institutions, re-establishing security, restoring social cohesion and rebuilding the domestic economy. International human rights organisations, including UN bodies and agencies and international non-governmental organisations (NGOs),[12] provide substantial assistance to post-conflict recovery. Frequently such assistance encompasses support to, and advice on, the transitional justice process. Where fragile, post-conflict states pursue a transitional justice policy that involves criminal prosecutions of minors, full compliance with binding juvenile justice standards and best practice presents significant, and arguably insurmountable, challenges. Whilst the state has primary responsibility for the implementation of, and compliance with, international standards, other actors do have a role in providing assistance, and thus an opportunity to enhance the rights of the child perpetrator.

This book explores how substantive international standards on child perpetrators of atrocities were, and can be, operationalised (i.e. put into practice through legal and policy initiatives) in a post-conflict society. Where a post-conflict state has decided to prosecute minors for atrocity crimes, what are the implications? Is it possible for a post-conflict state to comply with international standards? What do these standards require of states and do they make any allowances for the type of crime or for the specific context in which they are to be implemented? What mechanisms exist to promote and protect the rights of child offenders? How do international actors seek to enhance implementation of, and compliance with, international standards? What strategies and techniques do they use? By focusing on a state that was reportedly the first country to try, on a large scale, individuals for atrocities committed when they were minors, this book addresses those questions and provides an account of the operationalisation of juvenile justice standards in post-genocide Rwanda.

[11] Machel 1996: [250–251].

[12] These organisations are referred to collectively in this book as 'international actors'.

1.1 Child Perpetrators of Genocide: Mapping the Underexplored

Lucien, whose story opens this book, admitted to being present at a roadblock. But children participated in the whole range of acts committed during the genocide, both through the more organised structures of the Rwandan army and the *Interahamwe*[13] militia, and as part of the general mobilisation of the civilian population. Having taken a maximalist approach to accountability and thus the decision to prosecute all those who took part in the genocide, Rwanda tried many of these children over the next few years either before its formal courts or later before the *gacaca* courts, a more informal justice mechanism. Children who were too young to be prosecuted were sent to re-education centres. In all of its dealings with these children, Rwanda was obliged to comply with international standards: Rwanda is (and was at that time) a party to the CRC (and the ICCPR). Yet, Rwanda had been ravaged by conflict and a genocide that had devastated its institutions, including the penitentiary and judicial system, and ruptured the social fabric. The Rwandan government did not, however, operate in a vacuum. In the aftermath of the genocide, international actors were heavily involved in the reconstruction process, in particular by providing significant support to the justice system (including prisons). As pertains to children, UNICEF – the lead UN agency for children in conflict with the law – was the most active organisation. Rwanda thus provides an optimal opportunity to examine in detail how child perpetrators were dealt with, and also how international actors – with a particular emphasis on UNICEF – sought, and indeed may seek, to translate international juvenile justice standards into practice in a post-conflict society.

Whilst there is a significant body of literature dealing with child soldiers generally, and more specifically with the prohibition on, and crime of, recruiting children under 15 into armed forces and groups, comparatively little has been written on child perpetrators of atrocities. The limited legal scholarship that has addressed child perpetrators (often in tandem with a discussion on child soldier recruitment) has focused on whether such children *should* be held accountable (a debate that will not be entered into in any great depth in this book[14]), reviewed the

[13] The *Interahamwe* (which means 'those who work/fight together') was the youth wing of the ruling party.

[14] A comprehensive discussion would entail consideration of areas such as developmental psychology, penal theory and theories of agency and would constitute a book in itself.

jurisdiction of international courts and tribunals over children, or theoretically considered what standards apply where a state seeks to hold children accountable.[15] There has been very little empirical investigation into the implications (in particular as regards child rights) of a state's decision to pursue accountability measures for children accused of atrocities. With specific reference to Rwanda, there has been some research into children accused of involvement in the genocide, but this has been limited in terms of detail, the time period covered, or the particular accountability measure taken. For example, Morrill has considered juveniles and the *gacaca* jurisdictions as well as some administrative measures that were adopted,[16] Sullo has briefly addressed trials before the formal courts and the *gacaca* courts,[17] and Cantwell has examined the treatment of child *génocidaires* up until December 1996.[18] International human rights organisations have also produced analytical reports, either reviewing Rwanda's post-conflict judicial mechanisms in general but touching on child perpetrators, or dealing specifically with children affected by the genocide including child perpetrators.[19] There has been, however, no comprehensive exploration of how Rwanda approached the issue of child *génocidaires* or how international standards were operationalised.

This book thus addresses these lacunae in knowledge by synthesising data on law, policy and practice to provide a comprehensive account of

[15] Important contributions in this area are Drumbl 2012, Fisher 2013 (who focuses specifically on child soldiers who have perpetrated atrocities), Happold 2005 and Steinl 2017 (who also focuses on child soldiers involved in international crimes). Other works include: Amann 2001 (on the SCSL); Aptel 2010 (on the approach of international courts/tribunals to crimes against, and perpetrated by, children); Arts and Popovski 2006 (with contributions from academics and practitioners in law and psychology on children as victims, perpetrators and witnesses); Arzoumanian and Pizzutelli 2003 (on accountability of child perpetrators); Bakker 2010 (on responsibility of both recruiters of children and child perpetrators); Cohn and Goodwin-Gill 1994 (on child soldiers generally and their protection in international law); Freeland 2008 (on the prohibition and crime of child soldier recruitment and international criminal law's approach to child perpetrators); Grossman 2007 (on prosecuting child soldiers); Mezmur 2008 (on the prohibition and crime of child soldier recruitment and international criminal law's approach to child perpetrators). There are also numerous works on child soldiers in other disciplines, such as Grover 2012, Honwana 2006 and Wessells 2009, none of which examine in any detail the domestic prosecution of child perpetrators.

[16] Morrill 2004 and 2005.

[17] Sullo 2012.

[18] Cantwell 1997. Reports on the situation of child *génocidaires* (up to the year 2000) were also commissioned by UNICEF Rwanda. See Chorlton 1996; Racine 1998; van Krieken 2000.

[19] See in particular HRW 2003a.

Rwanda's treatment of 'child *génocidaires*' or 'genocide minors'. These terms are used interchangeably throughout the book to describe persons under 18 at the time of the genocide and in a neutral sense as to innocence or guilt (unless specified).[20] Where I use these terms in connection with any organisation, it should be noted that these are my own words, unless appearing in a direct citation.

The purpose of this book is not to resolve whether Rwanda's decision to prosecute minors was correct or justifiable or explore what the alternatives might have been (such as participation in a truth and reconciliation commission – TRC – or traditional justice ceremonies). This would require a detailed analysis of whether the Rwandan government's maximal approach to criminal accountability for all genocide perpetrators was appropriate, considering for example the extent to which a focus on individual criminal accountability in general is appropriate for collective crimes[21] and the implications of such an approach for post-conflict reconstruction.[22] It would also necessitate engaging in the debate as to whether children should be prosecuted for such crimes. Rather, working from the basis that the Rwandan government had adopted a policy that sought 'universal accountability' for genocide-related crimes through 'indiscriminate prosecution of all suspected perpetrators',[23] the book considers whether young age was a factor taken into account by the Rwandan government and whether child rights standards were broadly respected or violated. It reveals that child *génocidaires* were to some degree given preferential treatment on account of their age but, on the whole, were not granted the full protection envisaged under the CRC.

In addition to the detailed appraisal of Rwanda's approach to child perpetrators, the book explores and analyses the interventions of international actors in Rwanda. It focuses in particular on the activities and

[20] The term '*génocidaire*' is widely used in Rwanda without distinction between those accused, and those convicted, of genocide crimes although it must be stressed that some of those accused of genocide, and who spent years in pre-trial detention, were later acquitted. As will be seen, there were children who were accused of participating in the genocide but who were never convicted and thus these terms, in most instances, will denote those 'accused' or 'suspected' of genocide crimes.

[21] For a detailed discussion on this, see Drumbl 2007.

[22] On this in the Rwandan context, see Gahima 2013 (in particular 283–286), who suggests that universal accountability where a large section of the population has participated may jeopardise the development of the rule of law and peace building, as well as violate human rights, particularly where the justice system lacks resources and capacity; Sarkin 2001.

[23] Gahima 2013: 129.

approach of UNICEF to realising the rights (in particular pursuant to the CRC) of child perpetrators. Galligan and Sandler note in relation to the international human rights regime generally (as opposed to child rights specifically): 'How significant its institutions and strategies are, is a matter of empirical investigation which to date hardly exists.'[24] Whilst there is some limited literature on UNICEF's relationship with the CRC and its role in implementing child rights standards,[25] empirical studies on the implementation of, and compliance with, juvenile justice standards in a post-conflict society are lacking, particularly relating to the role of international institutions such as UNICEF.[26] One of the main goals of the book is thus to fill this gap in scholarship by exploring UNICEF intersectionally with child perpetrators in post-conflict zones. The book undertakes an institutional analysis of UNICEF, including a detailed review of its relationship with, and role under, the CRC, as well as its evolving commitment to the area of juvenile justice. Whilst UNICEF is now the lead UN agency for children in conflict with the law, it was only during the mid-1990s that child protection (considered a sensitive and controversial area) became a core concern for UNICEF at the global policy level – precisely around the time that UNICEF Rwanda[27] was encountering children detained in Rwandan prisons. With this context in mind, the book engages in a multi-disciplinary and empirically grounded examination and evaluation of the activities of UNICEF Rwanda, as well as of the strategic approach and techniques adopted to enhance implementation of, and compliance with, international standards in post-genocide Rwanda.

'Implementation' and 'compliance' are often used interchangeably in scholarly work on human rights as well as by human rights institutions but have different meanings. In this book, 'implementation' is used to mean the process of incorporating international norms into domestic law through legislative assimilation, judicial decision, executive decree,

[24] Galligan and Sandler 2004: 30.

[25] E.g. Himes 1993; Oestreich 1998 and 2007.

[26] Landgren (2007) provides a short review of UNICEF's child protection activities (including in juvenile justice) in post-conflict societies and mentions briefly its involvement in Rwanda and Sierra Leone, but does not provide a comprehensive, empirically grounded evaluation. See also the works referenced in note 18 above (which are limited in scope).

[27] This term is used to distinguish the Rwandan field office from the global agency or headquarters in New York (referred to as 'UNICEF headquarters'). Further, as will be illustrated later, much of UNICEF's work in Rwanda relied on the initiative of individual staff members (including consultants) and thus, when I use the term 'UNICEF Rwanda', it is in a broad sense to include such staff members.

or other process.[28] 'Compliance' is a broader concept and is 'concerned with factual matching of state behavior and international norms'.[29] Often, implementation is a 'critical step toward compliance',[30] but compliance may occur without any implementing measures having been taken: a state's behaviour may be consistent with a norm for reasons other than its commitment to that norm.[31] As the main focus here is on the approach adopted by UNICEF Rwanda to translate international standards into policy and practice, the book works from the premise that UNICEF Rwanda's ultimate objective was for Rwanda to comply with international standards. In some cases, however, UNICEF Rwanda explicitly sought changes to domestic legislation (thus 'implementation'), with the aim of inducing compliance (although this was not always the end result). As such, the terms are generally used in tandem throughout the book.[32]

The book argues that UNICEF Rwanda was principled yet pragmatic when seeking to enhance implementation of, and compliance with, international juvenile justice standards. This involved interpreting the international standards in light of the prevailing context, whilst remaining faithful to child rights principles, and using various strategies and techniques, which were broadly collaborative and constructive rather than coercive and critical. The book evaluates the extent to which, by using this approach, UNICEF Rwanda was able to exert some positive influence that increased recognition of, and respect for, the rights of child *génocidaires*. Acknowledging that UNICEF Rwanda's approach was very much shaped by the Rwandan context and UNICEF's institutional structure, the book then addresses how far this approach could be considered an appropriate and valid means of operationalising international standards in a post-conflict society.

1.2 Approach, Assumptions and Methodology

As stated earlier, the central objectives of the book are to investigate how Rwanda dealt with child *génocidaires*, in law, policy and practice, including

[28] Shelton 2000: 5. See also Murray and Long 2015: 27, who adopt this definition.

[29] Shelton 2005: 5. See also Murray and Long 2015: 27–28; Risse and Ropp 2013: 10.

[30] Indeed, implementation could be seen as 'legal' compliance (rather than compliance in practice).

[31] Raustiala and Slaughter 2002: 539.

[32] Note that, in some instances (particularly when referring to CRC Committee documentation), 'implementation' is used in a broader sense, as this is the term used by the relevant organisation or particular commentator.

a consideration of whether children benefited from special treatment as required by international law, and to examine and evaluate how international actors sought to operationalise international juvenile justice standards in a post-conflict context. The research proceeds from the basic premise that the current international standards on child perpetrators are appropriate and sufficient and does not aim to be normative by providing recommendations as to how the standards might be improved or in the sense of evaluating the usefulness of the standards themselves.

While it is an aim of this book to explain positively why certain steps towards greater compliance were taken when they were taken, my methodology does not allow me to provide an in-depth evaluation or theoretical exploration of the reasons why Rwanda fell short in complying with certain standards where shortcomings could be observed. There were numerous variables at play in Rwanda, including lack of capacity, political will (or lack thereof) to respect international law, the desire to put an end to impunity and also a hostile social context. These are all likely to have played a role in how Rwanda approached child perpetrators and it would be difficult to isolate the part played by each variable. Having considered the various challenges faced by Rwanda and the government's overall approach to accountability, I thus work from the assumption that all of these variables played a role, to a greater or lesser degree.

The research is also predicated on the assumptions that UNICEF Rwanda (and other international actors) intended to elicit implementation of, and compliance with, international standards; that international standards can be operationalised in the sense that international law can influence state behaviour; and that there are observable strategies and tactics that can be analysed. Whilst I seek to evaluate the approach adopted by UNICEF Rwanda, including the limitations and risks of the approach as well as the perceived results, the intention is not to quantify or measure actual impact. As will be elucidated in more detail in Chapter 8, there are significant difficulties in establishing causation, and measuring actual impact would require a much more detailed analysis than is possible given the data limitations outlined below. As such, the objective of the study is to identify the strategies and overall approach that UNICEF Rwanda considered useful, or even necessary, when seeking to enhance implementation and compliance, and some broad conclusions are drawn as to whether the data *suggest* that such an approach did have some positive influence.

Given the focus on the operationalisation of international standards on child perpetrators in post-conflict situations, the book adopts a multidisciplinary approach that draws upon literature from various fields and disciplines. These include scholarly works on child rights (and juvenile justice specifically), the promotion and protection of human rights, the UN, post-conflict transition and transitional justice. The book engages with theories from international law, international relations and to a lesser extent anthropology, but does not seek to explore in detail, critique, qualify or test these theories: rather they are used to provide the theoretical and conceptual backdrop to the arguments advanced. From a theoretical perspective, whilst I do not aim to prove any particular theory, or indeed develop a new theory, the findings here, namely that UNICEF adopted an approach of principled pragmatism, offer insights for incremental advances in theories on human rights promotion in post-conflict societies. From a policy perspective, the findings illuminate strategies that were used by, and found helpful for, UNICEF and that could thus be used to make inroads in extremely challenging circumstances elsewhere.

1.2.1 Collection of Empirical Material

Given the emphasis in the book on 'law in action', the research underpinning much of this book is empirically grounded, although doctrinal analysis of legislation and case law was undertaken to review international standards and Rwanda's domestic laws on child offenders. Additionally, I engaged in a detailed institutional analysis for the examination of mechanisms that promote child rights, in particular UNICEF, in Chapter 3. For the practical application of Rwanda's domestic laws, and a consideration of other criminal justice and administrative measures adopted by Rwanda, and for the approach adopted by international actors, I employed qualitative empirical research methods. These included, in particular, semi-structured interviews supported by archival research and documentary analysis of official publications, articles by scholars, published reports and policy papers by international actors, and 'grey literature'.[33] Although an element of caution must be observed when utilising grey literature on the basis that these documents may not reflect what happened in practice or be illustrative of an official approach, it has nonetheless been necessary to rely on such documentation given the dearth of published information. Efforts were made, however, to verify information from these documents

[33] 'Grey literature' in this book refers to policy documents, notes, memoranda, summary reports and other documents, usually unpublished and/or difficult to find through conventional sources.

through a process of triangulation using interviews with individuals from various organisations and backgrounds, and with different perspectives and interests.[34]

I undertook fieldwork in Rwanda from January to March 2013 and August to October 2013 to collect data. Authorisation was obtained from the Rwandan Ministry of Education to conduct the research, after obtaining ethics clearance and sponsorship of the project by the National University of Rwanda (NUR).[35] In addition to consulting the archives of various organisations for relevant documents,[36] I conducted in-depth semi-structured interviews with key stakeholders including judges, prosecutors, defence lawyers, government officials, policy framers and staff of NGOs and international agencies. Eighty-five individuals participated in interviews either in person or over telephone or Skype.[37] Interviews in Rwanda were conducted predominantly in Kigali, although some were conducted in the Western and Northern Provinces and also with participants travelling to, or based in, Kigali but who had worked in other regions. This was to ensure that views from outside the capital were included. I conducted the majority of interviews in French,[38] with the remainder in English. Interviews were conducted with the express consent of participants[39] and, where possible and with consent, I recorded and subsequently transcribed the interviews. For interviews that were not recorded, detailed notes were taken and written up the same day. Interviewees are referenced by name solely with their explicit consent. For most formal court judges, *gacaca* judges, lawyers, judicial defenders and NGO staff members, I do not reveal the interviewee's identity but for these participants, and for others who chose to remain anonymous, I do note their professional status and/or institutional affiliation to provide greater context. All individuals were questioned in a personal capacity and were not therefore speaking officially on behalf of the organisations or authorities for which they worked and, accordingly, any views expressed by them do not necessarily reflect those of

[34] See Shaffer and Ginsberg 2012: 4 for an explanation of triangulation.

[35] Ethics clearance for the research was also obtained from the University of Cambridge.

[36] See Annex 1 for a list of archives consulted.

[37] Participants were identified initially by purposeful sampling (drawing on desk-based research and advice from contacts at the NUR and UNICEF) and then snowball sampling.

[38] Note that all translations from French into English are my own.

[39] Prior to each interview, I provided each participant with an information sheet and a broad explanation of the research aims.

their organisation/authority.[40] Further, any conclusions drawn from interviews regarding the Rwandan state's response or an organisation's approach or viewpoint are my own – and, indeed, many participants may well disagree with my conclusions, evaluations and, in some cases, critical observations. Similarly, where names are provided, any errors in the name or position are my own.

1.2.2 *Methods Used in Data Evaluation*

Drawing on grounded theory approaches to analysing qualitative data,[41] the interviews were coded and analysed to generate concepts and theoretical categories, with further data being collected to develop and refine these theoretical categories through comparative analysis. Through this inductive process, it was possible to gather data for the descriptive analysis of what measures were taken by the Rwandan government, as well as identify the overall approach and the strategies and techniques adopted by UNICEF Rwanda, which ultimately form the basis of the review and evaluation in Chapters 6 to 8. Additionally, whilst this book does not seek to measure the impact of UNICEF Rwanda's approach, it utilises process tracing,[42] involving rigorous/close analysis of archival documents, interview transcripts and other sources, to suggest where UNICEF Rwanda appears to have exerted some positive influence on Rwanda's implementation of, or compliance with, international standards. The end product is thus an interpretative analysis of how international standards can be operationalised in a post-conflict society.

1.2.3 *Challenges and Limitations*

Conducting fieldwork in Rwanda posed a number of methodological challenges, particularly given the sensitive nature of the research topic. These ranged from obtaining research authorisation prior to commencing the research (with several contacts expressing surprise that authorisation had been granted for such a politically sensitive topic), to obtaining access to sources, establishing trust with participants and issues relating

[40] Note also – as later emphasised – the importance of individual initiative within UNICEF Rwanda, given UNICEF's decentralised structure as well as the lack of institutional guidance on juvenile justice at the time.

[41] Corbin and Strauss 2008; Gibson and Hartman 2014.

[42] See George and Bennett 2005: 6–7 and 206–207.

to reliability of information once in the field. I refer to some of these challenges throughout the book, but it is worth briefly outlining two principal constraints here.

The first relates to access to archival and official documentation, including information on genocide cases (both statistics and judgments). On several occasions, I submitted requests to government departments to consult specific documents, as well as requests for access to archival data more generally, but access was not granted. Frequently, the response was that the department did not have the specified document (despite it emanating from that department) or *any* relevant documents, or that the request should be submitted to another person within that department or to another department entirely (who/which then referred back to the first person/department).[43] In one case, I was informed that, given the relocation of the department and change in staff, no-one knew where the archives were kept. After contacting various former staff members, the archives were finally located, although unfortunately consisted of little more than some unlabelled folders and haphazardly piled documents. Inevitably, given the destruction caused during the conflict and genocide, the capacity for archiving and document management was lacking, at least in the first few years after 1994, and it would appear that systematic archiving has to some extent continued to be problematic. Additionally, given the time that has passed, it is possible that many physical documents were destroyed or mislaid and, due to the lack of technology at that time, were not electronically stored. When I was able to consult documents, they were sometimes incomplete and very rarely contained comprehensive information on legal and policy responses to child *génocidaires*.[44]

The difficulty in sourcing documents was not exclusive to government departments. International agencies and donors also responded to information requests that they did not have relevant documents. For example, a UNICEF Rwanda employee informed me that it was UNICEF's policy to destroy all documents after five years.[45] I was also unable to visit UNICEF's global archives located in New York. The archives were and currently remain closed to researchers whilst documents are 'reviewed

43 Similar problems have been experienced by other researchers, e.g. Doná 2011: 48.

44 As will be illustrated in Chapter 5, this is perhaps because children were not consciously singled out as a group in respect of which to formulate specific policies.

45 Interview with UNICEF Rwanda Staff Member A (at time of interview), Kigali, 5 February 2013. This was disputed by other UNICEF staff members who commented that only administrative and financial documents were destroyed and not project documents.

and assessed for archival value, and for sensitive and confidential information'.[46] Fortunately, a number of former or current UNICEF staff members and UNICEF's Innocenti Research Centre had retained some documents and these were made available to me. I also came across UNICEF documents in the archives of other organisations. However, it is quite possible that there were other documents containing relevant information which I have not been able to discover, or that interventions by international actors took the form of confidential communications with the government and are thus not accessible. To attempt to overcome these shortcomings, the research relies on interviews with key actors, but the lack of written data, in particular on UNICEF Rwanda's communications on this issue with the government, has inevitably limited the scope of analysis.

The second relates to interviews. Given that the research dates back to events in 1994, it was not easy to identify individuals who had worked on issues relating to child *génocidaires*. Additionally, there was reluctance on the part of some of those approached to participate fully, or at all, in the research, the response often being that they were not the appropriate person to respond to the questions. Frequently, the response to my questions would be, 'look at the law', 'look at the documents', 'check in the archives', even when the question concerned how things operated in practice or when a personal perspective was requested. It is possible that memories had faded given the time that had passed, or that there was an element of research fatigue, but it is also possible that some participants were being deliberately evasive or were anxious, given the sensitivity of the project. There was also some distrust towards me, as a researcher – and an outsider – several interviewees repeatedly asking whether the research was genuinely being conducted for academic reasons and not for a human rights NGO. One contact simply informed me that people 'did not give information to foreigners'.[47] Additionally, it is possible that participants were concerned about the potential personal and professional implications of providing information or proffering opinions that might

[46] Email correspondence with UNICEF's Division of Information and Communications Technology, 2 June 2017.

[47] This distrust of outsiders, particularly when the research topic is sensitive, has been noted by other researchers on Rwanda, see e.g. Clark 2011: 10. Cf. Murray (2010: 389–390), who conducted research on child rights and found little difficulty in securing access, but commented that 'access for more sensitive topics (notably the Rwandan genocide) may have been more problematic'.

be contrary to what they perceived was the official line.[48] In some cases, before agreeing to speak, participants wished to have express authorisation from their superiors and, in one case, a participant would speak only in the presence of his immediate boss.[49]

To overcome these difficulties, I sought to establish trust with participants, by fully explaining the purpose of the research and broad areas that would be discussed, and offered anonymity. Further, as with any qualitative research, there was a need to be reflexive as to the nature of the interview process (during the interview itself and subsequent analysis) and remain cautious about the reliability of responses, in particular responses that may have been considered socially or politically acceptable, or that exaggerated – or downplayed – roles, influences or visions. Part of this process included asking questions again in a different formulation or repeat interviewing, and corroborating responses through interviews with multiple sources and documentary analysis. An additional factor that had to be borne in mind was that, in many cases, the questions probed issues that the interviewee had worked on up to 20 years previously: not only might memories have faded, but perceptions might also have changed. However, whilst the passage of time since many of the events had occurred might be considered to have limiting effects on the research, it does provide the opportunity to consider the whole time frame in which the issue of child perpetrators was addressed, and thus enables the book to make a substantial contribution to the very limited existing work in this area.

1.3 Structure of the Book

As the book documents Rwanda's approach to child *génocidaires* in light of its obligations under international law and analyses how international actors sought to operationalise international standards, a necessary first step is to determine what *are* the international standards applicable to child perpetrators of atrocities. Chapter 2 thus begins with an examination

[48] Rettig (2011: 199), who conducted research on *gacaca* trials, reported similar experiences regarding interviewees' fears.

[49] See also Doná 2011: 48 (noting that, given the often-critical analyses of the Rwandan government, officials 'were reluctant to interact with anybody who did not have written formal approval by the highest echelons of command in order to "protect" themselves'); Ingelaere 2016: 102–104 (discussing the existence of an 'intelligence network' that verified that communications relating to *gacaca* aligned with government policy).

of international juvenile justice standards generally, before turning to the specific issue of child perpetrators of international crimes. It briefly considers whether children can be prosecuted for international crimes and argues that there is nothing in international law to prevent domestic prosecutions, but that there are various standards that must be upheld.

Given that these standards apply to all countries that have signed up to them (or are otherwise bound by custom), including post-conflict states or states otherwise with limited resources or facing socio-political challenges, Chapter 3 explores the legal accommodations inherent in the relevant legal instruments that allow for context to be taken into account. It also expounds factors that might affect the operationalisation of juvenile justice standards in particular. It then describes the mechanisms that exist at the international level to promote implementation of, and compliance with, children's rights. In particular, this chapter elaborates on UNICEF. It provides an overview of its institutional nature, its relationship with the CRC and its stance on juvenile justice, all of which are key to understanding UNICEF's involvement in Rwanda and its approach to child *génocidaires*.

The purpose of Chapter 4 is to set the context for this study on Rwanda. It first presents a brief outline of the civil war and genocide, including children's involvement as perpetrators. It then examines post-genocide Rwanda, in particular the impact of the genocide on Rwandan society and the judicial system, as well as the role of international and domestic actors in the recovery process. Finally, it addresses the position of the child offender under Rwandan law.

The book then presents in Chapter 5 how Rwanda dealt with child *génocidaires*. It explores whether children were held accountable for participating in the genocide in the same ways as adults, or whether they were given differential treatment on grounds of their age. These questions are explored in the context of arrests and detentions, criminal justice mechanisms (both formal courts and *gacaca* jurisdictions) and administrative measures taken to address genocidal acts.

In Chapters 6 to 8, the focus shifts to international actors. Chapter 6 briefly describes the interventions of UN bodies and international NGOs with regard to the rights of child *génocidaires* before turning the lens on UNICEF. It provides examples of how UNICEF Rwanda interpreted and applied international standards in the Rwandan context, drawing out the contention within UNICEF, and between UNICEF Rwanda and other actors, over how best to operationalise the rights of child *génocidaires*. It finds that UNICEF Rwanda took a contextual approach, relying in particular on the best interests of the child principle when interpreting the CRC (and related instruments). Chapter 7 then explores the strategic approach used by UNICEF Rwanda when seeking to enhance the implementation of, and compliance with, international standards. The empirical data suggest that UNICEF Rwanda was flexible and pragmatic, adopting a variety of strategies and techniques to fit the particular context, but which can broadly be categorised as collaborative and constructive.

These two chapters lay the foundation for the detailed evaluation in Chapter 8. After exploring the risks, criticisms and limitations of UNICEF Rwanda's approach, Chapter 8 presents examples of where the empirical data suggest that UNICEF Rwanda exerted a positive influence on Rwanda's implementation of, or compliance with, international standards on child perpetrators. It argues that UNICEF Rwanda's pragmatic yet principled approach was broadly valid, achieving some positive results, although there were shortcomings. The chapter concludes by analysing the factors that influenced UNICEF Rwanda's approach and suggests that the approach may be an appropriate means of operationalising international juvenile justice standards (or human rights standards more generally) in a post-conflict society.

The final chapter summarises the key findings of the book. It also gestures towards the implications of the research on a broader level as well as questions raised. Whilst each post-conflict state is unique and, given the scale of the violence and high degree of popular involvement in the genocide, it is arguable that Rwanda was exceptional, it is nonetheless hoped that the analysis and findings in this book will have relevance for post-conflict criminal justice initiatives in other states where children have been involved in any significant way in acts of violence, and perhaps for human rights promotion in post-conflict states more generally.

2

International Standards on Child Perpetrators of Atrocities

In this book, I focus specifically on children who were accused of committing genocide-related crimes in Rwanda, but children have perpetrated violence and committed gross human rights violations during many conflicts. National courts may try individuals for international crimes where this is envisaged under domestic legislation or for ordinary crimes[1] (i.e. the underlying offence) where international crimes have not been incorporated into domestic law. Children who come into conflict with the law have been identified as a distinct category of offender: they are accorded special protection under international human rights law which goes beyond the protection provided to adults. This is premised on children having a lower level of development and on their vulnerability. What follows is an overview of international standards on child perpetrators. I start by reviewing the normative framework relating to children who come into conflict with the law generally, before shifting the focus to *child perpetrators of international crimes*. After I establish that children can be prosecuted for international crimes, I will evince that a child who is accused of committing genocide, or any other international crime, is entitled to the same rights and protections as a child who has committed an ordinary crime.

2.1 The International Normative Framework Governing Child Offenders

Individuals accused of having infringed the criminal law are afforded protections under customary and conventional human rights law. Only certain human rights principles are recognised as binding on the basis

[1] 'Ordinary crime' is understood as a common crime under domestic law as distinct from an international crime having the special characteristics of crimes defined in the Rome Statute (ILC 1994: 58).

of custom:[2] the majority are binding through treaties. In this book, I take international treaties as the starting point, although reference will be made where appropriate to customary international rules (including treaty provisions that reflect or have attained customary status), general principles of law and also relevant soft-law or best practice (and thus non-binding)[3] instruments such as guidelines, principles and minimum rules adopted by organs of the United Nations, and general comments issued by the UN treaty bodies.

General human rights treaties such as the ICCPR, as well as related non-binding instruments that provide protection to persons accused or convicted of crimes,[4] apply to children as well as adults. However, children have been identified in international law as a group requiring specific legal protection. This approach to children originated in Europe and the US in the late nineteenth and early twentieth centuries and is characterised by age-based demarcations, with, in particular, the age of 18 now denoting the threshold to adulthood. Although originating in the West, it has morphed into a universal model, reflected in international law but also in most domestic legal systems throughout the world (albeit that practice frequently lags behinds). Despite this apparent universality, however, the definition of childhood, and relatedly the concept of child rights, remain contested ground. Childhood is a social construct and thus, whilst it is related to biological and psychological development, it 'changes according to local culture, the geographical environment and the prevailing social and economic conditions'.[5] It thus varies across time as well as within and across societies. Boundaries between adulthood and childhood may be more fluid[6] and arbitrary age distinctions may have little relevance in some societies, particularly where transition into

[2] The rights set out in the Universal Declaration of Human Rights (UDHR), for example, are frequently cited as constituting custom. See De Schutter 2014: 63.

[3] Note that 'soft' law can be categorised as non-binding law, as general norms or principles as opposed to rules, or as law that is not enforceable through binding dispute resolution. See Boyle 1999.

[4] E.g. Body of Principles for the Protection of All Persons under Any Form of Detention or Imprisonment; Basic Principles for the Treatment of Prisoners; UN Standard Minimum Rules for Non-custodial Measures (The Tokyo Rules); Basic Principles on the Use of Restorative Justice Programmes in Criminal Matters; UN Basic Principles and Guidelines on Remedies and Procedures on the Right of Anyone Deprived of Their Liberty to Bring Proceedings Before a Court; UN Standard Minimum Rules for the Treatment of Prisoners (The Nelson Mandela Rules).

[5] Van Bueren 1998: 6. See also Jenks 2005: 6–7.

[6] Honwana 2006: 40.

adulthood is marked by a social ritual or ceremony, or by the performance of particular labour or social roles irrespective of the individual's age.[7] In relation to African societies in particular, Twum-Danso asserts: 'The traditional African worldview of childhood (whatever that may be) and its termination sharply contrast with modern Western's society obsession with the age of eighteen as the entry into adulthood, as reflected in the Convention [on the Rights of the Child].'[8] This has led to assertions that standards based on the Western construction of childhood and on Western values cannot easily be transferred to, and translated into, non-western societies.[9] Further, even where domestic law in non-western societies enshrines age-based protections, this may not necessarily reflect local cultural understandings of the nature of childhood and the capacities of children: rather, it may simply be a relic of colonialism. I am not proposing to enter these extensive and contentious debates here, but I will revisit aspects of tensions between universal and local understandings of childhood and child rights elsewhere in the book.

The particular needs of children were first recognised in the Geneva Declaration of the Rights of the Child of 1924 and again in the UN Declaration of the Rights of the Child of 1959, but it was not until the ICCPR of 1966[10] that provisions addressing the child offender were incorporated into a global treaty. This was followed by the CRC of 1989[11] that contains more comprehensive provisions relating to child offenders.[12] These treaties are supplemented by non-binding guidelines and rules specifically relating to children that include the Beijing Rules,[13] the Havana Rules[14], the Riyadh Guidelines[15] and the Vienna Guidelines.[16]

[7] Wessells 2009: 5.

[8] Twum-Danso 2008: 400.

[9] Indeed, many non-western countries showed little interest in the drafting of the CRC, arguably because it was based on a notion of childhood that was alien to them.

[10] In force from March 1976.

[11] In force from September 1990.

[12] Note also the African Charter on the Rights and Welfare of the Child 1990 (ACRWC) at the regional level, which contains many provisions that largely mirror those of the CRC.

[13] UN Standard Minimum Rules for the Administration of Juvenile Justice (The Beijing Rules) (29 November 1985).

[14] UN Rules for the Protection of Juveniles Deprived of their Liberty (The Havana Rules) (14 December 1990).

[15] UN Guidelines for the Prevention of Juvenile Delinquency (The Riyadh Guidelines) (14 December 1990).

[16] Guidelines for Action on Children in the Criminal Justice System (The Vienna Guidelines) (21 July 1997).

A preliminary point to note is that none of the instruments, binding or otherwise, preclude the criminal responsibility of children. They do, however, contain detailed provisions on international standards that must be upheld when a child comes into conflict with the law. In this chapter, the emphasis is on those provisions that address the specific needs of the child and thus which go beyond, or in some other way differ from, the rights of the accused or detained adult: I do not, therefore, address in any detail general due process or prisoner rights. Nor do I provide an exhaustive analysis of all juvenile justice provisions in all instruments. The focus will be predominantly on the CRC given its subject-specificity and the fact that its provisions bind almost all UN member states,[17] although relevant ICCPR provisions will also be cited, and non-binding instruments will be referenced where these expand on CRC rights or are indicative of a common positioning. In the following analysis, and throughout the book, the status of the law (binding or non-binding) should be kept in mind.

2.1.1 *Juvenile Justice: The Rationale and Overarching Principles*

Article 40(1) of the CRC enshrines a child rights-centred approach to juvenile justice and the fundamental concept of differential treatment for children, which underlies all the juvenile justice provisions in the Convention. It provides that children in conflict with the law should be treated in a manner consistent with the promotion of their 'sense of dignity and worth', which reinforces their respect for human rights and takes into account their age and the desirability of promoting their reintegration and their assumption of 'a constructive role in society'. According to the Committee on the Rights of the Child (CRC Committee), differences between children and adults in terms of physical and psychological development and emotional and educational needs result in the lesser culpability of children and the requirement for different procedures and treatment: rehabilitation and restorative justice are the key aims, rather than the 'traditional objectives' of criminal justice, namely repression and retribution.[18] Some argue that this obligation to treat children

[17] The near universal ratification and the speed of ratification have led some to question whether the CRC as a whole, or at least certain provisions, constitute custom. See discussion in Van Bueren 1998: 53–57.

[18] CRC Committee 2007a: [10]. See also Cohn 1999: 130; Feld 2006: 426–429.

differently from adults in criminal proceedings is a norm of customary international law.[19]

Other key principles in the CRC are: non-discrimination (Article 2), the right to life, survival and development (Article 6), the right for children to express their views and have these views considered in all matters affecting them (Article 12),[20] and the obligation to act in the best interests of the child (Article 3(1)). The 'best interests' principle has been criticised for being vague and thus open to subjective interpretation.[21] However, the vagueness of the principle was intended to provide some flexibility given its broad application. Pursuant to Article 3(1) of the CRC, the best interests of the child shall be 'a primary consideration' in all actions undertaken by public or social welfare institutions, courts of law, administrative authorities or legislative bodies. It is both a substantive right and a principle of interpretation, and can be used 'to support, justify or clarify a particular approach' and as 'an aid to construction' in implementing other rights. It can also be used to resolve conflicts between different CRC rights.[22] The use of the indefinite article – '*a* primary consideration'[23] – indicates that the intention was not for the best interests of the child to trump all other considerations although they will prevail unless it can be shown that other interests should take precedence.[24] Indeed, during drafting discussions, it was noted that there were some situations where 'competing interests … of justice and of the society at large should be of at least equal, if not greater, importance than the interests of the child'.[25] In the context of juvenile justice, the interests of victims and, particularly in the case of mass violations, the desire to put an end to impunity, might constitute valid interests to be taken into account. Further, it is arguable that holding a child accountable might be in a child's best interests as this may aid

[19] Konge 2010: 55.

[20] This right includes the right to be heard in judicial and administrative proceedings.

[21] See discussion in Alston 1994: 18; Kilkelly 2011: 181. See also section 3.1.3.

[22] Alston 1994: 15–16.

[23] Cf. Art. 4, ACRWC (the best interests of the child shall be 'the' primary consideration); also Art. 21, CRC relating to adoption cases (the best interests of the child shall be 'the paramount consideration').

[24] For the negotiating history of this provision, see Alston 1994: 12–13; Detrick 1999: 91. See also Alston and Gilmour-Walsh 1996: 11.

[25] Working Group to the Commission on Human Rights 1989: [121]. See also Cantwell 2011: 49 (other interests might include 'upholding the rule of law, protecting the rights of others and reviewing material (including financial) issues').

reintegration into society, although the question remains as to whether such accountability must take the form of criminal responsibility.[26]

2.1.2 *The Importance of Age*

The CRC interprets the word 'child' as 'every human being below the age of eighteen years unless, under the law applicable to the child, majority is attained earlier'.[27] The CRC thus clearly demarcates 18 as the universal upper age limit of 'childhood'. In the context of juvenile justice, this means that, unless under their domestic judicial system the age of penal majority is higher than 18 or young adults are otherwise brought within the juvenile justice system, those over 18 will be subject to adult trial procedures whilst those below this age will benefit from special protections.[28]

The position is not clear, however, where an individual, under 18 at the time of the alleged offence, has reached 18 by the time his/her case is dealt with. The second sentence of Article 37(a) (relating to the death penalty and life imprisonment – see section 2.1.4) contains the only explicit reference in the juvenile justice provisions to age at the time of commission of the offence. The CRC Committee advises in its General Comment No. 10 on children's rights in juvenile justice that the 'rules of juvenile justice' – including 'procedural rules and … rules for diversion and special measures' – should apply to all children who were under 18 at the time of the alleged offence.[29] Draft General Comment No. 24, which is intended to replace General Comment No. 10 and which was under consideration at the time this book was finalised, contains similar wording.[30] It is more explicit on the issue of age, however, in a number

[26] See the discussion at notes 134–139 below and related text.

[27] Art. 1, CRC. During drafting negotiations, various ages were put forward: the compromise was struck to set an age of 18 but to allow for some flexibility by referring to applicable (national) laws. See Detrick 1999: 53; Van Bueren 1998: 36–37.

[28] See also Rule 11(a), Havana Rules (defining a juvenile as 'every person under the age of 18'). Note that Rule 3.3, Beijing Rules recommends that efforts be made to extend the principles to young adults.

[29] CRC Committee 2007a: [36]. The following paragraph provides that 'every person under the age of 18 years at the time of the alleged commission of an offence must be treated in accordance with the rules of juvenile justice'.

[30] CRC Committee 2018: [37] and [39]. At the time this book was finalised in December 2018, the CRC Committee had just invited comments on this draft general comment. As it is at draft stage and thus subject to change, I continue to refer to the (at the time of writing current) General Comment No. 10 (CRC Committee 2007a), and I reference the draft General Comment No. 24 (CRC Committee 2018) only where this indicates an evolution

of respects. It specifies: 'Juvenile justice systems should also extend protection to child offenders who were below the age of 18 at the time of the commission of the offence but who turn 18 during the trial or during the period of sentence.'[31] It also expressly provides that young people on probation or receiving education or curative treatment, or who are in a facility for children in conflict with the law, should continue to benefit from juvenile-specific measures once they turn 18 and recommends that they are not relocated to adult centres.[32] The issue of reaching majority is further addressed in relation to privacy, the draft General Comment stating that the right to privacy (see section 2.1.3) applies 'even if the child turns 18 during the course of the proceedings or release from custody'.[33] Clearly, then, in the Committee's view, a person who comes into conflict with the law when under 18 but who turns 18 during the relevant procedure remains entitled to all juvenile-specific rules. The Committee has not specifically addressed, however (either in its 2007 General Comment or the more recent draft replacement), the situation, such as occurred in Rwanda, where juveniles are tried several years after allegedly committing an offence, during which time they have attained majority.

The CRC Committee's approach seems to consist largely of recommendations regarding what it considers best practice, rather than a legal analysis of the scope and content of the obligations on states parties under Article 40 of the CRC.[34] Many of the rules in the CRC reflect the standards contained in the ICCPR for all persons coming into conflict with the law: it is only those that provide differential treatment for juveniles that are at issue. Whilst the CRC Committee has suggested that all juvenile justice rules should apply, the reasoning behind differential treatment for juveniles, in particular their psychological development, would seem to fall away to a certain degree in respect of some of these rules (such as special court procedures or the right to have parents/guardians present

in the CRC Committee's approach on specific issues. Any references to 'General Comment on juvenile justice' are thus to the 2007 document unless otherwise specified.

31 CRC Committee 2018: [41].

32 Ibid.: [46].

33 Ibid.: [78].

34 This is also the view of child rights expert, Dan O'Donnell (personal correspondence, 1 August 2015), who opined that the Committee's additional comment (in para. 38 of its General Comment No. 10) on extending juvenile justice rules to young adults, 'seems to confirm that this [the application of procedural rules to juvenile offenders who reach adulthood] is simply a policy that the Committee wished to endorse, regardless of whether it can be supported under the accepted rules on treaty interpretation'.

during proceedings), but perhaps not for others (such as the right to privacy, diversion and alternative dispositions) where other considerations, including stigmatisation, future impact and proportionality, would also play a role. In many cases, this particular situation will not arise, but in countries seeking to deal with atrocities, it may be that significant time passes between the alleged commission of the crime and the processing of cases.

As for the age from which children can be held criminally responsible, Article 40(3)(a) of the CRC requires states to promote the establishment of a minimum age below which children are 'presumed not to have the capacity to infringe the penal law'. The CRC does not provide any guidance on what this age should be. Cipriani argues that the lack of clarity of the provision[35] has led to 'wide conceptual interpretation' and to manipulation or disregard by many countries of their nominal minimum age, through for example punitive-oriented 'administrative' measures for children younger than that age (referred to in this book as 'non-responsible' children).[36] Rule 4.1 of the Beijing Rules provides some guidance, stating that the minimum age must 'not be fixed at too low an age level, bearing in mind the facts of emotional, mental and intellectual maturity'. The key question is whether 'a child can live up to the moral and psychological components of criminal responsibility', based on individual discernment and understanding.[37] Cipriani, drawing on his extensive analysis of state practice, suggests that there is a general principle of law that requires all states to set a minimum age of criminal responsibility and requires that the minimum age should not be set at a level where children cannot be expected to understand the consequences of their actions.[38] It is not possible, however, to make the same claim with respect to a mandatory age level; the question of what the minimum age should be thus remains. The CRC Committee concluded in its General Comment No. 10 that 12 years[39] should be the 'absolute minimum' age of criminal responsibility and encouraged states to raise it to a higher age, commending states that have adopted the age of 14 or 16.[40] In its draft General Comment

35 In particular, the reference to presumption suggests an element of discretion rather than an explicit right for the child below the minimum age not to be prosecuted.

36 Cipriani 2009: 56 and chapter 6 (in particular 136–139).

37 Commentary to Rule 4.1.

38 Cipriani 2009: 126–128. See also Happold 2005: 15; text at note 114.

39 This is also the median age worldwide (Cipriani 2009: 160).

40 CRC Committee 2007a: [30] and [32].

No. 24, the CRC Committee finds 12 to be 'still low', encourages states to increase the age to at least 14 and commends those states that have a higher minimum age of 15 of 16.[41] Clearly, the age of criminal responsibility must reflect capacity and protect those who have not developed the necessary discernment and understanding. Further, setting the age too low has implications for a child's ability to participate effectively in a criminal trial.[42] However, a high minimum age (depicting those below the age as innocent and, in the context of conflict, as victims) can lead to demands by society for changes to the law and for retribution against the 'evil' aberration where violent crimes are committed by non-responsible children.[43] And where a state fails to take any action at all in response to the non-responsible child (treating the minimum age as a cut-off for any response), the result can be vigilante justice.[44] A high age can also lead to the adoption of interventions for non-responsible children that, whilst nominally welfare-oriented, are in fact punitive, and thus implicitly attribute criminal responsibility.

A further issue relating to age is a practical one: many children do not have a birth certificate or other proof of age as many states lack an effective birth registration system or, in situations of conflict, such documentation may be destroyed or lost. Where there is no proof of age, investigations should be conducted to try to establish age;[45] if it cannot be established that the child is above the age of criminal responsibility, the child shall not be held criminally responsible.[46] In practice, however, juvenile justice

[41] CRC Committee 2018: [33].

[42] See e.g. *T* v. *United Kingdom* and *V* v. *United Kingdom*: [86–91]. In this well-known case (where the two defendants were aged 10 at the time they murdered the almost 3-year-old James Bulger), the court found a breach of fair trial provisions as the defendants, aged 11 at the time of the trial, had been unable to participate effectively.

[43] Ibid. (Although not the result of a high minimum age, public demand for tougher action followed these cases and arguably led to changes in the UK justice system.)

[44] See also Cipriani 2009: 161.

[45] The current General Comment No. 10 on children's rights in juvenile justice provides that the child is entitled to a 'reliable medical or social investigation' (CRC Committee 2007a: [39]). Draft General Comment No. 24 states that documentation other than a birth certificate (e.g. notification of birth, extracts from birth registries, baptismal documents or school reports) should be accepted as proof of age, and that parents or community/religious leaders should be consulted. An assessment of the child's physical and psychological development should only be conducted where other measures have been unsuccessful, and the Committee advises against the use of medical methods (such as bone or dental examination analysis) (CRC Committee 2018: [44–45]).

[46] CRC Committee 2007a: [35] and [39].

systems use various ways of assessing age, the most common of which is the judge's discretion.[47]

2.1.3 *Juvenile Justice System and Procedure*

International human rights instruments provide that the penal procedure must take into account a child's age.[48] States must 'seek to promote the establishment of laws, procedures, authorities and institutions' that apply specifically to children,[49] and the CRC Committee recommends that juvenile courts be established or, where not immediately possible, specialised judges be appointed.[50] Whenever 'appropriate and desirable', alternative measures to judicial proceedings (i.e. diversion) should be taken,[51] the aim being to protect juveniles from the negative effects of criminal proceedings, such as the stigma of conviction and sentence.[52] The Beijing Rules suggest that alternative measures might include 'community programmes, such as temporary supervision and guidance, restitution, and compensation of victims'.[53] Other initiatives include police warnings, family group conferencing and victim/offender mediation.[54] Arguably, diversion is intended for less serious offences rather than serious violent crimes: the CRC Committee stated in 2007 that the obligation to promote alternative measures applies but is not limited to children who commit minor offences such as shoplifting and other first-time child offenders;[55] and Rule 11 of the Beijing Rules provides that diversion may be appropriate '*even when* more serious offences have been committed' (emphasis added) depending on the merits of the individual case.

[47] Cipriani 2009: 132.

[48] Art. 14(4), ICCPR; Art. 40(1), CRC.

[49] Art. 40(3), CRC.

[50] CRC Committee 2007a: [93]. See also Guideline 14, Vienna Guidelines.

[51] Art. 40(3)(b).

[52] Commentary on Rule 11, Beijing Rules. See also Petty and Brown 1998a: 12 ('Once defined as a criminal in their own eyes and those of wider society, they find it much more difficult to change and adjust to the world of school, work and family life.').

[53] Rule 11.4, Beijing Rules.

[54] See e.g. Cappelaere, Grandjean, and Naqvi 2005: 403–414. See also Guideline 15, Vienna Guidelines (referring to mediation and also to the importance of family involvement).

[55] CRC Committee 2007a: [25]. In its draft General Comment No. 24, the CRC Committee states that diversion should be 'the preferred manner of dealing with child offenders in the majority of cases' and urges states to 'extend the range of offences for which diversion is possible, including serious offences where appropriate'. CRC Committee 2018: [24].

Where juveniles are subject to criminal proceedings, Article 40 of the CRC contains a series of minimum procedural guarantees. Whilst these mainly reflect the rights set out in Articles 9, 14 and 15 of the ICCPR,[56] juveniles have additional protections. These are the rights to have their parents or legal guardians involved in proceedings (for psychological and emotional assistance), to 'legal or other appropriate assistance'[57] (intended to reflect the informality of some juvenile justice proceedings) and to full respect for privacy at all stages of proceedings. The CRC Committee recommends that juvenile hearings be held behind closed doors,[58] which differs from adults where the press and public can be excluded only in particular circumstances.[59] Rule 8 of the Beijing Rules also recommends that, in principle, information that may lead to the identification of a juvenile offender should not be published, the aim being to protect juveniles from the adverse effects (such as impact on ability to access education or work) and stigmatisation that may result from media attention. This right to privacy extends to judgments, where an exception can be made to the requirement to make judgments public where this is in the interests of the juvenile.[60]

The General Comment on juvenile justice expands upon these due process guarantees and notes that the intention to hold a child criminally responsible implies that the child 'should be competent and able' to participate effectively in the trial. This includes being able to understand the charges, the possible consequences and penalties so as to provide instructions to legal counsel, challenge witnesses, provide an account of events, and put forward his/her views about evidence, testimony and the measures to be imposed. The child should also be able to express him/herself freely. Courtroom procedures and practices may also need to be modified depending on the child's age and maturity.[61]

[56] These include, for example, the right to be informed promptly of charges, the presumption of innocence, the principle of *nullum crimen sine lege*, the right not to be compelled to testify or confess, and the right to judicial review of decisions.

[57] It is left to states to determine how assistance is provided, but the CRC Committee (2007a: [49]) has stated that such assistance should be 'free of charge'. Art. 14(3)(d), ICCPR provides for free legal assistance for persons without means to pay for it, 'where the interests of justice so require'.

[58] CRC Committee 2007a: [66].

[59] Art. 14(1), ICCPR.

[60] Ibid.

[61] CRC Committee 2007a: [45–46] (reference is made to Rule 14, Beijing Rules). Note, however, that whilst modifications may go some way to assist participation, a child above the age of responsibility may not have developed the abilities necessary for full and effective participation. See note 42; Cipriani 2009: 144–148.

It is also arguable that juvenile proceedings must advance more quickly than adult trials. Article 40(2)(b)(iii) provides the right for the child to be heard 'without delay' and Article 10(2)(b) of the ICCPR provides that accused juveniles must be brought 'as speedily as possible' to adjudication.[62] The non-binding instruments expand on this: Rule 20 of the Beijing Rules recommends that each case be 'handled expeditiously, without any unnecessary delay'; and the General Comment on juvenile justice recommends the establishment of time limits for various periods between the commission of the offence and final adjudication, adding that these time limits should be 'much shorter' for juveniles than for adults.[63] The CRC Committee has also commented that there is an international consensus that, for children, 'the time between the commission of the offence and the final response to this act should be as short as possible'.[64]

2.1.4 *Sanctions and Measures*

In addition to greater judicial guarantees, youth also influences the measures that can be taken against offenders. The desirability of the juvenile's rehabilitation[65] or reintegration[66] must be taken into account and, whilst Article 10(3) of the ICCPR provides that the aim of treatment of prisoners (in general) is their 'reformation and social rehabilitation', it requires that juveniles be 'accorded treatment appropriate to their age and legal status'. The differential treatment of adults and juveniles is predicated on the view that juveniles need more protection against stigmatisation and should be subjected to educational, rather than punitive, measures.

The CRC and related documents place restrictions on the use of institutionalisation and emphasise the importance of proportionate responses. Under Article 37(b) of the CRC, deprivation of liberty 'shall be used only as a measure of last resort and for the shortest appropriate period of time'.[67] Deprivation of liberty covers juvenile detention but also detention

[62] Cf. Art. 14(3)(c), ICCPR which provides the right for adults to be tried without 'undue delay'.

[63] CRC Committee 2007a: [52]. Note, however, that it also emphasises that the 'decision-making process without delay' must respect other safeguards, including the right to legal assistance.

[64] CRC Committee 2007a: [51] (referring to Art. 37(d) – right to a prompt decision on any challenge to legality of deprivation of liberty – in support of this statement).

[65] Art. 14(4), ICCPR.

[66] Art. 40(1), CRC.

[67] See also Rule 19.1, Beijing Rules and Rule 2, Havana Rules which refer to institutionalisation/deprivation of liberty as 'a disposition of last resort and for the minimum necessary

in administrative and other settings[68] and could include welfare, education and health institutions.[69] The provision covers pre-trial[70] and post-conviction detention: the standard is thus higher than that for adults, where there should be no 'general rule' of detaining in custody persons awaiting trial,[71] but there are otherwise no restrictions on imposing lawful imprisonment. Specifically on pre-trial detention, the CRC Committee has voiced its concern that children 'languish' for extensive periods of time and stated that its use as a punishment violates the presumption of innocence.[72] The CRC suggests alternatives to institutionalisation that might be used where these are appropriate to the juvenile's well-being and proportionate both to the juvenile's circumstances and the offence. These include care, guidance and supervision orders, counselling, probation, foster care, and vocational or educational training programmes.[73]

The Beijing Rules provide greater detail on institutionalisation. Rule 17 provides that deprivation of liberty should be imposed only where there is no other appropriate response and where the juvenile has committed a serious violent act or is a repeat serious offender. It stresses the need for measures to be proportionate: not only to the juvenile's circumstances and the offence, but also the needs of society.[74] The Commentary notes that 'strictly punitive approaches are not appropriate' for juveniles, distinguishing adult cases but 'possibly also … cases of severe offences by juveniles' where just desert and retributive approaches might be appropriate. It stresses, however, that in juvenile cases, the interest of securing the well-being and future of the young person should prevail. The emphasis is thus on constructive rather than punitive sanctions in light of the young person's reformative ability, although there is some recognition

period'. Draft General Comment No. 24 on children's rights in juvenile justice (CRC Committee 2018: [101]) encourages states to set an age limit for the use of deprivation of liberty and recommends that no child in conflict with the law below the age of 16 be deprived of liberty.

68 CRC Committee 1996: [138]; Rule 11(b), Havana Rules; Guideline 19, Vienna Guidelines.

69 The provision would thus apply to measures taken against the non-responsible child.

70 Rule 13, Beijing Rules and Rule 17, Havana Rules expand on pre-trial detention issues (the latter states that pre-trial detention should be 'limited to exceptional circumstances').

71 Art. 9(3), ICCPR.

72 CRC Committee 2007a: [80].

73 Art. 40(4). See also Rule 18, Beijing Rules.

74 Note that the CRC Committee (2007a: [71]) has commented that whilst 'the need of public safety and sanctions' may be taken into account, they 'must always be outweighed by the need to safeguard the well-being and the best interests of the child and to promote his/her reintegration'.

that punitive responses might be appropriate in the most serious of cases.[75] According to the Beijing Rules, institutionalisation (in any form) should be avoided to the greatest extent possible on the basis that juveniles are more vulnerable to negative influences than adults because of their 'early stage of development'.[76] Where institutionalisation cannot be avoided for offenders, it should be in a correctional or educational institution rather than a prison.

Where deprived of liberty, the child has the right to prompt access to legal and other assistance, to challenge the legality of the deprivation of liberty and to a 'prompt decision' on any such challenge,[77] to maintain contact with his/her family, to be treated in an age-appropriate manner, and to be held separately from adults (unless this is not in the child's best interests).[78] This requirement for separation has been interpreted by the CRC Committee as meaning placement in separate facilities with distinct, child-centred staff and policies and not in an adult prison.[79] Once the individual reaches 18, there is no requirement to retain separation, although this should be made possible where it is in the individual's best interests and is not contrary to the best interests of the younger children in the facility.[80] The reasons behind separating children from adults include the risk of abuse or intimidation and criminal 'contamination', but also the need to place juveniles in an environment conducive to meeting their physical, psychological, educational and social requirements. The CRC has a holistic nature: all rights are considered interrelated, indivisible and applicable to *all* children (including those in detention) at all times.[81] Thus, whilst children might be deprived of their liberty, they remain entitled to the rights to healthcare, an adequate standard of living, education and vocational training and rest and leisure and access

[75] Cf. the CRC Committee (2007a: [71]), which has simply commented that a 'strictly punitive approach is not in accordance with the leading principles for juvenile justice' and then refers to 'proportionate' measures in respect of severe offences committed by children.

[76] Commentary to Rule 19. As Petty and Brown (1998a: 12) observe, offenders in penal institutions 'learn criminal skills, language and culture that is very likely to reinforce offending behaviour'.

[77] Art. 37(d), CRC (cf. 'without delay' in Art. 9(4), ICCPR).

[78] Art. 37(c), CRC; Arts. 10(2)(b) and 10(3), ICCPR. See also Rule 29, Havana Rules.

[79] CRC Committee 2007a: [85]. See also Rule 26.3, Beijing Rules (juveniles should be separated from adults, 'in a separate institution or in a separate part of an institution also holding adults').

[80] CRC Committee 2007a: [86].

[81] See e.g. CRC Committee 2003b: [6] and [18]. See also Guideline 10, Vienna Guidelines.

to recreational activities.[82] These provisions are also consistent with the overarching requirement to promote reintegration. The non-binding instruments flesh out these rights: the Beijing Rules state that children in institutions should be provided with 'care, protection, education and vocational skills, with a view to assisting them to assume socially constructive and productive roles in society',[83] and the Havana Rules contain very detailed provisions on the various rights whilst in detention.[84] Further, as would be applicable to all detainees, there is a prohibition on torture or other cruel, inhuman or degrading treatment or punishment.[85] Finally, Article 25 of the CRC provides all children in institutions with the right to a periodic review of their placement.

As regards the non-responsible child, the CRC Committee states that 'special protective measures' may be taken if necessary in the child's best interests,[86] although legal safeguards must be established to ensure fair and just treatment.[87] The CRC Committee has given some direction in its recommendations to states parties as to what special protective measures are acceptable, although this has been very context specific. It does not rule out the possibility of institutionalisation but emphasises the restrictions that apply where it is used.[88] In some cases, the Committee found that protective custody measures and detention in social welfare centres were inconsistent with the meaning of the minimum age of criminal responsibility.[89] Indeed, as noted earlier, many policies generally viewed as protection, education or welfare measures can constitute *de facto* punishment and thus implicitly attribute criminal responsibility to the child.

Differential treatment is also granted to children in relation to the death penalty and life imprisonment without possibility of release, neither of which can be imposed for crimes committed by persons under 18 years of age.[90] The age at the time of commission of the offence is

[82] Arts. 24, 27, 28, 29 and 31, CRC. See CRC Committee 2007a: [89] which sets out what is required by states to comply with these provisions in respect of children in detention.

[83] Rule 26.1.

[84] Rules 31–37 (physical detention conditions), 38–46 (education, vocational training and work), 47 (leisure and recreation), 49–55 (healthcare) and 79–80 (reintegration measures).

[85] Art. 37(a), CRC. See also Guideline 54, Riyadh Guidelines.

[86] CRC Committee 2007a: [31]. This also confirms that the non-responsible child 'cannot be formally charged and held responsible in a penal law procedure'.

[87] Ibid.: [33].

[88] Cipriani 2009: 62.

[89] Ibid.: 63.

[90] Art. 37(a), CRC. See also Art. 6(5), ICCPR regarding the death penalty.

the relevant age: thus a person who committed an offence when under 18 cannot be executed for that crime once he/she reaches 18.[91] The UN Human Rights Committee (HRC) contends that the prohibition on executing children reflects customary international law,[92] and the 2005 US Supreme Court decision in *Roper* v. *Simmons* provides further support for the customary nature of this rule. The prohibition is based on the perception of minors' diminished culpability[93] and also possibly their greater capacity for rehabilitation.

2.2 International Law and Child Perpetrators of International Crimes

It is clear from the above that children can be prosecuted for ordinary crimes, which may constitute the underlying offence of an international crime. As regards international crimes, these can be prosecuted before international courts and tribunals or national courts (where provided for in domestic law), although domestic prosecutions are intended to be the primary means of enforcement.[94] It has been suggested by some commentators that individuals under the age of 18 who have participated in international crimes should be viewed mainly as victims and should not be prosecuted for these crimes.[95] This push to exclude criminal responsibility is based on a conception of the child as a 'passive' or 'faultless' victim, an innocent vulnerable to brainwashing, threats and manipulation by adults or incapacitated through drugs or alcohol.[96] According to this narrative, the child lacks any type of agency and, as such, is deserving of protection rather than prosecution, or indeed any other accountability measure.[97] However, is there anything in international law that precludes holding children individually criminally responsible at the domestic

[91] See also CRC Committee 2007a: [75].

[92] HRC 1994: [8]. See also Schabas 2008a: 164–165.

[93] See *Roper* v. *Simmons*: [15–18]; Cohn and Goodwin-Gill 1994: 8–9.

[94] Cryer et al. 2010: 64.

[95] See e.g. Grossman 2007; No Peace Without Justice and UNICEF Innocenti Research Centre 2002: 34 ('Child perpetrators are … victims of criminal policies for which adults are primarily responsible.').

[96] See Drumbl 2012: 15 and 81. See also Steinl 2017: 26–34 for a discussion of the implications of the passive victim discourse.

[97] This narrative contrasts with the image of the child offender as 'evil', a 'deviant' or a 'demon', which often attaches to children accused of extremely violent, 'ordinary' crimes in Western societies but has also been particularly prevalent in discussions regarding children associated with 'terrorist' groups.

level for international crimes?[98] It has been argued that the Rome Statute establishing the International Criminal Court (ICC) sets the minimum age of criminal responsibility for international crimes at 18 and is intended to 'lead to decriminalization' at the domestic level of children who have committed such acts.[99] This section addresses, and essentially rejects, this argument by reviewing very briefly international criminal law and practice, before turning to the treaties that require states to prevent and punish core crimes to consider whether these expressly or implicitly exclude the prosecution of children.

2.2.1 International Criminal Law and Practice

The Rome Statute 1998 was the first international criminal law instrument to address the issue of young perpetrators specifically. Article 26 provides: 'The Court shall have no jurisdiction over any person who was under the age of 18 at the time of the alleged commission of a crime.' Eser argues that, although phrased in procedural terms, the exclusion in Article 26 can 'in substance, be considered as a ground for excluding criminal responsibility as well', on the basis that the main reason for the exclusion is lack of criminal responsibility of individuals under 18.[100] And Aptel asserts that the establishment of the ICC translated the practice of non-prosecution of juveniles by international courts into 'substantive international criminal law', and thus children should not be tried for international crimes by international courts.[101] As noted earlier, some

[98] Given this narrow focus, I do not review the various treaties and custom that provide the basis for these crimes or consider state obligations to prosecute. For a concise overview of state obligations, see Cryer et al. 2010: 69–73 and for a more detailed albeit dated account, see Orentlicher 1991.

[99] Grover 2012: 79; See also TRC 2004: [200].

[100] Eser 2008: 868. See also Clark and Triffterer 2008: 775 (commenting that Art. 26 'regulates an aspect of substantive criminal law from its procedural side ... thus showing the close connection between these two fields').

[101] Aptel 2010: 21–22 (noting that the International Military Tribunals of Nuremberg and Tokyo, the International Criminal Tribunal for the Former Yugoslavia and the International Criminal Tribunal of Rwanda (ICTR) have not tried children). She confirms, however (at 24) that Art. 26 does not fix the age of criminal responsibility for international crimes at 18; it 'merely' excludes children from the ICC's jurisdiction. See also Coomaraswamy 2009b: [14] (suggesting that there is an 'emerging consensus' that international courts should not prosecute children for war crimes and crimes against humanity); Clark and Triffterer 2008: 71 (suggesting that prosecutors 'perhaps assumed' criminal responsibility under international law began at the age of 18); Frulli 2002: 533 (arguing that the practice of international tribunals indicates that the age of 18 was considered a 'tacit threshold');

have suggested that Article 26 establishes 18 as the age of legal capacity for international crimes and that the intention is for domestic jurisdictions to follow suit.

However, an alternative and more convincing argument regarding Article 26 is that '[i]t is clear both from the language of the article and its drafting history that the provision is procedural rather than substantive in nature'.[102] The negotiating history of the Rome Statute indicates that there was clear support for the inclusion of jurisdiction over juveniles.[103] Time pressure and financing problems, a failure to agree on the minimum age and concerns that a separate juvenile justice system would need to be established, resulted in the exclusion of juveniles from the ICC's jurisdiction. It was also considered preferable by many to leave the question of criminal responsibility of juveniles to national jurisdictions.[104] It must also be recalled that the Rome Statute regulates the ICC only: whilst some provisions might be considered to codify customary international law, the Rome Statute is not a comprehensive international criminal code. Indeed, some 'mixed' tribunals,[105] established after the Rome Statute was adopted, had jurisdiction over juveniles. The Special Court for Sierra Leone (SCSL) had jurisdiction over persons aged 15–18 at the time of the alleged commission of the crime,[106] although the decision was taken by the prosecutor not to prosecute children.[107] The Special Panels for Serious Crimes in East Timor could try minors aged 12–16 for offences which, under applicable law, constituted murder, rape or a violent crime inflicting serious injury, those aged over 16 being subject to the ordinary rules of

Paris Principle 8.6 (referring to the Rome Statute and concluding that children should not be prosecuted by an international court or tribunal).

102 Happold 2005: 148. See also Cassese 2008: 267.

103 Various drafts presented a range of ages for criminal responsibility (from 12 to 21), with options for an absolute minimum age or a rebuttable presumptive age. See Clark and Triffterer 2008: 772–774; Preparatory Committee 1998: 52 and 119–120.

104 See Committee of the Whole 1998: 138–141.

105 Also referred to as 'hybrid' or 'internationalised' tribunals, or tribunals 'with international elements', these tribunals have a mixed composition of international and national judges and may have mixed applicable law.

106 Art. 7, Statute of the SCSL. Note that the issue of criminal responsibility of children was subject to intense debate (in particular between the UN Secretary-General and the Security Council – see correspondence: President of the Security Council 2000 and 2001; UNSG 2001a) given the number of child soldiers involved in the conflict and reports of atrocities committed by them. On the divergent views, see Amann 2001; Amnesty International 2000c: 13; Cohn 2001: 7–12; UNSG 2000b: [35–36].

107 SCSL 2002. See also IRIN 2002.

criminal procedure.[108] A 14-year-old juvenile, who had killed three persons with a machete but was allegedly involved with others in the extermination of 47 men, was tried by the Special Panels in 2002.[109] Initially charged with three counts of crimes against humanity, he pleaded guilty to an amended charge of murder without premeditation (manslaughter) under the Indonesian Penal Code. Although ultimately convicted of an ordinary crime, the decision is important in that a juvenile was tried by a mixed court for a serious offence committed in the context of a conflict. Finally, the War Crimes Chamber in the Court of Bosnia and Herzegovina, which began as a hybrid tribunal but has since become a court serviced by national staff, allows for the prosecution of persons over 14 (in accordance with Article 8 of the domestic criminal code). In August 2010, the Chamber convicted Elvir Jakupović of war crimes (after a guilty plea) and sentenced him to five years' imprisonment. Jakupović, a former member of the army of Bosnia and Herzegovina, had been 17 at the time he had shot a prisoner of war at point-blank range.[110]

In summary, at the most it *might* be arguable that there is an emerging consensus that persons under 18 should not be prosecuted before international criminal courts and tribunals (although I still hesitate to conclude that that is the case), but any argument that the Rome Statute establishes a minimum age of 18, and thus excludes criminal responsibility for child perpetrators of international crimes, is untenable. Article 26 merely excludes the jurisdiction of the ICC over those aged under 18: national courts can therefore prosecute the under-18s for international crimes where their laws permit this and assuming there is nothing precluding juvenile accountability in the treaties requiring states to criminalise such crimes.

2.2.2 *International Conventions and Custom*

Of the core international crimes, war crimes and genocide are the subject of global treaties requiring states to prevent and punish such conduct.[111]

[108] Sections 45.1 and 45.4, UNTAET Regulation No. 2000/30. Note, however, the requirement to uphold CRC rights, with the age of the juvenile being relevant to every decision. See also ss. 45 and 46, UNTAET Regulation No. 2000/30.

[109] *Prosecutor* v. *X*.

[110] *Prosecutor* v. *Elvir Jakupović*.

[111] The international legal prohibition on crimes against humanity is found in various international criminal law instruments and jurisprudence, and the position relating to child perpetrators was discussed in the preceding section.

With respect to war crimes, the main instruments are the four Geneva Conventions of 1949 and their Additional Protocols, none of which preclude the domestic prosecution of children. It has been argued that Article 77(2) of Protocol I (which establishes 15 as the minimum age of recruitment into armed forces or groups in an international armed conflict)[112] sets the same age (15) as the minimum age of criminal responsibility for war crimes. However, the text clearly does not refer to criminal responsibility, and the negotiating history reveals that a proposal to exclude penal proceedings against persons under 16 at the time of the alleged offence was rejected.[113] The committee discussing the final provision did refer to there being 'a principle of general international law that no person could be convicted of a criminal offence if, at the time the offence was committed, he was unable to understand the consequences of his act', but concluded that the application of this principle be left to domestic legislation.[114] The status of children (including those under 15) as combatants is recognised in Protocol I,[115] and like any other combatant (or indeed any civilian[116]), minors may incur individual criminal liability where they violate the laws of war. Children benefit from special protection, however, Article 77(4) requiring the separation from adults of children who are arrested, detained or interned for reasons related to the armed conflict,[117] and Article 77(5) prohibiting the death penalty for persons aged under 18 at the time of the offence related to the armed conflict. A similar preclusion on the use of the death penalty for the under-18s is found in Article 6(4) of Protocol II, governing internal armed conflicts.[118] Note that there is no prisoner of war status in internal conflicts and insurgents can be punished for taking up arms against their government and, where they kill members of the enemy forces, can be charged with murder under domestic law.

[112] Protocol II, which regulates non-international armed conflicts, contains a similar provision at Art. 4(3)(c). These provisions are norms of customary international law.

[113] See Brazilian Delegation 1978: 301 for the proposal and Committee III 1978a: 66–71 for the discussions. See also Happold 2005: 144.

[114] Committee III 1978b: 466.

[115] Art. 77(3) acknowledges that children under 15 may be taken as prisoners of war and thus can have combatant status.

[116] Since the Second World War, international law has recognised that civilians can commit war crimes.

[117] The Commentary links the question of separation with the domestic age of criminal responsibility (Sandoz, Swinarski and Zimmermann 1987: 903).

[118] Art. 68, Geneva Convention IV also prohibits the imposition of the death penalty on a protected person under the age of 18 at the time of the offence.

As regards genocide, the prohibition of genocide is universally recognised as a *jus cogens* norm (from which no derogations are permitted) giving rise to *erga omnes* obligations on states (owed to the international community as a whole). The 1948 Genocide Convention classified genocide, whether committed in times of peace or war, as a specific crime under international law and requires states parties to undertake actions to prevent and punish genocidal acts, although it is left to the state to enact legislation to give effect to the Convention provisions and, in particular, to provide effective penalties for individuals prosecuted domestically.[119] Nowhere in the Genocide Convention is there a reference to age limits for criminal responsibility: such issues are left to states when prosecuting the crime of genocide domestically or to international courts. However, genocide requires a specific intent to destroy a group or part of it, in addition to the material and mental elements to commit the underlying prohibited acts, and it has been argued that children will never possess this requisite specific genocidal intent and can thus not commit genocide.[120] This, however, is a matter of evidence rather than principle, and such intent would have to be considered on a case-by-case basis and would not exclude minors as a whole category from prosecution.

International law does not therefore preclude the domestic prosecution of minors for atrocities, charged either as international crimes or ordinary crimes, and there have been some instances where states have prosecuted minors.[121] Following the Second World War, persons under 18 (both at the time of the offence and trial) were tried for war crimes by the national military courts of the Allied Forces.[122] More recently, child soldiers have been prosecuted in the context of internal armed conflicts.[123] Between

119 As will be seen in Chapter 5, this was an issue that arose in Rwanda's response to the genocide. Note that the legal requirement to prosecute genocidal crimes was used to justify Rwanda's maximalist approach by both the Rwandan government and many international lawyers – at least initially (see Palmer 2015: 96–97).

120 On this, see Happold 2006: 71; Veale 2006: 97–98.

121 Note that some countries (e.g. Colombia and Mali) have expressly addressed the criminal responsibility of child soldiers in legislation or policy. See Steinl 2017: 170–189 for a discussion of the domestic implementation of international criminal law.

122 See *Oenning Trial*: 74 (the defendant's age of 15 was considered a mitigating factor by the British Military Tribunal but not a reason for excluding responsibility) and *Bommer Trial*: 62–66 (two young women, aged 16–18, were convicted by the French Permanent Military Tribunal, whilst a third, under 16, was acquitted on the ground of acting without judgment due to her age).

123 In Uganda, former child soldiers have been charged with treason for taking up arms against the government (but not atrocity-related crimes). See HRW 2003b and 2009.

1999 and 2002, military courts in the Democratic Republic of the Congo tried and sentenced to death seven child soldiers for various crimes, including criminal conspiracy, murder, manslaughter and weapons distribution.[124] And in the context of the 'war on terror', Omar Khadr (aged 15 at the time of the offence) was sentenced in October 2010 by a US Military Commission after pleading guilty to various crimes including violations of the laws of war.[125]

2.3 Juvenile Justice Standards on the Child Perpetrator of International Crimes

On the basis that minors can be prosecuted for international crimes, the next question to be addressed is: what are the international standards applicable to the child perpetrator of international crimes?

Section 2.1 explored in some detail the standards that apply to children who come into conflict with the law generally. As regards children accused of international crimes, the CRC does not contain any detailed provisions.[126] There are only two provisions in the CRC that relate to children in conflict or post-conflict situations: Article 38, which restricts children's participation in conflicts; and Article 39, which requires states to take measures to reintegrate child victims of various situations including armed conflicts (including child soldiers[127]). Similarly, the CRC's Optional Protocol on the Involvement of Children in Armed Conflict – which, given its subject matter, might have been expected to address explicitly children's involvement as 'perpetrators' – is silent on the issue. The accent in this instrument is primarily on the prohibition on child soldier recruitment and use, and, whilst there are provisions addressing the demobilisation, rehabilitation and social reintegration of child soldiers, no mention

124 Death sentences were commuted in respect of six, but the seventh was presumed to have been executed. See *Groupe de Travail sur les Dossiers Judiciaires Stratégiques* v. *Democratic Republic of Congo*: [4].

125 US Department of Defense 2010.

126 Nor do the ICCPR, the Beijing Rules, Havana Rules, Riyadh Guidelines or Vienna Guidelines.

127 See CRC Committee 1996: [130] and 2015a: 18. Note that UNICEF and the UN Special Representative for Children and Armed Conflict assert that Art. 39's 'focus on the well-being, recovery and reintegration of children affected by armed conflict applies to children involved in justice or reconciliation mechanisms, release and social reintegration programmes' (UNICEF and OSRSG-CAAC 2009: 59).

is made of justice concerns: children are cast solely as victims in need of protection.

Whilst neither the CRC nor its Optional Protocol explicitly expound on children accused of international crimes, Article 40(2)(a) of the CRC, which enshrines the principle of *nullum crimen sine lege*, does refer to infringements of international law. It can thus be concluded that the CRC does not preclude the prosecution of children for international crimes and that its juvenile justice standards are applicable to such children when tried in the domestic courts of a contracting state. This position has been affirmed by the UN, most notably through the 1996 expert study on the impact of armed conflict on children (the Machel report). Referring specifically to the Rwandan genocide, Machel commented: 'The severity of the crime involved … provides no justification to suspend or to abridge the fundamental rights and legal safeguards accorded to children under the Convention on the Rights of the Child.'[128] Veale comments that the Machel report establishes the CRC as 'the guiding framework for policy and practice with respect to children in conflict and post-conflict situations'.[129]

Additionally, many states have confirmed, through their endorsement of the Paris Commitments and Principles,[130] their commitment to apply international juvenile justice standards to children under 18 accused of international crimes. It is stressed in both documents that such children should be considered 'primarily as victims of offences against international law; not only as perpetrators' and that they should be 'treated in accordance with international law in a framework of restorative justice and social rehabilitation'.[131] The Paris Principles draw on the CRC, the Beijing Rules and the Riyadh Guidelines, as well as the ICCPR. The

128 Machel 1996: [251]. The report was commissioned by the UN and was 'welcomed' by the UN General Assembly (UNGA Resolution 51/77 (1996)). Note also that the CRC Committee's draft General Comment No. 24 on children's rights in juvenile justice affirms the applicability of the CRC to all children in conflict with the law 'regardless of the gravity or the context' when discussing the specific issue of children recruited and used by non-state armed groups, terrorist or violent extremist groups. CRC Committee 2018: [112].

129 Veale 1999: 106.

130 The Paris Commitments and Principles were adopted at an international conference in 2007 and built on the Cape Town Principles 1997 which did not contain any provisions relating to children accused of crimes.

131 Principle 3.6 and Commitment 11. See also Coomaraswamy 2009b: [75], 2011a: [29] and 2011b: [29–30] (acknowledging 'the need for some form of formal accountability' but commenting that detention and prosecution should be a measure of last resort); UNSG 2009: [171].

principles include: the need to seek alternatives to judicial proceedings (although no reference is made to the gravity of offences) and alternatives to institutionalisation (Principles 3.7 and 8.9 and Commitment 12), the prohibition on the death penalty and life imprisonment without the possibility of release (Principles 3.9 and 7.6.1), the prohibition on unlawful or arbitrary detention (Principle 7.6.2) and the prioritisation of juvenile cases where many people face prosecution as a result of armed conflict (Principle 8.10). Many of these standards are also referenced in the 'Key Principles for Children and Transitional Justice' (the outcome of a conference organised by UNICEF and the Harvard Human Rights Programme).[132] These Key Principles also note the contribution that local, traditional and restorative justice processes can make to accountability for crimes (although they rule out such mechanisms for more serious ordinary crimes and for international crimes), but stress the applicability of international child rights standards to such mechanisms. They advocate that the focus of these processes should be on a child's reintegration and psychosocial recovery.[133]

Whilst these best practice instruments are premised on the treatment of children as victims and 'not only' as perpetrators, and emphasise rehabilitation and restorative justice, they do not rule out accountability or domestic criminal trials, which in any event do not exclude rehabilitative or restorative approaches. As previously indicated, the focus of this book is not to consider whether children should or should not be held accountable for international crimes, but it is worth briefly returning to the suggestion that accountability could be in both the interests of the child as well as broader society. With specific reference to the commission of international crimes, the Coalition to Stop the Use of Child Soldiers commented:

> [I]t is reasonable to ask whether absolving children of responsibility for crimes they have committed is necessarily in the best interests of the child. In at least some cases, where the individual was clearly in control of their actions, and not coerced, drugged, or forced into committing atrocities, acknowledgement and atonement, including in some instances prosecution, might be an important part of personal recovery. It may also contribute to their acceptance by families, communities and society at large.[134]

[132] UNICEF 2010.

[133] Ibid.: 412–414. See also Coomaraswamy 2011a: [31–33] discussing TRCs, reintegration and traditional justice.

[134] Coalition to Stop the Use of Child Soldiers 2008: 36.

Similar comments have been made by others. Amann refers to the potential for criminal trials to contribute to reconciliation, promote rehabilitation of the child and provide redress to victims.[135] Fisher suggests that failure to hold accountable an 'adolescent child soldier' who was not coerced and was in control of his/her actions 'would arguably deny justice to victims and could be communicatively detrimental to the community and to the particular individual suspected of wrongdoing'.[136] She argues in favour of accountability, with criminal prosecutions (compliant with juvenile justice standards) being warranted in some cases, but notes that for most child soldiers, accountability approaches other than formal prosecutions and punishment may be more appropriate.[137] Doek considers that '[i]t is in line with respect for the child as a rights-holder also to hold him/her responsible for the serious violations of the rights of others he/she may have committed'.[138] In Doek's view, however, alternative measures focusing on restorative justice, rather than penal sanctions and judicial proceedings, should be used for these children. And Steinl, who 'hold[s] the view that child soldiers can benefit from accountability under the condition that the accountability measures are crafted and executed in a child-adequate fashion', similarly locates such appropriate measures in what she refers to as the 'restorative transitional justice' paradigm rather than criminal prosecutions.[139]

135 Amann 2001: 182 (note that Amann is referring to trials by the SCSL rather than domestic prosecutions).

136 Fisher 2013: 150. She also provides (in chapter 2) a comprehensive account of difficulties faced by former child soldiers in reintegrating into communities where there is a lack of accountability.

137 Fisher 2013 (generally, but in particular chapter 7).

138 Doek 2012: xix. See also Cohn 2001: 11–12 (citing a briefing by the Special Representative for Children and Armed Conflict, Olara Otunnu in 2000); Otunnu 2001: [26]; Veale 2006: 107. Cf. Grover 2012: 31 who argues against any form of accountability.

139 Steinl 2017: 36–37, and generally. She argues that restorative transitional justice is 'particularly well-suited' to deal with child soldiers, who in many cases are 'victim-perpetrators *par excellence*' (at 367) and explores the potential of various justice modalities including TRCs, amnesties and traditional justice. See also Coomaraswamy 2011b: [31] (acknowledgement of past wrongdoing 'plays a crucial role in psychosocial development' and restorative justice can lead to rehabilitation and reconciliation); Cohn 1999: 181 ('determinations of moral culpability' in e.g. truth commissions, can 'advance the child's moral development and reinsertion into a family or community'); Lima Declaration on Restorative Justice 2009 ('restorative justice is very often the only way of bringing reconciliation to victims and offenders alike in a war-torn society where victims of offences suffer as do child offenders, having been forced to commit offences').

In summary, the corpus of international standards referred to in section 2.1 above apply equally to children accused of international crimes: whatever charges are levelled at a child, he/she will benefit from the special treatment provided by the CRC and the ICCPR (where ratified by the relevant state) and the related non-binding instruments. It is also worth highlighting that this observation remains valid for children accused of 'terrorist' crimes. This is despite the retreat from child rights principles – and indeed from the 'faultless victim' image of the child soldier – by Western powers when dealing with children implicated in atrocities directed against their own populations.[140]

2.4 Conclusion

International law relies on chronological age markers to distinguish between 'adults' and 'children', the age of 18 delineating the threshold of adulthood. Many would argue that this arbitrary age distinction does not reflect societies where socio-cultural factors are more determinative of entry into adulthood. This could have particular ramifications where a 'child' under the age of 18 commits an atrocity. In such circumstances, international law does not preclude the prosecution of persons under the age of 18, although increasingly activists – as well as some academics – argue that criminal prosecution is an inappropriate response. However, where states decide to hold children accountable, either for international crimes or ordinary crimes, there are a number of international standards and principles that apply. These standards apply to all children coming into conflict with the law, although there is a lack of clarity (which the recent draft General Comment addresses to some degree) as to what standards remain applicable where an individual under 18 at the time of the alleged crime has crossed the threshold into adulthood by the time his or her case is processed. The emphasis in the standards is on taking a child-sensitive approach at all stages of the process (from investigation through to detention or alternative measures) and involves taking account of the child's age as well as the desirability of promoting his/

[140] The treatment of children captured by US forces in the 'war on terror' and their subsequent trial by US military commissions (including Omar Khadr referred to earlier) offer a compelling example of this regression. On the paradoxical perception of the child perpetrator as a 'faultless victim' when targeting his/her own population in a distant land, but as 'an intentional author of purposeful violence' when targeting Westerners, see Drumbl 2012: 128–130.

her reintegration into society. The standards set out in the CRC require states to establish a minimum age of criminal responsibility and to put in place juvenile-specific laws, procedures and institutions, establish minimum procedural guarantees (in addition to the due process guarantees granted to all persons) and prohibit certain sanctions for juveniles. A key principle underlying all of these standards is the obligation to act in the best interests of the child. A number of non-binding instruments expand on these rights. However, how are these international standards put into practice? It is to this question the book now turns.

3

Putting International Standards into Practice

The responsibility for implementing and complying with international standards rests firmly with a state that has signed up to these standards or is otherwise bound by custom. The CRC sets out implementation obligations for states parties in Article 4, requiring states to 'undertake all appropriate legislative, administrative, and other measures for the implementation of the rights recognized in the present Convention'. The methods through which implementation takes place are left to the state, although the CRC Committee has outlined measures that it considers key to effective implementation.[1] Such measures include the harmonisation of laws, the provision of effective remedies, monitoring, sufficient resource allocation, training on child rights and general awareness-raising.

However, as was mooted in the introduction, and as will become evident throughout this book, a post-conflict state will often be bereft of resources and may not be in a position to implement or comply fully with its international obligations. That raises the question as to whether international child rights standards make any allowances for the context in which they are to be implemented: does the CRC, or the non-binding instruments, permit derogations from the provisions or otherwise accommodate local conditions? In this chapter, I address this question and also expound particular challenges to implementation and compliance in the field of juvenile justice.

The state does not, however, operate in vacuum. There is a range of international mechanisms that promote implementation of, and compliance with, human rights law. Some are judicial bodies or specialist bodies that evaluate a state's compliance with its international obligations, whilst others are more operational in nature and are involved in providing technical or other forms of assistance to the state. This chapter will provide an overview of these mechanisms as they relate to children's rights, examining

[1] See CRC Committee 1999 and 2003b.

in particular the CRC Committee established by the CRC to monitor state compliance with the treaty, before focusing in some detail on UNICEF. As I will evince later in this book, UNICEF had significant involvement with child *génocidaires* in Rwanda, and a key objective of this book is to elucidate and evaluate the role it played in operationalising international juvenile justice standards: it is thus essential to have an understanding of the organisation's institutional ethos, its role under the CRC and the impact of the CRC on its work, and its stance on juvenile justice. It is these issues that will be the focus of the final part of this chapter.

3.1 Legal Accommodations

International standards on child perpetrators contained in the CRC apply to all children in states that have ratified the treaty. This includes post-conflict states, which may be in turmoil, with no functioning apparatus and limited or no resources. This section looks at whether international law accommodates the relevant context. It first considers the 'escape' route of derogations, then explores whether the economic, social and cultural context may be taken into account, before finally addressing textual flexibility. Although these mechanisms relate to evaluating a state's compliance on a legalistic basis (and are thus more related to enforcement by judicial or quasi-judicial bodies), the existence or lack of legal accommodation indicates the nature of child rights and provides the background against which international standards on child perpetrators are operationalised.

3.1.1 Derogations

Some international treaties allow for states to derogate temporarily from some of their commitments in times of emergencies.[2] Whilst the CRC provides for denunciation of the Convention (Article 52), it does not contain any derogation provision. The derogations mechanism was discussed during the drafting process[3] but ultimately no provision was included. It is arguable that derogation is permitted even where not expressly provided for in a treaty, on the basis that the right to derogate 'is inherent in any human rights law system'.[4] Conversely, the claim has

2 For an overview of the derogation mechanism, see Fitzpatrick 1994; Gross and Ní Aoláin 2006.

3 See Price Cohen 1987: 98–105.

4 Giacca 2014: 83 (referring to the various proponents of this approach).

been advanced that the absence of such a provision means that all the treaty provisions remain in full force.[5] The CRC Committee has indicated that the general provisions in Articles 2–4 of the CRC are not subject to derogation in times of war or emergency and also emphasised that the entire 'framework of the realization of the rights of the child' should be ensured in times of armed conflict.[6] UNICEF takes the view that derogation is not permitted under the CRC in times of crises, and that it therefore applies at all times, in all circumstances, to all children.[7] The HRC has commented on the lack of a derogations clause in the CRC, and stated: 'As article 38 of the Convention clearly indicates, the Convention is applicable in emergency situations.'[8] In contrast to the CRC, the ICCPR does allow for temporary derogation 'in time of public emergency … the existence of which is officially proclaimed', although there are restrictions, and certain articles are excluded.[9] The list of non-derogable rights does not include Articles 10 and 14 which provide specific protection for juvenile offenders. However, the HRC has confirmed that a state cannot derogate from ICCPR provisions where this would result in a breach of that state's other international obligations.[10]

A strong argument can thus be made that international standards on child perpetrators apply in full in emergency situations. Given the focus in this book on the operationalisation of international standards in post-conflict situations, rather than on the state's responsibility for failing to respect standards, I do not address whether states should be able to derogate from their obligations under the CRC. However, the question of derogation will be revisited briefly in Chapter 5. Further, it is worth noting White and Odello's observations that a post-conflict state may be reluctant to declare a state of emergency 'for reasons of credibility', and also that a state of emergency situation may differ from the 'immediate post-conflict situation'.[11]

[5] This is the view of Cohn (1999: 193), who argues that the absence of such a clause in the CRC means that the 'entire Convention remains in effect regardless the level of national emergency'. See also the discussion in Cohn 1991: 105–106.

[6] CRC Committee 1992c: [67] and [73]. See also Hodgkin and Newell 2007: 660.

[7] UNICEF 2007a: [27].

[8] HRC 2001: note 5.

[9] Art. 4.

[10] HRC 2001: [9–10].

[11] White and Odello 2007: 61–62. They argue that a state of emergency framework can provide guidance but note that a country in a state of emergency may have a functioning infrastructure in contrast to a post-conflict state.

3.1.2 Recognition of Relevant Conditions

The non-binding instruments relating to juvenile justice (the Havana Rules, Beijing Rules and Riyadh Guidelines) expressly allow for contextualisation by providing that economic, social and cultural conditions are relevant to the implementation of the rules.[12] O'Donnell argues that this wording should not be perceived as a 'ready-made excuse' for non-implementation on the basis of 'unfavourable' local conditions, but as 'an affirmation' of the obligation to implement the standards 'in some appropriate way' that takes account of prevailing conditions.[13] The CRC does not contain the same wording. Its preamble refers to 'the importance of the traditions and cultural values of each people', and Article 4 allows for consideration of resources, but in respect of economic, social and cultural rights only.[14] In its General Comment on implementation measures, the CRC Committee notes that Article 4 introduces the concept of 'progressive realization' for economic, social and cultural rights to reflect 'a realistic acceptance that lack of resources … can hamper the full implementation' of such rights.[15]

A distinction is thus made between civil and political rights and economic, social and cultural rights, which some child rights experts have called 'flawed' or have found to be unhelpful for public policy or human rights work.[16] A detailed analysis of the differences between these two sets of rights is beyond the scope of this book. It is sufficient to note that progressive realisation usually proceeds from the premise that economic, social and cultural rights are resource-demanding and require positive action, whilst civil and political rights are not resource-intensive and are negative in nature. However, whilst this may be the case, for example, for the prohibition on the death penalty for the under-18s, it is not the case for the separation of children from adults in detention, juvenile courts or fair trial guarantees, where significant resources (defined broadly to include financial, human, material and organisational resources) and

[12] Rule 16, Rule 1.5 and Guideline 8 respectively. The Vienna Guidelines do not contain similar wording.

[13] Cited in Veerman and Waldman 1996: 156.

[14] Note that, in initial drafts, both categories of rights were subject to 'available resources'. This 'available resources' wording was later restricted to economic, social and cultural rights after UNICEF expressed concern that there would be 'radical diminution of the standards contained in existing instruments'. See OHCHR 2007a: 349–356.

[15] CRC Committee 2003b: [7].

[16] Himes 1993: 13 (referencing Alston and others). See also Van Bueren 1998: 381–383.

action will be required on the part of the state. With particular reference to children accused of international crimes, Petty and Brown recognise the 'resource implications' of certain standards contained in the ICCPR and CRC (including separation from adults, humane conditions of detention and fair trial guarantees) and note that such resources may not be available in a post-conflict state.[17] Yet no allowance is made in either instrument for lack of resources in respect of these standards.[18] In reports to the CRC Committee (and the HRC), states are required to report on any factors and difficulties which have affected implementation and, to this extent, are able to raise issues such as economic difficulties, violence or political instability. However, whilst committees have taken note of these factors, Brems comments that they are not accepted as a justification for failure to implement the provisions, and committees have frequently stressed that states must take measures to overcome these obstacles.[19] As will be illustrated in Chapters 5–7, in practice the resource constraints in post-genocide Rwanda significantly impeded state compliance and also had an impact on how UNICEF Rwanda approached implementation and compliance with the result that arguably both sets of rights were in effect treated as being subject to progressive realisation.

3.1.3 Textual Indeterminacy or Flexibility?

Alston comments that international human rights norms 'must be sufficiently clear, comprehensive and inflexible to provide the international community with some basis on which it might seek to constrain a government which undermines or circumvents minimum standards of decent behaviour'.[20] The absence of a clear standard can impede evaluations of compliance as well as advocacy efforts aimed at encouraging compliance.

[17] Petty and Brown 1998b: 106–107. See also Lubell 2012: 325–330 (arguing in favour of a contextual approach and noting – at 330 – that detention and trial rights are 'far from cost-free'); Galligan and Sandler 2004: 34–35 (noting that freedom from torture requires a sophisticated system with accountability and controls and that 'positive' rights such as fair trial rights require even more resources).

[18] And indeed, the HRC (1992: [13]) has stressed the 'mandatory' nature of the requirement to separate juveniles from adults in detention facilities.

[19] Brems 2001: 346–352.

[20] Alston 1994: 17–18. See also Chayes and Chayes 1995: 10 (citing ambiguity and indeterminacy of treaty language as one potential reason for non-compliance); Franck 1988: 714 (textual determinacy is one of four characteristics identified as being key to the legitimacy of a rule); Shelton 2000: 14 (noting that '[a]mbiguity and open-endedness of international standards can limit efforts to secure compliance').

Imprecision can also lead to subjective application of a provision and may result in it being (mis)used to justify a particular action. However, it can be argued conversely that a level of imprecision is necessary for universal application. Donnelly, for example, asserts that a 'fairly high level of abstraction actually helps to assure that human rights remain a progressive force', arguing that there needs to be 'space' within the provisions to allow for differences in implementation.[21] With respect to the CRC, Alston similarly notes that any instrument which is 'avowedly universalist in its aspirations' and encompasses so many rights and issues must retain flexibility and be able to adapt to change.[22] Indeed, given the desire to attract universal ratification and thus the need to take account of various particularities (as well as the requirement for consensus during the drafting stage) many of the CRC's provisions are vague.[23]

In the area of juvenile justice, Cantwell highlights two indeterminate provisions: Article 37(b) that requires detention to be used 'only as a measure of last resort and for the shortest appropriate period of time' and Article 40(3)(b) that requires the setting of a minimum age of criminal responsibility but fails to specify that age.[24] And, as will be recalled, the best interests principle has been considered especially vague. Kilkelly comments that the imprecision of the best interests principle 'risks undermining its contribution to the rights approach to children's issues', yet concludes overall that Article 3 of the CRC is a useful advocacy tool.[25] Zermatten refers to there being advantages of having 'a broad, flexible and responsive (relative to time and space) concept' that is adaptable to cultural and socio-economic variance across different legal systems, and asserts that it provides the 'link between the theory and the reality'.[26] And Alston indicates that localised 'understandings' during the application of the best interests principle can mitigate against indeterminacy, and that the CRC 'as a whole' contributes to the elaboration of the principle by providing a 'broad ethical or value framework' within which those applying

[21] Donnelly 2006: 70.

[22] Alston 1994: 18 (he notes that some of the core human rights norms, such as due process rights, are by nature indeterminate).

[23] Interestingly, the ACRWC's provisions are frequently less flexible, including its 'rigid' definition of childhood, which 'leaves no space for local interpretations'. See Twum-Danso 2008: 393.

[24] Cantwell 2011: 52 (note 22).

[25] Kilkelly 2011: 181.

[26] Zermatten 2010: 495.

the principle can seek guidance.[27] Lack of precision can thus be viewed more as a lack of prescription, allowing local particularities to be taken into account during implementation whilst remaining faithful to the underlying normative value of the standard. This appears to be the way in which the CRC Committee has used the best interests principle, applying it 'as a dynamic concept that requires an assessment appropriate to the specific context'.[28] Indeed, Cantwell has argued that the CRC as a whole should be viewed as a 'living document' able to adapt to new issues that were not in the contemplation of its drafters at the time.[29] As I argue later in this book, the textual flexibility inherent in the CRC enabled UNICEF Rwanda to interpret the provisions non-restrictively, and thus to adopt a pragmatic yet principled approach when operationalising international standards on child perpetrators.

3.2 Juvenile Justice – The 'Unwanted Child' of Human Rights?[30]

As indicated above, the CRC does not expressly allow for the consideration of local conditions (which may include lack of resources or social challenges) in respect of civil and political rights. In comparison to other areas of human rights, children's rights are often viewed as fairly uncontroversial. In the words of Smith: 'It is difficult to be an opponent to the goal of making a better world for children.'[31] The rate at which the CRC was ratified together with the level of ratification would support this viewpoint, constituting 'evidence of the consensus possible with regard to children'.[32] It might thus be thought that children's rights are largely impervious to pressures arising from unfavourable local conditions. Indeed, Abramson notes that states parties have taken 'meaningful steps' to comply with their obligations under the CRC through reviewing their laws, institutions and policies, and are also complying with their state reporting obligations.[33] He further asserts that the 'power of the CRC is its catalytic effect in stimulating activism at all levels of society'.[34] Simmons,

[27] Alston 1994: 19.
[28] CRC Committee 2013a: [1].
[29] Cantwell 2011: 52–53.
[30] This phrase is borrowed from Abramson 2006.
[31] Smith 2009: 109.
[32] UNICEF 1999c: 2. UNICEF suggests that this consensus 'can help to create a more positive climate for the acceptance of other human rights standards'.
[33] Abramson 2006: 16.
[34] Ibid.: 17.

who explores the impact of treaty ratification on state behaviour and stresses the importance of domestic mobilisation in enhancing compliance, comments: 'If there is any group around whom most societies can mobilize to protect, it is children … Thus … the more protective measures for children are fairly uncontroversial in principle.'[35]

However, states ratify international treaties for a whole host of reasons. These may include genuine commitment to the principles of the treaty (albeit often without the ability to fulfil these commitments), international pressure and/or a desire to enhance their status in the international community with no intention to fulfil their treaty obligations. This undermines the argument that near universal ratification of the CRC equates with universality in attitudes towards children's rights. The fact that African states have been much slower to sign up to the regional child rights treaty (the ACRWC) than the CRC further suggests that not all states are on the same page when it comes to children's rights: states may have been more concerned about their international (compared to regional) reputation rather than being committed to child rights principles.[36] Additionally, there may be a disconnect between the official national approach and local communities. As Twum-Danso underscores, 'due to the long history of imperialism and colonization, states may be more universal than their societies, as in many countries the gap between the state and its society is significant'.[37] Thus, whilst a government may have endorsed and accepted a treaty's provisions, the population may actively reject them, and thus impede implementation.

It is certainly the case that some child rights are accepted in all societies as legitimate (although they may not always be conceived or constructed as 'rights'). These may include in particular those that address the basic needs of the child such as the food, shelter and health. However, universality of the conception of rights is a different proposition entirely from universal implementation: even where a society's views may correspond with international standards, the practical realisation of such rights may be hindered by local conditions, in particular lack of resources. Additionally, some child rights are still subject to considerable contestation at the domestic level. These include participation and protection

[35] Simmons 2009: 358.

[36] A further reason for the slower adoption of the ACRWC may be that, whilst the ACRWC contains similar provisions to the CRC, some of its provisions are more stringent and thus demanding on states parties. See Twum-Danso 2008: 398.

[37] Twum-Danso 2008: 396 and Twum-Danso Imoh 2011: 381.

rights, which are often more politically sensitive than survival and development rights. And juvenile justice is perhaps the most controversial area of all. Whilst Simmons postulates that societies can be mobilised around the issue of child rights, she makes the observation (in general, as opposed to relating to juveniles) that the mobilisation effect is likely to be weaker where the beneficiaries are alleged criminals. She explains that it may be difficult to garner support for fair trial rights as 'alleged criminals … typically are not well positioned to mobilize to demand better treatment by law enforcement authorities and the local court system … Moreover, alleged criminals do not enjoy the natural sympathy of a broad segment of most societies.'[38] Not only does this make it difficult for the victims of violations to assert their rights, but it can also make advocacy on their behalf more challenging as human rights advocates may be seen as an extension of this group.[39]

This tension can be perceived with respect to juvenile justice and children's rights. Hamilton and Harvey highlight public opinion towards juveniles (often based on lack of information or misconceptions) as being a key challenge to the implementation of juvenile justice standards.[40] Odongo, presuming political will on the part of the government to implement children's rights given that they protect a vulnerable group, comments that juvenile justice 'challenges the perception that children's rights are apolitical in nature' and thus may result in a 'retreat in political commitment'.[41] Abramson, noting the success in all other key areas addressed in the CRC, comments that juvenile justice has been neglected and marginalised. He provides a number of explanations for juvenile justice being the 'unwanted child' of human rights. These include: society's unsympathetic or hostile response to child offenders; the structure of juvenile justice, in that it involves several overlapping systems (i.e. the police, prison service, prosecutors, defence lawyers and judges) and functions (i.e. prevention, diversion and imprisonment); the rhetoric, presenting 'children' as innocent victims which marginalises older juveniles; and adopting a 'salami' or piecemeal approach to the CRC despite its holistic nature by focusing on specific articles addressing particular themes rather than factoring in that there is, for example, a right to

[38] Simmons 2009: 357.
[39] See Jetschke and Liese 2013: 41.
[40] Hamilton and Harvey 2004. See also UNICEF 1998a: 17.
[41] Odongo 2005: 122.

education and health for juveniles in detention.[42] Abramson suggests that one way of mitigating these factors is by getting juvenile justice reform on the international agenda. He refers to international development and support as being essential, noting that the lack of financial capability in developing countries is frequently cited as a reason for failure to implement juvenile justice standards.[43] Odongo similarly notes that the lack of financial (and also human) resources is often raised as an impediment to implementation,[44] and, according to Van Bueren, the 'fundamental problem' with juvenile justice standards is the cost of implementation: 'How can states which regard themselves as being unable to afford universal child education and health services devote scarce resources to improving a juvenile justice system which only affects a minority of the child population. Until this issue is confronted universal improvement in the administration of juvenile justice will remain only a distant goal.'[45]

The challenges to the implementation of, and compliance with, juvenile justice standards are not confined to developing countries: 'Western' states have confronted 'moral panics' with respect to youth crime which have frequently resulted in a shift towards more punitive responses,[46] and have also pointed to lack of resources for failure to implement or comply with CRC provisions.[47] However, these challenges are more likely to be pronounced in a post-conflict society such as Rwanda, where institutions are not functioning fully and where the alleged crimes are particularly serious and emotive and there is thus stronger societal pressure for retributive measures. The particular challenges faced by Rwanda after the genocide will be explored in Chapter 4.

3.3 Mechanisms for the Promotion of Child Rights

There are various mechanisms at the international level that seek to promote human rights implementation and compliance. These include

[42] For the full list and discussion, see Abramson 2006: 23–32.

[43] Ibid.: 34–36.

[44] Odongo 2005: 419–422.

[45] Van Bueren 1998: 171.

[46] See e.g. Jensen and Jepsen 2006: 446–451; Jenks 2005: chapter 6 (commenting on the James Bulger case and observing that children committing violent crimes 'disassemble the traditional binary opposition between the categories of "child" and "adult" ' – at 128).

[47] E.g. the UK entered a reservation (since removed) to Art. 37(c) (requiring separation in detention) on the basis that mixing might be mutually beneficial or might be necessary in the event of lack of suitable accommodation/adequate facilities.

the complaints procedure and special procedures of the Human Rights Council,[48] resolutions by the General Assembly, measures by the Security Council and, at the field level, programmes of the Office of the UN High Commissioner for Human Rights (OHCHR) – which may themselves address child rights issues. There are also some that are specifically concerned with child rights.[49] The Office of the Special Representative of the Secretary-General for Children and Armed Conflict[50] and the Security Council Working Group on Children and Armed Conflict[51] are two such mechanisms, although their focus has been more on child soldier recruitment and children targeted during attacks, rather than child perpetrators.[52]

3.3.1 The CRC Committee

The main mechanism for the promotion of child rights is the CRC Committee, established by the CRC to monitor and promote specifically the rights set out in the Convention.[53] The primary method of work is the state reporting procedure under Article 44, pursuant to which states parties must submit periodic reports to the Committee on measures adopted to 'give effect' to CRC rights and 'on the progress made on the enjoyment of those rights'. They must also report on any factors and difficulties which have impeded implementation. To facilitate a constructive dialogue between the Committee and state party during formal examination of the report, the Committee sends the state party a list of issues and questions arising from the report and from information gathered from other organisations, including UNICEF and NGOs, during a presessional meeting. The list indicates which issues will be raised during

48 The Human Rights Council replaced the Commission on Human Rights in 2006.

49 See Van Bueren 1998: 383–412 for an overview of mechanisms that pertain to children's rights.

50 UNGA Resolution 51/77 (1996) established the mandate and recommended the appointment of a Special Representative, and the first Special Representative, Olara Otunnu, was appointed in 1997.

51 Established in 2005 by UNSC Resolution 1612.

52 Although note that the detention of children for alleged association with armed groups has been identified as an emerging challenge (see e.g. Coomaraswamy 2010a: [8–11]) and, as referenced in section 2.3, various reports have addressed briefly the prosecution and detention of children.

53 Art. 43. Note that many of the comments in this section are relevant to all UN treaty bodies, including the HRC that monitors compliance with the ICCPR (and thus those articles containing juvenile justice standards).

examination and requests additional information. There is then a formal examination of the report between Committee members and delegates of the state party. Following this, the CRC issues its concluding observations in which it comments on compliance by the state, notes areas of concern and makes recommendations.

There are diverging views on the effectiveness of the state reporting system. Some commentators argue that the process can stimulate legal review and reform and raise awareness of child rights issues, and that the concluding observations can be utilised to benchmark state law and practice and used as an advocacy tool by other states or organisations.[54] The process is seen as a means of promoting social mobilisation and encouraging collaborative action and thus aims 'to strengthen the national capacity to monitor children's rights and not to replace it'.[55] Others highlight that states frequently fail to file reports on time (if at all – for which there are no real sanctions[56]) and that reports, where filed, are often 'insufficient, politically doctored, and unreliable'.[57] Further, the concluding observations and recommendations do not create any binding obligations. As regards post-conflict states, O'Flaherty considers that the value of treaty bodies exists 'more in potential than in reality', commenting that conflict and post-conflict states are 'among the worst culprits in failing to submit timely reports (whether because of the chaos of conflict, the lack of skills and capacities or through sheer unwillingness on the part of key elements of government)'.[58] Treaty bodies, including the CRC, have developed procedures to attempt to overcome these limitations, which include the ability to undertake urgent actions in serious situations. These may include requesting a special report from the state, examining a situation in the absence of a report or requesting a state visit. Such actions are considered to be part of the obligation to report, but the invocation of the procedure is subject to a number of criteria and must embody the spirit of dialogue between the state and the Committee.[59] However, as O'Flaherty

[54] See e.g. Alston 1997: 21–24; Kilkelly 2011: 184; O'Flaherty 2002: 1–3; Tomuschat 2008: 188–189; Van Bueren 1998: 384.

[55] Lansdown 2000: 114.

[56] The CRC Committee can refer to a state's failure to comply in its annual report to the General Assembly which can call on states to comply, but these calls are largely 'ineffectual' (Crawford 2000: 4). See also LeBlanc 1995: 234.

[57] Galligan and Sandler 2004: 46.

[58] O'Flaherty 2003: 67.

[59] See CRC Committee 1992b. Pursuant to Art. 44(4) of the CRC, the CRC Committee can request further information from states on the implementation of the Convention, but

notes, 'these practices have, with regard to post-conflict situations, only been invoked in a highly sporadic manner'.[60]

In addition to the reporting process, the CRC Committee issues general comments which provide interpretative guidance on implementing and complying with particular treaty provisions. It also has, although only since April 2014, the mandate to consider individual and inter-state complaints.[61] An individual complaints mechanism had been rejected during the drafting process of the CRC: it was felt that individual complaints would 'transform an implementation mechanism based on cooperation to one fraught with confrontation', and that such a mechanism was appropriate for civil and political rights only.[62] Like the state reporting procedure, the views issued by treaty bodies on communications are non-binding, although the mechanism can have a positive influence particularly in states concerned about their international reputation.[63] However, there has been little use of individual complaints procedures (before other treaty bodies) in conflict and post-conflict states, as such states have often not ratified the relevant provisions or protocol allowing for the procedure.[64]

A further key method of 'foster[ing] the effective implementation' of the CRC is the role assigned to actors other than the state and an emphasis on international cooperation. Under Article 45, UNICEF and other UN organs can be present when state reports are under consideration, may be invited to submit reports and provide expert advice to the CRC Committee, and may also receive requests to provide technical assistance. Further, UNICEF may be invited by the Committee to participate in private meetings.[65] In the words of O'Donnell: 'In effect, these provisions provide the legal basis for a system for promoting implementation of the Convention which goes far beyond mere monitoring, and which could make a valuable contribution to stimulating and co-ordinating

'[t]here is an understanding that this provision will be used rarely and only in cases which appear grave'. Hammarberg 1994: 86.

60 O'Flaherty 2003: 67. See, however, section 6.1 regarding the HRC's request to Rwanda to submit urgently a special report.

61 Optional Protocol to the Convention on the Rights of the Child on a Communications Procedure 2011.

62 Van Bueren 1998: 411. See also Van Bueren 2011: 120–124; Tomuschat 2008: 198–199.

63 Tomuschat 2008: 229.

64 O'Flaherty 2003: 67. Rwanda, for example, has not ratified the relevant optional protocols to the ICCPR and CRC.

65 CRC Committee 2015b: Rule 41.

bilateral and multilateral co-operation in favour of the rights of children.'[66] Treaty body recommendations for future action 'almost invariably' include references to technical cooperation or assistance, and the CRC Committee produces the 'most comprehensive' recommendations in this regard.[67] According to Van Bueren, technical assistance 'was intended from the beginning to be central to the implementation procedure' and is considered 'crucial' to domestic implementation of the substance of the CRC. She asserts: 'This approach to implementation underlies the whole philosophy of the Convention on the Rights of the Child, which is implementation through cooperation. It adds an important dimension to the standard reporting procedures.'[68] Balton, however, underlines that agencies providing assistance 'will serve … strictly at the pleasure of the governments of those states, and will likely have little leverage to enforce compliance with the Convention'.[69]

Arguably, these procedures are fairly weak implementation methods, particularly given the non-binding and unenforceable nature of concluding observations and views. However, as noted by Hammarberg, the CRC aims to 'encourage progress rather than pass judgement', thus the CRC Committee is to identify problems, propose remedies and encourage discussion: 'The thrust is not finger-pointing.'[70] That the CRC adopts a constructive and non-confrontational rather than critical orientation to implementation and compliance has been highlighted by many commentators. LeBlanc states that the CRC's task is seemingly to 'assist' rather than 'penalise' states,[71] and Santos País refers to the 'non-adversarial approach' of the CRC and the emphasis on 'the need for dialogue rather than a punitive attitude'.[72] Regarding CRC Committee practice, Black identifies a policy of fostering constructive dialogue; persuasion as opposed to confrontation being considered the best strategy given that CRC provisions must be implemented through legal and policy reform at the national or even subnational level.[73] Fottrell comes to a similar

[66] O'Donnell 1992: 26.

[67] Gallagher 2000: 218 and 220.

[68] Van Bueren 1998: 395–396.

[69] Balton 1990: 128–129.

[70] Hammarberg 1994: 85. See also Donnelly 2013: 166 (commenting that complaints regarding the 'weakness' of the reporting system assumes that the goal is 'coercive enforcement', whereas the aim is 'promotion' and thus to encourage and facilitate compliance).

[71] LeBlanc 1995: xxi.

[72] Santos País 1997: 498. She goes on to highlight the advantages of this approach.

[73] Black 1996: 295.

conclusion, referring to 'constructive and creative suggestions' rather than coercion as the *modus operandi* of the Committee, but suggests that this system is likely to be more effective where a state generally has good human rights practices.[74] Whether this promotion of cooperation over confrontation is to be seen as a hindrance or an opportunity depends on the theoretical position taken on human rights promotion, protection and compliance, and will be discussed in more detail in Chapter 8.

3.3.2 UNICEF

Initially created by the UN General Assembly in 1946 as a temporary UN programme to provide emergency assistance to children following the Second World War,[75] UNICEF's mandate was made permanent in 1953.[76] It was the first intergovernmental agency to have an exclusive focus on children. Whilst not established with the explicit mandate to promote children's rights, it has embraced its role under the CRC (albeit gradually), adding rights to its humanitarian and development mandate. In the following subsections, I explore these developments in the context of UNICEF's institutional nature and its relationship with the CRC, before concluding with an overview of the place of juvenile justice in UNICEF's activities.

a UNICEF's Institutional Nature

According to LeBlanc, 'UNICEF was created by governments and, for the most part, remains a creature of governments. Governments prescribe its mandate, establish much of its agenda, and provide most of its budget – all of which can serve to limit its independence or autonomy.'[77] Further, the founding General Assembly resolution provided that UNICEF would operate in a particular country only 'in consultation with, and with the consent of, the Government concerned.'[78] This suggests that UNICEF is constrained by its founders, funders and host governments, which inevitably could dictate its *modus operandi*.

[74] Fottrell 2000: 6–7.

[75] UNGA Resolution 57(1), 11 December 1946. Its term was renewed for three years in 1950. See UNGA Resolution 417(V), 1 December 1950.

[76] UNGA Resolution 802(VIII), 6 October 1953.

[77] LeBlanc 1995: 40. See also Beigbeder 2001: xii. Note, however, that UNICEF funds are derived from a range of sources, at least a quarter of contributions coming from individuals and private sources.

[78] UNGA Resolution 57(1) (1946): [2(c)].

UNICEF's mandate derives from General Assembly resolutions, as interpreted by UNICEF's Executive Board. As such, its mandate maintains some flexibility and is capable of being adapted to address new challenges. The mandate has dynamically evolved over time, largely as a result of practical experience but, as evinced below, particularly following the entry into force of the CRC. Established initially to develop relief programmes for children in war-torn countries (primarily in Europe but also Japan and China) and also more generally for child health purposes, UNICEF's reach expanded both geographically and operationally in 1950: UNICEF was henceforth to develop programmes and policies of long-term benefit to children in developing countries. In response to this change in focus, the words 'international' and 'emergency' were removed from UNICEF's name (United Nations International Children's Emergency Fund) in 1953. However, whilst UNICEF can now be viewed predominantly as a child development agency, it has nonetheless retained an emergency and humanitarian mandate.[79] Additionally, UNICEF adopted a rights-based approach in the mid-1990s and has thus further expanded its responsibilities which, as will be illustrated below, has not been without contention.

Whilst its headquarters is based in New York, UNICEF is an operational organisation with country offices or other representation in 190 countries.[80] A Basic Cooperation Agreement between UNICEF and the host country provides the legal basis for UNICEF's operations. UNICEF and the relevant government develop a five-year 'country programme', based on a situation analysis, that identifies the priorities that will be addressed during this period. UNICEF's activities in a particular country are 'necessarily selective', the country programme 'commit[ting] UNICEF to support a limited, strategic set of activities that are chosen … for their catalytic and advocacy effect, as well as for their direct impact on a specific number of beneficiaries'.[81] The emphasis is on supporting and building national and local capacities for action: in the words of Jolly, 'Support could be catalytic but not more.'[82] Indeed from its very early work, it is clear that UNICEF saw its role as assisting governments rather than taking on responsibility itself for the administration of operations.[83] The

[79] For an overview of UNICEF's policy on emergencies over the years, see Beigbeder 2001: chapter 6.
[80] There are also seven regional offices that provide support and guidance to country offices.
[81] UNICEF 1995b: [27].
[82] Jolly 2014: 33.
[83] See e.g. UNICEF 1953: [16].

country programme approach is seen as a major UNICEF asset on the basis that programmes and activities can be tailored to the reality on the ground and are developed in cooperation with governments and other key national partners. As such, the approach enables responsiveness to rapidly changing local conditions.

Also considered a crucial UNICEF attribute is the organisation's decentralised structure on which the country programme approach is founded. The New York headquarters is responsible for the overall coordination and management of the organisation and also for UNICEF's global policy. But it is at the national, or sometimes also the subnational, level that UNICEF is most operationally active. At the country level, UNICEF employs international staff but also a large number of national professionals who not only speak the local language but are also culturally sensitive. Considerable authority and responsibility are invested in UNICEF's country representatives, who operate with a significant degree of autonomy and flexibility in making decisions, the headquarters' role kept to a minimum.[84] As Oestreich sums up:

> As an organization, UNICEF places considerable emphasis on its decentralized operations and the limited interference from New York in the activities directed by its field representatives. It is left to each office to determine which areas are to be considered priorities and which strategies are appropriate. There are, of course, strategy documents created in New York. Nevertheless, allowing maximum freedom for country offices to find their own path remains part of the organization's culture and standard operating procedures.[85]

This decentralised structure has been lauded by commentators: Quesnel asserts that it 'allows UNICEF to perceive and respond to diverse needs, audiences and demands emanating from local realities',[86] whilst Beigbeder describes it as the 'strength of UNICEF and at least one of the keys to its success'.[87]

One final feature that UNICEF seeks to promote is its impartiality, neutrality and non-political stance. UNICEF has historically sought to provide humanitarian assistance and development aid to all those in need

[84] Over the years, UNICEF has sought to enhance its decentralised structure whilst also ensuring sufficient checks and balances. See e.g. UNICEF 1996f (for delegation to field operations); Jolly 2014: 115 (for tightened procedures).

[85] Oestreich 1998: 188.

[86] Quesnel 2002: 17.

[87] Beigbeder 2001: 48.

without taking sides in any conflict, to avoid being used for political means, and to refrain from engaging with politically sensitive issues. This commitment to political neutrality was a major sticking point when it came to UNICEF's engagement with the CRC.

b UNICEF and the CRC: A Framework for Action

The CRC was described in 1997 by Carol Bellamy, UNICEF's Executive Director at that time, as 'a document that is at once the core of UNICEF's work, and the torch that lights the way'.[88] The CRC was not always central to UNICEF's work, however. UNICEF initially had been reluctant to support the Convention given its concerns that a set of binding rights could compromise its relationship with states – one based on collaboration rather than confrontation, with UNICEF operating in a particular country only with consent. It was also concerned that involvement with the CRC would politicise UNICEF and could draw it into controversial issues. Before the adoption of the CRC, UNICEF's advocacy 'was not a matter of exposure, critique and campaigns for political or legislative reform', and UNICEF was 'inhibited by its intergovernmental character from engaging, or wishing to engage, in … confrontational campaign[s]' on rights issues.[89] A particular concern was child protection – a major feature in the draft Convention: 'UNICEF was originally reluctant to join an initiative which would include child protection, a sensitive area where the agency might find itself in confrontation with governments, compromise its tradition of impartiality, and thus jeopardize its global child survival and development programmes.'[90] Consequently, 'UNICEF treated the Working Group on the Convention with "benign neglect" for several years'.[91]

However, during the 1980s, UNICEF changed tack, seeking to influence the drafting of the CRC. Both Beigbeder and Oestreich suggest that the decision to engage with the drafting process was at least partly a result of UNICEF's increasing interest during the mid-1980s in a new area of children's issues – children in especially difficult circumstances (see below).[92] These issues were seen by some in UNICEF as closely related to the rights set down in the draft convention and they, together with

[88] Cited in UNICEF 1997b: [400].
[89] Black 1996: 137.
[90] Beigbeder 2001: 147–148.
[91] Ibid.: 148.
[92] Ibid.: 148 and Oestreich 1998: 185.

NGOs (who had significant involvement in the drafting of the CRC)[93] persuaded the Executive Board to support the drafting process. Under the leadership of James Grant (Executive Director 1980–1995), who became a 'passionate and effective advocate' of the CRC,[94] UNICEF subsequently promoted the Convention's adoption and universal ratification through mobilising public opinion and advocacy and awareness-raising activities. Indeed, a report of the Secretary-General in 1998 referred to UNICEF's 'sustained efforts to encourage ratification' of the CRC contributing to almost universal ratification.[95]

As outlined earlier, the CRC explicitly assigns UNICEF a role in the promotion of the effective implementation of the Convention and facilitation of international cooperation. There were proposals to name UNICEF as 'the designated lead agency on children', for UNICEF to 'collaborate' with UN specialised agencies/organs and NGOs 'to establish and carry out programmes of action to further the implementation' of CRC rights, and for UNICEF to be informed of measures taken by specialised agencies for the realisation of CRC rights.[96] However, during drafting discussions, many delegates argued that states parties were primarily responsible for implementation and only they were 'entitled to control compliance with the convention'. Further, some questioned whether UNICEF should be mentioned at all in the text for various reasons, including that UNICEF was not specialised in legal matters and should not be involved in judging compliance (the implication being that UNICEF should not be present during the examination of state reports).[97] The wording ultimately adopted removed the phrase 'designated lead agency' but retained the reference to UNICEF.[98] As such, 'for the first time in any international treaty, the organization was named as having special responsibilities in fostering the effective implementation of the Convention nationally and internationally'.[99] Writing in 1992, O'Donnell asserted that, as the only UN

[93] See Türkelli and Vandenhole 2012.

[94] Beigbeder 2001: 36.

[95] UNSG 1998: [41].

[96] Extracts from document E/CN.4/1987/WG.1/WP.2, page 18, reproduced in OHCHR 2007b: 825. See also extracts from document E/CN.4/1988/WG.1/WP.2, pages 23–24 reproduced in OHCHR 2007b: 834–835.

[97] Working Group to the Commission on Human Rights 1988: [170–171].

[98] Note, nonetheless, that UNICEF is frequently referred to as the lead agency for children (see e.g. Coomaraswamy 2007: [61] and 2009b: [47]; UNSG 2003: [88]; Zerrougui 2013a: [55]).

[99] UNICEF 1995b: [6].

body with an exclusive focus on children, and 'the only United Nations agency expressly mentioned in the Convention', UNICEF 'has a special responsibility to ensure that this innovative advance in the international protection of human rights does not remain a dead letter or, worse still, become perverted into an empty bureaucratic exercise'.[100]

Over the years, UNICEF has worked collaboratively with the Committee: it has participated in the state reporting process,[101] has provided advice to the Committee and has participated in the Committee's days of general discussion, in the development of general comments and in meetings discussing progress made in the implementation of the CRC and future challenges.[102] In this regard, UNICEF's Innocenti Research Centre has played a major role through providing support and advice based on thematic research and data-driven policy analysis. As previously mentioned, in its concluding observations and recommendations, the CRC Committee also frequently calls upon UNICEF (and other agencies) to provide technical support. In seeking to enhance implementation of the CRC, UNICEF has assisted governments in reviewing legislation and policy initiatives for compliance with its provisions, supported law reform (particularly children's codes and juvenile justice systems), assisted governments with state reporting obligations, and provided training and awareness-raising on the content of CRC provisions for key national stakeholders such as the police and the judiciary.[103] This technical assistance was provided within the framework of UNICEF's country programmes, which look to the CRC and the Committee's concluding observations for guidance, and it is indeed at the country level that UNICEF's contribution is most widely felt. Oestreich, underscoring the national dimension, notes that, whilst the role assigned by the CRC to UNICEF is not unique (other organisations having similar positions with

[100] O'Donnell 1992: 26.

[101] Oestreich (1998: 190–191) concludes that UNICEF has 'carved out a role for itself as an informal monitoring body, although not the only agency providing materials to the committee'. See also UNICEF 1999c: 22 for UNICEF's own positive assessment of its role in this process.

[102] In the course of these discussions 'UNICEF shared lessons learned from its policy analysis and studies' and also 'drew on its work in more than 160 countries'. UNICEF 2000: [24]. Concomitantly, CRC Committee members have also participated in UNICEF events such as trainings, awareness-raising activities and field visits. See e.g. UNICEF 1996c: [87].

[103] For a summary of areas in which the need for technical assistance has been identified by the CRC Committee, and where it has frequently requested the assistance of UNICEF, see CRC Committee 2002.

respect to other legal instruments), it is unusual because of UNICEF's 'national, and in many cases subnational, presence in states'.[104] With offices throughout the world, the significance of UNICEF's role 'comes from its potential to promote effective implementation of the rights of the child on the national level'.[105]

The wholehearted adoption of the CRC as an advocacy tool or normative frame of reference for UNICEF's activities was not, however, immediate: it took until 1996 for UNICEF to formally adopt a rights-based approach and, in 2000, UNICEF reported that, although progress had been made, there were still challenges in mainstreaming the rights-based approach through all programme areas.[106]

UNICEF had expressly addressed its role in the implementation of the CRC in 1991. In a report to the Executive Board, the secretariat affirmed that UNICEF should support the CRC as an inherent component of its country programmes and global advocacy. The CRC was seen as providing 'a new opportunity to demonstrate how the principles of human rights can become an integral part of the daily work of development agencies'.[107] The emphasis was on monitoring the situation of children, rather than monitoring compliance with the Convention, 'a function in which UNICEF has no direct role': UNICEF could contribute by strengthening the capacity of governments to evaluate their own progress towards realisation of CRC rights.[108] The country programme was identified as the main vehicle for supporting countries 'in their efforts to transform Convention ideals into legal safeguards and practical programmes benefiting children'.[109]

Over the next few years, efforts were made to align UNICEF's programming and advocacy activities with the CRC: 1996 saw the adoption of the UNICEF Mission Statement that described UNICEF as 'guided by' the CRC, UNICEF 'striv[ing] to establish child rights as enduring ethical principles and international standards of behavior towards children'.[110] It thus committed UNICEF to formulating policies and programmes

[104] Oestreich 1998: 184–185.

[105] O'Donnell 1992: 27. See also Smith 2009: 113.

[106] UNICEF 2000: [202]. See also Oestreich 2007: 44–45 who affirmed in 2007 that 'the process of transformation within UNICEF has not yet been completed'.

[107] UNICEF 1991a: [58].

[108] Ibid.: [30–31]. See also UNICEF 1991b: 7.

[109] UNICEF 1991a: [21].

[110] UNICEF 1996a. Jolly (2014: 125) comments that the Mission Statement 'had for the first time explicitly mentioned the promotion of child rights'.

firmly grounded in children's rights. It further provided that UNICEF was mandated by the General Assembly to 'advocate for the protection of children's rights, to help meet their basic needs and to expand their opportunities to reach their full potential',[111] a mandate considerably broader than its initial purpose of developing programmes for children in war-torn countries and for child health generally. In 1998, UNICEF issued guidelines for human rights-based programming to all its field offices, in which it outlined the implications of the approach for UNICEF's operations and how UNICEF's work could contribute to the realisation of child rights.[112]

UNICEF thus officially adopted a rights-based approach, the CRC becoming a 'semiofficial statement of principles' or 'an unofficial constitution of UNICEF, with almost every facet of its operations directed toward the convention's implementation'.[113] Jolly observes that adopting a rights-based approach 'involved some difficult and fundamental changes from UNICEF's traditional style of country programming approach'.[114] Whilst much of UNICEF's development work had been consistent with human rights principles, the rights-based approach required a more holistic approach and added new dimensions to UNICEF's work, particularly in the areas of child participation and protection. Pursuant to a rights-based approach, CRC standards and principles broaden the conceptual framework for the country situation analysis, facilitating a detailed review of the status of child rights and needs and informing the identification of priority areas for the duration of country programme. Additionally, they serve as a basis for advocacy interventions and policy dialogue with governments and are also used as a benchmark for assessing the impact of projects and programmes.

As clearly evinced, over time the CRC took on more importance within the organisation as UNICEF progressively expanded its remit. Carol Bellamy remarked in 1998: 'The force and clarity of [UNICEF's] mandate grows out of the guiding power of the Convention on the Rights of the Child and its ever-evolving relevance to UNICEF's day-to-day work. Whether in the field or at headquarters, the Convention is the bedrock foundation of everything we do.'[115] There remained, however, concerns

111 UNICEF 1996a.

112 UNICEF 1998d.

113 Oestreich 1998: 184 and 186–187. See also Black 1996: 281–282.

114 Jolly 2014: 125.

115 UNICEF 1998b: 2.

regarding the potential impact on UNICEF's relationship with states. For example, UNICEF commented in 1995 that, whilst some governments and NGOs were positive about UNICEF's support for implementing the CRC and its monitoring of state progress, others were 'concerned that the publicized denunciation of violations of children's rights (as opposed to behind-the-scenes advocacy) may compromise the historic neutrality that has enabled UNICEF to assist children in some very difficult circumstances'.[116] Yet UNICEF had to 'respond both to growing public expectations that it serve as the "world's conscience" on all matters relating to children, and to the need to work constructively with Governments to improve the situation of children'.[117] It was thus a question of striking a balance between a 'favoured partnership' when providing services and supplies and a 'critical partnership' when promoting (and in some cases monitoring and addressing violations of) human rights, particularly in the area of child protection. James Grant affirmed in 1993 that UNICEF had 'developed methods' to work constructively with governments on sensitive issues, 'using its favoured partner relationship as a foundation for its critical partner role which it plays continuously in many ways today'.[118] He subsequently stated that the two roles are 'really two sides of the same coin of "concerned dialogue"', and added:

> UNICEF has built itself as a favoured partner to most governments through the effectiveness of our programme delivery and the validity and reliability of the experience which we share and the advice we offer. As a favoured partner, we are given greater liberty to be a critical partner: based upon the experience which we have garnered over the years and from many countries, we are able to identify shortcomings and express our views.[119]

Grant's comments would prove to be particularly prescient a couple of years later in the context of Rwanda.

Whilst the CRC was perceived by some as potentially causing difficulties at the national level, the legally binding nature of the CRC, the international consensus surrounding its adoption by the General Assembly and the speed and breadth of its ratification are seen by UNICEF as providing legitimacy to its operations. The CRC 'legally reinforces the mandate of UNICEF' and provides 'a platform for advocacy that is founded

[116] UNICEF 1995b: [32].
[117] Ibid.: [32]. See also Beigbeder 2001: 197.
[118] UNICEF 1993a: [8].
[119] UNICEF 1993b: 8–9.

on international law'.[120] As children's rights become legal obligations on states, the CRC provides a 'legal foundation for the ethical and moral principles that have always guided UNICEF's work'.[121] It 'strengthens the UNICEF mission, by providing an added source of legitimacy to reinforce the organization's mandate to raise difficult issues with governments, for instance, when children are at risk or "in especially difficult circumstances"'.[122] It is also seen as simplifying programming given that it provides a 'clear guide to standards and a framework for decision-making'.[123] Nonetheless, whilst the CRC contains minimum standards that are binding on states, Cantwell asserts that its 'limitations' as a treaty must be recognised: it may provide a 'common reference point' or a 'springboard for programme response', but it should not be considered a blueprint.[124] A final point to note is that, given the wide-reaching and holistic nature of the CRC, it also influenced UNICEF's relationships with governments in a positive sense, in that it resulted in UNICEF cooperating with an increasing number of government departments. Indeed, as will be seen later in this book, in the area of child protection alone, UNICEF Rwanda worked with numerous Rwandan bodies including various ministries, the police, the judiciary and the prison authorities.

c UNICEF and Juvenile Justice

Child protection, which includes juvenile justice, is currently one of UNICEF's focus areas. However, it is only since the mid-1990s that juvenile justice has been a core concern for UNICEF and an integral part of its activities. Juvenile delinquency had been identified as an issue in the 1970s, but there does not appear to have been any global focus on juvenile justice as an area, it being left to UNICEF representatives responsible for country programmes to work with those countries that wanted more support for children with 'special problems'.[125]

The 1980s saw an increasing interest in the area of 'children in especially difficult circumstances' (or CEDC), with an extensive policy review on CEDC and an Executive Board decision in 1986[126] that O'Donnell

120 UNICEF 1991a: [9]. See also UNICEF 1995b: [23], noting that 'near universal ratification' has given UNICEF's advocacy role 'a clearer ethical basis and greater urgency'.

121 UNICEF 1999c: 18.

122 UNICEF 1991b: 8.

123 Ibid.: 8.

124 Cantwell 1997: 5 and 21.

125 See e.g. UNICEF 1980: [50–51].

126 UNICEF 1986a, 1986b and 1986c.

asserts marked 'a major change in the UNICEF interpretation of its mandate'.[127] The decision expanded UNICEF's remit beyond child health and education and beyond young children,[128] it brought about a realisation that industrialised as well as developing countries were affected, and it resulted in UNICEF's involvement in a number of new areas, including participation in standard-setting (in particular supporting the CRC drafting process).[129] CEDC issues were to be included in the scope of the country programmes, UNICEF was to engage in awareness-raising about CEDC both at the national and international level, and technical assistance and training to improve implementation of projects relating to CEDC were to be provided to countries upon request.

However, the key areas for action within CEDC were children affected by armed conflict and natural disasters, children in exploitative work conditions and street children, and children subject to abuse and neglect: juvenile justice was not officially on UNICEF's agenda.[130] Further, implementation of the CEDC policy was patchy. UNICEF saw its role in this area primarily as one of advocacy, and the overall priority still remained, at that time, child survival, particularly at UNICEF headquarters. Indeed, James Grant (Executive Director until 1995) 'never really enthusiastically supported programmes focusing on children in especially difficult circumstances': child survival and development were paramount.[131] Black cites the political sensitivity of CEDC issues as well as the fact that a focus on CEDC would have necessitated a shift in UNICEF's emphasis from infants and young children to all children aged up to 18 as reasons for CEDC not being prioritised.[132] Few resources were directed at CEDC activities, which were seen largely as 'a programmatic add-on'[133] or "'stand-alone" activities' for most country offices, relying 'almost exclusively on non-formal approaches outside national efforts to improve major social sectors'.[134]

[127] O'Donnell 1992: 29.

[128] The young child (aged 0–5) had previously been accorded priority status in UNICEF's assistance policies.

[129] O'Donnell 1992: 29–30.

[130] See UNICEF 1986a and 1986b. See also van Krieken 2000: 5.

[131] Racelis 2001: 128.

[132] Black 1996: 289–290.

[133] UNICEF 1996b: [13].

[134] UNICEF 1998c: [3]. See also Black 1996: 136 and 289–90; Oestreich 2007: 48 (noting that rights work, particularly on CEDC, between 1990 and 1997 was 'largely confined to field offices, on a haphazard basis'). O'Donnell (1992: 31) notes that some country offices made 'valuable efforts' in relation to CEDC, but that 'many of those experiences are poorly

Improved protection of CEDC was cited as one of seven key goals at the World Summit for Children in 1990 (organised at UNICEF's initiative), with 'juvenile delinquents' receiving very brief mention in the accompanying Plan of Action.[135] However, as O'Donnell notes, in comparison to other sectors, for which there were numerous targets, CEDC received 'short shrift', states simply being asked to 'provide improved protection' for CEDC and 'tackle the root causes'.[136] It was not until the mid-1990s that CEDC or 'child protection' as it gradually became known, assumed greater importance as a UNICEF focal point. Reports from 1995 drew particular attention to child protection in the context of emergencies, but children in conflict with the law, including children in detention, were also identified as a group requiring special protection and care in this context. Indeed a report on UNICEF's emergency operations refers explicitly to UNICEF's work in Rwanda in this regard, including its support for the establishment of a special department focusing on women, children and juvenile justice.[137] UNICEF's work in emergencies would include 'strengthening of legal norms and judicial systems to ensure children's protection; … supporting implementation of the Convention on the Rights of the Child and monitoring major violations; and identifying children at risk and mobilizing assistance for children in need of special protection'.[138] The link between the CRC and CEDC was clear: CRC provisions on child protection were 'becoming increasingly useful tools for worldwide efforts to address problems of children in especially difficult circumstances (CEDC)'.[139]

In 1996, UNICEF adopted a new policy on child protection, moving beyond the notion of 'children in especially difficult circumstances' (which was felt to negatively label children) towards the need for 'special protection measures', a concept developed by the CRC Committee. The policy referred specifically to 'deficient laws and juvenile justice system' as amongst the categories of circumstances that 'put children [at] special

known, even within UNICEF itself' – see Chapter 8 for a brief discussion of institutional memory.

135 UNICEF 1990b: [22]. The World Summit for Children brought together world leaders to discuss issues and set goals relating to the survival, protection and development of children.

136 O'Donnell 1992: 31.

137 UNICEF 1995d: [20]. See section 7.1 for details of this.

138 UNICEF 1995c: [34].

139 UNICEF 1995a: [102]. See also UNICEF 1997a: [1], noting the protection policy as 'grounded' in the CRC, with CRC principles 'reflected' in strategies and activities.

disadvantage'.[140] The following year, juvenile justice was explicitly noted as an 'emerging area of concern for UNICEF' in a report on steps taken to implement this new special protection policy, reference also being made to this topic being 'given high priority' by the CRC Committee.[141] A framework for UNICEF's priorities on child protection in conflict and emergencies was set out in a 1997 report on strategic priorities and operational concerns. This addressed the various phases of emergencies, suggesting actions that could be taken at each stage. In respect of juvenile justice, this included: supporting legislative and institutional review during the pre-emergency prevention and preparedness phase; monitoring children in detention, and identifying separate facilities for juveniles in the onset of emergency and in the crisis/early rehabilitation phases; and ensuring compliance with international standards for custody and trials and monitoring trials in the recovery and post-emergency phases.[142] In its report to the Economic and Social Council that year, UNICEF stated that it had 'some competence in the area of child justice', referencing specifically the Rwandan situation and UNICEF's work in separating juveniles from adults in detention.[143]

Nonetheless, UNICEF's scope of action was still interpreted narrowly. A follow-up report on the implementation of the policy on children in need of special protection measures noted that UNICEF's 'comparative advantage' in juvenile justice was in developing preventative measures, UNICEF having 'limited capacity to assist in the areas of legal protection and law enforcement'.[144] Further, whilst juvenile justice, and child protection more broadly, were increasingly integrated into UNICEF's work in the mid-1990s, child protection issues were still seen as very sensitive by some UNICEF staff members, who were concerned that involvement in human rights (rather than development only) could compromise impartiality.[145] By 2000, juvenile justice was more firmly on the UNICEF programme map: reform of juvenile justice systems had 'emerged as a further significant area of UNICEF support',[146] and in 2001, UNICEF included child protection amongst five priority areas for UNICEF's work for

140 UNICEF 1996b: 3.
141 UNICEF 1997a: [46].
142 UNICEF 1997c: 24. It also referred to advocating for legal/institutional frameworks for children accused of war crimes.
143 UNICEF 1997b: [81].
144 UNICEF 1998c: [39].
145 Landgren 2007: 188.
146 UNICEF 2000: [91].

2002–2005.[147] Yet still in 2005, UNICEF was cognisant of the sensitivity of child protection issues, underscoring the need for guidance on policies to be provided by headquarters to field offices, together with training on media relations and how to navigate child protection issues with governments and other partners.[148] Despite ongoing concerns, UNICEF is identified, and indeed views itself, as the lead UN agency for children in conflict with the law.[149]

3.4 Conclusion

The CRC applies to all children, including child perpetrators of atrocities, in all states that have ratified the Convention, with no explicit allowance being made (at least in respect of civil and political rights) for the context in which the standards are to be implemented. However, as recognised by Machel, a post-conflict state that is willing to prosecute offenders may not have a functioning judicial system or the resources to do so adequately.[150] And Cohn notes: 'The state of the national justice system is of particular concern when child perpetrators are to be prosecuted.'[151] Not only is a post-conflict state likely to have serious resource and infrastructural limitations, but public opinion may also militate against any political will to provide children with preferential treatment and comply with juvenile justice standards.

Operationalising international juvenile justice standards in a post-conflict society is thus likely to present significant challenges. At the international level, the main mechanism for child rights promotion and protection is the CRC Committee, but this is unlikely to have much influence in post-conflict states. However, the CRC also provides a role for agencies, including UNICEF, in the implementation process. This includes the provision of technical assistance to states parties, which is intended to assist states in meeting their obligations under the Convention, and which is thus consistent with the overall constructive and non-confrontational approach of the CRC. The relationship between UNICEF and the CRC Committee has been close, with UNICEF participating actively in the

[147] See Landgren 2007: 191.
[148] UNICEF 2005a: 42.
[149] See UNICEF 2008b: [61], referring to the UN Secretary-General identifying UNICEF as the lead agency for 'juvenile justice'.
[150] Machel 1996: [252].
[151] Cohn 1999: 186.

state reporting process and in the Committee's standard-setting activities, and the Committee's concluding observations and recommendations concomitantly having an impact on UNICEF's programmes. This cooperation has been identified 'as an example that might be followed by other components of the United Nations system and human rights treaty bodies in their mutual contacts'.[152]

UNICEF, whilst not designated the 'lead agency' by the CRC, has embraced the Convention, which has become the guiding framework and touchstone for UNICEF's activities. As such, UNICEF has added a rights-based approach to its development and humanitarian mandate. As Quesnel comments, child rights 'represent the essential value of UNICEF's mandate and, in fact, of the identity of the organization itself. This identity is captured in the UNICEF Mission Statement.'[153] The 1998 guidelines on a rights-based approach further encapsulate this shift. The role assigned to UNICEF under the CRC 'is not a large one'[154] and, as highlighted earlier, UNICEF perceives its role in any particular state as one of facilitative support. However, UNICEF's decentralised structure and national presence together with its commitment to integrating the CRC into all of its activities have arguably resulted in it going beyond simply promoting and advising on the rights of the child to adopting a more active role in translating the principles of the CRC into practice and in monitoring a state's progress. There is a risk, however, that assuming a greater role in implementing international standards can compromise an organisation's independence as well as the principles on which it relies – an issue that will be revisited in Chapter 8.

As illustrated, the progression to a rights-based approach has not been easy and has 'exposed UNICEF to occasional dissent or opposition'.[155] Child protection, which had initially caused concern at the drafting stage of the CRC, has continued to be a problematic area, given its political sensitivity and thus the risk of confrontation with governments and of compromising UNICEF's neutrality. Nonetheless, UNICEF has adopted child protection (including juvenile justice) as a key area for its activities and has sought to balance the requirement for a more critical orientation in this area with its traditionally supportive development role. How this has played out in practice will be under examination in this book.

[152] UNSG 1998: 59.
[153] Quesnel 2002: 15.
[154] Oestreich 1998: 186.
[155] Beigbeder 2001: 173.

At the very same time that UNICEF started to take a greater interest in child protection at the global policy level, UNICEF Rwanda was coming face to face with children detained in Rwandan prisons. Indeed, Landgren comments that UNICEF's involvement with Rwandan child *génocidaires* (and other vulnerable children) constituted a 'bookend' to the pre-1995 period (characterised by the provision of essential services to war-affected children) and a 'curtain-raiser' to the next, in which UNICEF assumed greater responsibility for child protection.[156] In Chapters 6 to 8, I examine how UNICEF Rwanda sought to enhance the rights of child *génocidaires* in the post-conflict state of Rwanda, and thus how UNICEF's role under the CRC and its adoption of a rights-based approach played out in practice. Before this, however, the next chapter will introduce the case study of Rwanda, following which, Chapter 5 will review Rwanda's responses to child perpetrators.

[156] Landgren 2007: 186. She identifies a third period from 2001 in which child protection became a UNICEF priority.

4

Rwanda: Setting the Context

Tens or even hundreds of thousands of children are currently involved in conflicts throughout the world,[1] and some, although certainly by no means all, will have become implicated in the perpetration of international crimes. Post-genocide Rwanda, however, offers a paradigmatic example of what happens when thousands of minors are accused of, and pursued for, committing acts of atrocity, in a post-conflict state that has been thoroughly decimated. This chapter, which introduces the case study for this book, throws light on the context, the aim being to equip the reader with an appreciation of children's involvement in the genocide and of the social, economic and political challenges facing post-conflict states when dealing with the past and facing international actors when seeking to enhance compliance with international standards. The initial part of this chapter provides a synopsis of the civil war and genocide in Rwanda, describing in particular the role of minors. It then turns to post-genocide Rwanda to explore the impact of the genocide on the social fabric (in particular the perception of the child) and the judicial system and outlines the involvement of international and domestic actors in the reconstruction process. Finally, it briefly examines the position of the child offender under Rwandan law, noting also Rwanda's international obligations at the time covered by this book. In addition to setting the scene, the chapter draws out the challenges generated primarily by the genocide (recognising that some issues were latent) so as to contextualise Rwanda's responses to child perpetrators (the focus of Chapter 5) as well as the approach adopted by international actors, in particular UNICEF (the focus of Chapters 6 and 7).

[1] The figure of 300,000 child soldiers worldwide is frequently cited, but, as Rosen notes, this figure is not corroborated by independent statistics. Rosen 2019. See also Wessells 2009: 9–10.

4.1 Civil War and Genocide

4.1.1 An Overview

In just over 100 days, between 6 April and 18 July 1994, an estimated 800,000 people (approximately 10 per cent of the total population) were killed as part of an orchestrated plan to eliminate the Tutsi in Rwanda.[2] Whilst the pretext and trigger for the violence and massacres was the shooting down of a plane carrying the Hutu Rwandan President, Juvénal Habyarimana, the genocide was the culmination of years of increasing discrimination against the Tutsi and the result of months of planning.

Rwanda, with a significant Hutu majority and Tutsi minority,[3] had been colonised by the Germans in 1897 and placed under Belgian administration from 1916. Prior to colonisation, Rwanda was a highly structured and organised society, ruled by a Tutsi monarchy. Whether Tutsi and Hutu are distinct ethnicities, socio-economic groups or political identities has been extensively debated elsewhere, as has the question of whether conflict existed between the groups before colonisation.[4] It is generally accepted, however, that before colonisation, the distinction was at least to some extent fluid, with some movement between the two groups and occasional intermarriage. The colonial powers institutionalised the racialisation of the groups, particularly the Belgians who introduced identity cards (requiring ethnicity to be specified) in 1933 that permanently fixed the identities and subsequently facilitated the execution of the genocidal plan.[5] Formal independence was declared in 1962 after a Hutu 'social revolution' from 1959 to 1961 that removed the Tutsi from power. In the lead-up to independence, there was increasing alienation of, and systematic violence towards, the minority Tutsi population, resulting in the exodus of many

[2] Estimates of victims are widely discrepant although the figure of around 800,000 has been cited frequently. See e.g. Gourevitch 2000: 3 (at least 800,000); Prunier 1995: 265 (between 800,000 and 850,000); UN Independent Inquiry 1999: 3 (approximately 800,000). Cf. Des Forges 1999: 15–16 (at least 500,000); MINALOC 2001a: 7 and 16–18 (over 1 million – at least 94 per cent Tutsi); Reyntjens 2004: 178 (over 1 million).

[3] The often-cited figures are 85 per cent Hutu, 14 per cent Tutsi, with a very small third group (the Twa) making up 1 per cent, although these figures are also disputed (for a discussion, see Kuperman 2001: 19–20).

[4] For an overview of the main narratives on these issues, see Ingelaere 2008: 25–26; Mamdani 2001: 41–75; Pottier 2002: 110–123.

[5] Mamdani 2001: 87–102. See also Gourevitch 2000: 56–57; Straus 2006: 20–22.

Tutsi to neighbouring countries. The post-independence period, first under Grégoire Kayibanda and then Habyarimana (both Hutu) was similarly marked by widespread discrimination and periodic violence against Tutsi, often in response to attacks by Tutsi guerrillas and later the more organised Rwandan Patriotic Front (RPF) through its armed wing, the Rwandan Patriotic Army.[6]

On 1 October 1990, the RPF launched an invasion into Rwanda from Uganda, triggering a civil war. Hutu hardliners, promoting an ideology of 'Hutu Power' that presented the Tutsi as foreign invaders, encouraged Hutu to defend their homes and eliminate the Tutsi '*inyendi*' (cockroaches). Following peace talks, the Habyarimana government and the RPF entered into the Arusha Peace Agreement in August 1993, pursuant to which they agreed to a power-sharing arrangement to be overseen by a UN peacekeeping force (UNAMIR). However, in the following months, both the Rwandan government and RPF made preparations for a resumption of war. Preparations for the genocide were also taking place in the background, with youth militia (in particular the *Interahamwe*) undergoing intensive training and weapons being stockpiled and distributed.[7]

Within hours of the plane being brought down on 6 April, Hutu extremists took control of the government, road blocks were set up throughout Kigali and the massacres of Tutsi began, rapidly spreading throughout the country. In addition to killings by the Rwandan Armed Forces (FAR), the Presidential Guard and the *Interahamwe*, there was mass involvement of the civilian population. Incited or coerced by politicians, the media[8] and the military, ordinary citizens killed (with basic weapons such as clubs, hammers and machetes), tortured, raped, pillaged, denounced those in hiding, manned roadblocks, or provided resources to those directly involved.[9] As Martin comments: 'The enormity of the genocide lies first in the number of its victims, slaughtered by

[6] See Mamdani 2001: 129–130, 134–135 and 137–142; Waldorf 2006: 30. For ease, this book uses the abbreviation RPF to refer to both the political and armed wings of the primarily Tutsi movement.

[7] Commission of Experts 1994: [65]; Degni-Ségui 1994a: [26] and 1995a: [9(b)]; UNSG 1994: [11]. See also Dallaire 2004: 142–144, 164–165 and 199–203; Des Forges 1999: 9, 127–130 and 143–172; Gourevitch 2000: 103–104; Ingelaere 2008: 29; Melvern 2008; Prunier 1995: 204–206.

[8] Dallaire (2004: 272) talks of the radio being 'akin to the voice of God', Rwandans responding to the call to violence in the belief that they were being 'sanctioned to commit these actions'.

[9] For comprehensive accounts of the genocide (including public participation) see Dallaire 2004: chapter 10 onwards; Des Forges 1999: 180–302; Prunier 1995: 237–268.

primitive methods, in a short space of time ... But the enormity lies also in the numbers of its perpetrators: tens of thousands, possibly hundreds of thousands, were the direct perpetrators of murder.'[10] Although the genocide targeted the Tutsi, tens of thousands of Hutu who opposed the genocidal regime, were seen as Tutsi sympathisers or refused to participate in the genocide, also fell victim to the massacres.[11] On the other side, but to a far lesser degree, Hutu civilians (as well as FAR soldiers and militia) were killed by the RPF after it resumed its military operations and advanced across Rwanda, but also after the end of hostilities.[12] Thousands of Hutu (including many *génocidaires*) fled Rwanda into neighbouring countries.

RPF troops from northern Rwanda reached Kigali on 11 April 1994, and the battle for the capital lasted three months. The RPF ultimately defeated the genocidal regime, bringing an end to both the genocide and civil war, and formed a Government of National Unity on 19 July 1994. Although the UN had been present in Rwanda in the form of UNAMIR and was aware that preparations were being made for genocide, it had failed to intervene sufficiently to prevent or put an end to it.[13] Indeed, the UN Security Council initially reduced the number of peacekeepers from 2,400 to 270 just two weeks after the start of the genocide.[14] It later revised UNAMIR's mandate to provide for 5,500 troops but they only began to arrive in August 1994. In the interim, France (with the support

[10] Martin 1998: 3. Like the number of victims, estimates of perpetrators also vary considerably. See e.g. Drumbl 2000: 1250 (as many as a million 'direct' and 'indirect' participants); Gourevitch 2000: 244 (referring to President Kagame's estimate of 1 million and a former presidential adviser's estimate of 3 million); Straus 2004 and 2006: 115–118 (175,000–210,000 perpetrators); Waldorf 2009a: note 9 (referring to government estimates of 800,000–3 million).

[11] Some of the first to be killed were Hutu moderates including the Prime Minister. See Des Forges 1999: 187–191 and 205–206; Eltringham 2004: 95–97; Prunier 1995: 230–232 and 265.

[12] There is debate as to the magnitude of the killings of civilians and also whether killing civilians was a deliberate policy by the RPF or the unsanctioned actions of soldiers. See e.g. Degni-Ségui 1994b: [38–42] and 1995b: [40]; Des Forges 1999: 13–14, 16 and 701–735; Eltringham 2004: 101–110, 118–119 and 124–142; Gahima 2013: 223–229; HRW 2008: 89; Martin 1998: 3 and 10–15; Prunier 1995: 175 and 322–325; Reyntjens 2004: 194–195.

[13] There are many accounts of inaction by the international community and the UN in particular. See e.g. Des Forges 1999: 16–27, 172–179, 595–668; Destexhe 1995: 48–51; Gourevitch 2000: 149–151; Martin 1998: 1–2; Melvern 2000; Prunier 1995: 273–277; UN Independent Inquiry 1999. For a detailed and first-hand account, see Dallaire 2004 who accuses the UN of aiding and abetting genocide (at 323) and also places significant responsibility on the United States and France, as well as on the RPF which he believes pursued total victory at the cost of the deaths of many Rwandans.

[14] UNSC Resolution 912 (21 April 1994).

of the UN) had established a 'safe humanitarian zone' under its *Opération Turquoise*, which facilitated the safe passage not only of civilians but also *génocidaires* and members of the FAR into (then) Zaire.[15] Sporadic killings continued in 1995 and 1996, and armed confrontations between the FAR and *Interahamwe* militia on the one side and the RPF on the other continued well into 1998 in the north-west of Rwanda.

4.1.2 Children's Participation

As indicated above, a key, and distinguishing, feature of the Rwandan genocide was participation by ordinary citizens, and children were amongst the perpetrators. Degni-Ségui, the Special Rapporteur for the UN Commission on Human Rights, reported that the massacres were a 'mass phenomenon' designed to involve all levels of the population, 'including the children, as killers "manipulated by their handlers", often with the encouragement of their parents or members of the militias'.[16] A preliminary point to note is that, whilst it is clear from documentary evidence and interviews conducted for this study that children did participate in the genocide, they were far fewer in number than adults: the overwhelming majority of *génocidaires* were adult men, with young adults playing a major role.[17]

Most child perpetrators were part of the general mobilisation of the civilian population, but some, in particular older adolescents, were involved within the more organised structure of the *Interahamwe* militia.[18] Minors were also recruited into the armed forces of both parties to the civil war,[19] and whilst many of these recruits may not have committed atrocities, there are reports that FAR child soldiers actively participated in the genocidal massacres and that RPF child soldiers (to a lesser extent) committed acts of revenge following the massacre of their families.[20] As will be discussed in Chapter 5, the Rwandan government took measures

[15] See e.g. Dallaire 2004: chapter 14; Des Forges 1999: 668–690; Destexhe 1995: 51–55; Prunier 1995: chapter 8.

[16] Degni-Ségui 1996: [27].

[17] Confirmed by Lawyer C (interview, Kigali, 8 March 2013). See also Des Forges 1999: 11.

[18] See e.g. Dallaire 2011: 36–39.

[19] Degni-Ségui (1996: [28]) estimates 2,000 child soldiers in the RPF and 2,820 in the former FAR. See also UNICEF Rwanda 1996b: 16. Note that officials in the Rwandan Demobilisation and Reintegration Commission (RDRC) asserted that the RPF did not actively recruit child soldiers (interviews with two RDRC officials, Kigali, 19 September 2013).

[20] Degni-Ségui 1996: [29].

(penal or administrative) to address genocide-related acts perpetrated by children (at least those who did not flee Rwanda[21]). Those children who were associated with the RPF, however, attended a special school (the *Kadogo* School[22]) and were not subject to any screening to determine whether they had committed acts of atrocity,[23] leading to assertions of preferential treatment.[24]

Children as young as five were involved in the whole range of acts committed during the genocide. A survey conducted south of Kigali found that 56 per cent of children had seen other children used in various ways in the genocide, and 47 per cent had seen children killing other children.[25] A wider trauma study conducted across 11 prefectures[26] found that almost 36 per cent had seen children participating in killings or physical violence.[27] Research participants spoke of children being used to kill other children and babies, this appearing to be a deliberate policy by those ordering the massacres,[28] or to 'finish off' the dying with crude weapons such as hammers or clubs.[29] African Rights reported various incidents in which children were involved in killings and other acts of violence.[30] In Cyangugu Prefecture, for example, Tutsi boys aged between 13 and

[21] Children (and adults) who left Rwanda and later went through demobilisation programmes were not subject to any screening process (confirmed by RDRC officials, interviews, 19 September 2013). See also Waldorf 2009b: 22–23.

[22] *Kadogo* means 'little ones' in Swahili. See Cantwell 1997: 51–52 for an overview.

[23] Skype interview with Mima Perisic, former CEDC Project Officer, UNICEF Rwanda, 13 November 2013. As this book focuses on perpetrators of atrocities, it does not address the *Kadogo* School or demobilisation programmes, given that these did not involve any determination of wrongdoing.

[24] E.g. Isabella Castrogiovanni, former Human Rights Field Officer for UNHRFOR and former Consultant on Juvenile Justice for UNICEF Rwanda (Skype interview, 21 August 2013) commented that these children 'benefited from rehabilitation' whilst those who participated in the genocide 'were treated as criminals, according to the criminal law'. Former Judicial Defender E (Skype interview, 22 December 2013) made similar comments.

[25] UNICEF Rwanda 1995a: 1. See also Degni-Ségui 1996: [27]; UNICEF 1995e: 28.

[26] Until 2001, Rwanda was divided into 12 prefectures, each further divided into communes, then sectors and cells.

[27] Dyregrov et al. 2000; UNICEF Rwanda 1996c: 23.

[28] E.g. Interview with Jean de Dieu Mucyo, former Director of National Judicial Police, former Minister of Justice and former Chief Prosecutor, Kigali, 13 September 2013. See also *Ministère Public c/ Nsabamungu* [*Nsabamungu*]: 58; *Ministère Public c/ Nsabimana* [*Nsabimana*]: 142–144 which provide support for this statement.

[29] Interview with Ray Torres, former Child Protection Officer, UNICEF Rwanda, Kigali, 28 September 2013.

[30] In addition to the examples cited here, see African Rights 1995a: 625 and 851–853 and 1995b: 36–39. See also Dallaire 2011: chapter 2.

15 were selected and then killed by boys of a similar age, although some attackers were reportedly younger than 10.[31] In a massacre at Ntarama Church (Greater Kigali Prefecture), one survivor reported that young boys aged approximately 11–14 were amongst the *Interahamwe* which came into the church 'carrying spears and sharpened sticks' that were used to beat many children to death.[32] A survivor of massacres in Kibeho referred to her fellow students being amongst the killers of Tutsi who were forced to dig their own graves, as well as to 'young boys' killing in a 'brutal fashion' on the orders of the militia.[33] And in an attack in Gikongoro Prefecture, a boy of 10 killed someone with a *masu* (a club studded with nails), whilst a student was given money and a radio cassette in recognition of his successful murder of many refugees.[34]

Whilst minors were not among the planners and organisers of the genocide, there were some who distinguished themselves as killers, either through the number of their victims or excessive malice they showed. For example, in one reported case, a 16-year-old had gouged out the eyes of children he had killed and then partially buried the bodies.[35] In another case, a juvenile, nicknamed 'The Child Eater', had confessed to killing 31 and leaving many others half-dead.[36] Minors also committed torture and degradation of bodies[37] as well as rape, an NGO worker referring to children copying their older siblings during gang rapes.[38] One woman who was raped repeatedly said: 'Small boys would come with grenades. They had no shame in taking a grown woman like me to sleep with them. I could be their mother.'[39] Children were present at the checkpoints and roadblocks throughout the country,[40] a young boy of around nine reportedly 'bouncing a grenade' at a checkpoint that was littered with bodies.[41]

[31] African Rights 1995a: 522 and 851.

[32] Ibid.: 263 and 851.

[33] Ibid.: 311–312.

[34] Ibid.: 323.

[35] *Ministère Public c/ Kabirigi et consorts* [*Kabirigi*]: 150.

[36] Interview with Judge H, former Minors' Judge in Specialised Chamber (Western Province), Western Province, 1 October 2013.

[37] Interviews with former ASOFERWA Staff Member A, Kigali, 24 September 2013; Faustin Murigo, former Prison Director, Kigali, 6 September 2013.

[38] Interview with NGO Staff Member, Kigali, 22 February 2013.

[39] African Rights 1995a: 789.

[40] Recall Lucien's story, and his report that 'everyone' was at the roadblock in his village.

[41] African Rights 1995a: 851. See also Dallaire 2011: 39–41 (referring to the 'ubiquitous' presence of teenagers and boys, who were at every checkpoint in Kigali).

They also looted and denounced those in hiding by 'nos[ing] out the fugitives'.[42]

In many cases, children followed orders issued by the militia or authorities. Children were not only easier to manipulate, but also Rwandan culture teaches children to obey adults.[43] Other children were forced to kill or commit other atrocities,[44] whilst many imitated adults in a context 'where violence and hatred had become the norm'.[45] Research participants spoke of children being more susceptible to propaganda, becoming involved in massacres because 'everyone else was killing' and seeing it all as a game.[46] Some commented that children had been more active than adults given their levels of endurance and energy,[47] and that they were more dangerous given their lack of fear.[48] Indeed, a judge stated that, whilst he saw child perpetrators as victims drawn into the genocide by adults, 'il apparaîtrait que les enfants ont été plus atroces que les vieux, parce que tu sais pourquoi – les enfants, c'est comme si vous envoyez les chiens pour mordre, en suivant des exemples notamment des grands'.[49] Although frequently children had either followed orders or the examples of their elders without fully understanding what they were doing or the consequences of their actions, there are reports of older children being more active members of the *Interahamwe*[50] and that some 'acted alone and even directed other killers'.[51] Many of those subsequently arrested showed no

42 Hatzfeld 2008: 125.

43 See e.g. HRW 2003a: 13; Prunier 1995: 244–248 (noting a strong tradition of obedience to authority).

44 See e.g. *Ministère Public c/ Minani* [*Minani*].

45 Orr 1995. See also Hatzfeld 2008: 34–35 and 44.

46 Interviews with former IPJ/Prosecutor, Kigali, 26 September 2013; Dativa Ngaboyisonga Mukanyangezi, former Social Assistant for SCF-USA and ASOFERWA, at time of interview, Commissioner in Charge of Social Correction, Human Rights and Cooperation, Rwanda Correctional Service, Kigali, 8 October 2013; Judge H, 1 October 2013.

47 Interviews with Naphtal Kisakye, former District Coordinator of *gacaca* courts, Kigali, 12 September 2013; former Prosecutor D, Kigali, 26 September 2013.

48 Interview with Mukanyangezi, 8 October 2013.

49 ['Children seemed to be crueller than adults – you know why? Because with children, it's like sending in the dogs to bite, following the example of adults.'] Interview with Judge I, former Judge in Specialised Chamber (Kigali Province), Kigali, 2 October 2013. This perception tallies with Shepler's (2014) findings on child soldiers in Sierra Leone, where children were seen as 'the most dangerous' and occupying a liminal space between animality and madness (at 51).

50 UNICEF Rwanda 1995c: 4. See also UNICEF Rwanda 1997b: 2; Briggs 2005: 18.

51 Moussalli 2000a: [117] (describing children's participation as 'one of the most shocking aspects' of the genocide).

remorse for their actions and were 'ready to do it again'.[52] A youth worker at the Gitagata Re-education and Production Centre (Gitagata) for child genocide suspects under 14[53] commented that children seemed to 'really believe the genocide was justified',[54] although a former staff member of ASOFERWA,[55] the organisation that ran Gitagata, referred to the children 'regretting what they had done'.[56] Whether acting voluntarily or not, the participation of children in the genocide had a profound impact on the concept of the Rwandan child.

4.2 Post-Genocide Rwanda

4.2.1 Rwandan Society and the Perception of the Child Perpetrator

The mass participation of the population in the genocide, involving all levels of society, resulted in social disruption and dislocation. Following the genocide, victims and survivors (*rescapés*) demanded justice, and significant numbers of Hutu civilians, including children, were rounded up and detained, most frequently on the basis of (sometimes unsubstantiated) denunciations. Additionally, revenge attacks were committed by Tutsi civilians as well as RPF soldiers.[57] Social polarisation continued to be a feature of Rwandan society resulting in a highly charged socio-political context, which led to intimidation of lawyers, witnesses and judges who were involved in genocide trials, to threats and violence against defendants and to harassment of, and violence against, genocide survivors.[58]

As noted in Chapter 2, at the international level the child perpetrator has often been conceptualised primarily as a victim. Whilst many international actors continued to emphasise the victimhood of child *génocidaires*,[59] the participation of children in the genocide challenged

[52] Degni-Ségui 1996: [27].

[53] See section 5.3.1.

[54] African Rights 2000: 93.

[55] Association de Solidarité des Femmes Rwandaises.

[56] Interview with former ASOFERWA Staff Member A, 24 September 2013.

[57] See e.g. African Rights 1995a: 1181; Amnesty International 1997b: 19; HRW 1994: 3–5. See also note 12 and related text.

[58] See e.g. Amnesty International 2002: 16; HRW 2008: 77 and 2011: 84–94.

[59] See e.g. HRW 2003a: 1 ('Although they garner less sympathy, children who took part in the genocide are also victims. Their rights were first violated when adults recruited, manipulated, or incited them to participate in atrocities, and have been violated again by the Rwandan justice system.').

the notion of childhood held by many of those coming into contact with these perpetrators and inevitably had a bearing on their interventions.[60] For Rwandans, the ramifications were significant, an NGO staff member observing that, prior to the genocide, Rwandans did not believe that children were capable of killing.[61] Afterwards, 'public opinion and beliefs shifted dramatically ... from general support or understanding of the special needs for children who have committed offenses, to a completely different set of values for those children accused of crimes committed in conjunction with the genocide'.[62]

A seminal study by Save the Children Fund-USA (SCF-USA) in 1995, which used focus groups in different parts of Rwanda, revealed that ordinary Rwandans' understanding of children's culpability and punishment differed from the principles enshrined in the Rwandan Penal Code, and that a distinction was made between 'children's misdeeds under normal circumstances' and genocide-related acts.[63] SCF-USA had conducted the study given their concern that 'the application of *legal justice* might not serve the requirements of the *social justice* expected at the popular level' which could give rise to difficulties for the reintegration of child perpetrators.[64] Whilst participants in the SCF-USA study cited various reasons for children's involvement in the genocide, the majority considered that children had 'committed these atrocities of their own free will'.[65] Even where a child had been forced to commit a crime, this did not 'negate the criminal aspect of the act' and the child should be punished.[66] Further, in contrast to their approach to sanctions for acts committed in normal circumstances, almost all participants rejected the excuse of minority for genocide crimes, believing that children who were capable of committing atrocities should be held accountable and punished in the

60 See, in particular, Chapter 6.

61 Interview with Jean-Pierre Hitababyaye, former coordinator of PRI's *gacaca* monitoring programme, Kigali, 10 September 2013 (although he stressed that children, and indeed most adults, had committed acts during the genocide without knowing what they were doing). The reaction to child *génocidaires* is similar to that seen in the James Bulger case in the UK, where the murder of a young child by two 10-year-old boys was considered 'inconceivable' (see Jenks 2005: 119).

62 MINIJUST and UNICEF Rwanda 1997b: 15.

63 SCF-USA 1996: 3. Note: a version of the study was released in French in 1995. For ease, this book refers to a revised version in English from 1996.

64 Ibid.: 4.

65 Ibid.: 9.

66 Ibid.: 10.

same way as adults: the view being that they were no longer children.[67] This finding was echoed by others:

> You will hear Rwandans say very often that if a child was able to kill, if a child was able to discriminate between two ethnic groups, to decide who was a Hutu moderate and who wasn't, and was able to carry out murder in that way, why should that child be considered differently from an adult? And therefore the punishment should be the same.[68]

Most participants in the SCF-USA study felt that children who had killed during the genocide should receive the death penalty, one group commenting that, if the Rwandan state did not impose the death penalty, they would kill the children themselves.[69] For crimes other than murder (except theft), the feeling was that children should be punished severely. Only a small number of participants (mainly university students) considered that children should always be treated leniently. For participants in the study, one aim of punishing child *génocidaires* was to eradicate impunity: children who had committed atrocities since 1959 had benefited from impunity and gone on to become adult *génocidaires*. Further, punishment was considered a way of showing empathy with survivors, thus giving them 'the justice they are due', but also 'protect[ing] the perpetrators from the vengeance of their erstwhile victims'.[70]

That victims might seek revenge against child perpetrators was an issue raised by participants interviewed for this book. Isabella Castrogiovanni, who worked for UNHRFOR[71] and then UNICEF, recalled a victim telling her that these children were criminals, had committed 'horrific things' and, if released, would be killed by the community. She considered that this spoke volumes of the 'bouleversement' of social rules after the genocide, in which 'normal categories', including those relating to children, were rendered irrelevant. She considered that this was inevitable given the scale of the genocide and level of victimisation.[72] Whether, in practice, these strong feelings would have translated into actual violent revenge attacks against minors is unknown. One participant in this research vehemently denied that there was any risk to child perpetrators on the basis

67 Ibid.: 11. See also Moussalli 2000a: [117], who noted the 'strong pressure to treat them like normal criminals'.

68 Ray Torres cited in Hackel 1995.

69 SCF-USA 1996: 12.

70 Ibid.: 14.

71 United Nations High Commissioner's Human Rights Field Operation in Rwanda.

72 Skype interview with Castrogiovanni, 21 August 2013.

that there were few survivors: 'What survivors there were, were struggling to survive!'[73] There were, however, reports of revenge attacks against genocide suspects particularly in the first few years after the genocide,[74] and a minors' judge recalled cases where released individuals were attacked by victims.[75] The Rwandan NGO, LIPRODHOR,[76] reporting in 1999 on the reintegration of persons provisionally released, noted continuing hostility towards those released (including minors) and reported that some were threatened.[77]

The SCF-USA study does not indicate whether participants were victims or *rescapés*, only referring to whether a focus group was in an area that was 'more' or 'less' affected. However, persons interviewed for this book frequently referred to victims and *rescapés* being unable to accept that children were less culpable, a minors' judge recalling that victims could often not understand why children appearing in court received reduced sentences.[78] Further, some victims and *rescapés* were resentful of organisations and individuals who were defending the rights of child perpetrators, a former staff member of ASOFERWA – a *rescapé* herself – commenting that some failed to comprehend why she was helping *génocidaires* in the Gitagata centre, wanting them to be prosecuted.[79]

Other elements from the SCF-USA study are also worth comment. First, the majority of its participants used socio-cultural factors as determinative of the transition from childhood to adulthood, although a minority (see below) used chronological age as the defining factor.[80] Some commentators have submitted that the concepts of childhood and adulthood in Rwanda were less dependent on chronological age than on social (im)maturity, adulthood being marked by events such as leaving home, getting married and having financial independence.[81]

[73] Interview with former ASF Staff Member, Kigali, 5 February 2013. See also Amnesty International 2002: 20 (questioning the risk of reprisals).

[74] Rwandan Human Rights Lawyer (Skype interview, 29 August 2013) recalled that the first persons released by screening committees were attacked – some murdered – and that, subsequently, reports were received of attacks and re-arrests. See also African Rights 1995a: 1181.

[75] Interview with Judge F, former Minors' Judge in Specialised Chamber (Western Province), Western Province, 30 September 2013.

[76] Ligue Rwandaise pour la Promotion et la Défense des Droits de l'Homme.

[77] See LIPRODHOR 1999b and 1999c.

[78] Interview with Judge F, 30 September 2013. Other judges related similar accounts, e.g. Judge I, interview, 2 October 2013.

[79] Interview with former ASOFERWA Staff Member A, 24 September 2013.

[80] SCF-USA 1996: 6–7.

[81] See Cantwell 1997: 59.

This chimes with anthropological and sociological paradigms of the concept of childhood. Honwana, writing on child soldiers in Angola and Mozambique, highlights that childhood is 'centrally linked to social roles, expectations, and responsibilities' and 'may have little to do with age'.[82] And as Twum-Danso explains: 'In numerous African societies, as in other non-western cultures, chronological age as an indicator for the termination of childhood is perceived as an arbitrary concept.'[83] In Cantwell's opinion, the Rwandan concept of childhood 'has obvious repercussions for attitudes towards some "categories" of children, in particular those who are accused of having participated in the genocide' and does not fit well with the general principle of special treatment contained in the CRC for all children under the age of 18.[84] Indeed, it would seem that it also did not fit well with existing Rwandan law which set the age of penal majority at 18.[85]

Second, the results of the SCF-USA study suggest different perceptions according to level of education. Those with a higher level of education on the whole (but not in every case) defined childhood in terms of chronological age – some using the legal definition of childhood – and considered that children should be treated more leniently than adults. This distinction between the well- and lesser-educated was also made by some of those interviewed for this book, one participant identifying a higher level of acceptance amongst the educated for differential treatment of minors on the understanding that they had been manipulated by adults.[86] That members within society would have different conceptions of children and childhood is consonant with the idea of childhood as a social construction. Several other participants referred to differences between those in the government and the general population, a former senior Rwandan justice official commenting that the government was 'very firm' in stressing that minors had been pushed by adults into committing genocidal acts and should thus benefit from special treatment, whilst a 'proportion of the population' thought age was no excuse.[87] The official

82 Honwana 2006: 41.

83 Twum-Danso 2008: 400–401.

84 Cantwell 1997: 59.

85 See section 4.3. Civil majority was set at 21 (Arts. 360 and 431, Loi No. 42/1988 portant création du titre préliminaire et livre premier du code civil [Book I, Civil Code 1988]).

86 Interview with a former Executive Secretary of a Survivors' Organisation, Kigali, 21 February 2013.

87 Skype interview with former Senior Rwandan Justice Official, 24 July 2014.

further asserted that the Rwandan government was conversant with its international obligations to young perpetrators, a point also made by a judicial defender who stated that the general population's level of comprehension of laws was very different to that of government officials: the government knew about child rights, even if such rights were not always respected.[88] This disconnect between the government and the general population in their perception of the capacity of the child and the appropriate response lends support to the argument that a government may be more 'universal' than its society.[89]

Rwanda thus faced the challenge of dealing with this conflict between notions of social and legal justice. Whilst there was a need to protect the rights of minors and apply the law, the government also faced demands from society that children be punished for the acts they had committed. Whilst it is possible that, over time, the risk of reprisals against child perpetrators (and other *génocidaires*) declined (either as a result of emotions becoming less acute or the sensitisation of society), for the first few years after the genocide, the risk was palpable. Added to this challenge was the impact of the genocide on Rwanda's institutions.

4.2.2 *Rwandan Judicial System*[90]

Upon taking power in 1994, the RPF-led government declared its intention to prosecute all perpetrators of genocide, adopting a maximalist approach to accountability.[91] As Schabas notes, Rwanda is perhaps the 'paradigm' of the rare situation in which a state 'seems uncompromisingly willing to try to prosecute', there being a 'keen and truly unquestionable commitment to bringing perpetrators to justice'. He added, however, that this approach was found to be 'quite unrealistic'.[92] One of the key challenges facing the Rwandan government was the lack of a functioning judicial system.

88 Skype interview with former Judicial Defender B, 28 August 2013.

89 See Chapter 3.

90 I use the terms judicial system and justice sector generally in a broad sense to encompass the judiciary and courts, legal profession, police and other law enforcement personnel and penal institutions.

91 Palmer (2015: 97) notes that justifications for this approach drew on 'international law and a legalist perspective on transitional justice', referring to the legal requirement to prosecute the crime of genocide.

92 Schabas 2008b: 531–532. See also Sarkin 2001 (arguing that Rwanda prioritised justice over truth and reconciliation in dealing with the past); Teitel 2000: 27–28 (noting that criminal justice is often eschewed by transitional states or takes the form of the 'limited criminal sanction' in which prosecution processes do not result in full punishment).

Even before the genocide, Rwanda's judicial system was characterised as a 'caricature of justice'[93] in which corruption was rife and the courts were highly politicised and under the control of the Executive.[94] The civil war and genocide exacerbated the already deficient system: there were no functioning courts, public prosecution authority, police or prisons. Judicial infrastructure across the country including the Ministry of Justice (MINIJUST) itself, court buildings and prisons had been ransacked during the genocide, with windows blown out, documents burnt and equipment stolen or destroyed. UNHRFOR reported that MINIJUST and prosecutors did not have a single working vehicle between them, and that they lacked basic office materials such as pens and paper.[95] In addition to destruction of property, many lawyers and judicial personnel had been killed, fled the country, or were themselves implicated in the atrocities.[96] Of around 1,200 judicial personnel before April 1994, including judges, prosecutors, judicial police inspectors (IPJs)[97] and court clerks, fewer than 400 remained in place in October 1994.[98] Schabas reported that there were approximately only 20 legally trained lawyers in Rwanda in November 1994;[99] the Rwandan government estimated that only 27 out of 150 MINIJUST officials remained at their posts;[100] and UNHRFOR reported that there remained under 40 per cent of judges (only a minority of whom were legally trained), 14 out of 75 prosecutors, 24 out of 193 IPJs and 30 out of 382 prison guards.[101] The military thus took over prisons and policing functions until the police, prosecutor's office and prison service were rebuilt.

Dealing with the significant number of people arrested would have been beyond the capacity of almost any judicial system, let alone one that had been decimated. With considerable assistance from donors and NGOs, the Rwandan government set about (re)constructing the judicial

[93] Schabas 1996: 531.

[94] See Clark 2012: 216; Mutagwera 1996: 18–20.

[95] UNHRFOR 1996b: [12]. See also African Rights 2000: 1; UNDP 1999: 21.

[96] See e.g. Des Forges and Longman 2004: 58; UNDP 1999: 21.

[97] IPJs (*inspecteurs de police judiciaire*) were investigators within the public prosecution. There were also judicial police officers (OPJs) (*officiers de police judiciaire*) who were part of the gendarmerie.

[98] Reyntjens and Vandeginste 2005: 108.

[99] Schabas 2005: 883.

[100] Degni-Ségui 1994b: [36].

[101] UNHRFOR 1996b: [52] and annex 1. De Beer (1997b: 6) cites 17 IPJs and 19 legally qualified judges.

system, refurbishing buildings, procuring basic materials and equipment and recruiting and training personnel. By 1996, whilst far from being fully functional, the judicial system had improved considerably,[102] and the next few years saw the number of judicial personnel increase, leading the UN Development Group (UNDG) to conclude in 2000 that the criminal and civil courts were sufficiently staffed so as to function (having approximately 800 judges[103] and 220 prosecutors). Concerns remained however regarding the competence and performance of many personnel given the brevity of their training.[104] A further issue related to defence lawyers: whilst their numbers increased from just 20 in 1994 to 55 in 1999,[105] many were reluctant to represent alleged *génocidaires*, as their family or friends were genocide victims, they feared that they would be tarred with the same brush through association or they were concerned about their own safety.[106] Efforts were made to improve access to lawyers. The international NGO, Avocats Sans Frontières (ASF), provided support through expatriate lawyers and financed Rwandan lawyers, and a Bar Association was established in 1997 as well as a body of 'Judicial Defenders' (trained by the Danish Centre for Human Rights – DCHR).[107] The number of lawyers nonetheless remained inadequate.[108]

Trials of genocide suspects in the formal courts began in December 1996. However, as will be discussed further in Chapter 5, it soon became clear that it would not be possible to process the increasing number of detainees through the ordinary court system and thus alternative solutions were sought. The result was the establishment of the *gacaca* jurisdictions, which began operating in 2002.

[102] RCN 1996: 37.

[103] Note that less than 15 per cent of this total was assigned to work on genocide cases in the Specialised Chambers. See ASF 2000b: 5.

[104] UNDG 2000a: 17. See also Degni-Ségui 1997: [69]; Moussalli 1999a: [39] (reporting that only 15 out of 800 magistrates in 1999 had a law degree, most of the remainder having received three or six months' training).

[105] Moussalli 2000a: [143].

[106] See ASF 1997b: 13; de Beer 1997a: 2; HRW 2008: 80–82; Mutagwera 1996: 23. Research participants spoke of some lawyers disappearing after representing alleged *génocidaires* and others being accused of genocide (Skype interviews with Rwandan Human Rights Lawyer, 29 August 2013; former Judicial Defender B, 28 August 2013). This supports the argument referenced in section 3.2 that human rights advocates may be viewed as an extension of the alleged criminals they represent.

[107] Law No. 03/97 Establishing a Bar Association in Rwanda.

[108] ASF 2000a: 10.

4.2.3 *International and National Actors in Rwanda*

Whilst international actors were present in Rwanda before 1994, the genocide resulted in a mass influx of foreign aid workers and a proliferation of international NGOs and agencies. As one research participant commented, 'They came in droves!'[109] A commentator remarked, 'Rwanda, "a land of 1,000 hills", has been dubbed "a land of 1,000 foreign aid workers"'.[110] In the summer of 1994, between 200 and 250 NGOs were operating in Rwanda. Many NGOs left towards the end of 1994 and during 1995,[111] with just a core group remaining for the long term. Some international NGOs were strongly criticised for being inexperienced and unprofessional and also for failing to coordinate their activities.[112] West distinguishes between well-established NGOs with financing, experience and professional staff, and 'nascent' NGOs which often had no experience at all, their objectives being 'much closer to Band Aid songs such as "We Are the World" or "Do They Know It is Christmas?" than any juridical text'.[113] As regards domestic NGOs, like other components of Rwandan society, these had been implicated in, or wiped out during, the genocide. They began to reappear from 1995 onwards,[114] but were often considered to be in opposition to the government (particularly those funded from overseas) and given little political space, or were essentially co-opted by the government or exercised self-censorship.[115] Further, given the political situation, it was extremely difficult for anyone (and in particular domestic organisations) to promote the rights of alleged *génocidaires*.

Relations between the Rwandan government and international actors were frequently strained for a number of reasons including: distrust of 'anything international', given the international community's failure to intervene in the genocide;[116] lack of coordinated assistance; donors' preference to direct funds through international agencies and NGOs;[117]

[109] Interview with NGO Staff Member, 22 February 2013.
[110] Linden 1999: 282.
[111] West 2001: 172–173 and 192.
[112] See Cantwell 1997: 6 and 74; Linden 1999: 289.
[113] West 2001: 174–175.
[114] Ibid.: 176.
[115] Peter and Kibalama 2006: 139 and 141. See also Kimonyo, Twagiramungu and Kayumba 2004: 52.
[116] Skype interview with former Judicial Defender B, 28 August 2013.
[117] For an analysis of donor activity in Rwanda after the genocide, see Oomen 2005; Zorbas 2011.

perceived inadequacies of the ICTR to prosecute alleged *génocidaires*; and the perception that international actors protected only *génocidaires*, preferring to promote the rights of criminals over victims.[118] Forty-three foreign NGOs were expelled from December 1995,[119] and NGO (foreign and domestic) operations were tightly regulated from 2001.[120] The run up to the national elections in 2003 saw a greater narrowing of the political space, and in 2004 a report was issued accusing some domestic and international NGOs of divisionism.[121] International agencies were not immune from ill-feeling, Cantwell referring to 'official ambivalence towards the intergovernmental community as a whole'.[122] Gahima went further, noting the 'sense of betrayal' many felt in Rwanda that 'generated very strong resentment towards international institutions in general, and United Nations institutions in particular'.[123]

Yet Rwanda required significant international assistance following the genocide. Whilst seeking to maintain self-reliance and policy independence in the reconstruction process[124] and control over justice and accountability,[125] it actively sought the help of donors, international agencies and NGOs.[126] The involvement of these international actors in the rehabilitation of the Rwandan justice system in particular (including the penitentiary system) cannot be overstated,[127] but the complexity of the dynamics playing out in Rwanda must always be borne in mind when considering the role and *modus operandi* of these actors. Given the focus on child perpetrators, this book does not detail the aid and technical support provided generally to post-genocide Rwanda, nor single out all those actors who provided support or built capacity. However, some

[118] Interview with Judge J, former President of Court of First Instance (Northern Province), Kigali, 4 October 2013. See also Cantwell 1997: 7, 63 and 71–75 and West 2001: 209–210 referencing many of these reasons.

[119] See Office of the Resident Co-ordinator 1996: 7. See also Peter and Kibalama 2006: 63–64.

[120] Loi No. 20/2000 relative aux associations sans but lucratif.

[121] See Demay et al. 2005: 26; Peter and Kibalama 2006: 129–134.

[122] Cantwell 1997: 63.

[123] Gahima 2013: 104.

[124] See Kimonyo, Twagiramungu and Kayumba 2004: xix (referring to the government 'jealously guard[ing] for itself the leading role'); Zorbas 2011: 107.

[125] Schabas (2008b: 536) stresses that Rwanda 'clung stubbornly to its view that justice should be done by Rwandans to Rwandans'.

[126] Moussalli 2000b: [20]. See also van Krieken 2000: 29 (referring to Rwanda's 'dual feeling' towards the international community: it was aware of the need for assistance but felt 'deeply frustrated and shocked' by the lack of intervention).

[127] Cf. Schabas 2008b: 536 (commenting that, whilst there was a significant level of assistance to the justice sector, it was 'on the margins').

organisations featured prominently in reports and commentaries and were recognised by participants in this research as particularly active in the justice sector. Their activities thus merit a brief mention, although their involvement with child *génocidaires* will only be discussed (where relevant) in Chapter 6.

In terms of international agencies, UNHRFOR, operational in Rwanda from September 1994 until July 1998, played a key role in implementing technical cooperation programmes in the justice sector.[128] In addition to promoting legal reform and institution building, it provided education and training for the judiciary, law enforcement personnel and NGOs, sought to promote a human rights culture through educational and promotional activities in Rwandan society, monitored and sought to improve detention conditions and also monitored genocide trials.[129] Other UN agencies, including the UN Development Programme (UNDP), UN High Commissioner for Refugees (UNHCR) and UNICEF were also very active, working on detention issues and facilities, providing resources and training to law enforcement and judicial personnel and, in the case of UNDP, later providing support to the *gacaca* jurisdictions. Other instrumental organisations included the International Committee of the Red Cross (ICRC), ASF, DCHR, Réseau de Citoyens (RCN) and Prison Reform International (PRI). ICRC, with its accent on detention facilities, rehabilitated buildings, provided materials, registered detainees and trained law enforcement personnel. The projects of ASF, RCN, DCHR and PRI covered various aspects of the judicial and penitentiary systems. Their main activities included: training judges, clerks and prosecutors (ASF and RCN), prison staff (PRI) and police officers (DCHR); providing legal aid (both to alleged perpetrators and victims) and training legal representatives (ASF and DCHR); providing material, logistical and financial support to judicial and law enforcement bodies (RCN); producing and disseminating legal manuals and guides (ASF, RCN and PRI); improving prison conditions and the prison administration (PRI); providing support to sensitisation campaigns (RCN); monitoring formal trials (ASF); and advising on, assisting with the implementation of, and monitoring, *gacaca* proceedings (ASF and PRI).[130] International NGOs also supported their

[128] For an overview of UNHRFOR generally, including its deficiencies and the difficulties it faced, see Martin 1998.

[129] See various reports by OHCHR and UNHRFOR.

[130] For more detail on the work of international actors in the justice sector (as well as other areas), see various reports by ASF, Moussalli, OHCHR, PRI, RCN and UNDP.

domestic counterparts, Trocaire, for example, running a 'Human Rights Capacity-Building Programme' and also funding, together with the Irish government, prison and trial monitoring conducted by LIPRODHOR.[131] There were also large NGOs such as HRW and Amnesty International that were not involved in facilitating the implementation of projects, but were monitoring developments (including arbitrary arrests, detention conditions, extrajudicial killings and trials before the formal courts and *gacaca* jurisdictions), raising concerns and making recommendations.[132] The Rwandan government, as well as domestic NGOs, also received assistance (financial, material and technical) from multilateral and bilateral donors, in particular the European Union, Belgium, Canada, Germany, Ireland, the Netherlands, Sweden, Switzerland, the UK and the US.[133]

As mentioned above, there were few domestic NGOs in operation following the genocide. There were however some that worked on justice and human rights issues and that maintained independence from the government (giving rise in some cases to allegations of divisionism). CLADHO,[134] an umbrella human rights organisation, and LIPRODHOR, a constituent member of CLADHO, are two that were particularly prominent. LIPRODHOR monitored genocide trials before the formal courts (producing a monthly report called *Le Verdict*) and *gacaca* proceedings, followed up on the reintegration of persons released from detention, and monitored detention facilities with the aim of improving conditions and ensuring respect of prisoners' rights.[135] CLADHO also monitored trials and ran various training, sensitisation and education programmes on human rights.[136]

It is incontestable that international actors played a major role in the reconstruction of Rwanda's state systems and institutions in the first few years after the genocide, although it must be recalled that all hinged on the Rwandan government's approval and acceptance of this assistance. Once Rwanda decided upon a different course of justice to deal with

See also Chakravarty 2006; Demay et al. 2005; Kimonyo, Twagiramungu and Kayumba 2004: chapter III; Oomen 2005.

131 Moussalli 2000b: [66] and [80]. Trocaire also provided training for social workers and supported court and prison officials with the processing of defendants' files.

132 See various reports on Rwanda by Amnesty International and HRW.

133 Degni-Ségui 1997: [65–66]; Moussalli 1997: [24] and 2000a: [130]. See also Oomen 2005.

134 Collectif des Ligues et Association de Défense des Droits de l'Homme au Rwanda.

135 See various reports by LIPRODHOR.

136 See various reports by CLADHO.

génocidaires, in the form the *gacaca* jurisdictions, it is arguable that their role diminished. Whilst some commentators posit that donors and international actors exerted considerable influence on the elaboration and implementation of *gacaca*,[137] and whilst it is clear that various donor states provided support,[138] the government exercised tight control over *gacaca*, including the *gacaca*-related activities of domestic and international NGOs, particularly once the jurisdictions began operating. Gready, observing a breakdown in PRI's relationship with the government during the transition from policymaking to policy implementation, concluded: 'There is a general sense that the space for civil society influence shrank as *gacaca* entered the implementation phase.'[139] ASF's role was also constrained; an evaluation of its activities indicated a move from relative independence from the government when it was providing judicial assistance, to greater collaboration with the authorities once it redirected its efforts to *gacaca*, a shift that resulted in its criticisms of the *gacaca* legislation becoming increasingly muted.[140]

The balance between collaboration and criticism was precarious for most international actors in post-genocide Rwanda, and not only after the *gacaca* jurisdictions had begun operating. Given the inaction of the international community to intervene prior to, or during, the genocide, there was an element of guilt, leading one commentator to refer to a 'genocide credit' that he asserts was exploited by the Rwandan government to divert criticisms away from its own violations.[141] An analysis of how different actors approached this dilemma in general is beyond the parameters of this book, although this issue will be revisited in Chapters 6–8 when examining international actors', in particular UNICEF's, interventions in respect of child *génocidaires*.

4.3 The Position of the Child Offender under Rwandan Law

Before the genocide, there were very few provisions in Rwandan law dealing expressly with children. Cantwell explains: 'Rwanda's legislation

137 Bornkamm 2012: 3–4, 27 and 90 (who also emphasises the influence of domestic NGOs); Oomen 2005.

138 In particular, Austria, Belgium, Canada, Germany, the Netherlands, Sweden, Switzerland, the UK and the US provided support. See Digneffe and Fierens 2003: 78; HRW 2011: 127–129; Oomen 2005: 903; Schotsmans 2011; Uvin and Mironko 2003: 228.

139 Gready 2011: 96–97. See also Schotsmans 2011: 399 on problems encountered by PRI.

140 Demay et al. 2005: 55–56.

141 Reyntjens 2004.

on child-related issues is minimal and often outdated, inspired by colonial laws or even unchanged since that era … Its lacunae have been supplemented, moreover, by the need to deal with new situations resulting from the genocide, including the penal response to the crime itself …'[142] For children coming into conflict with the law, there was no special juvenile justice system or procedure, although the law provided for reduced sentences for those aged under 18 and an implicit minimum age of criminal responsibility of 14,[143] as well as the separation of children from adults in prisons.[144] Children under 14 who committed wrongs would generally be dealt with within their family, unless it was a serious crime, in which event they may have been taken to a re-education centre. However, there were no formal arrangements enshrined in the law for this category of minors: the authorities would often classify them as vagabonds who could be placed in custody.[145] The Rwandan Penal Code of 1977 is largely modelled on the French Penal Code of 1810. Odongo notes that, as many juvenile justice laws in Africa are colonially inherited, 'the philosophy of how to manage child offenders reflected the social construction of childhood as conceptualised by the colonizing countries'.[146] Research participants had different views as to whether the age categories in the Rwandan Penal Code corresponded with the reality of Rwandan society. A former Director General of Social Affairs in the Ministry of Labour and Social Affairs (MINITRASO) considered the age divisions to be very 'European' and not reflective of Rwandan 'thinking',[147] whilst a prosecutor[148] and a defence lawyer,[149] although recognising that the age categories derived from Belgian and French law, believed that they did

[142] Cantwell 1997: 57.

[143] Art. 77, Décret-loi No. 21/77 instituant le Code Pénal [Penal Code 1977]. UNICEF Rwanda (1996c: 33) commented that, with the exception of this article, 'special provisions concerning children in conflict with the law … were almost non-existent'.

[144] Art. 40, Penal Code 1977 and Art. 28, Ordonnance No. 111/127 organisant le service pénitentiaire du Ruanda-Urundi [Penitentiary Service Statute 1961].

[145] Interview with Judge D (various courts)/former Prosecutor, Kigali, 18 September 2013. The relevant law on vagabonds dates back to 1896 (Décret sur le vagabondage et la mendicité). In 1975, special re-education centres were established to accommodate vagabonds (see also section 5.3.1).

[146] Odongo 2005: 39. See also discussion in section 3.2.

[147] Interview with Straton Nsanzabaganwa, former Director General of Social Affairs, MINITRASO and former Director of Social Affairs/Protection, MINALOC, Kigali, 8 October 2013. Judge D/former Prosecutor (interview, 18 September 2013) expressed a similar view.

[148] Interview with Prosecutor B (public prosecution officer), Kigali, 10 September 2013.

[149] Interview with Lawyer E, Northern Province, 1 October 2013.

reflect Rwandan society. As indicated earlier, the SCF-USA study had highlighted that many Rwandans saw socio-cultural factors as demarcating childhood and adulthood, yet most considered that children who had committed acts in normal circumstances should be treated differently than adults. It was children's participation in the genocide that had a significant influence on society's perception of the child and of appropriate responses for this particular set of children: through their violent acts, these perpetrators were no longer 'children' and thus deserved to be punished as adults.

Subsequent chapters will examine the various measures that were taken to deal with child perpetrators and that sought to balance the interests of the child and of society. Some of these measures would also lay the foundations for a future system that would be more sensitive to juvenile justice considerations.[150] Whilst this book analyses only those laws and policies relevant to child *génocidaires*, and thus does not examine in detail more recent legislation and practice, there has been a discernible increase in the commitment to children's rights, at least on paper.

Very briefly, in addition to the Constitution of 2003 that contained provisions relating to children and the family,[151] a law was passed in 2001 that specifically addressed the rights of the child (including the right to be heard in judicial matters and to legal assistance) and the protection of the child against violence.[152] This was repealed by a more comprehensive law in 2011 which contained a chapter on children in conflict with the law.[153] This confirmed 14 as the minimum age of criminal responsibility, provided that a child's 'personality' must be taken into account during criminal proceedings, restricted pre-trial detention, provided for alternatives to imprisonment (such as deferred sentence or placement in a rehabilitation or re-education centre), and provided for the right of privacy at all stages of proceedings. Similar provisions are contained in the current law on child protection passed in 2018, although this law does not specify the age of criminal responsibility or contain provisions on alternatives

[150] NGO Staff Member (interview, 22 February 2013) directly linked the increase in juvenile justice protections with the awareness resulting from the genocide that children were capable of committing serious crimes.

[151] In particular, Art. 28 recognises the right of the child to 'special measures of protection … that are necessary … under national and international law'.

[152] Law No. 27/2001 Relating to the Rights and Protection of the Child Against Violence.

[153] Chapter VII, Arts. 58–64, Law No. 54/2011 Relating to the Rights and the Protection of the Child.

to detention.[154] In 2003, the government established a national policy for orphans and other vulnerable children which proposed juvenile justice strategies, including the establishment of appropriate detention facilities, models for alternatives to imprisonment, a child protection unit in the police and a juvenile chamber in courts.[155] In 2004, provision was made for a juvenile chamber in certain courts that, in addition to sentencing juvenile offenders, was to 'ensure appropriate measures for their safety, support, supervision and education'.[156] Specific provisions were included in a new Criminal Procedure Code of that same year covering the investigation of juvenile cases as well as court proceedings.[157] Note, however, that the Criminal Procedure Code 2004 created some confusion by providing that children over 12 could be detained and tried by juvenile chambers, suggesting a lower age of criminal responsibility.[158] Article 100 of the 2012 Penal Code removed this confusion by expressly stipulating that children under 14 cannot be criminally liable,[159] and the Criminal Procedure Code of 2013 confirms that children under 14 cannot be prosecuted, but allows in exceptional circumstances for children aged 12–14 to be held in custody for a maximum of 72 hours for the purposes of investigation.[160] Prisons also underwent reform, a law in 2006 providing that prisoners would be separated according to age, sex, health status and sentence, with juveniles aged between 14 and 18 being supervised by 'competent employees'.[161] This 2006 law also referred to the establishment (by subsequent Presidential Order) of special rehabilitation centres for convicted

154 Chapter III, Arts. 23–26, Law No. 71/2018 Relating to the Protection of the Child.

155 MINALOC 2003: 17. In its report to the CRC in that year, Rwanda referred to the establishment of two police units specifically to deal with children (CRC Committee 2003a: [64]).

156 Arts. 9, 74 and 75, Organic Law No. 07/2004 Determining the Organisation, Functioning and Jurisdiction of Courts (later replaced by similar provisions of Organic Law No. 51/2008). This law was part of an extensive reform of the judicial system in 2004.

157 Arts. 184–192, Law No. 13/2004 Relating to the Code of Criminal Procedure [Criminal Procedure Code 2004].

158 Arts. 184 and 192.

159 Organic Law No. 01/2012 Instituting the Penal Code. A similar provision is included at Art. 85 of the new Penal Code of 2018 (Law No. 68/2018 Determining Offences and Penalties in General).

160 Art. 198, Law No. 30/2013 Relating to the Code of Criminal Procedure.

161 Art. 24, Law No. 38/2006 on the Establishment and Organisation of the National Prisons Service [National Prisons Service Law 2006]. Similar provisions were repeated in Art. 31 of Law No. 34/2010 on the Establishment, Functioning and Organisation of Rwanda Correctional Service (RCS) and remain in force pursuant to Law No. 19bis/2017 Modifying and Complementing Law No. 34/2010.

minors.[162] Finally, a National Commission for Children was established in 2011 to promote children's rights.[163]

In addition to its domestic laws, Rwanda was also bound by obligations under customary international law and the international treaties it had ratified, the most relevant for this book being the ICCPR[164] and the CRC.[165] Rwanda's Constitution of 1991[166] made only brief reference to international law, its preamble expressing concern to protect and promote human rights in accordance with the UDHR and the African Charter on Human and People's Rights, and its Article 44 setting out the President's power to negotiate, sign and ratify international treaties and conventions. The 2003 Constitution went further, reaffirming its adherence to human rights principles and explicitly referring to the CRC (as well as the other key human rights treaties) in its preamble. Amendments to the Constitution in 2015, however, removed these explicit references, referring simply to the commitment to building a state based on rule of law and respect for human rights. As a monist state, international treaties were automatically applicable in Rwanda and could be invoked before the courts. However, as Goonesekere observes in respect of the CRC, even in monist countries there is generally no procedure to invoke directly its provisions before the courts, and thus 'legislative assimilation or incorporation can be vital in integrating treaties in domestic law'.[167] In any event, invoking rights before courts or tribunals primarily addresses only one aspect of implementation: the provision of effective remedies to redress violations that have already occurred. As will be illustrated in the rest of this book, efforts to implement and comply with the CRC (and related standards) were directed more at translating the rights into policy and practice.

[162] Art. 51, National Prisons Service Law 2006. There is no reference to rehabilitation centres specifically for minors in subsequent legislation.

[163] Law No. 22/2011 Establishing the National Commission for Children and Determining its Mission, Organisation and Functioning.

[164] Accession date: 16 April 1975.

[165] Ratification date: 24 January 1991. Rwanda also ratified the African Charter on Human and People's Rights in 1983 and signed the ACRWC in 1990 (although ratification did not occur until 11 May 2001). In 2002 Rwanda ratified the first and second Optional Protocols to the CRC. Note also that Rwanda had ratified the Genocide Convention but had not enacted legislation to give effect to its provisions (see section 5.2.1).

[166] In force until 2003, although modified by the Arusha Peace Agreement and the RPF Declaration of 17 July 1994.

[167] Goonesekere 2007: 6.

4.4 Conclusion

The genocide in Rwanda gave rise to numerous challenges for the new government. Given decades of impunity, the decision was taken to prosecute all of those who took part in the genocide. Yet the government had inherited a completely devastated country, at all levels: not only had all state machinery, including the judicial system, been destroyed, but also the social fabric of the state. In particular, children's participation in the genocide had significantly affected the perception of the child in Rwanda, with the result that even very young child perpetrators were not exempt from demands for accountability. Indeed, the SCF-USA study suggested that societal demands for these children to be held responsible were such that, had the government failed to take accountability measures in respect of these children, their security would have been at risk. Rwanda thus faced a number of competing demands including institution building, social reconstruction and reconciliation and accountability, at the same time as trying to ensure stability and security and begin its economic development. Financial, material and technical assistance were available from international actors, and the Rwandan government readily accepted assistance in the justice sector whilst making it clear that justice was to be done on Rwanda's terms. Arguably, the influence of international actors waned once the *gacaca* jurisdictions were instituted but it seems that, at least in the first few years following the genocide, their role was important. Nonetheless, significant tensions persisted between international actors (in particular the UN) and the Rwandan government. As will be elucidated in subsequent chapters, this influenced the manner in which actors such as UNICEF were able to operate and moulded their interventions. Working within the confines of the maximalist approach to accountability dictated by the Rwandan government, international actors also had to navigate the socio-political context and be cognisant of the significant resource constraints of the Rwandan government.

Whilst this chapter has suggested that, over time, there has been an increasing commitment to children's rights in Rwanda's legislation, the aim of this book is to explore how international standards on *child perpetrators of atrocities* can be operationalised in post-conflict societies. Chakravarty has argued that the requirements on post-genocide Rwanda 'render the absolute application of human rights principles virtually impossible',[168]

[168] Chakravarty 2006: 139.

and Schabas noted that Rwanda was 'simply incapable of respecting the provisions of its own criminal law, not to mention its obligations under international human rights law'.[169] In the next chapter, I examine whether this was indeed the case in respect of child perpetrators in Rwanda, before I explore, in Chapters 6 and 7, how international actors, in particular UNICEF, sought to enhance the application of children's rights in this difficult context.

[169] Schabas 2008c: 213.

5

Rwanda's Responses, in Law, Policy and Practice, to Child *Génocidaires*

Following the genocide, the Rwandan government adopted a policy that sought to hold accountable all those suspected of participating in the genocide, including minors. This chapter provides a comprehensive account of how these child perpetrators were dealt with in Rwanda in law, policy and practice. It examines how children were held accountable for participating in the genocide, whether they were given differential treatment on grounds of their age (and if so, what the relevant age thresholds were) and, broadly, whether Rwanda complied with its international obligations. The intention is not to evaluate Rwanda's actions against a checklist of the international standards referred to in Chapter 2,[1] although it will be indicated where particular measures conformed with, or deviated from, international law; rather, the aim is to explore how Rwanda, a post-conflict state with international obligations, approached child *génocidaires*, in light of its decision to pursue accountability measures for all perpetrators. These issues are explored in the context of arrests and detentions, criminal justice mechanisms (both formal courts and *gacaca* jurisdictions) and administrative measures taken to address genocidal acts. Whilst the emphasis is on child perpetrators – and particularly on spotlighting any age-related differential treatment – many of the findings in this chapter relating to shortcomings in the treatment of *génocidaires* are equally applicable to those aged over 18 at the time of the genocide.

[1] Chapter 2 provides the current status of international standards on child offenders. It thus includes the CRC Committee's guidance on CRC provisions, in particular its General Comment No. 10 on children's rights in juvenile justice (currently under review), which was issued in 2007 and thus some years after the genocide and after most children had gone through the accountability process.

5.1 Arrests and Detentions

The earliest reports of children detained in Rwandan prisons on suspicion of participating in the genocide came in November 1994, after representatives from the international community were permitted to enter prisons.[2] The reported number of child *génocidaires* in detention varies considerably according to the source and across time given the lack of systematic, consistent and accurate record-keeping and reporting procedures. MINIJUST reported that 1,600 minors (the majority accused of genocide) were in detention[3] in 1995; 2,566 in 1996; 3,832 in 1997; 4,533 in 1998; and 4,454 in 1999.[4] By 2002, the total number of children detained had decreased to around 3,000, and had almost halved by 2004, there being 1,516 in central prisons.[5] In 2008, the Rwandan government informed the UN HRC that all child *génocidaires* had been released provisionally and were thus no longer in detention.[6] Although children under 14 could not be held criminally responsible under Rwandan law, a child as young as seven was seen in Kigali prison in 1995,[7] and more than 500 detainees under 14 at the time of the genocide were in detention in 1999.[8] Some of these children were, over the years, transferred to re-education centres before being reintegrated into society, but whilst many of the under-14s had been released by December 2000, some remained in prison beyond this date, in clear violation of Rwandan and international law.[9] To put the number of child detainees in context, the total number of detainees in 1999 was approximately 121,500;[10] thus minors accounted

2 Cantwell 1997: 48; Chorlton 1996: 27; UNICEF Rwanda 1995c: 5.

3 In prisons, *cachots* (local detention centres intended to hold detainees temporarily for up to 48 hours before transfer to prisons, but that were, in effect, used as prisons following the genocide) and 'special detention centres' or gendarmerie *brigades* (also intended to be temporary).

4 Referenced in UNDG 2000b: 5.

5 LIPRODHOR 2005: 122–123 (the decrease being the result of releases following the 2003 Presidential Communiqué – see section 5.3.2).

6 HRC 2008: [110]. See also CRC Committee 2012: [339].

7 Degni-Ségui 1995b: [70] and [72].

8 ASF 1999a: 13. See also UNICEF Rwanda 1996a: 3, noting an increase of more than 100 per cent (from 207 to 430) in the number of under-14s in prison between 29 March 1995 and 9 May 1995.

9 HRW 2003a: 29–30 and Moussalli 2001: 29 refer to several hundred non-responsible children in prisons after the December 2000 releases. See also Rwanda's report to the CRC Committee (CRC Committee 2003a: [331]). In 2004, the Rwandan government reported that all non-responsible children had been released (CRC Committee 2004a: 7).

10 Moussalli 2000a: [97].

for just under 4 per cent of the prison population. Whilst this is not a huge proportion, it is nonetheless a significant number of children that could not simply be disregarded.

Rwandan law provided for the separation of minors (at least males) from adults in prisons.[11] However, children were initially held together with adults in most prisons[12] in breach of domestic and international law. Even where there were separate minors' wings, access for adults was often not restricted. This facilitated physical and sexual abuse of children by adult prisoners and increased the risk of children becoming hardened criminals. The discovery of hundreds of children held in deplorable conditions in Kigali initiated UNICEF's engagement with child *génocidaires*, and it started a 'hard-core advocacy' to separate minors from adults.[13] Working with MINIJUST, it sought the transfer of the under-14s from prisons to re-education centres and the separation from adults of minors who remained in prisons, through the restoration or construction of new minors' wings. By 2000, six out of 18 prisons had minors' blocks, but 1,097 minors continued to be detained with adults.[14] An additional complicating factor was that many child genocide suspects had turned 18 whilst in pre-trial detention. Rwandan law did not specify what should happen in these circumstances. Jens Matthes, a legal consultant for UNICEF Rwanda's child protection team who worked on these issues with the Rwandan government, reported that MINIJUST had suggested that juveniles remain separated from adults until they reached 21, or until the conclusion of their trial if later, but noted that, in practice, it depended on the prison.[15] A former juvenile detainee arrested after he had turned 18 was placed in the adult wing,[16] but Tertsakian found child *génocidaires* (by then in their mid-20s) in minors' blocks in 2004,[17] and a former prison director stated that genocide minors who had reached

[11] Art. 40, Penal Code 1977 and Art. 28, Penitentiary Service Statute 1961 (albeit that the latter provides for separation to the extent to which facilities permit).

[12] Degni-Ségui 1996: [91]. Former Juvenile Detainee (Skype interview, 24 August 2013), under 18 at the time of arrest, was placed with adults in prison.

[13] Skype interview with Daniel Toole, former Deputy Resident Representative and Resident Representative, UNICEF Rwanda, 16 May 2013. See also Cantwell 1997: 48 and 86.

[14] UNDG 2000a: 14 and 2000b: 5.

[15] Matthes 1997a: 5 and 9. See section 6.2.2b for details of UNICEF Rwanda's advocacy on this point.

[16] Skype interview with Chaste Gahunde, former juvenile detainee, 19 August 2013.

[17] Tertsakian 2008: 174 and 182. See also Moussalli 2000b: [114] (finding a 22-year-old genocide minor in the minors' wing of Gitarama prison).

18 remained in the minors' wing.[18] ASOFERWA reported that, in some prisons, only genocide minors under 18 at the time of detention were in minors' wings, whilst in others all those under 18 at the time of the alleged offence remained in the minors' wing,[19] and a former detainee commented that it depended on the availability of places in his prison – if the minors' block was crowded, the oldest detainees would be moved to the adult wing.[20]

Overcrowding was a serious issue for all prisoners, the prison population vastly overwhelming prison capacity, sometimes by eight times.[21] As a result, conditions were 'extremely rudimentary', prisoners 'piled in practically on top of one another', everyone thrown together irrespective of age or health condition.[22] Minors' detention conditions were described as 'atrocious', failing to meet the most basic of needs, including water, sanitation, health care, clothing and food.[23] Conditions in *cachots* were reportedly worse: given their intended temporary nature, there was no food or healthcare budget: the families of detainees had to supply food.[24] Many detainees, including minors, died as a result of the overcrowding and poor conditions, but also from torture and inhuman treatment, including severe beatings.[25] Training was provided to prison staff on special requirements for children in detention (with specific reference to the CRC and other international standards)[26] and conditions improved over the years. However, UNDG reported in 2000 that minors' detention conditions were 'far from meeting the basic minimal standards (as specified in the CRC and Beijing Rules, for example)'.[27] Commenting in 2004, MINIJUST acknowledged poor prison conditions but stated that Rwanda did not have the financial capability to meet 'international norms on the

[18] Interview with Murigo, 6 September 2013.

[19] See e.g. ASOFERWA 1998d: 16 and 19 and 1998e: 3 and 9–11.

[20] Interview with former Detainee of Kigali Central Prison (KCP), Northern Province, 30 September 2013.

[21] Degni-Ségui 1995b: [71]. See also PRI 2005: 5.

[22] Degni-Ségui 1994b: [32]; Tertsakian 2011: 213.

[23] Chorlton 1996: 43. See also UNICEF Rwanda 1996b: 15.

[24] Moussalli 1999b: [107–108].

[25] Degni-Ségui 1995b: [73–79] and 1997: [125]; HRW 2003a: 36–39; Tertsakian 2008: 45–46 and 239–241. Former Juvenile Detainee (Skype interview, 24 August 2013) reported that he was beaten by soldiers and police during arrest and detention.

[26] Murigo (interview, 6 September 2013), a former prison director, received training from PRI, and Mukanyangezi (interview, 8 October 2013), a former social assistant, received training from the penitentiary services in collaboration with NGOs and UNICEF Rwanda.

[27] UNDG 2000b: 5.

treatment of prisoners. Conditions are as good as the GOR [Government of Rwanda] can afford.'[28]

As regards activities, from May 1995, UNICEF Rwanda and UNESCO were authorised by MINIJUST to run an emergency education programme in the main prisons. This was followed by the more formal 'Protégez-moi' project run initially by SCF-USA and then by ASOFERWA (with support from UNICEF Rwanda), which provided minors in central prisons (at least those in separate minors' blocks) with literacy and numeracy training, language courses, vocational training, educational talks, social activities and psychosocial support.[29] Following the introduction of *gacaca* jurisdictions, genocide minors also received information on *gacaca* and the advantages of pleading guilty, on national reconciliation and peaceful coexistence in society and, after January 2003, on the Presidential Communiqué (see section 5.3.2).[30] However, not all prisons, and almost certainly not *cachots*, had such programmes, and in detention facilities (even within the project) teaching was largely left to adult prisoners.[31]

In terms of procedural requirements, the Criminal Procedure Code 1963 contained the process for preliminary investigation and arrest, and conditions for preventative and provisional detention,[32] but no reference was made to minors. In the immediate aftermath of the genocide, arrests were conducted primarily by the military or local administration authorities rather than legally competent judicial personnel and were most frequently made on the basis of denunciations rather than investigation.[33] In most cases, there was no arrest warrant, and persons were detained beyond legally mandated periods, amounting to clear breaches of both domestic

[28] MINIJUST 2004: 26.

[29] See various reports by ASOFERWA on the Protégez-moi project. See also CRC Committee 2003a: [342]; van Krieken 2000: 15–16. Mukanyangezi (interview, 8 October 2013), who worked on the project from 1995, stated that she also advocated for legal representation for these minors and for their cases to be expedited.

[30] See ASOFERWA reports on the Protégez-moi project from 2002 and 2003; UNICEF Rwanda 2002: 15 and 32 (reporting that 3,295 genocide minors received support under the project in 2002). Juveniles also received information on juvenile justice and the Genocide Law from judicial defenders. See section 5.2.1c.

[31] Confirmed by former Detainee of KCP (interview, 30 September 2013); Murigo (interview, 6 September 2013). See also ASOFERWA reports on Protégez-moi project.

[32] Arts. 21–36 and Arts. 4 and 37–57 respectively, Loi portant Code de Procédure Pénale [Criminal Procedure Code 1963].

[33] This process was heavily criticised by human rights organisations, who noted that many denunciations were false. See Tully 2003: 389; Waldorf 2006: 41–42.

and international law. Derogations from arrest and detention procedures and extensions to the pre-trial detention limits in the Criminal Procedure Code were subsequently permitted by law with retrospective effect.[34] Of interest, whilst Rwanda expressly referred to the ICCPR in the preamble to this legislation, it did not formally declare a state of emergency with respect to its obligations under the ICCPR, which appears consistent with White and Odello's comment (see Chapter 3) that post-conflict states may be reluctant to declare a state of emergency. The legislation led to considerable criticism by the UN Special Rapporteur, Degni-Ségui, who considered that, whilst special measures might have been necessary 'until early 1995', by the time of his state visit in late 1996, it was not 'materially impossible to respect certain forms and procedures of criminal legislation'. He thus considered that Rwanda was failing to meet international standards.[35] He did not, however, as Schabas notes, propose that genocide suspects be released from prison.[36]

The Office of the UN High Commissioner for Human Rights (OHCHR), reporting in 1998, determined that it was impossible to comply with arrest and detention procedures given the depletion of judicial personnel, and noted that measures were being taken by the government to improve capacity.[37] UNICEF Rwanda came to a similar conclusion with respect to minors, commenting that the lack of trained personnel meant 'even minimum safeguards cannot be respected'.[38] Efforts were made, mainly within the framework of the joint MINIJUST/UNICEF Children in Conflict with the Law Project,[39] to train judicial personnel on investigation techniques, the preparation of minors' files and international juvenile justice standards in an attempt to expedite minors' cases.[40] Minors were also prioritised in

[34] Law No. 09/96 Relating to Provisional Modifications to the Criminal Procedure Code; Law No. 16/97 Modifying the Law No. 09/96. A 1995 law that sought to suspend procedural rules was declared unconstitutional by the Constitutional Court, leading to an amendment to the Constitution. See Degni-Ségui 1996: [79–83]; Schabas and Imbleau 1997: 173–174.

[35] Degni-Ségui 1997: [104–117]. See also UNHRFOR 1996b: [58] (referring to a possible breach of the ICCPR). Note, however, Moussalli's (2000a: [138]) comments in February 2000 that the extension of these legislative derogations was 'regrettable', but that there was 'no real alternative'.

[36] Schabas 2008b: 545.

[37] OHCHR 1998a: [7].

[38] UNICEF Rwanda 1997d: 86.

[39] This project, formulated in 1995, aimed to accelerate the processing of juvenile cases, secure the removal of under-14s from prisons/*cachots* and ensure legal representation for juveniles.

[40] See CRC Committee 2003a: [331]; UNICEF Rwanda 1995c: 9; UNDG 2000b: 5. Confirmed by former Prosecutor E (public prosecution officer) (interview, Kigali, 27 September

the various initiatives established to accelerate the preparation of case files: *commissions de triages* (screening committees established as an extra-judicial measure to review cases and release detainees where there was insufficient evidence) were ordered to prioritise the cases of the elderly, women and minors;[41] and some *groupes mobiles* (mobile investigation units comprising judicial police from both the public prosecution and gendarmerie) were assigned specifically to minors' cases.[42] Minors who were released received some reintegration assistance from ASOFERWA under the 'Protégez-moi' project.[43]

Despite efforts to accelerate processing, minors' cases continued to move slowly: in 1997, UNICEF Rwanda recorded that, of more than 3,000 juvenile cases, 11 files had been submitted to courts with a further 70 files completed and due to be submitted.[44] By 2001, the situation had improved, yet still only 35 per cent of detained genocide minors had complete files.[45] Reasons for the delay included the lack of judicial personnel working exclusively on minors' cases,[46] the introduction of group trials in which juveniles were tried alongside adult co-defendants and problems in obtaining legal counsel to represent juveniles. Many minors, in some cases wrongly arrested, were thus held in pre-trial detention for lengthy periods and without case files,[47] contrary to various international child rights standards, in particular Articles 37(b) and 40(2)(b) of the CRC.

2013) who received training and former MINIJUST/UNICEF (Children in Conflict with the Law) Project Coordinator A (interview, Kigali, 7 October 2013).

41 UNHRFOR 1996b: [72] (noting however that this stipulation was not followed in practice) and OHCHR 1996b: [26]. Confirmed by Lawyer B (interview, Kigali, 15 February 2013); Prosecutor A (interview, Kigali, 14 February 2013).

42 ASF 2000b: 19. Confirmed by former IPJ/Prosecutor (interview, 26 September 2013), Prosecutor B (interview, 10 September 2013) and former Prosecutor E (interview, 27 September 2013), all of whom worked on these teams that would take detainees to the 'hills' to collect testimonies from the local population.

43 Interview with ASOFERWA Staff Member B, Kigali, 27 September 2013. However, note Briggs' (2005: 24) report that Minani (the first juvenile tried) received 'no counselling support from the government, nor was there any type of coordination with his home community'.

44 UNICEF Rwanda 1997c.

45 Moussalli 2001: [29].

46 In practice, investigators and prosecutors on the 'minors' team' were sometimes assigned to cases involving adults. See ASF 1999b: 40 and DCHR 1999: 7 (both also referring to no prosecutor being available to take juveniles' confessions).

47 Former Juvenile Detainee (Skype interview, 24 August 2013) said he was arrested in January 1995, held without a case file/formal charges until 2001 and released in 2005; Gahunde (Skype interview, 19 August 2013) reported that he was imprisoned in 2002 and

5.2 The Criminal Justice Response

5.2.1 The Formal Courts

Although the RPF-led government made the prosecution of genocide suspects a priority, and whilst Rwanda had ratified the Genocide Convention,[48] national law did not provide expressly for the punishment of the crime of genocide. Considering it essential to have the crimes committed during the genocide symbolically categorised as 'genocide', yet also cognisant of the need to avoid violating the principle of retroactivity, the government passed the Genocide Law of 1996.[49] Article 1 provided that persons could be prosecuted for 'acts set out and sanctioned under the Penal Code and which constitute: (a) either the crime of genocide … as defined in the [Genocide] Convention … ratified by Rwanda; or (b) offences set out in the Penal Code which … were committed in connection with the events surrounding the genocide …' Rwanda thus adopted what has been termed a 'double/dual incrimination' approach, pursuant to which a person could, for example, be found guilty of murder and genocide, but the applicable penalty would be that prescribed by the Penal Code for murder (or more lenient sentences where foreseen under the Genocide Law). Daniel de Beer, involved in drafting the Genocide Law, affirmed that dual incrimination required elements of both crimes to be made out, and that it was therefore necessary to establish the specific intent to destroy the Tutsi group for a finding of genocide.[50] However, Madeline Morris, also involved in the drafting process, interpreted the approach differently. She considered there to be no legal basis in Rwandan law in force at the time of the genocide to try individuals for the crime of genocide: the Genocide Law simply introduced special procedures and courts for crimes already codified under the Penal Code at the time of their commission. Thus there was no requirement to show specific intent.[51] In practice, as will be

detained for three years without receiving any information on his detention, and was later acquitted by the *gacaca* courts.

48 Décret-loi No. 08/75 approuvant et ratifiant diverses Conventions Internationales.

49 Organic Law No. 08/96 on the Organization of Prosecutions for Offences Constituting the Crime of Genocide or Crimes against Humanity Committed since 1 October 1990.

50 de Beer 1997b: 32–35. Confirmed also in personal correspondence, 22 October 2014.

51 Skype interview with Madeline Morris, Former Adviser on Justice to the President of Rwanda, at time of interview, Professor of Law, Duke Law School, 13 May 2014.

seen in section 5.2.1d, individuals were generally convicted of 'genocide' in conjunction with the related ordinary crime.

The Genocide Law created Specialised Chambers in the courts of first instance and military courts to try genocide cases and, whilst existing laws including the Penal and Criminal Procedure Codes continued to apply (save where expressly provided),[52] introduced some novel approaches. It created four categories of crimes to reflect the perpetrator's degree of culpability: category 1 encompassed persons involved in planning and organising the genocide, people in positions of power who committed or encouraged crimes, 'notorious murderers' and those who committed acts of sexual torture; category 2 applied to persons who committed or were accomplices of murder; category 3 comprised persons who committed serious assaults against the person; and category 4 covered property crimes. The Genocide Law departed from the Penal Code in terms of sentences[53] for some of these categories, such as life imprisonment for category 2 offences (which included 'intentional homicide' and thus could be punishable by death).[54] In addition to imprisonment, a further penalty (under Article 17) was the withdrawal of 'civic rights', the extent and duration of withdrawal dependant on the offender's category.[55] The Genocide Law also introduced a confession and guilty plea procedure (Articles 4–13) providing for sentence reductions that varied according to when the confession was made and the category of offence.[56] Defendants could rely on defences and excuses provided in the Penal Code,[57] and mitigating circumstances (at the complete discretion of the judge) could further

[52] Art. 39.

[53] Annex 2 sets out the sentences pursuant to the Genocide Law.

[54] Art. 14. Under Arts. 311–312, Penal Code 1977, premeditated murder was punishable by death, and voluntary homicide by life imprisonment – category 2 encompassed both of these acts. ASF (2004a: 113) commented that, given the special nature of genocide, most intentional homicides were classed as premeditated murder.

[55] 'Civic' rights (the term used in the legislation) include the right to serve in the armed forces or police or to hold public office and electoral and political rights (see Annex 2).

[56] Arts. 15 (confessions made 'prior to prosecution') and 16 (confessions made 'after prosecution'). The word 'prosecution' is vague: De Beer (1997b: 64) suggests that Art. 15 applied where a confession was made before an accused was informed officially of the right to participate in the confession procedure pursuant to Art. 4. Accordingly, Art. 16 would have applied to a confession made after official notification but before the case was transmitted to the court.

[57] E.g. Irresistible constraint would negate criminal responsibility, and minority status would result in a reduced sentence (Arts. 70 and 77, Penal Code 1977 respectively).

reduce sentences.[58] Article 36 of the Genocide Law gave defendants the right to legal representation when prosecuted but not at government expense. In practice, not all detainees had legal representation as many were impecunious and, as previously mentioned, there remained very few lawyers after the genocide, most of whom refused to act for alleged *génocidaires*.[59] Efforts were made to improve access to lawyers, as detailed in section 4.2.2 and in the discussion on trial procedure below.

The courts began to try suspects from 27 December 1996, and the first judgment against a juvenile (the *Minani* case) was handed down on 23 September 1997. Progress was very slow, only 346 persons being tried in the first year.[60] The rate did increase over the years, partly due to the use of itinerant trials (holding court sessions where the crimes were committed) and group trials (having more than ten accused), and by mid-2006, approximately 10,000 persons had been tried by the formal courts.[61] However, it had become clear in the first few years that it would take considerably longer than a lifetime to complete the prosecutions at the rate at which cases were proceeding.[62] Alternative solutions were sought, culminating in the introduction of the *gacaca* jurisdictions (see below). The majority of genocide suspects went through this more informal judicial mechanism.

Unfortunately, it was difficult to obtain official comprehensive information on juvenile trials – both statistics[63] and judgments. There is no comprehensive database of reported genocide cases, and despite making requests to individual courts for relevant documents (with the full case citation, once names of defendants had been identified from other sources), I received only a few positive responses and just six cases. Given this difficulty in identifying and procuring cases, I rely significantly on the 'Recueil de Jurisprudence Contentieux du Génocide' produced by ASF in collaboration with the Supreme Court of Rwanda, as well as interviews

[58] Arts. 82–83, ibid.

[59] Over time, Rwandan lawyers became more willing to take on genocide cases (see ASF 1998b: 7–14; Moussalli 1999a: [36]).

[60] LIPRODHOR 2001a: 6.

[61] Waldorf 2009b: 19.

[62] Moussalli (2000b: [14]) commented that it would take 200 years, noting that some estimated 400 years.

[63] I was informed by an official in the National Public Prosecution Authority (NPPA) that the NPPA held no data on genocide cases, on the basis that these cases were dealt with by *gacaca* courts: this despite the fact that around 10,000 people were tried by the formal courts.

with former judges and others involved with juvenile cases. As regards statistics, the only official information found is in the state report to the CRC Committee that 33 juvenile cases were tried before the formal courts in 1998, representing 3.3 per cent of total judgments that year.[64] As such, it has not been possible to determine the total number of individuals under 18 at the time of the genocide tried by the formal courts. What is clear, however, is that the number of such minors tried by the formal courts is significantly lower than the number tried by *gacaca*, due to the vast difference in the total numbers tried by the two mechanisms.

a Age of Criminal Responsibility and Sentencing Provisions

The Genocide Law contained only one provision (the requirement for juvenile benches – see below) expressly dealing with minors accused of participating in the genocide. The issue of child perpetrators does not appear to have been very high on the agenda: Matthes commented that children were 'simply forgotten' in initial drafts of the genocide legislation,[65] and Morris did not recall any occasion where a different track or special provisions for child perpetrators were discussed.[66] There was some debate, however, on the accountability of children. Gerald Gahima, MINIJUST's Secretary-General from February 1996 to February 1999 and, prior to that, part of the leadership of the RPF, recalled discussions on child perpetrators in the context of the general debate within the RPF about how to deal with the genocide: some (in particular *rescapés*) wanted all children involved to be prosecuted (thus changing existing law), whilst others stressed the importance of dealing with them in ways that complied with international standards.[67] De Beer recalled that some, including Gahima at first, wanted to lower the age of criminal responsibility for child *génocidaires*,[68] and Torres referred to proposals to lower the age, or remove it entirely, noting that UNICEF Rwanda fought strongly against this.[69]

64 CRC Committee 2003a: [331].

65 Matthes 1996b: 3.

66 Skype interview with Morris, 13 May 2014.

67 Skype interview with Gerald Gahima, former Secretary-General of MINIJUST and former Prosecutor General of Rwanda, 5 November 2013.

68 Interview with Daniel de Beer, former Director, RCN and ASF and former adviser to MINIJUST, at time of interview, Professor of Law, Saint-Louis University, Brussels, Belgium, 15 October 2014. He noted that Gahima later became more open to child rights, and Gahima was amongst those identified by UNICEF Rwanda staff members as being very open to, and a good ally on, child rights issues (see Chapter 7).

69 Interview with Torres, 28 September 2013. See also UNICEF Rwanda 1995c: 8.

What seems clear is that excluding children from accountability through any kind of amnesty was not on the table. A judge commented: 'Personne ne pouvait en tout cas brandit cette idée d'amnistie même pour les mineurs. Je crois le pays était encore sous un choc. Ça aurait été interprété comme une sorte de négationnisme.'[70] Other research participants made similar comments, noting that an amnesty was not appropriate given the Rwandan context.[71] The end result was to apply existing law, in particular the Penal Code of 1977.

Article 77 of the Penal Code provided that convicted minors 'over 14 and less than 18' at the time of the offence would be liable to 10–20 years in prison for crimes that would have received a death sentence or life imprisonment had the offender been over 18. For crimes with a determinate prison sentence or fine, minors would receive a sentence not greater than half of that which would have been imposed had they been over 18 (i.e. a lesser sentence than half the adult sentence could be imposed). The Penal Code envisaged imprisonment (or fines for minor offences) only: it did not foresee any alternative sanctions to detention.[72] Reading the Penal Code together with the Genocide Law, minors over 14 and less than 18 would face a maximum sentence of 20 years if in category 1 or 2, and half the adult sentence if in category 3. Category 4 offences gave rise to civil liability, and thus a juvenile's parents/guardians would be responsible for any civil damages. Individuals aged 18 or over at the time of the offence were adults under the law and would not benefit from any special sentencing regime.[73] Article 77 did not expressly provide that those under 14

[70] [No-one could broach the idea of an amnesty, not even for minors. I think the country was still in shock. Raising this idea would have been interpreted as genocide denial.] Interview with Judge J, 4 October 2013.

[71] Interviews with Augustin Nkusi, former Chief Legal Adviser to the Département des Juridictions *Gacaca*/Director of the Legal Support Unit, NSGC and Prosecutor, Kigali, 22 September 2013; former Prosecutor D, 26 September 2013. See also Palmer 2015: 97, referring to many proponents of international criminal law being opposed to an amnesty in Rwanda.

[72] Cf. Art. 37(b), CRC (deprivation of liberty should be a measure of last resort) and Art. 40(4), CRC (alternatives to institutionalisation). Alternative measures were introduced in Art. 190, Criminal Procedure Code 2004. Although this provision had immediate effect, most child *génocidaires* were dealt with by the *gacaca* courts after this date, which did not apply the Criminal Procedure Code.

[73] Research participants confirmed that the over-18s at the time of the genocide did not benefit from any preferential treatment by virtue of their youth, one commenting: 'il a traversé le pont: il n'est plus mineur' ['he's crossed the threshold: he's no longer a minor'] (interview with Judge A (various courts), Kigali, 18 February 2013). However, some defence lawyers commented that they would raise young age, or lack of education, in mitigation for the

attract no criminal responsibility but can be read implicitly as establishing a minimum age of 14. Further, a minor who turned 14 on the day the acts were committed would benefit from the excuse of minority.

A significant problem, however, was the difficulty in determining age, particularly important for those born in 1976 or 1980. First, birth certificates or other identifying documents usually referenced the year of birth only, without specifying the day or month. Second, many documents were destroyed during the genocide. Where there was doubt over age, it was incumbent on the prosecutor or court to obtain a birth certificate from the Registry Office; where this was not available, an affidavit or court judgment on the date of birth should have been obtained.[74] A prosecutor also referred to visiting the parish in which the child was born to check any baptism records and checking when the child began primary school.[75] In the case of continued uncertainty, benefit of the doubt was to be given to the accused.[76] In practice, this principle was applied in some cases, but not all. In one case, a defendant's file stated 1980 as year of birth but the prosecutor argued that his sources had confirmed the year of birth as 1975. Despite uncertainty, the court continued to hear witnesses without investigating further.[77] In another case, an accused had two conflicting pieces of evidence: a census form stating 1974 as the year of birth and an identity card showing 1976. The court relied on the census form as this pre-dated the identity card, and the accused was sentenced as an adult.[78] In contrast, an appeal was allowed where the Specialised Chambers had concluded that a non-responsible defendant was over 14 without thoroughly investigating his age.[79] And in the *Niyoniringiye* case, the court undertook a site visit to verify age, following which the defendant was given the benefit of the doubt that he was under 14 and sent to a re-education centre. Note, however, that in this case, the accused was questioned during the trial before the site visit took place and was subsequently found '*coupable*'

over-18s (e.g. interviews with Lawyer A, Kigali, 14 February and 6 March 2013; Lawyer D, Kigali, 25 September 2013; Lawyer E, 1 October 2013).

74 Arts. 138 and 147–149, Book I, Civil Code 1988.

75 Interview with Prosecutor A, 14 February 2013. Scientific methods to determine age (such as bone age assessments) were considered beyond the means of Rwanda (see Doulliez 1998a: 6; Racine 1998: 24).

76 Art. 20, Criminal Procedure Code 1963. See also ASF 2010: 14.

77 LIPRODHOR 2001b: 11.

78 *Kabirigi*: 148.

79 *Mugabo c/ Ministère Public*: 157.

of the offences charged but criminally non-responsible due to his age.[80] A lawyer interviewed for this study asserted that many minors were acquitted by judges applying the 'benefit of the doubt' principle,[81] and a judge reported that, in one case, a defendant erroneously benefited from application of the principle, being sentenced as a juvenile on the basis of a document found during a site visit which stated his year of birth as 1976, when it was later discovered that he had been born in 1974.[82]

b Minors' Judges

The only provision in the Genocide Law that specifically related to child genocide suspects was Article 19(3) which stipulated that one or more benches (consisting of three magistrates) had to be 'composed of magistrates for minors which shall have exclusive jurisdiction over the offenses set out in Article 1 committed by minors'. Prior to the genocide, there had been no specific juvenile courts or benches and thus this provision marked an innovation in the Rwandan justice system.[83] Matthes asserts that the inclusion of this provision was a result of UNICEF Rwanda's advocacy efforts,[84] and de Beer's account of the drafting history supports this.[85]

As detailed in Chapter 4, the judicial system had been destroyed during the genocide with the result that very few judges remained in Rwanda. To facilitate trials (both of genocide and ordinary crimes), new judges, often without any legal background, received an accelerated training over six months, followed by practical court experience.[86] Eighty-six minors' judges as well as prosecutors were provided with special training by UNICEF Rwanda on how to apply Rwandan law in accordance with international juvenile justice standards.[87] The training, which took place over

[80] *Ministère Public c/ Niyoniringiye* [*Niyoniringiye*]: 111–112. See also *Auditorat Militaire c/ Pte Habimana*: 283 (defendant was given benefit of the doubt that he was aged 16 at the time of the genocide, despite initially stating he was born in 1975 during interrogations).

[81] Interview with Lawyer C, 8 March 2013.

[82] Interview with Judge I, 2 October 2013.

[83] There was no provision for special judges for minors accused of non-genocide-related crimes until 2004.

[84] Skype interview with Jens Matthes, former Legal Consultant on Child Protection, UNICEF Rwanda, 28 November 2013. See also UNICEF Rwanda 1997b: 2.

[85] Skype interview, 28 November 2013. See also section 6.2.2d and section 7.5.

[86] ASF 1997b: 9–10. Confirmed by Judge I (interview, 2 October 2013).

[87] UNICEF Rwanda 1997b: 2. See also MINIJUST and UNICEF Rwanda 1997b: 20, which notes also that training on child rights was later provided to defence lawyers (confirmed by Lawyer E, interview, 1 October 2013).

three days in July and August 1997,[88] included lectures, debates and practical group exercises, and covered four main themes: (1) an overview of the differences between trying juveniles and adults (noting the difficulties of testing a child's memory and the importance of considering adult influence); (2) the concept of minority;[89] (3) reparation for damages caused by minors; and (4) the different stages in a juvenile case, including confirmation that the elements of the crime of genocide (including specific intent) were substantiated, consideration of any aggravating or mitigating circumstances, and imposition of the sentence.[90] Between 2001 and 2003, further training was provided to judges, lawyers and judicial defenders on the Genocide Law (as amended) by ASF,[91] and a certificate from a training session in 2002 referred to a module on 'la minorité pénale' (criminal responsibility of minors).[92] A coordinator of the MINIJUST/UNICEF project also spoke of training provided to judges by child rights experts engaged by the project, which encouraged judges to use the CRC.[93]

There has been some debate over the application of Article 19(3), the UNDG reporting in 2000 that the juvenile bench 'was still not operational',[94] whilst Morrill reported that juvenile benches had been 'functioning with some regularity by the fall of 1997' but were used less frequently after the introduction of group trials.[95] Indications are that juvenile benches were operational in some courts but not others. The Specialised Chamber of a Northern Province court[96] did not incorporate any 'specialisation for

[88] Copies of certificates from this 'Seminar on "Juvenile Justice"' received by two judges are on file with the author. Cf. HRW 2003a: 24 (stating that the session on juvenile justice lasted just a few hours and did not go into detail).

[89] A judge who attended the training recalled instructors informing participants that the relevant age was at the time of the acts and not the trial (given the delay in cases coming to trial) and that, where the exact birth date was unknown, 31 December of the birth year should be applied (Judge F, interview, 30 September 2013).

[90] Habimana 1997: 2–5. Attendees of the training confirmed that it covered relevant domestic and international provisions (interviews with Judge E, former Minors' Judge in Specialised Chamber (Northern Province), Northern Province, 20 September 2013; Judge F, 30 September 2013; Judge G, former Minors' Judge in Specialised Chamber (Northern Province), Northern Province, 1 October 2013; Judge H, 1 October 2013; Judge K, former Judge in Specialised Chamber (Northern Province), Kigali, 11 October 2013.

[91] Demay et al. 2005: 28. Confirmed also by de Beer interview, 15 October 2014.

[92] Certificate dated 22 November 2002 (copy on file with author).

[93] Interview with former MINJUST/UNICEF Project Coordinator A, 7 October 2013.

[94] UNDG 2000b: 4 (note 1). See also ASF 2004a: 196 (note 329) and 207.

[95] Morrill 2005: 110.

[96] In order to protect anonymity, I do not refer to the specific location of the court but refer only to the post-2006 province in which the court is located.

minors': who tried a particular case depended on the availability of the judges.[97] Similarly a former judge of the Specialised Chamber of a Kigali Province court reported that he could not recall any judges specifically for minors: he himself had judged juveniles in group trials but had not received any special training.[98] And a lawyer who represented alleged *génocidaires* (including juveniles) in a number of different locations did not recall any specialisation, believing specialisation was not possible given the small number of lawyers and judges, and commenting that sacrifices had to be made everywhere given the extreme challenges.[99] In the Specialised Chamber of a Western Province court, however, judges were designated as 'minors' judges' and any case involving a minor had to be tried by the minors' bench.[100] This was also the case in a second Northern Province court, where it was confirmed that three out of seven judges were nominated to hear minors' trials, and all three had to be sitting to hear a juvenile trial.[101] Indeed, in one trial involving a juvenile before that chamber, the hearing was adjourned to enable the minors' bench to convene.[102] In the event of a group trial, the minors' bench would judge the whole group.[103] It appears that minors' judges were not assigned solely to juvenile cases (despite a possible interpretation of the law to this effect[104]): minors' judges of Specialised Chambers in the Western Province Court and second Northern Province court confirmed that they would also deal with adult cases in the absence of any juvenile cases.[105]

[97] Interview with Judge K, 11 October 2013. Confirmed by Judge J (interview, 4 October 2013).

[98] Interview with Judge I, 2 October 2013.

[99] Interview with Lawyer D, 25 September 2013.

[100] Interviews with Judge F, 30 September 2013; Judge H, 1 October 2013. It appears to have been the intention behind the provision that, in any case involving a number of defendants where one of the accused was a minor, the whole case would be directed to the minors' bench. See de Beer 1997b: 67.

[101] Interview with Judge E, 20 September 2013. Although note that a lawyer who appeared before this court did not recall there being special judges for minors (Lawyer E, interview, 1 October 2013).

[102] Interview with Judge E, 20 September 2013. De Beer (1997a: 6) also reported two cases that were adjourned in Gikongoro for this reason.

[103] Interview with Judge G, 1 October 2013. Confirmed by former Judicial Defender B (Skype interview, 28 August 2013).

[104] See Rutazana 1998: 82–83, who refers to the Kinyarwanda text supporting this interpretation. Cf. de Beer 1997b: 67, who, referring to parliamentary debates on Art. 19, comments that the intention was to have judges specialised in juvenile justice to preside over juvenile cases, but that these judges would not be limited only to cases involving minors.

[105] Interviews with Judge E, 20 September 2013, Judge F, 30 September 2013; Judge H, 1 October 2013.

As for juveniles who had turned 18 by the time of the trial, there were no specific provisions in the Genocide Law or Criminal Procedure Code. It has not been possible to ascertain what happened in practice in every case where this occurred, but in the Specialised Chamber of the second Northern Province court referred to above, the President organised the bench to include minors' judges when trying an individual who was under 18 at the time of the alleged crime, regardless of the age during the trial.[106] As noted in Chapter 2, it is, in any event, arguable that special courts/procedures for juveniles who have reached majority is more a matter of good policy than a requirement under international law.

c Trial Procedure

Whilst some judges received specific training on juvenile justice, there was no provision for a modified trial procedure. The Criminal Procedure Code 1963 set out procedures from the initial referral of the case to the court, through to execution of the sentence but contained no juvenile-specific provisions.[107] Contrary to international standards,[108] all hearings were held in public irrespective of whether juveniles were amongst the defendants.[109] Some judges reported that, whilst the procedure was the same, in practice they modified the way they approached juveniles. For instance, one minors' judge spoke of trying to put minors at ease,[110] another reported that he was more careful and less harsh with minors because he saw them more as victims of adult manipulation,[111] and a third commented that minors' judges adapted their 'attitude' when trying juveniles, and that the questions put to a minor were different 'as a child is a child'. This was even the case where a juvenile at the time of the genocide was tried after turning 18.[112] De Beer, who had attended a number of trials, observed that some judges took account of age during the hearing,

[106] Interview with Judge E, 20 September 2013.

[107] The Criminal Procedure Code 2004 introduced greater protection for minors and had immediate effect, although see comment at note 72.

[108] Art. 40(2)(b)(vii), CRC and Rule 8, Beijing Rules.

[109] It would certainly be contrary to international standards in respect of defendants under 18 at the time of the trial. The position regarding those who had turned 18 is less clear, although the recent draft General Comment No. 24 goes some way to addressing this. Judge H (interview, 1 October 2013) noted that it would have been preferable to have had private sessions, but that this was not feasible at the time as juveniles were tried alongside adults in group trials.

[110] Interview with Judge F, 30 September 2013.

[111] Interview with Judge I, 2 October 2013.

[112] Interview with Judge G, 1 October 2013.

explaining to juveniles that it was in their interests to tell the truth and that influence of adults would be taken into account.[113] HRW, in contrast, reported that courts failed to pay sufficient attention to 'the social background of the minor, to his or her mental state at the time of the alleged crimes, and to his or her emotional and mental immaturity and susceptibility to external influence and manipulation'.[114]

Despite measures adopted to expedite juvenile cases, ASF found that minors were judged three times more slowly than adults and alleged that judges did not share the view that juveniles should benefit from speedy trials.[115] LIPRODHOR similarly found juvenile cases to be slow to come before the courts, expressing its concern regarding this situation and asserting that it constituted a flagrant violation of Article 40 of the CRC.[116] A minors' judge from the Western Province, however, asserted that his court simply dealt with the cases forwarded by the prosecutor's office and, where there were juvenile cases, they would commence with those.[117] It is also arguable that the very measures introduced to speed up trials generally had an adverse effect for juveniles: with the advent of group trials, juveniles were often tried together with adult co-defendants, which – as noted above – frequently resulted in processing delays.

Delays were also caused by the desire to ensure that juveniles had legal representation.[118] Pursuant to the MINIJUST/UNICEF Children in Conflict with the Law Project, UNICEF Rwanda had earmarked funding for ten Rwandan lawyers to work exclusively on juvenile cases, but initially only four full-time lawyers and one part-time lawyer could be found.[119] Financial and organisational problems hampered the ability of the project to meet demand, the project assisting only 80 out of 150 juveniles tried in 1999.[120] A coordinator of the project commented that, whilst the provision of legal aid was positive, it sometimes caused 'a blockage' where juvenile trials were postponed for lack of a defence lawyer.[121]

113 de Beer 1999: 41 (confirmed during interview, 15 October 2014).
114 HRW 2003a: 33.
115 ASF 2000a: 34 and 2000b: 19. See also CLADHO 1997 and 1998.
116 LIPRODHOR 1999d: 10–13.
117 Interview with Judge H, 1 October 2013.
118 Recall, in this respect, that the CRC Committee, when commenting on the expeditious handling of juvenile cases, highlights the need to respect other safeguards including the right to legal assistance.
119 Cantwell 1997: 50. See also UNICEF 1995e: 29.
120 DCHR 1999: 6. See also van Krieken 2000: 10 and 14; Sullo 2012: 144.
121 Skype interview with former MINIJUST/UNICEF (Children in Conflict with the Law) Project Coordinator B, 19 February 2014.

Indeed, a case in Kibungo was postponed for almost a month for this reason.[122] As explained above, most legal representation was provided by or through ASF or by judicial defenders. ASF had not generally intervened in juvenile cases given the MINIJUST/UNICEF project, but became involved in 1999 given its concern that many minors continued to have no effective representation.[123] Judicial defenders, who were not legally qualified but had undergone six months of theoretical training from June–December 1998 (provided by DCHR in collaboration with MINIJUST) followed by two months of practical training in early 1999, provided advice to genocide minors in central prisons on juvenile justice standards (including restrictions on pre-trial detention, the right to be separated from adults and the right to be assisted) and all aspects of the trial.[124] They also represented juveniles before the courts from January 2000. Five judicial defenders (out of 87) were assigned specifically to minors' cases. Whilst they did not receive any training on juvenile justice, they were selected based on their professional experience with children and their personal motivation to work with juvenile suspects, and they expanded their knowledge of child rights through their own research.[125] In cases reported by ASF, most juvenile defendants had legal representation, there being just two cases where it was expressly recorded that the defendant represented himself, but where no further comments were made regarding the right to legal representation.[126] Many participants in this study confirmed that, in most cases they had participated in, juveniles were represented,[127] although some commented that minors were tried (and sometimes convicted) without a lawyer being present,

[122] *Ministère Public c/ Niyonsenga* [*Niyonsenga*]. Other cases were adjourned to allow the juvenile's counsel time to prepare the defence (*Kabirigi*; *Ministère Public c/ Karangwa*).

[123] ASF 1997b: 3 and 13 and 1999a: 7.

[124] DCHR 1999: 3 (reporting that defenders reached 2,324 of the estimated 4,500 minors in detention). Also confirmed by former Judicial Defender A, interview, Kigali, 26 February 2013; former Judicial Defender B, Skype interview, 28 August 2013; former Judicial Defender D, interview, Kigali, 8 October 2013.

[125] DCHR 1999: 2; Interviews with former Judicial Defender A, 26 February 2013; former Judicial Defender B, 28 August 2013 (Skype); former Judicial Defender D, 8 October 2013.

[126] The two cases were *Minani* and *Ministère Public c/ Nzabonimpa* [*Nzabonimpa*]. Most of the other cases identified the juvenile(s) counsel, and a few cases were silent on legal representation.

[127] E.g. Former Judicial Defender E, Skype interview, 22 December 2013; Judge I, interview, 2 October 2013; Jules Marius Ntete, former National and Chief Prosecutor, at time of interview, Inspector General, NPPA, interview, Kigali, 21 February 2013; former Prosecutor D, interview, 26 September 2013.

simply because there were not enough lawyers.[128] Clearly, where legal assistance was denied, there was a breach of Article 40 of the CRC and Article 14(3)(d) of the ICCPR.[129]

As referenced earlier, the Genocide Law introduced a confession and guilty plea procedure, pursuant to which a valid confession would result in a sentence reduction.[130] ASF noted that, of the 25 cases involving minors in which it had intervened during 1999, 15 juveniles had entered guilty pleas,[131] and a judge recalled that most, if not all, juveniles in his cases had confessed.[132] Tertsakian reported that younger prisoners were considered more likely to confess (even if innocent) than older ones, as they had their whole life ahead of them,[133] and a prosecutor with responsibility for juvenile cases at the time, commented that most juveniles pleaded guilty, as they were 'actually remorseful'.[134] A former prosecution officer affirmed that he would take time to explain the procedure to minors, as most would confess once they understood the benefits and provided others were not trying to throw them off course.[135] However, minors were particularly susceptible to pressure and intimidation from other prisoners not to confess. In *Nsabimana*, two minors who confessed at the start of the trial reported that they had not confessed whilst in detention as they had been told that anyone who confessed would be deprived of food.[136] A minor, aged 12 at the time of the genocide, reported

128 E.g. Judge K (interview, 11 October 2013); Prosecutor C (interview, Northern Province, 20 September 2013).

129 Note also that there would be a breach of Art. 37(d) where children in detention were denied access to legal and other appropriate assistance.

130 The procedure was retained in the *gacaca* legislation. Many commentators reported that false confessions were frequently made and that the procedure inverted the concept of justice: people who confessed to serious crimes were released, whilst those who were innocent remained in prison. See e.g. ASF 2005b: 11; Ingelaere 2016: 63–64; Tertsakian 2008: 396–423; Waldorf 2006: 72–73; various PRI *gacaca* reports. See also Palmer 2015: 131–132, who, in her discussion of *gacaca* jurisdictions, refers to various reasons for confessions, including self-interest (to receive a reduced sentence) but also personal atonement and conforming to a new understanding of the right thing to do.

131 ASF 1999b: 29.

132 Interview with Judge H, 1 October 2013.

133 Tertsakian 2008: 407.

134 Interview with Jean Bosco Siboyintore, former IPJ and Public Prosecutor (responsible for minors' cases), at time of interview, Head of Genocide Suspects Tracking Unit, NPPA, Kigali, 9 October 2013.

135 Interview with former Prosecutor F (public prosecution officer), Kigali, 9 October 2013.

136 *Nsabimana*: 142.

significant threats directed at minors in both Gitarama prison (where he was initially detained) and Gitagata:

> In the prison at Gitarama, there were around 150 juveniles, of whom four confessed. When someone confessed the others called him a 'coward'; they say he has 'sold out'. It was difficult for a child to confess. The adults would dissuade them by saying that the one who confessed would be shot.
>
> In Gitagata there are 208 juveniles. I only know two juveniles who dared to confess. Here, like in prison, the situation and the consequences of confession are the same. We are treated by our colleagues as 'traitors', as having 'sold out' and as being 'children of the authorities' and other things of the kind.[137]

Another Gitagata resident attested to harassment and acts of intimidation against minors, saying that he was hit the day after he confessed.[138] According to a youth worker in Gitagata, some non-responsible minors were reluctant to talk about what they had done as they saw 'silence as a way of protecting their assumed innocence in the face of society' and knew they would be returned to their communities after their stay in Gitagata.[139]

d Trials in Practice

As discussed above, it is arguable that the intention of the legislators was to allow for individuals to be charged with an ordinary crime under the Penal Code and genocide under the Genocide Convention (arising from the same conduct). The cases analysed suggest that this was the approach adopted in charges issued against defendants and in court judgments. However, despite the requirement to show specific intent to destroy the group (or part of it) for the crime of genocide, in some cases judges failed to deal explicitly with this element. In *Kabirigi* for example, intent (or lack thereof) was discussed only in relation to acquitted defendants. In *Ntahondi*, a minor was found guilty of genocide, the court noting that the victim had been targeted because he belonged to the Tutsi ethnic group, and this reflected what was happening throughout the country, but no further analysis took place.[140]

In cases where defendants had pleaded guilty (the position in most cases reviewed), more detailed findings were set out regarding intention. For example, a court concluded that three juveniles had participated in an attack clearly knowing that the aim was to hunt out

137 Cited in African Rights 2000: 34–35.

138 Ibid.: 34.

139 Ibid.: 93. Note that, since the under-14s could not be prosecuted, there were no legal benefits to confessing.

140 *Ministère Public c/ Ntahondi*: 237. See also *Niyonsenga*.

and exterminate Tutsi according to a nationwide plan, and that the juveniles had indeed hunted out and killed the young victims after being told by a soldier that children should be killed by other children. Further, they had also been convinced that there would be no consequences to their actions.[141] And in *Nzabonimpa*, a juvenile, who had confessed to killing five children of a similar age to him because of their Tutsi ethnicity after being ordered to do so on the basis that children should kill other children, was found to have committed the crimes voluntarily, with awareness of their gravity. It was also held that the crimes were committed with the sole aim of exterminating Tutsi and opponents of the regime.[142]

A former prosecutor commented that specific intent could be inferred from the facts: 'Si on analyse les faits on va se rendre compte que l'ordre qu'il a reçu de tuer, malgré son jeune âge, malgré son niveau d'éducation, il a pu distinguer entre Hutu et Tutsi, et il a mis sur la liste des victimes les Tutsi.'[143] Thus, in this prosecutor's view, if a child was capable of distinguishing a Tutsi from a Hutu for the purposes of killing that person, it would be possible to establish specific intent.[144] A former Justice Minister made similar observations regarding the targeting of people on the basis of their perceived 'race' and added:

> [A] lot of children knew that when they were killing it was bad. The children may not have known precisely what the written law was, but they had to have known they were doing something serious. They knew that they were supposed to kill a specific race of people, and as a result they must have known that what they were doing would have real implications. In interviews the children were saying that they thought their group was the only group that should be in the world.[145]

[141] *Nsabimana*: 143–144. See also *Ministère Public c/ Nsabamungu*, in which similar findings were made, and *Ministère Public c/Mudaheranwa*, in which the court, finding the defendant guilty of genocide and rape, relied on the explanation of the defendant that he had raped a woman because she was Tutsi, knowing that this was happening throughout the country.

[142] *Nzabonimpa*: 114–115.

[143] [Analysing the facts, you can see that he received the order to kill, and that, despite his youth and level of education, he was able to distinguish between Hutu and Tutsi, and he put the Tutsi on the list of victims.] Interview with former Prosecutor D, 26 September 2013.

[144] As outlined in Chapter 2, for the crime of genocide, there must be specific intent to 'destroy' the group or part of it; merely being able to identify a person as part of a group would not meet this legal requirement.

[145] Jean de Dieu Mucyo cited in Briggs 2005: 21.

Other research participants, however, considered it extremely difficult to prove that a minor had the specific intent to destroy the Tutsi, unless perhaps the minor was particularly active in the killings.[146]

Although many participants in this study considered it highly unlikely that juveniles would come within category 1 (which included planners of the genocide, perpetrators in positions of authority and notorious killers),[147] a 16-year-old in Kibuye was deemed a notorious murderer and placed in category 1 given the excessive malice he had shown in gouging out the eyes of children he had killed and then partially burying them. He failed to confess to his acts and was sentenced to 18 years' imprisonment (an adult accused of the same acts was sentenced to death).[148]

In some cases, minority status was not taken into account. RCN reported that four minors under 14 at the time of the genocide were sentenced to six years in prison by a court in Nyamata, the President of the court stating that, given the individuals were adults at the time of trial, they could be held criminally accountable.[149] Although Article 77 of the Penal Code clearly provided that the death penalty and life imprisonment could not be imposed on minors, a juvenile *génocidaire* was sentenced to life imprisonment in Byumba,[150] and another, aged 15 during the genocide (his age clearly recorded in the case file), received a death sentence in Nyamata.[151] In *Banzi Wellars*, the court held that a juvenile born in 1976, but whose exact date of birth was unknown, should benefit from a reduction of sentence pursuant to Article 77, yet then appears to have sentenced him to life imprisonment.[152] Mistakes were sometimes rectified on appeal, a juvenile's sentence being reduced in Ruhengeri after the Specialised Chamber failed to take into account his minority status.[153] A Rwandan human rights lawyer, who monitored juvenile trials for CLADHO

146 E.g. interviews with Judge C, former Court of First Instance Judge (Southern Province), Kigali, 17 September 2013; Lawyer D, 25 September 2013.

147 Indeed, former Prosecutor D (interview, 26 September 2013), who had been involved in drawing up the list of category 1 perpetrators, thought there were very few, if any, minors on the list given the definition of category 1 offences, and Siboyintore (interview, 9 October 2013), responsible for juvenile cases at the time, also could not recall any minors being on the category 1 list. Cf. HRW 2003a: 20.

148 *Kabirigi*: 150 and 157.

149 RCN 2003b: 22.

150 DCHR 1999: 6.

151 ASF 2000b: 19. This case was pending before the Kigali Appeal Court in 2000 but unfortunately it has not been possible to confirm the outcome.

152 *Ministère Public c/ Banzi Wellars*: 142 and 146.

153 ASF 2000a: 19.

(financed by UNICEF Rwanda), commented that he did not see many irregularities in juvenile cases and suggested that this might have been because judges knew they were being observed by someone reporting back to UNICEF, and because juvenile cases were often straightforward.[154]

The provisions of the Genocide Law relating to the withdrawal of civic rights did not refer to minors, but this sanction was imposed on convicted juvenile *génocidaires* which, given their young age, could have a significant impact on their future. In *Kabirigi*, all of those convicted were deprived of civic rights: for the category 1 juvenile offender, all civic rights were withdrawn for life, and for the remaining three category 2 offenders, selected civic rights in accordance with Article 17(b) were withdrawn (thus for life).[155] And Minani (a category 2 offender) lost selected civic rights for five years after completion of his prison sentence.[156] Civil damages were also awarded against convicted juveniles.[157] Under Article 260 of Book III, Civil Code, parents are civilly responsible for acts committed by their minor children and accordingly, in *Kabirigi*, the parents of the convicted juveniles were ordered to pay civil damages.[158] It was reported that, in some cases, parents were held civilly responsible and required to pay damages without having been asked to appear before the court to mount a defence to the civil action.[159]

As regards sentence reductions, it appears that reductions for minority status and any guilty plea were applied before making any further reduction for mitigating circumstances. In *Minani*, where the defendant had pleaded guilty 'after prosecution'[160] to murdering his four nephews, the prosecutor had requested a 6-year prison sentence (applying a 50 per cent reduction under Article 77 of the Penal Code to what would have been a 12–15-year sentence under Article 16 of the Genocide Law). The court sentenced Minani to five years (thus below the sentence range)

[154] Skype interview with Rwandan Human Rights Lawyer, 29 August 2013 (noting that juveniles were generally not political figures, had legal representation and had often made use of the confession and guilty plea procedure).

[155] *Kabirigi*: 157. Whilst the judgment does not expressly state that all civic rights of the category 1 juvenile were withdrawn for life, this is implicit, and the summary of the judgment expressly refers to the sanction.

[156] *Minani*: 92. According to Art. 17(b), withdrawal should have been permanent.

[157] In accordance with Art. 258, Décret du 30 juillet 1888 relatif aux contrats ou obligations conventionnelles [Book III, Civil Code].

[158] *Kabirigi*: 157–158.

[159] Digneffe and Fierens 2003: 68.

[160] See note 56 on this wording.

after applying a third reduction for the mitigating circumstance of duress, accepting that Minani had had no option but to follow orders to kill the children to save his own life.[161] As mentioned earlier, mitigating circumstances were at the complete discretion of the judge. Cooperation with the court appears to have played a key role in sentencing: a Rwandan human rights lawyer who monitored trials commented that juvenile cases were amongst the 'smoothest you could get', as juveniles generally admitted their involvement, and that this was taken into account by judges.[162] A lawyer agreed with this assessment of juvenile cases, noting that juveniles generally told everything to the judge.[163] Other factors in juvenile cases included an incomplete or late guilty plea,[164] and duress or pressure. In *Niyonsenga*, the court appears to have accepted incitement by adults as a mitigating factor,[165] yet in *Kabirigi*, a plea of duress was rejected (both as a defence and in mitigation) as the defendants had failed to show that the constraint was 'irresistible': others had refused to participate in killings and there was no evidence they had suffered consequences.[166]

On the whole, judges appeared more receptive to arguments raised in mitigation for juveniles than for adults, including where the juvenile had turned 18 by the time of the trial: a minors' judge commented that, whilst they often raised the same defences and mitigating circumstances, 'we had more pity for minors'.[167] De Beer observed a clear recognition among judges that the young were influenced by adults,[168] and both a lawyer and a judicial defender confirmed that judges were more likely to accept an argument of duress pleaded by a juvenile than an adult.[169] A judge confirmed that being 'dragged' into the genocide and forced to commit acts by adults would be a valid argument for a juvenile (except

[161] *Minani*: 90–92. It is not clear why this was not accepted as 'irresistible constraint' and thus a complete defence.

[162] Skype interview with Rwandan Human Rights Lawyer, 29 August 2013.

[163] Interview with Lawyer E, 1 October 2013.

[164] See e.g. *Kabirigi*: 154 and *Ministère Public c/ Rwagakiga*: 230–232 (sentences were reduced for some juveniles in both cases below the sentence range specified in the Genocide Law, after taking account of a late guilty plea).

[165] *Niyonsenga*: 115 (the lawyer argued that Niyonsenga was incited by adults and lacked the will to commit the crimes; the judges applied a reduction for 'mitigating circumstances' but did not enumerate these circumstances).

[166] *Kabirigi*: 151.

[167] Interview with Judge F, 30 September 2013.

[168] de Beer 1999: 41 and interview, 15 October 2014.

[169] Interviews with former Judicial Defender C, Kigali, 17 September 2013; Lawyer D, 25 September 2013.

where the juvenile had distinguished him/herself in performing acts of atrocity), whereas a similar argument (such as being forced to act by the *Interahamwe* or authorities) would generally be rejected when raised by an adult.[170] For one judge, if minors argued that they were following what everyone else was doing, 'it could sound reasonable', whereas for adults, evidence of coercion would be required. However, age was relevant: a court would likely make a greater sentence reduction for a minor aged 14 at the time of the genocide than aged 17, on the basis that the former's understanding was much lower.[171] Another judge noted that minors, in effect, benefited in two ways from their age: first, the excuse of minority automatically resulted in a reduced sentence, and second, mitigating circumstances linked to their age – such as reduced capacity to resist pressure or threats – would also be taken into account.[172]

Prosecutors and defence lawyers/judicial defenders also adapted their arguments to take account of age. A prosecutor stated that, in summing up, he would try to contextualise participation: submissions in respect of a juvenile who had received orders to commit a crime would differ from submissions in respect of an adult who had received the same orders, on the basis that it was difficult for a juvenile to resist.[173] In *Kabirigi*, the defence lawyer asked the court to show clemency to juveniles found guilty and to impose an educational sanction.[174] And a judicial defender confirmed that she would emphasise that minors were forced into acting or that they had followed their elders (not being sufficiently mature to make a decision), stressing the collective nature of the genocide and mass popular participation. For adults, it was extremely difficult to adduce these arguments.[175] One issue she encountered, however, was due to the passage of time: she represented juveniles from 2000 and found, in some cases, that when she introduced the accused as a minor, some judges would laugh. LIPRODOR, reporting in 1999, noted that, after five years in detention, a juvenile would have grown up and that his/her reasoning and behaviour would have developed. It was alleged that judges therefore

[170] Interview with Judge I, 2 October 2013.

[171] Interview with Judge C, 17 September 2013.

[172] Interview with Judge J, 4 October 2013.

[173] Interview with former Prosecutor D, 26 September 2013.

[174] *Kabirigi*: 147.

[175] Skype interview with former Judicial Defender B, 28 August 2013. Similar comments were made by Lawyer D (interview, 25 September 2013); Lawyer E (interview, 1 October 2013). For a discussion on the collective nature of atrocity crimes as a ground for diminished culpability in child perpetrator cases, see Fisher 2013: 76–80.

tended to treat and sentence the juvenile like an adult.[176] Judges who participated in this research affirmed that they had taken into account the age of the accused in 1994, but that the public, in particular victims, had difficulties accepting reduced sentences and preferential treatment for these children who had grown up and who were often considered to be more sadistic or savage than adults.[177]

5.2.2 *The* Gacaca *Jurisdictions*

After it became clear that the formal court system would be unable to process the large number of genocide suspects, a series of 'reflection meetings' were held to consider alternative mechanisms. The result was the adoption of the Gacaca Law in January 2001.[178] An evaluation of the *gacaca*[179] system is beyond the scope of this book: much has been written elsewhere on whether it was an indigenous and informal justice mechanism meting out restorative justice or an 'invented' tradition that was fundamentally retributive in nature, whether or not it achieved its aims, how it affected Rwandan society, the extent to which it complied with international standards, and the degree of state control over, and the influence of local dynamics on, the system.[180]

176 LIPRODHOR 1999a: 35. Sentencing as an adult was a clear contravention of Rwandan law. Arguably it also breached international standards, although as noted in Chapter 2, with the exception of the imposition of the death penalty, the applicability of other standards (particularly procedural) to those who have reached 18 may be more a matter of best practice than a strict legal requirement.

177 Interviews with Judge F, 30 September 2013; Judge I, 2 October 2013; Judge K, 11 October 2013.

178 Organic Law No. 40/2000 Setting Up 'Gacaca Jurisdictions' and Organising Prosecutions for Offences Constituting the Crime of Genocide or Crimes against Humanity Committed between 1 October 1990 and 31 December 1994 [Gacaca Law 2001]. The initial legislation has been modified five times, the most notable changes occurring in 2004, 2007 and 2008. Organic Law No. 16/2004 Establishing the Organisation, Competence and Functioning of the Gacaca Courts Charged with Prosecuting and Trying the Perpetrators of the Crime of Genocide and Other Crimes against Humanity Committed between 1 October 1990 and 31 December 1994 [Gacaca Law 2004] repealed Gacaca Law 2001. Gacaca Law 2004 was subsequently modified by Organic Law No. 10/2007 Modifying and Complementing Organic Law No. 16/2004 [Gacaca Law 2007] and Organic Law No. 13/2008 Modifying and Complementing Organic Law No. 16/2004 [Gacaca Law 2008]. The term 'Gacaca Laws' is used to refer to this body of laws governing the *gacaca* jurisdictions, with any notable differences between the laws being specified.

179 *Gacaca* is derived from the Kinyarwandan word, *umucaca*, which describes a soft species of grass on which people would gather to sit. Ingelaere 2016: 19.

180 For detailed academic monographs on *gacaca*, see Bornkamm 2012; Clark 2011; Ingelaere 2016. See also Amnesty International 2002; HRW 2011; Ingelaere 2008; Karekezi,

Gacaca Law 2001 provided for the establishment of *gacaca* courts across the country, presided over by lay judges. It retained the dual incrimination approach under the 1996 Genocide Law,[181] as well as the four categories of genocide crimes and reduced sentences for guilty pleas (see Annex 3 for the *gacaca* sentencing scheme). Alleged perpetrators in categories 2 to 4 were to be heard by the *gacaca* jurisdictions – those who had committed property crimes being tried at the cell level and those who had committed crimes against persons at the sector level – whilst those in category 1 were to be handled by the formal courts. Changes were made in subsequent legislation to the *gacaca* court structure as well as categories of offences (being reduced to 3 categories in 2004)[182] and to the sentences that could be passed. A novel sentencing approach of the Gacaca Laws was the use of community service (TIG: *travail d'intérêt général*) for certain categories of offenders in lieu of imprisonment for part of the prison term.[183] From 2007, part of the overall sentence could also be suspended. Like the Genocide Law, the Gacaca Laws included, as an additional penalty, the loss of civic rights.[184] The extent of the withdrawal depended on the category of offence, and later, on the offender's willingness to confess. Gacaca Law 2004 also provided that the names of category 1 and 2 offenders be posted at the local sector offices.[185] A 2007 amendment required further details (including a description of the offender's identity and the crimes committed) to be posted at the local sector offices and in the history section of genocide memorials, registered in the offender's criminal record and published on the Internet.[186]

The *gacaca* process consisted of three main steps: collation of information (in public); categorisation of the accused (in private); and trial (in public). There was no express right to, nor prohibition on, legal representation in the Gacaca Laws. The National Service of Gacaca

Nshimiyimana and Mutamba 2004; NHRC 2005a and 2005b; Palmer 2015; Rettig 2011; Waldorf 2006; and the reports by ASF and PRI on *gacaca*.

181 Note that the dual incrimination wording was dropped in Gacaca Law 2004, which referred to prosecutions for 'the crime of genocide' (i.e. without reference to the Penal Code) 'or other crimes provided for in the Penal Code' carried out with the intention of committing genocide.

182 Categories 2 and 3 were merged in 2004 (Art. 51, Gacaca Law 2004), and Gacaca Law 2008 extended the jurisdiction of *gacaca* courts over some category 1 cases.

183 Arts. 69, 70 and 75, Gacaca Law 2001 and Arts. 73, 74, 78, 80 and 81, Gacaca Law 2004 (as amended).

184 Art. 72, Gacaca Law 2001, replaced by Art. 76, Gacaca Law 2004 (as amended).

185 Art. 76(3), Gacaca Law 2004.

186 Art. 15, Gacaca Law 2007.

Courts (NSGC)[187] asserts that, whilst rare, defendants sometimes engaged lawyers, but it is not clear whether this was during the trial itself or in preparation for trial.[188] Clark comments that lawyers were 'barred from all hearings', but explains that some participants did consult lawyers for advice on presenting evidence and testifying.[189] The Rwandan government, in its response to the UN HRC's Concluding Observations, reported that legal counsel were authorised to attend *gacaca* courts and could provide information, but they were not authorised to represent parties.[190] If defendants were denied legal representation at any stage of the proceedings, which seems to have been the case certainly during the hearings, this would contravene Article 14(3)(d) ICCPR and Article 40 of the CRC (in the case of minors), which provide for the right to legal assistance in the determination of any criminal charge.

The investigatory stage (or 'collecting information' phase) of *gacaca* proceedings was launched on a pilot basis in June 2002 and extended to the rest of Rwanda in January 2005. The first trials began in the pilot sectors in March 2005, the trial stage going nationwide by July 2006. Over 11,000 courts operated across the country from 2002 until *gacaca* proceedings were officially closed on 18 June 2012. The NSGC reported that 1,958,634 cases had been processed, although the number of individuals tried was cited as 1,003,227, some defendants appearing in more than one case.[191] Ninety per cent of defendants were men and 10 per cent were women,[192] but no statistics are available for juveniles. Thus, as for the formal courts, it has not been possible to determine the total number of juveniles tried by *gacaca* jurisdictions.

Similarly, there is, as yet, no comprehensive public database of *gacaca* records and, in any event, official transcripts do not exist for *gacaca* proceedings.[193] Whilst I obtained some records of cases involving minors following an official request to the National Commission for the Fight against Genocide (CNLG),[194] these contained only a very brief description of proceedings. This section thus relies on monitoring and evaluation

[187] The NSGC, previously the Département des Jurisdictions Gacaca within the Supreme Court, became an independent body in 2004.

[188] NSGC 2012: 186–187.

[189] Clark 2011: 83 and 162–163.

[190] HRC 2010: 6.

[191] de Brouwer and Ruvebana 2013: 950. See also Clark and Kaufman 2012: 989.

[192] de Brouwer and Ruvebana 2013: 950.

[193] Waldorf 2006: 1 (note 2).

[194] The CNLG holds hard-copy records; digitalisation of the archives is underway.

reports from the NSGC, PRI, ASF and other organisations, as well as articles by academics for accounts of *gacaca* court proceedings. Additionally, to enhance the description and analysis of trials in practice, interviews were conducted with former judges in the *gacaca* jurisdictions, as well as others involved in this justice mechanism.

a Age of Criminal Responsibility and Sentencing Provisions

During the 'reflection meetings', reference was made to the 'big and particular role' of young people (and women) in the genocide and massacres,[195] yet no mention was made in the report of any special treatment for those who were minors at the time of the genocide. Gahima did not recall any discussion regarding minors during these meetings, as he believed that most minors were already out of the prison system by then: by 1999, minors were not 'a big issue'.[196] Indeed, a MINIJUST official confirmed that the excuse of minority had not been raised at all during early discussions on *gacaca*, although it had been agreed that the procedure for juveniles would be the same as that for adults.[197]

The Gacaca Laws did, however, include provisions relating to minors, drawing on the Penal Code 1977 for the age categories as well as the notion of reduced sentences.[198] In contrast to both the Penal Code and Genocide Law, the Gacaca Laws explicitly provided for a minimum age of criminal responsibility of 14. There were some ambiguities, however, in the different language versions of the 2001 and 2004 laws as to the position of a minor who turned 14 on the date of the alleged acts.[199] These ambiguities (of interest academically but unlikely to be at issue in practice – particularly given the difficulties in determining age) were resolved by Article 20 of Gacaca Law 2008. This provided that reduced sentences applied to those

[195] Office of the President 1999: 71.

[196] Skype interview with Gahima, 5 November 2013.

[197] Coopération Belge 1999.

[198] Van Krieken (2000: 26) postulates that these provisions were included as a result of 'active Unicef lobbying'.

[199] The English version provided that those 'more than fourteen years old but less than eighteen' would benefit from reduced sentences, whilst those 'less than 14' could not be prosecuted. The French version contained similar language. The English version of Gacaca Law 2004 seemed to resolve this ambiguity providing in Art. 78 for reduced sentences for those who 'were fourteen (14) years or more ...' but the French retained the lacuna. ASF (2004a: 208–209) argued that, given the ambiguity in the French version (no mention is made of the English version), the most favourable position should be applied to minors.

who were, at the time of the commission of the offence, aged 14 exactly, thus deviating from the Penal Code and retroactively lowering (by one day) the age of criminal responsibility for genocide crimes. For those under 14, the Gacaca Laws expressly provided for rehabilitative measures, Article 74 of Gacaca Law 2001 providing that the under-14s could be placed in rehabilitation centres (changed in 2004 to 'solidarity camps'[200]).

In terms of reduced sentences, Article 74 of Gacaca Law 2001 provided that a category 1 juvenile (tried by the formal courts) would be liable to 10–20 years' imprisonment; for category 2 and 3 juveniles, the sentence would be 'equal to half the sentence … for mature defendants of the same category', thus providing judges with less discretion than under the Penal Code (and thus the Genocide Law). Whilst on the face of it, the sentencing regime appears straightforward, there were some uncertainties. For category 2 juveniles who had not confessed, the sentence would be half the adult sentence of 25 years to life imprisonment.[201] No guidance was given on how to calculate half a life sentence. Also, this category 2 juvenile's sentence (minimum 12.5 years) could exceed the sentence imposed on a category 1 juvenile who had not confessed (minimum 10 years). It could also exceed the sentence that could have been imposed for category 2 juveniles under the 1996 Genocide Law (10–20 years). A further lacuna relates to the category 1 offender who had confessed, there being no reference to the confession procedure in Article 74. Some of these issues were resolved by the 2004 law which entered into force before the *gacaca* trial phase began. Gacaca Law 2004 stated the minimum and maximum sentences for juveniles in each category, taking into account any confession (see Annex 3), although some uncertainty remained regarding category 1 juveniles who had confessed after appearing on the *gacaca* list. Article 16 of Gacaca Law 2007 ultimately resolved this.

Under Gacaca Law 2001, it was not clear whether there could be further reductions for mitigating circumstances. Article 81 of Gacaca Law 2004, however, provided that mitigating circumstances could not result in a lower sentence being imposed than the minimum specified for the relevant category.[202] ASF commented that this could have a

200 Art. 79, Gacaca Law 2004. Note, the French version of Art. 79 referred to a stay of three months, whilst the English version contained no time reference.

201 Art. 69(a).

202 Cf. Arts. 82 and 83, Penal Code 1977 which gave judges the discretion to reduce sentences significantly.

significant impact on juveniles tried by *gacaca*, noting that a number of decisions under the Genocide Law had taken account of mitigating circumstances to reduce juvenile sentences below the specified minimum.[203]

As noted earlier, a novel approach of the *gacaca* sentencing scheme was the use of TIG (community service). In addition to reducing the prison population, TIG was intended to assist the rehabilitation and reintegration of offenders and contribute to reconciliation by being of benefit to Rwandan society (including survivors). Gacaca Law 2001 did not include any reference to TIG being used for juvenile offenders, whereas the later laws included TIG in the sentencing provisions for juveniles (see Annex 3). Presidential Orders that regulated TIG initially contained references to juveniles, providing that age would be taken into account when assigning minors to TIG and that 'labour laws relating to women and minors' would govern TIG.[204] These references were, however, removed from a later TIG Order of October 2005[205] and, given that the trial stage began in the pilot sectors only in March 2005 and the rest of the country in July 2006, it is possible that age did not play any role when assigning the now grown-up juveniles to TIG.

Over the years, successive amendments to the *gacaca* legislation saw a reduction in the penalties that could be imposed. Gahima refers to a number of reasons for this trend, including the desire to reduce the number of people in prison and facilitate reintegration into the community, and notably 'ensuring the treatment of juveniles in a manner that more closely conforms to relevant international human rights standards'.[206] It appears that a more lenient approach to juveniles was adopted, in that Gacaca Law 2004 generally provided that juveniles would receive half the adult sentence, whilst Gacaca Law 2007 reduced the sentence for juveniles to less than half the adult sentence (with the exception of the final category 2 offences).

[203] ASF 2004a: 212. See also section 5.2.1d.

[204] Arts. 35(3) and 37, Presidential Order No. 26/01 Relating to the Substitution of the Penalty of Imprisonment for Community Service. Presidential Order No. 10/01 Determining the Modalities of Implementation of Community Service as Alternative Penalty to Imprisonment of March 2005 retained the reference to labour laws in Art. 37 but removed the reference to age from Art. 35.

[205] Presidential Order No. 50/01 Modifying and Complementing Presidential Order No. 10/01.

[206] Gahima 2013: 164.

b *Gacaca* Judges

Gacaca judges (or *inyangamugayo* – persons of integrity) were elected in October 2001, and training took place between March and May 2002, over six days, for six hours each day.[207] Training was based on a manual containing explanations of the law and forms to be completed. The manual explicitly stated that an accused under 14 at the time of the alleged crime could not be tried but could be placed in a re-education centre. Where such a minor was incarcerated, the bench had to complete a Warrant of Immediate Release.[208] For those aged 14–18 at the time of the genocide, the manual simply outlined the sentences that could be imposed under Gacaca Law 2001.[209] To assist with the training of judges, a 'Gacaca Kit' was prepared by MINIJUST, which had pictorial representations of the process with accompanying notes. This included one information sheet on sentences to be given to those aged between 14 and 18 (namely half the sentence that would be given to an adult if in categories 2 or 3 and restitution of property if in category 4).[210]

Further training was provided in 2004 and 2005 following changes to the law and in preparation for the judgment phase.[211] One of the themes addressed was the criminal responsibility of minors before the *gacaca* jurisdictions. This covered the reasoning behind different sentences for minors (including minors' lower level of discernment and the influence of adults) and the two categories of minors: the under-14s (who could not be tried but could be placed in solidarity camps) and those aged 14–18 (who would receive lighter sentences than adults). It was stressed that the relevant age was the age at the time of the alleged crime rather than trial and that, where no day or month of birth was indicated, the date to be applied was 31 December, on the basis that the accused should have the benefit of the doubt.[212]

A former Court of Appeal judge, who provided training to *gacaca* judges, explained that the training was very condensed and that it was

207 This was considered inadequate by some, given the different backgrounds, level of education and abilities of the judges. See e.g. African Rights 2003: 4–12; PRI 2005: 18 and 41.

208 Département des Juridictions Gacaca 2001: 87–88.

209 Ibid.: 131.

210 MINIJUST 2001.

211 ASF 2005a: 1 and 5. Additional training took place in March 2007 after amendments to the Gacaca Law. See ASF 2007b: 18.

212 ASF 2004b: 13–14. See also ASF 2005a: 11, 19 and 21. Many of those receiving the training who had been judges during the pilot phase had asserted that, in the event of doubt, 1 January of the birth year ought to be used.

necessary to find a very simple formulation that was accessible to the population. As a result, the specificities relating to minors concerned sentencing only, as the procedure was the same for all.[213] The former chief adviser to the Department of the Gacaca Jurisdictions, Augustin Nkusi, echoed that age was relevant to sentencing only. Further, he did not recall discussions during the training on reintegration or reinsertion of released detainees into the community: this was left to the administrative authorities.[214] In relation to the under-14s, African Rights reported that during training sessions, some judges who were genocide survivors were unable to understand why 'children couldn't be punished even though they had played an active role in the genocide'.[215] Indeed in one training session, participants argued that Article 79 of Gacaca Law 2004 ought to be changed to provide for custodial sentences as well as placement in solidarity camps.[216] In addition to training, support was provided to *gacaca* judges by 'Gacaca coordinators' and also through booklets that provided a simplified overview of the Gacaca Law, in particular the procedures (see below).

c Trial Procedure

In brief, the trial procedure as set out in the Gacaca Laws,[217] applicable to both adults and juveniles, entailed the confession or collected testimonies being read, and the parties, victims and any witnesses then having the opportunity to speak. The judges then deliberated and subsequently delivered their verdict. The only potential protection for juveniles was in Article 24 of Gacaca Law 2001 (repeated in Article 21, Gacaca Law 2004), which referred to the possibility of *in camera* hearings when 'requested by any interested person and pronounced by judgement for reasons of public order or good morals'. There was, however, no reference to age being a consideration and no evidence of juveniles being tried in closed hearings, and it is clear from records and from various conversations I had with attendees of *gacaca* hearings that juvenile cases were held in public.

213 Interview with Judge B, former Court of Appeal Judge (Northern Province), Kigali, 5 September 2013.

214 Interview with Nkusi, 22 September 2013.

215 African Rights 2003: 27.

216 ASF 2005a: 18.

217 See Arts. 64 (confession before trial) and 65 (no confession), Gacaca Law 2001 and Gacaca Law 2004 (which were broadly similar). Later legislation did not change the general procedure.

Having reviewed the guidance booklets on the procedure produced by the NSGC, there are few references to the age of the accused and no mention of any special procedure for juveniles. In the 'Collecting Information' booklet,[218] only in the sample forms contained in the Annex to the booklet is specific reference made to minority. The sample Charge Sheet requires the bench to specify whether the accused was under 14 'at the time of committing crimes' and, if so, to order his/her immediate release. The File Sheet also includes this information, and the Warrant of Immediate Release includes age under 14 as a reason for release. There is no place on the forms completed at this stage to specify whether the accused was a juvenile aged between 14 and 18 at the time of the alleged crime. The 'Trial Procedure' booklet sets out a specific order for trials, which privileges those who have confessed.[219] Juveniles (as a general category) were not given priority over *génocidaires* who had confessed, or the very ill, but did take priority over other defendants.[220] This booklet provides that, during deliberation by the judges *after* the hearing, the bench 'verifies whether the defendant was not below 14 or if he was 14 years and above but below 18 years old at the time he/she committed the crime charged', and the sentence would then be decided based on age and other factors (such as any confession, and any aggravating or mitigating circumstances).[221] This, however, conflicts with the forms in the Collecting Information booklet, where the bench is required to confirm at the information collection stage whether the individual is under 14.

The former Legal Director of the NSGC, Gratien Dusingizimana, confirmed that age was verified at the beginning of the trial stage: any minor under 14 at the time of the alleged acts would remain present and could be asked questions during the hearing. He asserted, however, that

218 NSGC 2004.

219 See comments made regarding confessions and the inversion of the concept of justice at note 130.

220 NSGC 2005: 2. Gratien Dusingizimana (former Director of the Legal Support Unit, NSGC, interview, Kigali, 5 September 2013) and Kisakye (former District Coordinator of *gacaca* courts; interview, Kigali, 12 September 2013) stated that those who had confessed could facilitate proceedings by providing details of their crimes/accomplices and would thus be tried first; the sick would be next given concerns they may die before their trial; and juveniles would then be tried before other defendants to avoid them spending longer in prison than the possible sentence that could be passed, and so that they could return to, and contribute to, society.

221 NSGC 2005: 12. These factors (including the accused's minority status) are also reflected in the section 'Motivation of the Decision' in the 'Copy of Judgement' annexed to the booklet.

it was more a truth-telling procedure (the minor was not treated as a 'pure accused') to discover what the individual knew and for the court to decide if there was sufficient evidence to send him/her to a re-education centre. Judges were instructed to moderate their questioning.[222] However, it is difficult to see how this differed in practice from the trial procedure. ASF found that the issue frequently arose during the *gacaca* hearings it monitored and noted a lack of consistency in the approach of the different jurisdictions: some decided to send the non-responsible minor as a matter of course and without trial to a solidarity camp, whilst others first determined the culpability of the minor before taking the decision.[223] A review of case reports indicates that some *gacaca* courts certainly took the latter approach: a *gacaca* court in Kigali heard all testimony before it found two minors under 14 (the youngest aged 9) guilty ('*coupable*') and sent them to a solidarity camp.[224]

Whether or not the under-14s went through the trial phase, it is clear that those aged between 14 and 18 at the time of the alleged crime were subject to the same process as adults. Dusingizimana stated that, whilst judges were asked to modify their approach when questioning those aged under 14, those above 14 were to be 'asked questions like adults' but were to be given enough time to express themselves as they were minors under the law. He considered it would be too complex to require judges to follow a different procedure.[225] Note, however, that *gacaca* judges interviewed for this research reported that they had tried to 'have consideration' towards minors,[226] and had 'more pity',[227] and a monitor of *gacaca* courts for the National Human Rights Commission (NHRC) found that *gacaca* judges in cities were more likely to take into account that 'a child is a child'.[228]

222 Interview with Dusingizimana, 5 September 2013.

223 ASF 2005b: 24. A former *gacaca* monitor reported that, in the trials he had observed, all minors went through the procedure as each piece of information was considered useful (interview with former ASF Staff Member, 5 February 2013).

224 *Ntihabose* and *Ugeziwe*: 22–24 and 30. Similarly, a non-responsible minor, placed in category 2 for his role in a murder, was asked to present his 'defence' before a *gacaca* court in Gitarama, after which he was sent to a solidarity camp for three months (*Mwenedata*:18 and 23), and a minor, aged 13 at the time of the genocide, was found 'guilty' of participating in a fatal attack. He was not, however, sent to a solidarity camp: the *gacaca* court simply determined that he could not be held criminally responsible (*Havugimana*: 22–24).

225 Interview with Dusingizimana, 5 September 2013.

226 Interview with former *Inyangamugayo* A, Kigali, 3 October 2013.

227 Interview with former *Inyangamugayo* B, Kigali, 3 October 2013.

228 Interview with Legal Adviser, National Human Rights Commission, Kigali, 2 October 2013.

The CRC Committee expressed 'extreme' concern in 2004 about the lack of a special procedure in the *gacaca* courts for those aged under 18 at the time of their alleged crime.[229] Sullo, arguing that the *gacaca* jurisdictions do not respect fair trial standards as children were treated the same as adults (except for penalties), comments that 'the best interests of the child were not considered a parameter when the *gacaca* law was drafted'.[230] Van Krieken, however, postulates that, as the genocide minors were in their 20s by the time they faced trial by the *gacaca* jurisdictions, there was 'no need for special procedures'.[231] A legal officer of NSGC came to a similar conclusion: 'If somebody who committed a crime when they were a child is being tried at the age of 25, does that person need assistance you normally give to juveniles? In my view, they do not.'[232] As discussed in section 2.1.2, the legal position regarding procedural rights for minors who have reached majority is not clear-cut. The practical implications of trying such juveniles are discussed in the next section.

d Trials in Practice

From a review of reports by NGOs, in particular monitoring reports prepared by ASF and ten cases selected at random from national archives, it has been possible to draw out some common themes. The failure to address the requirement of specific intent for genocide was more prevalent in the *gacaca* jurisdictions than in the formal courts. Indeed, in the cases reviewed, there appears to have been no discussion of intent whatsoever, although given the frequent lack of reasoning in judgments, it has often not been possible to understand the grounds for conviction or why a particular sentence was imposed.[233] In a small number of cases, the precise category and/or whether a valid confession had been made were recorded, and the law on sentencing was applied correctly.[234] However, it was not uncommon for judges to fail to record (or possibly verify) when a confession had been given, rendering it difficult to determine the legal

229 CRC Committee 2004d: [70].

230 Sullo 2012: 147.

231 van Krieken 2000: 27.

232 Interview with Alphonse Muleefu, former Legal Officer, NSGC, Kigali, 5 March 2013.

233 On this, see ASF 2005b: 13–14 and 2007b: 23–26. In some of the files obtained from national archives, the forms (e.g. Charge Sheet, Judgment and Arrest Warrant) were not completed in full.

234 E.g. *Kanyamugara*: 33.

basis for the sentence passed, as it was not possible to apply the sentencing scale established in the law.[235]

A key concern arose from the delay in bringing suspects to trial, genocide minors being in their mid-20s or even over 30 when appearing before *gacaca*. There was a risk that *gacaca* judges, without formal legal training and often only with basic education (if any at all), would find it difficult to perceive these individuals as minors at the time of the alleged crime.[236] As outlined in Chapter 4, an SCF-USA study had found level of education to be an important variable in the perception of young *génocidaires*. Of course, perceptions may have changed over time, particularly in light of sensitisation campaigns: this was the view of the former Executive Secretary of NSGC who considered that the position relating to minors was very clear and had been explained in detail to the community.[237]

The former coordinator of PRI's *gacaca* monitoring programme was of the impression that many minors failed to raise their minority status, and that *gacaca* judges simply looked at age at the time of trial. In the couple of cases he observed where minority was raised, the accused were judged as adults, *gacaca* judges not believing they had been under 18.[238] In some of the reported cases, juveniles whose year of birth was clearly recorded during proceedings were nonetheless sentenced as adults, a minor born in 1977 being sentenced to 26 years' imprisonment for murdering a child.[239] In some instances where minors were sentenced as adults, this was rectified on appeal/review.[240] For example, a minor (born in 1978) was convicted of rape, sexual torture and murder, and sentenced to life imprisonment. Following a review of his case, his sentence was amended to 20 years.[241] Another minor (born in 1978) was sentenced

[235] ASF 2005b: 22 and 26 and 2007b: 25–26.

[236] Morrill 2005: 109 (reporting that ASF also raised this concern).

[237] Interview with Domitilla Mukantaganzwa, former Executive Secretary of the NSGC and former Project Officer, UNICEF Rwanda, Kigali, 3 September 2013.

[238] Interview with Hitababyaye, 10 September 2013. Former Juvenile Detainee (Skype interview, 24 August 2013) reported that he had not been asked about his age during a *gacaca* meeting.

[239] *Mutabazi alias Gitarama* (the sentence should have been 8–10 years). Another minor born in 1977 and aged 30 at the time of the trial, but whose minority status was acknowledged throughout proceedings, also appears to have been sentenced as an adult (*Nyirimbabazi*). Note, however, that in many cases reviewed, minority status appears to have been accepted without any documentary evidence of age being produced (see also ASF's comments in *Habyarimana*: 4).

[240] Confirmed by former *Inyangamugayo* A, B and C (interviews, 3 October).

[241] *Joseph M.*

initially to 27 years' imprisonment for various crimes (including murder, torture and dehumanising acts on dead bodies) despite the judges noting his minority status and recording his valid confession. Following appeal, he was sentenced to 7 years.[242] In trials observed by ASF between October 2005 and September 2006, sentences imposed on juveniles were generally in accordance with the law, although some (possible) juveniles were sentenced as adults.[243] Between October 2006 and April 2007, ASF saw an improvement in the recognition of minority status, finding only one case where it was not applied.[244]

It is clear from the sentencing provisions of the Gacaca Laws (post 2004) as well as the TIG Orders that minors could be sentenced to TIG, and a review of cases confirms that this sanction was in practice passed in juvenile cases.[245] It has not been possible to determine what activities were carried out by juvenile *génocidaires*. Some participants in this study, however, were of the view that, given that these juveniles were tried 10 years after the genocide, they were physically strong and could thus do the same TIG as adults.[246] As regards the withdrawal of civic rights, *gacaca* jurisdictions frequently failed to impose this sanction expressly, possibly on the assumption that the sanction applied automatically.[247] The other additional sanction from 2004 was the publication of names. No reference was made in the relevant provision to juveniles, but a former district coordinator for the NSGC commented that lists of convicted perpetrators including juveniles (in particular those tried *in absentia*) were posted at sector offices, but had not been included at genocide memorials or on the Internet, although he thought this might happen in the future.[248] The

242 *Jean Baptiste N.*

243 ASF 2007a: 34 (citing a case where an accused's charge sheet recorded the year of birth as 1976 – without specifying the month – but the *gacaca* court failed to investigate his age).

244 ASF 2007b: 60 (ASF also reported another case, in which it was simply accepted that an accused had been under 18 based on his own assertions and those of some witnesses).

245 E.g. *Habyarimana*: 19–20; *Kanyamugara*: 33; *Mutabazi C.*: 19; *Ngabonzima*: 33. See also IRIN 2007.

246 Interviews with Lawyer B, 15 February 2013; former Executive Secretary of a Survivors' Organisation, 21 February 2013.

247 ASF 2007b: 58. ASF suggest that this may be a result of judges relying on the Kinyarwanda text which provides that this sanction would apply automatically. Note also that the 'Copy of Judgement' form provided: 'Convicted persons are also liable to withdrawal of their civil rights as stipulated in Article 76' (NSGC 2005).

248 Interview with Kisakye, 12 September 2013. Cf. Dusingizimana (interview, 5 September 2013) who commented that lists had not been put up in practice anywhere.

publication of juvenile offenders' names is contrary to Rule 8 of the Beijing Rules, and thus this would amount to a breach of that (non-binding) Rule, if we can assume that privacy is a right that a juvenile would retain after reaching majority.

As regards defences and mitigating circumstances, ASF documented that 'irresistible constraint', which would exonerate an accused, was frequently invoked by defendants (not just juveniles), but rarely accepted. When it was accepted, it was considered a mitigating circumstance rather than a defence.[249] In one case, a juvenile (at the time of the genocide) argued that he had revealed someone's hiding place after being threatened with death, yet this did not appear to have been considered at all by the judges.[250]

As indicated earlier, over time, the sentences that could be passed by *gacaca* jurisdictions were reduced in the legislation. According to Gahima, *rescapés* saw the changes brought about from the Genocide Law 1996 through to Gacaca Law 2008 as 'some kind of incremental amnesty'. He considered that they did not have strong feelings about minors specifically, but about the accountability process more generally.[251] In the view of a former NSGC legal officer, whilst victims were unhappy generally with the leniency of *gacaca* sentences, some found it especially difficult to understand why individuals, who had killed their relatives when they were under 14 but were now adults, could not be punished.[252] Others, however, were of the view that the population at least understood (and possibly accepted) the differential treatment as this had been made clear through sensitisation.[253] The length of time between the genocide and trial also had the result that juveniles had often spent longer in prison than the maximum term that could be imposed by law. For example, a category 2 juvenile sentenced to 5 years' imprisonment had already served this sentence, having spent 7 years and 8 months in detention by the time of his trial.[254]

[249] ASF 2005b: 22.

[250] *Nyirimbabazi*: 19–22. As noted earlier, he was also sentenced as adult.

[251] Skype interview with Gahima, 5 November 2013.

[252] Interview with Muleefu, 5 March 2013.

[253] E.g. Interviews with Kisakye, 12 September 2013; Mukantaganzwa, 3 September 2013. See also section 7.2.

[254] *Twagirayezu, Habyarimana and Ndahayo*: 45. Another genocide minor, who had spent 6 years and 8 months in prison was sentenced in the same judgment to 4 years.

5.3 Administrative Measures

5.3.1 Children under the Age of Criminal Responsibility – Re-Education Centres

As outlined earlier, many children under 14 were amongst those arrested. Whilst they could not be held criminally responsible, Rwandan law – at least until Gacaca Law 2001 – was silent as to what could, or should, happen to them. UNICEF Rwanda initially lobbied for their release, but the Rwandan government argued that 'there had to be a process of getting them to a point where society would accept them as cleared, having done some punishment or civic education or whatever it would take'.[255] The risk to these children was underscored by the SCF-USA study, which revealed that a majority of participants was in favour of the death penalty for child *génocidaires* who had killed.[256] Given the gravity of their alleged crimes, it was also considered essential to re-educate these children, so as to reduce the risk of recidivism and so that they could play a part in the future of Rwanda.[257] UNICEF Rwanda thus concluded that transferring these children from prisons and *cachots* to a re-education centre would be in their best interest[258] and worked with the government to identify appropriate centres: Gitagata, in Nyamata District, was chosen for boys and the Miyove Centre (Miyove), in Byumba District, for girls (as well as women with infants).[259]

Gitagata, established in 1975 to receive, *inter alia*, child vagrants,[260] had been completely destroyed during the genocide. After being rebuilt, it opened in July 1995, with 152 boys initially being transferred from prisons, a further 45 later joining them.[261] The ages of these children at the time of the genocide ranged from 5 to 14.[262] Over the next few years,

[255] Skype interview with Toole, 16 May 2013.
[256] SCF-USA 1996: 12. See section 4.2.1.
[257] Interviews with former ASOFERWA Staff Member A, 24 September 2013; Nsanzabaganwa, 10 October 2013; Ntete, Kigali, 21 and 27 February 2013.
[258] See section 6.2.2a regarding UNICEF Rwanda's extensive deliberations on this issue.
[259] UNDG 2000b: 4. See also Chorlton 1996: 43; UNICEF Rwanda 1995c: 7.
[260] Pursuant to Arrête Présidentiel No. 234/06 portant création de centres de rééducation et de production. Three other centres were also established: two for adults and one for female minors at Miyove.
[261] Cantwell 1997: 48. See also Degni-Ségui 1997: [37]; UNHRFOR 1996a: 3 and 1996b: [49].
[262] Letter from ASOFERWA to UNICEF Rwanda, 3 December 1997 (copy on file with author). See also Doulliez 1998b: 16.

some children were reintegrated into society, whilst more arrived at the centre. As with statistics generally, it has been difficult to obtain authoritative figures. Véronique Doulliez, an ASF expatriate lawyer on mission in Rwanda, reported that almost 400 boys were in Gitagata in January 1998.[263] By 1999, Gitagata had reintegrated 297 boys and continued to hold 170.[264] By mid-2000, 392 children had been reintegrated, with a reported 684 minors having spent time in Gitagata.[265] The Miyove Centre opened in August 1997. Doulliez, who visited Miyove in April 1999, found there to be 383 residents, including just one accused of genocidal acts who had been under 14, and 51 aged 14–18 at the time of their alleged crimes (only a few of whom were accused of genocide).[266] There is very little information available on Miyove, and thus this section focuses on Gitagata. In November 2000, more than 500 non-responsible minors were transferred from prisons, *cachots* and re-education centres (including 262 from Gitagata) to the Busogo solidarity camp, where they spent 6 weeks before returning home.[267] Gitagata was henceforth used to accommodate children who had been associated with armed groups.

For children sent to Gitagata, there was generally no judicial process or systematic and comprehensive review of the charges against them: it was simply ascertained from their case file whether there was a *prima facie* case, or as a prosecutor said 'indices de culpabilité'.[268] As the response was administrative, criminal judges did not have competence to review their cases, a minors' judge noting that his bench had sent home a child (under 14 during the genocide) who had come before the court by error and had confessed to killing many people.[269] Recall, however, that in the *Niyoniringiye* case, a non-responsible minor was questioned during a

263 Doulliez 1998b: 16.

264 Moussalli 2000a: [118] and [121].

265 van Krieken 2000: 10. See also ASOFERWA 2001: 2–3 (reporting similar figures).

266 Doulliez 1999: 10.

267 See ASOFERWA 2001: 3–4; LIPRODHOR 2001b: 11; van Krieken 2000: 13. Not all non-responsible children were released, however – see section 5.1.

268 Interview with Prosecutor B, 10 September 2013. This approach was confirmed by former Prosecutor F (interview, 9 October 2013) and former MINJUST/UNICEF Project Coordinator A (interview, 7 October 2013). UNICEF Rwanda (1996d: 15) reported that it was advocating for the creation of juvenile benches in civil courts to deal with non-responsible children, but no further information on the outcome has been discovered.

269 Interview with Judge H, 1 October 2013. The minor was subsequently sent to Gitagata after his mother had insisted to the public prosecutor that he could not remain in the village because of what he had done.

hearing about his participation in the genocide before being sent to a re-education centre.

Initially, Gitagata was under the responsibility of MINIJUST but was transferred to MINITRASO in August 1996. Much of the day-to-day running of the centre was managed by ASOFERWA (a local NGO), with support from UNICEF Rwanda and other international agencies and NGOs, although from February 1997, responsibility for re-education activities within the centre was assumed by MINITRASO, with ASOFERWA focusing on reintegration and follow-up activities.[270] Although Gitagata had been rebuilt, its facilities remained (and in fact more recently still remain[271]) fairly basic, but it was 'more spacious and clean' than the prisons from which children had been transferred.[272] Children were provided with basic education as well as psychosocial care and recreational activities, although Cantwell, reporting up to December 1996, comments that primary education was more or less the only structured activity.[273] Few of the older children were motivated to follow the school programme, resulting in discipline problems, and there were reports of physical and sexual abuse, of gangs organised by older juveniles and of older children spreading negative propaganda amongst younger children.[274] A primary school was built adjacent to Gitagata in 1997 and was attended by Gitagata residents and local children. By 2000, activities had been expanded to include vocational training and courses on social aspects, such as rights, duties and responsibilities.[275] At the centre, instructors worked with groups of approximately 20 children, their main objective being to teach 'the difference between good and evil'.[276] The aim of the activities was to assist minors with the transition back into

[270] ASOFERWA 1998a: 2, 1999b: 2 and 2001: 2.

[271] I visited Gitagata in October 2013.

[272] UNICEF Rwanda 1996b: 15. See also Moussalli 2000a: [119] and 2000b: [127]. Note, however, that Doulliez, visiting Gitagata in 1998, referred to the repulsive filthiness and foul odour of the dormitories as well as problems with the water supply and limited food. She also reported that her interpreter had seen a soldier beat a child (Doulliez 1998b: 17–18). Conditions in Miyove were better, although she noted a significant problem with the water supply (Doulliez 1999: 10–11). See also HRW 2003a: 28 reporting that by mid-1998, conditions were getting worse and that UNICEF had described them as 'abominable' in 2000.

[273] Cantwell 1997: 49.

[274] Chorlton 1996: 46; van Krieken 2000: 17. See also section 5.2.1c regarding threats/violence against those who confessed.

[275] See Biseruka 1999: 32; CRC Committee 2003a: [339]; van Krieken 2000: 16.

[276] Moussalli 2000a: [120] and 2000b: [128]. See also Briggs 2005: 29–30.

the community and facilitate their return to education or assist with their finding employment once released.[277]

The approach was thus, ostensibly, rehabilitative rather than punitive, although some questioned the nature of the detention. A child's stay in Gitagata was a condition for his ultimate release. Tertsakian asserts that, whilst 'not technically a prison, the children were not free to leave and were effectively in a detention centre by another name',[278] and van Krieken's view was that, although Gitagata was an open centre, very few children left, seemingly seeing their stay there as 'part of the "package deal"'.[279] SCF Rwanda sums it up neatly: 'Until the children are released they are in effect serving an indeterminate sentence, or being held for care and protection, depending on one's point of view.'[280] To the extent that the stay in Gitagata could be considered a punitive sanction, it would amount to attributing penal responsibility to children under the minimum age of criminal responsibility and thus violate Rwandan law and Article 40(3)(a) of the CRC. Further, Gitagata received considerable attention from donors (in terms of support and funding) but also from the media: children at Gitagata were frequently filmed and photographed, having their 'identities known for reasons other than their rehabilitation'.[281] In Cantwell's opinion, '[i]t would have been far more in keeping with the CRC to have taken this initiative in a less publicly-oriented manner'.[282]

Time spent in Gitagata varied, some children spending two years or more at the centre. The decision to release a child was taken by a Case Review Committee following an assessment of the child (including education or knowledge of a trade/craft, health, behaviour and psychological status), of the family (to assess willingness to receive the child, capacity to pay school fees or training fees and family history) and of the community (to assess perception and potential threats towards the child and support available).[283] The Committee also drew up a care plan for each child. The views of the child on where he wished to live and what he wished to do were taken into account during the personal assessment.

[277] Note, however, Cantwell's (1997: 49) comments in 1997 that if Gitagata were to be rehabilitative, it would have to create an environment and lifestyle which reflected this aim.

[278] Tertsakian 2008: 176.

[279] van Krieken 2000: 17.

[280] SCF Rwanda 1998: 113.

[281] Cantwell 1997: 49.

[282] Ibid.

[283] MIGEFASO 1997. See also ASOFERWA 1998a: 10, 1999b: 2, and 2001: 1; Biseruka 1999: 35. Confirmed by former ASOFERWA Staff Member A, interview, 24 September 2013.

Additionally, the child was entitled to participate in the Case Review Committee meeting during the discussion on the care plan. The process was thus individualised with the child able to offer his views, and thus, to some extent, was in accordance with the child's right to participate under Article 12 of the CRC and the best interests principle.

Steps were taken to facilitate reintegration. ASOFERWA collaborated closely with local authorities, traced the family and mediated between children and their parents or other community members.[284] Where a family was reluctant to accept a child, a relative in the extended family who lived further away would be approached.[285] ASOFERWA also held 'days of reflection' with selected members of the community (including survivors) in which it explained the objectives of Gitagata, the rights of the child and the reintegration process.[286] Other methods used to sensitise the community included newspaper articles and a radio programme on the activities of the centre, as well as a 'Mayor's Initiative' project in which mayors were provided with guidelines on how to protect child rights, including the rights of those released from Gitagata or prisons.[287]

The reintegration process began in 1998 and, by the end of 1999, ASOFERWA had followed up on 100 out of 297 cases. Whilst it found that there had been no reprisals against the released children,[288] it nonetheless noted that many communities continued to be hostile and reluctant to accept children who had participated in the genocide, and that the released children were often too old to be accepted back into school.[289] The government reported similar problems following visits to 480 of 512 children reintegrated in December 2000, noting that, given the passage of time, 'these children have grown so much that it is becoming difficult to make people understand that they are not criminally liable' (seven were re-arrested) and for the children to reintegrate into society and school.[290]

284 See ASOFERWA 1998a: 3–4; UNICEF Rwanda 1997b: 2. Confirmed by former ASOFERWA Staff Member A, interview, 24 September 2013.

285 Interview with ASOFERWA Staff Member B, 27 September 2013.

286 ASOFERWA 1998a: 9. See also van Krieken 2000: 17.

287 See ASOFERWA 1998a: 10; UNICEF Rwanda 1997d: 87. See also section 7.2.

288 See Moussalli 2000a: [120] and 2000b: [128].

289 ASOFERWA 1998a: 13 and 1998b: 2. See also LIPRODHOR 1999b: 12 noting that some *rescapés* considered that all those (including minors) who had participated in the genocide should receive exemplary punishment.

290 CRC Committee 2003a: [339]. See also ASOFERWA 2001: 4 (noting continuing hostility in some regions).

Van Krieken also reported that some had been returned to prison after the community had informed the authorities that the individual was not under 14 at the time of the crime, and that many had relocated (usually to Kigali) due to family problems or to find employment.[291] However, he opined that, whilst many people found it difficult to understand that these children, now grown up, could not be held responsible, 'the general climate has developed to such an extent ... that proper explanations suffice'. He thus concluded that, on the whole, the reintegration programme had been successful.[292] ASOFERWA similarly observed an increasing acceptance over time, which it attributed to human rights mobilisation campaigns.[293]

5.3.2 The 2003 Communiqué from the Office of the President

Before 2003, detainees (including some minors) held in pre-trial detention had been released provisionally on an *ad hoc* basis by the government, where there was insufficient evidence or given their vulnerable status.[294] A Communiqué from the Office of the President, broadcast on 1 January 2003 on national radio, ordered the release of a much larger number of detainees.[295] The fairly brief Communiqué was followed by a written directive on 9 January 2003, which provided further details.[296] The Communiqué identified for provisional release (to be tried subsequently) those who had made a valid confession and were at risk of being imprisoned for longer than the sentence set by the law, minors aged between 14 and 18 at the time of their alleged crimes and those accused of infiltration or of ordinary crimes. Additionally, the elderly and very sick were to be released in accordance with earlier government orders. Those provisionally released, with the exception of the elderly and seriously ill, were to be sent to *ingando* (solidarity camps – see below) before

[291] van Krieken 2000: 18. See also Briggs 2005: 30–31 (noting issues regarding the real age of the children).

[292] van Krieken 2000: 18.

[293] ASOFERWA 2000: 2. Confirmed by Mukantaganzwa (interview, 3 September 2013), who had worked on the Gitagata project whilst working for UNICEF Rwanda. See also PRI 2003b: 56.

[294] See e.g. Amnesty International 2002: 19–20; ASF 1998b: 18 and 1999a: 13; HRW 2003a: 1; RCN 1996: 63–64; OHCHR 1998a: [33] and 1998b: [35].

[295] Communiqué émanant de la Présidence de la République, Kigali, 1 January 2003 (copy of transcript on file with author).

[296] Parquet Général 2003.

being reintegrated into society.[297] PRI reports that around 2,360 people were provisionally released shortly after the Communiqué, and a further 19,500 were released in a second wave.[298] Further releases pursuant to the Communiqué occurred in 2004, 2005 and 2007.[299] Minors (at the time of their alleged crime) were amongst those released: around 1,100 minors in January 2003 (a further 200 due to be released later that year),[300] 1,900 in July 2005 and a further 78 in March 2007.[301]

From the wording of the Communiqué, it was not clear whether *all* juveniles were to be released or just those who had confessed and whose period of pre-trial detention exceeded the sentence set by law. The written directive shed some light on this, although there were some inconsistencies. This stated that all minors under 14 at the time of the genocide who remained in prison would be released, and juveniles between 14 and 18 at the time of the genocide would be released according to the categories established by law *and* if they had confessed. It then went into more detail, providing that category 1 juveniles, and juveniles in category 2 who had not made a valid confession, were not eligible for release on the basis that their time in prison had not exceeded the minimum sentence. Category 3 juveniles who had not made a valid confession would be released (in contradiction to the earlier wording requiring a confession) if they had spent more than half the maximum sentence in prison. Juveniles in categories 2 and 3 who had spent more than half of the maximum sentence in prison and had confessed *before* being placed on the *gacaca* list would be released. The directive was silent, however, on those who had confessed *after* being placed on the list. According to Morrill, the Communiqué was a 'persistent source of confusion' for juvenile suspects, who had understood from the radio broadcast that all minors would be released

297 Note that detainees released on an *ad hoc* basis did not attend *ingando* but reportedly received sessions in prison to prepare them for release into their communities (interview with AJPRODHO Staff Member, Kigali, 15 February 2013).

298 PRI 2010: 21. See also Cacioppo 2005: 6 (reporting that 22,000 prisoners were released in January 2003).

299 Tertsakian (2008: 427–428) reports that 4,500 were released in 2004, most of whom were accused of common crimes; 22,000 were released in the summer of 2005; and a further 6,700 in 2007.

300 Coalition to Stop the Use of Child Soldiers 2004; LDGL 2006:34. See also RCN 2003c:38 (reporting that 1,147 minors attended solidarity camps after being released pursuant to the Communiqué).

301 Coalition to Stop the Use of Child Soldiers 2008. See also LDGL 2006: 36 and Morrill 2005: 116, both relating statistics from the prosecutor's office that 1,880 of 22,000 detainees released in 2005 were minors.

without condition, yet later were informed that only those minors who had confessed would be released, and then only provisionally and after spending some time in *ingando*.[302] Further, the Communiqué appears to have been implemented (by prosecutors) differently in different areas and over time, with releases in 2005 not requiring any confession.[303]

As indicated above, the releases pursuant to the Communiqué were provisional: those released would subsequently come before the *gacaca* courts. Some Rwandans approved of the Communiqué, although there were those who considered it unjust to grant provisional liberty to those who had confessed whilst many innocents remained in prison;[304] others however perceived the releases as a form of pardon. Some participants in this research considered the release of those who had been minors at the time of the genocide to be less controversial than the release of the elderly, noting that many saw older people as leading figures in the genocide and responsible for teaching ethnic hatred to their children.[305] Indeed, many elderly prisoners interviewed by Tertsakian in 2004 had been re-arrested almost immediately after being provisionally released, often on the same charges.[306] But this was also true for some juveniles interviewed by Morrill in 2005. For example, a female arrested in 1995 (aged 15) was released from prison on 22 February 2003 only to be re-arrested on 4 May 2003 without explanation. She was then released again on 29 August 2005.[307] Some juveniles who were released found it difficult to reintegrate, feeling animosity from others and discovering that survivors were not 'in agreement' with their release (in contrast to what they had been told in *ingando*).[308]

302 Morrill 2005: 107. This was confirmed by Gahunde (Skype interview, 19 August 2013); Former Juvenile Detainee (Skype interview, 24 August 2013).

303 Personal correspondence with Gahunde, 22 February 2014.

304 LIPRODHOR 2005: 37. See also LDGL 2006 for a study of perceptions and consequences of the Communiqué.

305 E.g. Former Executive Secretary of a Survivors' Organisation, interview, 21 February 2013; Muleefu, interview, 5 March 2013; Rukundakuvuga (Judge of the Supreme Court in the department in charge of coordination and supervision of Gacaca Courts' activities), interview, Kigali, 13 February 2013. See also African Rights 2000: 60–63 (many considered old age not to be a mitigating factor, whereas some thought that minors were 'children, acting unconsciously'); LIPRODHOR 1999c: 33 (referencing a *rescapé* who considered that old age should be an aggravating circumstance given the key role played by the elderly in inciting and leading the genocide).

306 Tertsakian 2008: 198–199 and 428–434.

307 Morrill 2005: 116.

308 Morrill 2005: 107–108. Also confirmed by Gahunde, Skype interview, 19 August 2013.

5.3.3 Ingando *(Solidarity Camps)*

Ingando were run formally by the National Unity and Reconciliation Commission (NURC) from 1999, although some had taken place as early as May 1996 under the Ministry of Youth, Sport and Culture.[309] Initially for new university students, returning refugees and released prisoners, they were later extended to other categories of society. There were specific *ingando* for child genocide suspects. In November–December 2000, over 500 non-responsible children released from detention (including Gitagata) attended a six-week workshop at Busogo camp (in Ruhengeri).[310] The following year, a second phase of *ingando* took place over an eight-week period for non-responsible minors in Gacuriro (a suburb of Kigali).[311] Both of these programmes were organised by NURC and MINIJUST with support from UNICEF Rwanda. Detainees provisionally released in January 2003 spent three months in *ingando*,[312] whereas minors released in 2005 stayed for one month or 45 days.[313] Approximately 1,875 individuals aged under 18 at the time of the genocide participated in an *ingando*, specifically for minors, at Duha in Kibungo from August to September 2005.[314]

The aim of *ingando* was to provide civic education to facilitate unity and reconciliation. Whilst the syllabus varied according to the target audience, common features across all *ingando* were lectures and cultural activities, with the focus being on discipline and uniformity.[315] According to Moussalli, non-responsible children at the Busogo camp received counselling, education and training for reintegration into society,[316] and the NHRC reported providing lectures on the rights and duties of children.[317] HRW noted that minors were taught Rwandan history and human rights, but also that they performed military exercises 'and were

309 See UNICEF Rwanda 1996c: 8–9 (UNICEF provided financial support to youth solidarity camps).

310 ASOFERWA 2001: 2–4; See also NHRC 2001: 39–40.

311 NURC 2002: 15.

312 Tertsakian 2008: 435; Clark 2011: 102.

313 Former Juvenile Detainee (Skype interview, 24 August 2013) reported spending one month in the Duha *ingando*; Gahunde (Skype interview, 19 August 2013) recalled spending 45 days there; Mukantaganzwa (interview, 3 September 2013) spoke of minors spending one to two months in the Duha *ingando*.

314 Interviews with Gahunde, 19 August 2013 (Skype); Mukantaganzwa, 3 September 2013.

315 Purdekova 2011: 16–17 and 36. See also Tertsakian 2008: 436; Thomson 2011: 334–336.

316 Moussalli 2001: [29].

317 NHRC 2001: 47.

encouraged to accuse adults in the *gacaca* proceedings'.[318] A participant in the 2005 Duha *ingando* recalled that classes covered national policy, reconciliation and history ('their version') and that in the evening, there was morale building through, for example, singing songs (which he stated were selected to convey the ideology of the RPF).[319] From other reports on *ingando* for former prisoners, it is clear that the focus was on promoting the unity of Rwandans and eradicating genocide ideology. Both Thomson and Mgbako also refer to an aim being to obtain further details from former prisoners on events during the genocide.[320]

Whilst *ingando* was intended to facilitate reintegration, assessments diverge as to its impact on detainees and the broader society. PRI found that ex-prisoners were often positive about their *ingando* experiences,[321] and detainees in Clark's study considered it would assist with reintegration.[322] Cacioppo, however, concluded that many survivors considered *ingando* to be ineffective, believing that a simple apology could not heal the wounds caused by the genocide, whilst former prisoners felt that their motivations for apologising were continuously questioned.[323] Tertsakian and Thomson reported that participants saw *ingando* as an attempt at brainwashing,[324] and Morrill found that released minors who had attended *ingando* felt 'disenfranchised', 'fear' and 'paranoia' and found it difficult to interact with persons who had not been in prison. She asserted that Rwanda had failed to take sufficient steps to facilitate the reintegration of these young people: 'Two months of re-education in the *ingando* will not undo the damage that ten years of prison have done.'[325] HRW

318 HRW 2003a: 29.

319 Skype interview with Gahunde, 19 August 2013. A similar account was provided by former Juvenile Detainee (Skype interview, 24 August 2013). See also Mgbako 2005: 202 and Thomson 2011: 334–336 who speak of pro-RPF ideology and political indoctrination; Ingelaere 2016: 111–112, noting the use of songs, often quite militaristic, that were used to reinforce concepts promoted during re-education sessions.

320 Mgbako 2005: 222; Thomson 2011: 334.

321 PRI 2004a: 18–22 (although noting at 43–44 that many *ingando* participants feared reprisals).

322 Clark 2011: 107.

323 Cacioppo 2005: 11–16.

324 Tertsakian 2008: 437–439; Thomson 2011: 331. Two participants in this research who attended the Duha *ingando* were of the same opinion (Skype interviews with Gahunde, 19 August 2013; former Juvenile Detainee, 24 August 2013).

325 Morrill 2005: 107, 114 and 118. The two attendees of the Duha *ingando* confirmed that they had faced difficulties reintegrating, 'feeling animosity' from and 'seeing hostility in the eyes' of people. Both subsequently left Rwanda.

reported similar concerns as to whether the Busogo camp had sufficiently prepared the under-14s for reintegration into society, given that they had spent their 'entire adolescence' in detention.[326]

5.4 Conclusion

The genocide destroyed all facets of Rwandan life, including the judicial system and social fabric, and the Rwandan government's response was to seek to prosecute all those who took part. This overall context influenced the way in which Rwanda dealt with young perpetrators. Whilst child perpetrators were, to some degree, given preferential treatment on account of their age and some progress was made in implementing international standards, on the whole, child perpetrators were not granted the full protection provided by international law. Of course, no detainee in Rwanda – young or old – was granted the full protection provided by international law (or indeed existing Rwandan law). However, as a particularly vulnerable population, and bearing in mind the risks associated with children languishing in prisons – risks both for the child and for the future of society more broadly – children in conflict with the law should arguably be prioritised where resources are scarce.

Existing Rwandan criminal law made clear distinctions between individuals on the basis of age: those under 14 could not be held responsible, those aged 14–18 could be prosecuted for crimes but their age mitigated their sentence, whilst those over 18 were considered adults. These age divisions were retained after the genocide, being carried over into the Genocide Law and Gacaca Laws and being the reference for the administrative measures adopted. Some existing domestic law provisions complied with international standards, for example, an acceptable minimum age of criminal responsibility, different sentencing for juveniles and the separation of (male) minors from adults in prisons. Rwanda did not, however, have a comprehensive juvenile justice system. Following the genocide, various initiatives were taken to deal with the issue of child perpetrators. These did not result in wholesale legislative reform: some limited juvenile justice provisions were inserted into the genocide-specific legislation, efforts were made to ensure that existing provisions that *were* compliant with international standards were respected in practice and steps were

[326] HRW 2003a: 29.

taken to adopt practical measures and policies that would enhance the rights of child *génocidaires*. In many cases, however, there continued to be violations of both domestic and international law.

In the aftermath of the genocide, children (including those under 14) were arbitrarily arrested and detained. Whilst the government sought to regularise the situation domestically through retrospective legislation, it remained in violation of international standards, and many children were held for lengthy periods in deplorable conditions in pre-trial detention. Efforts were made to separate minors from adults in detention and to remove the under-14s as quickly as possible from prisons and *cachots*. However, given the socio-political climate as well as the gravity of their alleged crimes, non-responsible children were placed in re-education centres (ostensibly a social welfare measure aimed at rehabilitation, but that some allege were akin to prisons) before being released into society. It appears that in some jurisdictions, particularly after the introduction of *gacaca*, those under 14 at the time of the genocide went through the same trial procedure as adults, their age coming into play only at the end when the decision was taken whether or not to send them to a re-education centre or solidarity camp. Possibly, this change in approach was due to the time that had passed between the genocide and proceedings, but, whatever the reason, any 'trial' of a non-responsible child would violate the minimum age of criminal responsibility.

For those aged between 14 and 18, their participation in the genocide was a matter for the criminal justice system. Before the formal courts, there was provision for minors' judges that was implemented in some, but not all, jurisdictions. Trials were conducted in public (contrary to international standards – at least certainly where the juvenile was under 18 at the time of trial) and there was no provision for any special procedure, although there is some evidence that judges made accommodations when dealing with, and sentencing, juveniles. In some cases, juveniles were sentenced as adults, but, on the whole, they benefited from reduced sentences (in law and practice) on the basis of their age. Many minors had free legal representation, although it appears that some represented themselves: if they were denied legal assistance, this would be in contravention of their rights. Whilst measures were adopted to accelerate juvenile trials, in practice these had little effect, in one part due to the very desire to secure legal representation for juveniles. The Gacaca Laws did not provide for special judges or any different procedure for juveniles and, in practice, minors went through the same, public, trial procedure as adults. If specific juvenile justice procedural guarantees *do* apply to individuals who were minors at the time of the alleged crime but who are tried after they have reached majority (the position on this is not clear, particularly where many years have lapsed), this would be a violation of international standards. Additionally, like all suspects, juveniles did not have legal representation before this more informal mechanism. Juveniles continued to benefit from reduced sentences, with the later Gacaca Laws providing much more explicit language relating to minors than the Genocide Law. However, at all stages, the criminal justice system did not provide for diversion and proceeded on the basis that imprisonment was the appropriate sanction for those aged 14–18 at the time of the genocide, the only exception being the introduction of TIG and suspended sentences, which were applied across the board without distinction as to age. Specific measures that took account of the perpetrator's young age and that aimed at rehabilitation and reintegration were thus lacking.

The decision to release those who were minors at the time of the genocide, particularly pursuant to the 2003 Communiqué, might at first glance appear to be privileging them due to their age, but a closer examination reveals that the releases, in 2003 at least, were contingent on them having confessed and being at risk of spending longer in prison than the sentence provided for by law. Thus the same criteria were applied as to adults (the only advantage being directly linked to their reduced sentence). The early *ingando* for non-responsible minors (those under 14 at the time of the genocide) possibly had more child-oriented programmes, but the later *ingando* in Duha, whilst nominally for 'minors', appears to have differed little from *ingando* for former prisoners generally. This is feasibly due to these minors being (by 2005) at least 25 years old. Indeed, a key issue in the treatment of all minors was the passage of time between the genocide and trial. Given the number of years taken to process files, it was difficult for judges and, more widely, the community, to conceive that these individuals, now grown up, should be treated as minors. This resulted in difficulties during trials as well as reintegration and also led to many minors being held in pre-trial detention (contrary to international standards) for periods longer than the maximum sentence they would incur if found guilty.

Overall the approach taken to young perpetrators was driven by the resolve of the Rwandan government to end impunity: the gravity of the crimes was such that any kind of amnesty was inconceivable for the government and Rwandan society, and also rendered it essential that these children underwent a process of re-education and/or accountability. Some preferential treatment was accorded to minors drawing on existing age divisions in Rwandan law, but in many cases, there was a failure to comply with international standards. Whether this failure can be attributed to lack of political will as well as lack of capacity on the part of the Rwandan government is debatable,[327] but it is undeniable that efforts to give practical effect to child-sensitive laws and policies were hampered by the context. For example, the huge number of suspects in prisons made it difficult, if not impossible at least initially, to separate minors from adults. It also, together with the debilitated judicial system, made processing of cases exceptionally slow – for all detainees – resulting in long-term pre-trial detention. Another key factor was the breakdown of society and the hostility of public opinion towards child *génocidaires*. This significantly influenced the decision not to release the under-14s, and, at least for the first few years after the genocide, placed considerable pressure on judges in the Specialised Chambers seeking to apply juvenile justice standards. Whilst some of the challenges, in isolation, might have been surmountable, their accumulation made full respect of international standards impossible. These challenges posed problems not only for the Rwandan government, but also those actors seeking to enhance child rights in Rwanda. As Cantwell commented:

> The situation of children arrested – for whatever reason – in Rwanda during the post-genocide period is surely unique. While virtually all its individual facets have been – or are being – experienced elsewhere to some degree, their combination in the case of Rwanda has constituted an unprecedented challenge on a number of fronts, posing fundamental ethical dilemmas for all organizations and their staff that become involved.[328]

It is to the actions of these organisations that this book now turns.

[327] On this, see section 7.5.
[328] Cantwell 1997: 48.

6

International Actors and the Rwandan Child *Génocidaire*

This chapter explores the approach of international actors to child *génocidaires* and to the Rwandan government's legal and policy responses to such children. It begins by describing briefly the approach of UN bodies (non-operational and those with a field presence in Rwanda) and international NGOs. It then turns to examine UNICEF Rwanda's[1] involvement. As we saw in Chapter 3, the CRC grants a role to UNICEF in the promotion of the effective implementation of its provisions. This chapter will hone in on UNICEF's pivotal role, as the UN's lead agency for children in conflict with the law, in safeguarding child rights in post-genocide Rwanda. It will provide an account of UNICEF Rwanda's involvement with child *génocidaires*, first examining how it became involved and then providing an overview of its activities, before drawing upon specific issues to exemplify how UNICEF Rwanda interpreted and applied international standards in the Rwandan context. It draws out the contention within UNICEF, and the friction between UNICEF Rwanda and other actors, over how best to implement the CRC, particularly as regards institutionalisation. In addition to illustrating UNICEF Rwanda's contextual application of, and pragmatic approach to, the standards, this chapter also sets the scene for the further analysis of UNICEF Rwanda's policy and advocacy strategies in Chapter 7 and provides the context for a broader evaluation in Chapter 8 of UNICEF Rwanda's approach to operationalising international standards on child perpetrators in a post-conflict state.

6.1 International Actors and the Rwandan Child *Génocidaire*

Chapter 3 profiled briefly the mechanisms at the UN level involved in the promotion of child rights. As noted in that chapter, the UN treaty

[1] As noted in Chapter 1, this term is used to distinguish the Rwandan field office from the global agency or headquarters. Note also the importance of individual initiatives within the field offices given UNICEF's decentralised structure.

bodies (the CRC Committee and HRC) rely mainly on the state reporting system to monitor compliance. Generally, these bodies consider a situation in a state only when the state has submitted its report, although special procedures have been instituted to allow for urgent examinations in serious situations. In the case of Rwanda, the HRC issued a request on 27 October 1994 to Rwanda to submit a report by 31 January 1995, addressing the application of specified articles of the ICCPR, including Articles 10 and 14, which are relevant to children accused of genocide.[2] Rwanda, however, failed to respond to this request,[3] and it was not until 2009 that its third periodic report[4] (due in 1992 but submitted in 2007 – thus more than 15 years late) was considered by the HRC. At this point, the HRC expressed concern at 'reports of appalling prison conditions' as well as 'the fact that there appears to be no guarantee that detained children will be held separately from adults'.[5] However, the Rwandan government had informed the Committee in its replies to the list of issues that all child *génocidaires* had been released provisionally and were thus no longer in detention,[6] thus this comment was likely directed at children suspected or convicted of ordinary crimes. The HRC also 'note[d] with concern' that *gacaca* jurisdictions did not comply with fair trial guarantees, referring to lack of legal training for judges and concerns over the rights of defence and the equality of arms principle.[7] It did not, however, refer to juveniles going through the process.

The CRC Committee does not appear to have invoked its urgent action procedure in respect of Rwanda, examining the situation in Rwanda only in 2004 after the government had submitted its periodic report.[8] The summary records of Committee meetings indicate that members were concerned regarding the treatment of child *génocidaires*, with various questions being put to the Rwandan delegation on court procedures and detention. One Committee member stated that the 'lack of a special juvenile justice system and the fact that children were prosecuted under

[2] HRC 1995: [55].
[3] HRC 2009b: [65].
[4] HRC 2007.
[5] HRC 2009a: [15].
[6] HRC 2008: [110].
[7] HRC 2009a: [17].
[8] CRC Committee 2003a. Rwanda had submitted a brief initial report in 1992 (CRC Committee 1992a), leading the Committee to request the submission of a more comprehensive initial report within one year (see CRC Committee 1993b). This report was never submitted.

the same procedures as adults and placed in the same prisons were very worrying', whilst another commented that not allowing legal representation before the *gacaca* courts 'appeared to constitute a violation of the right to a fair trial'.[9] In its Concluding Observations, the Committee recognised the 'long-term negative consequences on the implementation of the Convention' caused by the genocide.[10] In addition to raising general concerns (and making recommendations) regarding the lack of progress in establishing a functioning juvenile justice system in respect of 'other alleged children in conflict with the law',[11] the Committee expressly addressed the situation of minors accused of 'war crimes' (used to refer to alleged *génocidaires*). It noted that it was 'extremely concerned' that individuals under 18 at the time of their alleged 'war crime' continued to be detained without trial in very poor conditions and were not provided with services that would assist them in their rehabilitation. It also commented on the *gacaca* courts, expressing 'deep concern' that there was no special procedure for persons under 18 at the time of their alleged crime, asserting that this is required by Article 40(3). It recommended that, in accordance with Articles 37, 39 and 40 of the CRC, the Rwandan government take all necessary measures to complete legal proceedings within six months against all persons under the age of 18 at the time of their alleged 'war crimes'.[12]

As regards other UN bodies, such as the General Assembly, the Commission on Human Rights (now the Human Rights Council) and the special procedures, these reported or passed resolutions on the situation in Rwanda generally, raising issues that pertained also to child *génocidaires* or drawing attention to the specific situation of these children. For example, various resolutions of the General Assembly and the Commission on Human Rights expressed 'deep concern' regarding arbitrary arrests and detention conditions that did not conform to international standards, welcomed domestic prosecutions of alleged *génocidaires* and improvements made over time in terms of the trial process, and encouraged the Rwandan government to continue efforts to

[9] CRC Committee 2004b: [60] and [62].

[10] CRC Committee 2004d: [4].

[11] Ibid.: [72–74]. Concerns included the lack of juvenile courts and trained personnel, poor detention conditions, overuse and long periods of pre-trial detention and lack of rehabilitation and reintegration measures. The Committee suggested that Rwanda seek technical assistance from UNICEF and other agencies.

[12] Ibid.: [70–71].

improve detention conditions and strengthen fair trial guarantees and the judicial process generally, in accordance with international standards.[13] The General Assembly also 'welcome[d] and encourage[d] the release of minors … who were detained for their alleged involvement in genocide and other abuses of human rights, and urge[d] the Government of Rwanda to establish adequate measures to facilitate the reintegration of released persons into society'.[14] The Commission on Human Rights made similar comments, encouraging the Rwandan government to continue efforts to reduce the prison population by releasing minors and other vulnerable groups and 'affirming' the urgent need to complete a file for each detainee.[15]

These resolutions drew on the information obtained from the Special Rapporteur (Degni-Ségui) and Special Representative (Moussalli) of the Commission on Human Rights who visited Rwanda from 1994 to 1996 and 1997 to 2001 respectively. As illustrated in Chapter 5, the reports of these two experts contained various references to the treatment of child *génocidaires* in addition to the human rights situation generally. Degni-Ségui reported on the arbitrary arrest and detention of minors, on efforts made to separate juveniles from adults in detention and on the transfer of non-responsible minors to the Gitagata Re-education Centre.[16] He also reported on deplorable conditions of detention and inhuman treatment, going so far as to refer to the 'torture' of juveniles.[17] He advised the UN to call for an end to violations (including arbitrary arrests and detentions) and made recommendations, but did not suggest that those who were arbitrarily detained be released immediately.[18] Moussalli made a number of observations and recommendations relating to children accused of genocide. He commended efforts made by the government to prioritise their cases and separate them from adults in detention, but also

[13] See for example UNGA Resolutions 49/206 (1995), 50/200 (1996), 51/114 (1997), 52/146 (1998), 53/156 (1999), 54/188 (2000); UN Commission on Human Rights Resolutions 1995/91, 1997/66, 1999/20, 2000/21.

[14] UNGA Resolution 53/156 (1999). See also UNGA Resolution 54/188 (2000) 'encouraging' efforts to reduce the prison population by releasing minors and others.

[15] UN Commission on Human Rights Resolutions 1998/69, 1999/20 and 2000/21. It also commended government efforts to improve the situation of children (generally – as opposed to *génocidaires* specifically) and encouraged further efforts 'in collaboration with UNICEF, guided by a concern for the best interests of children' pursuant to the CRC (Res. 2000/21).

[16] See Degni-Ségui 1994b: [30], 1995b: [66], [70] and [72] and 1997: [37] and [120].

[17] Degni-Ségui 1997: [125].

[18] Degni-Ségui 1994b: [72–73] and 1995b: [139–140].

highlighted problems such as difficulties in securing legal representation for minors and sexual violence against detained minors. He further welcomed the release of minors from detention, whilst stressing the need for measures to ensure their security and assist with their reintegration.[19] Moussalli recommended that 'serious consideration' be given to releasing 'on humanitarian grounds … minors and children for whom alternatives to imprisonment can be found', given the deplorable conditions in detention facilities, and that authorities treat as a priority for release 'children who are without files or who are confirmed to be innocent'.[20] However, he did not suggest that all minors be released unconditionally. Indeed, whilst reporting that children under 14 were being detained 'illegally' under Rwandan and international law, he referred to 'opposition to their unconditional release' and urged the government to transfer more children to Gitagata (an initiative which he 'fully supported') after which they would be returned home.[21] It would seem that his advocacy regarding the under-14s had some success, with more than 500 non-responsible children being released (after attending a solidarity camp) in December 2000.[22] In his final report in 2001, Moussalli referred to discussions with the Minister of Justice regarding non-responsible children still in detention in 2001, and noted that he 'was promised that every effort would be made to identify and release these outstanding cases'. He had also been informed that all genocide minors' cases would 'have priority'.[23]

Moussalli, in many cases, drew attention to international standards. For example, he 'recall[ed] the obligations' of Rwanda to protect children's rights under the CRC[24] and 'urge[d] that all actions affecting [child *génocidaires*] be guided by a concern for the interests of the child, as specified under the Convention on the Rights of the Child'.[25] He also noted in 2000 that many minors continued to be detained with adults 'in clear

[19] Moussalli 1998b: [51], [61] and [74]. He later recommended the continuation of community-sensitisation programmes to prepare for the release of these children (Moussalli 2000a: [220]).

[20] Moussalli 1999a: [77], 2000a: [220] and 2000b: [229].

[21] Moussalli 2000a: [118] and [121].

[22] See section 5.3.1. HRW (2003a: 30) commented that, whilst international officials had frequently raised the issue of illegally detained minors, they had 'rarely achieved success', but in this 'exceptional case', Moussalli had secured a promise, that was honoured, from President Kagame to release the under-14s by the end of the year.

[23] Moussalli 2001: [29–30].

[24] Moussalli 1998b: [61].

[25] Moussalli 1999a: [59].

violation' of the CRC,[26] and stated that 'every effort' should be made to separate them. He further asserted that, 'according to international standards, minors should not be imprisoned', and thus recommended that they be moved to Gitagata.[27] Whilst he did refer to violations of the Convention, his key approach was to call on the international community to provide assistance to Rwanda in seeking solutions to problems rather than harshly criticising the government's (in)action, and he frequently acknowledged the challenges Rwanda faced.

The Special Representative for Children and Armed Conflict, Olara Otunnu, who took office in 1997, visited Rwanda in February 1999. He expressed concern regarding the slow pace of juvenile trials, but was encouraged by Rwanda's efforts to deal with child genocide suspects, including provision for minors' benches in the Specialised Chambers, the construction of minors' wings in prisons and the training of juvenile justice officials.[28] After the introduction of the *gacaca* system, Otunnu recommended the prioritisation of young persons who had been aged between 14 and 18 in 1994[29] and later expressed support for the *gacaca* jurisdictions.[30] Later reports by the Special Representative to the Human Rights Council and General Assembly make no reference to child *génocidaires*.[31]

As regards the OHCHR, it expressed concerns, in general, regarding fair trials and long-term pre-trial detention, with very few references to child genocide suspects.[32] The main contribution made by this office was through its field presence, the UNHRFOR, on whose activities its reports were based. In Chapter 4, I briefly outlined the assistance provided by UNHRFOR to the Rwandan government in rehabilitating the justice system. UNHRFOR's mandate included monitoring the ongoing human rights situation and implementing programmes of technical cooperation in human rights, in particular the administration of justice.[33] It

[26] Moussalli 2000a: [117] and [220].

[27] Ibid.: [220]. Recall, however, that the CRC does not prohibit imprisonment: rather, it states that it should be a measure of last resort and for the shortest appropriate period of time.

[28] Otunnu 1999: [91].

[29] Otunnu 2002: [36].

[30] Otunnu 2003: [12].

[31] See various reports by Coomaraswamy, Gamba, Otunnu and Zerrougui.

[32] OHCHR 1998b: [35–36] referred to the release of minors (and other vulnerable persons) by *groupes mobiles* and welcomed the government's intention to continue the release of vulnerable detainees.

[33] OHCHR 1995: [9]; Martin 1998: 4–5. Note that the monitoring function proved to be a source of tension, the Rwandan government wishing to restrict UNHRFOR's mandate to

thus monitored trials, arrests and detention (including of minors) and the broader human rights situation, informed the government of alleged violations of international human rights standards, and proposed means of addressing shortcomings.[34] It also provided training to officials and NGOs, and conducted educational seminars (in particular on the rights of women and children) in Rwandan society.[35] Given its broad remit, it did not have a specific focus on child *génocidaires* but they did come within its activities, and field officers, at least initially, made use of a manual on the 'Protection and Promotion of Children's Rights in the Field'. This contained information on the minimum age of criminal responsibility and the sentencing provisions of the Rwandan Penal Code.[36]

Similarly, other international actors in Rwanda following the genocide worked on children's issues, but not exclusively, and only a core group's activities directly covered child *génocidaires*. This group included: ASF, DCHR, ICRC, PRI, RCN and UNDP and, with a specific focus on children, SCF and UNICEF. Additionally, there were organisations such as Amnesty International and HRW that were not involved in the implementation of projects but were monitoring developments. The activities of these organisations in general were outlined in section 4.2.3 and some of their interventions relating to child *génocidaires* were highlighted in Chapter 5. Both the UNDP and the ICRC were involved significantly in improving detention conditions generally, but also specifically for minors. Research participants spoke in particular of ICRC's work: Howland considered the ICRC to be very effective in expanding and improving detention facilities, which he believed led to minors being separated from adults,[37] and a former prosecutor recalled visits from an ICRC representative 'almost 2 days a week talking about the rights of children' in detention.[38]

providing technical assistance rather than 'policing' the government. UNHRFOR's activities were terminated on 28 July 1998, after failure of the High Commissioner and the Rwandan government to agree on a revised mandate (see OHCHR 1998b: [10–14]).

34 OHCHR 1998a: [45] and 1998b: [8]. See also Martin 1998; UNHRFOR 1997b and 1997c (commending progress made with genocide trials but noting where it considered trials to have violated the ICCPR).

35 OHCHR 1995: [25], 1996d: [12] and [25–33] and 1997b: [29–30]. See also Martin 1998.

36 Cohn 1999: 186–187 (Cohn notes, however, that the manual stopped being used given the turnover of staff – at 161–162).

37 Skype interview with Todd Howland, former Head of Legal and Human Rights Promotion Unit, UNHRFOR, 7 February 2014.

38 Interview with Ntete, 27 February 2013. Siboyintore (interview, 9 October 2013) also recalled the ICRC, as well as UNICEF, addressing prosecutors on children in detention.

The international NGOs that were operational in Rwanda played a key role in training law enforcement, prison and judicial personnel on human rights in general, and children's rights in particular. They also provided other significant technical and material assistance to Rwanda's judicial system, which directly or indirectly benefited child perpetrators. To provide just a few examples of their work, PRI's training of prison guards from 1998 addressed 'international conventions and the requirement to separate children from men, and men from women',[39] and PRI highlighted '*jeunes génocidaires*' as being one category of vulnerable detainees it would continue to focus on in its country programme.[40] It also provided material supplies for juvenile detainees and gave training on 'juvenile trauma' in prisons.[41] RCN's training to IPJs covered the minimum age of criminal responsibility and reduced sentences for minors in the Penal Code,[42] and its training to prosecutors addressed international treaties ratified by Rwanda as well as the differential treatment accorded to juveniles during investigation and prosecution.[43] RCN assisted the prosecutor's office in taking juvenile detainees to the site of the alleged acts to obtain evidence, following which some were released for lack of evidence, and it listed genocide minors as one category of intended beneficiaries of its programme to support itinerant trials.[44] DCHR and ASF's role in securing the provision of legal assistance (judicial defenders or lawyers) for juveniles accused of genocide before the Specialised Chambers was detailed in Chapter 5.[45] As also outlined in that chapter, ASF provided training to judges in the formal courts and also monitored proceedings before the formal and *gacaca* courts, including cases involving minors (the reports of which have aided significantly the research for this book). Further, it 'pressured the government to consider the vulnerable situation of female prisoners and those prisoners who were minors at the time they allegedly participated in the genocide'.[46] As regards SCF's activities, its survey on the perception of child perpetrators was highly influential on the development of policies towards child *génocidaires*, in particular non-responsible

[39] Interview with Lawyer B, 15 February 2013.
[40] PRI 2002a: 3.
[41] PRI 2003c.
[42] Mugenzi 1995.
[43] RCN 2005: 10.
[44] RCN 2005: 8.
[45] ASF lawyers reportedly referenced international juvenile justice standards in their court advocacy before the Specialised Chambers (interview with Ntete, 27 February 2013).
[46] Chakravarty 2006: 136–137.

children. SCF also supported minors in detention, through the provision of material supplies to the Gitagata centre and through the 'Protégez-moi' project which provided education, care and psychosocial support in prisons. To the extent that their activities concerned child *génocidaires*, the aim of all of these operational NGOs was to improve the situation of such minors predominantly through the provision of technical or other assistance to Rwanda. Thus the emphasis was on collaboration rather than criticism.[47]

Non-operational international NGOs, in particular Amnesty International and HRW, produced reports highlighting shortcomings in the treatment of child *génocidaires*, usually in the context of a more general report on post-genocide justice. HRW's report, 'Rwanda: Lasting Wounds', included a detailed section on child *génocidaires*, noting where it considered the Rwandan government to have violated international standards. It made a number of recommendations which clearly drew on the CRC. For example, it recommended that Rwanda establish a juvenile justice system that 'emphasizes the best interests of the child and provides children with a fair hearing and equal protection of the law' and that children in conflict with the law be treated 'in a manner consistent with the promotion of their sense of dignity and worth, taking into account their age and the desirability of promoting their reintegration into society'. It also recommended that minors (at the time of their alleged crime) in the formal justice system have access to legal assistance 'and other due process protections afforded them under international human rights law', as well as separate trials and reduced penalties in accordance with Rwandan law. In relation to *gacaca*, it advised that the government amend the relevant laws to ensure that accused child *génocidaires* 'receive additional protections as required by the Convention on the Rights of the Child' (although it did not enumerate what these were).[48]

Brief mention should also be made of the few domestic human rights NGOs that were functioning after the genocide. CLADHO's sensitisation programmes included seminars on 'youth' and the rights of

[47] Indeed, RCN (2005: 16), reporting on its activities in general, asserted that one of its assets was the ability to explain the law and support measures that were moving towards the respect of human rights rather than denouncing violations (distinguishing itself from other NGOs that focused on monitoring and/or denouncing). See also Demay et al. 2005: 55–56 regarding ASF's approach.

[48] HRW 2003a: 3. See also Amnesty International 2000a: 20–21 (which refers to violations of the CRC).

the child under international law.[49] It also entered into an agreement with UNICEF (under the 'Programme for Monitoring the Situation of Children Accused of Genocide') to collect data on children detained on suspicion of genocide and to monitor trials before the Specialised Chambers involving minors.[50] LIPRODHOR also monitored trials, including those involving minors, and followed up on the reintegration of people (including minors) who were released provisionally, were acquitted by the courts or had served their sentence.[51] And the role of ASOFERWA in the Gitagata centre and prisons has already been discussed in some detail in Chapter 5. As will be recalled, it was extremely difficult for domestic NGOs (or indeed any organisation in Rwanda) to promote the rights of alleged *génocidaires* (including minors) given the political situation, and over time increasing restrictions were placed on NGO activities.

6.2 UNICEF's Involvement with Child *Génocidaires*

6.2.1 *Child* Génocidaires*: An Unprecedented Undertaking*

UNICEF first became involved with the issue of child *génocidaires* in November 1994 after international observers visited prisons and reported that children were amongst those detained. Dealing with child *génocidaires* was a first for Rwanda, for UNICEF and for the international community as a whole. As will be recalled, whilst UNICEF's remit had included children in especially difficult circumstances (CEDC) from the mid-1980s, the accent had been on other vulnerable children rather than children in conflict with the law. Indeed, it was UNICEF's involvement with child genocide suspects in Rwanda that 'brought to the fore' UNICEF's 'relatively new' approach to juvenile justice.[52] As a result, 'there were no "institutional" guidelines to which reference could readily be made'.[53] Children in detention also did not fall within the remit of the

[49] CLADHO 1995.
[50] CLADHO 1997 and 1998.
[51] See various reports by LIPRODHOR. Confirmed by Rwandan Human Rights Lawyer, Skype interview, 29 August 2013. Note that LIPRODHOR frequently drew attention to the relevant provisions of the CRC in its reports.
[52] UNICEF 2002: 121.
[53] Cantwell 1997: 77.

agreements initially signed between UNICEF and the Rwandan government.[54] Cantwell reports that, after discovering the existence of children in Kigali prison, UNICEF Rwanda debated 'whether or not it should work in this sphere … and if so, how'.[55] Additional complicating factors were the lack of any functioning judicial system and the social context, UNICEF Rwanda noting that society's perception of child suspects would circumscribe UNICEF's 'amplitude of movement'.[56]

UNICEF Rwanda thus had no legal precedents or other resources to consult and no expertise within the organisation yet was faced with the prospect of working with a government (that had adopted a maximalist approach to accountability) to protect the rights of children perceived by the community as culpable of heinous crimes affecting the entire nation. UNICEF Rwanda, however, took up the challenge. In the absence of capacity on the part of the government and the lack of a strong, independent civil society, UNICEF Rwanda's involvement in matters pertaining to minors in the justice and penitentiary systems was significant (Matthes referred to it as 'unprecedented'[57]). It worked very closely with the Rwandan government, cooperating also with other international actors, as well as local NGOs, on specific projects. Given the lack of formal institutional guidance, it was mainly through the individual initiative of UNICEF Rwanda staff within the 'child protection' programme (which included children in conflict with the law) that approaches and policies were developed and implemented.[58]

The CRC was central to UNICEF Rwanda's approach. Whilst for NGOs working on child rights in Rwanda the CRC was 'almost universally the *sine qua non* of their mission statement and programme justification', in practice, the impact of the CRC on their work varied.[59] For UNICEF Rwanda, however, the CRC constituted the 'guiding principle' and framework for all its programmes on CEDC (i.e. including child *génocidaires*).[60]

[54] Ibid.: 86. Note that the Government of Rwanda and UNICEF had entered into a Basic Cooperation Agreement in December 1993. UNICEF's support to Rwanda was wide-reaching, child protection being just one of its programmes.

[55] Cantwell 1997: 86.

[56] UNICEF Rwanda 1996a: 2.

[57] Matthes 1996b: 3.

[58] According to former UNICEF Rwanda Child Protection Staff Member A (interview, 15 October 2014), the lack of institutional memory continued to be an issue, given the turnover of staff and lack of documentation.

[59] Cantwell 1997: 74.

[60] UNICEF Rwanda 1996b: 16. See also Cantwell 1997: 77.

It was used as 'a tool for planning, implementing and monitoring child protection programmes', and making the CRC 'a reality' for children was 'at the centre' of UNICEF Rwanda's programming.[61]

As discussed in some detail in Chapter 3, UNICEF had adopted the CRC as the basis for all of its activities in the mid-1990s, around the exact time that UNICEF Rwanda became involved with child *génocidaires*. At the operational country level, UNICEF's interventions aim at enhancing a state's implementation of, and compliance with, the CRC. However, whilst the CRC clearly provides the framework, Cantwell asserts that UNICEF should not engage in an 'ideological' campaign on children's rights: governments should be allowed to navigate their own way in achieving compliance with the CRC.[62] Arguably this includes the decision on whether or not to hold minors accountable. Petty and Brown comment that child rights agencies should not 'pass judgment' on the extent to which children committed war crimes voluntarily or on personal culpability. Rather, agencies should 'monitor and promote action on the part of national authorities that is in accordance with … international standards … and promote the reintegration of children by giving them the skills and motivation to join mainstream society'.[63] As illustrated in Chapter 5, the Rwandan government's decision to prosecute all those responsible for genocide resulted in the arrest, and subsequent prosecution, of minors. UNICEF Rwanda, becoming involved with the issue of child *génocidaires* after discovering minors already in detention, worked within this overall approach, seeking to steer Rwanda into greater compliance with international standards. However, as will be illustrated in the next section, the post-conflict situation presented UNICEF with significant challenges in how best to operationalise the CRC, particularly as regards detention.

As will be recalled, the CRC has a holistic nature, all rights being interrelated and being applicable to all children (including those in detention) at all times. In addition to the CRC, some of the non-binding child rights instruments deal exclusively with children in conflict with the law, and these were also utilised by UNICEF Rwanda. The next section will provide a brief overview of UNICEF Rwanda's interventions that draws together, and adds to, the references made throughout Chapter 5 to UNICEF Rwanda's contributions. It will then focus on

[61] UNICEF Rwanda 1996c: 4 and 23.

[62] Cantwell 1997: 78.

[63] Petty and Brown 1998b: 107.

a number of interventions on specific issues that exemplify UNICEF Rwanda's approach.

6.2.2 UNICEF Rwanda's Interventions

After identifying child perpetrators as an issue requiring a response, UNICEF Rwanda established a joint project with MINIJUST in 1995[64] with the aims of enhancing 'enforcement' of the CRC by ensuring that the rights of children in conflict with the law were protected and by assisting with their reintegration into the community. The project's objectives targeted detention conditions, judicial and legal issues and community-based actions.[65] Over the following years, UNICEF Rwanda undertook a number of activities working towards these objectives, including: providing a consultant to draft rules and regulations for children in detention on the basis of the Havana Rules;[66] providing support to NGOs to train prison directors on child rights; monitoring detention conditions; building or reconstructing facilities for the re-education of children under 14 and for the detention of those aged 14 to 18; identifying the under-14s in prisons and *cachots* and requesting their transfer to re-education centres; providing supplies, education and psychosocial activities to children in detention; advocating for minors' benches within the formal courts and training minors' judges and court clerks; advocating for the acceleration of juvenile trials and training IPJs and prosecutors to deal specifically with juvenile cases; providing legal assistance to juveniles; monitoring trials before the formal courts; advocating for the release of minors held without formal charge; assisting with the community reintegration of the under-14s; and conducting or assisting with community sensitisation and social mobilisation.[67] Much of this work took place before the introduction of the *gacaca* system.

In relation to the *gacaca* jurisdictions, UNICEF Rwanda advocated for an express minimum age of criminal responsibility in the Gacaca Laws; for the provision of legal assistance to minors; for minors to be prioritised before the *gacaca* courts; for minors to do community service appropriate to their age (as opposed to remaining in detention); for training

[64] The MINIJUST/UNICEF Children in Conflict with the Law Project.

[65] UNICEF Rwanda 1995a.

[66] The end product is Matthes 1997a and 1997b. See section 6.2.2b.

[67] See MINIJUST and UNICEF Rwanda 1997a; UNICEF Rwanda 2000; van Krieken 2000: 7–9.

to be provided to *gacaca* judges on child rights; and for a handbook to be produced for paralegals to be able to explain the *gacaca* process to minors.[68] Its interventions during this phase were thus more advocacy-based, although it was also involved in community sensitisation, in which key child rights were explained to local communities.[69] However, whilst the Gacaca Laws explicitly provided for a minimum age of criminal responsibility of 14, the other recommendations do not appear to have been taken on board (although community service was introduced ultimately as a partial sentence for most genocide offenders).[70] Further, once the *gacaca* courts started operating, UNICEF Rwanda's involvement with child perpetrators appears to have diminished. A child protection staff member suggested that this was because child protection was not (and, in this person's view, is still not) a priority for UNICEF.[71] However, it is also possible that UNICEF Rwanda's attention shifted to other matters, given that genocide minors would have been over 25 when tried by *gacaca* and given the competing priorities facing UNICEF Rwanda.[72] Further, another UNICEF Rwanda staff member's personal view was that, once *gacaca* began to be rolled out, the government did not 'give us the space to do much other than being interested'.[73]

a Institutionalisation of Child Genocide Suspects

Perhaps the most contentious of UNICEF Rwanda's decisions, and one which would have an impact on its overall approach to child *génocidaires*, was to support the institutionalisation of children. This decision was not made lightly, one commentator referring to the 'soul-searching' that went on within UNICEF Rwanda,[74] and was made only after careful

[68] Interview with former UNICEF Rwanda Child Protection Staff Member A, 15 October 2014. See also PAPG 2003: 19.

[69] Interview with former UNICEF Rwanda Child Protection Staff Member A, 15 October 2014; Skype interview with former UNICEF Rwanda Programme Officer, 31 October 2014.

[70] A 'Master Plan of Operations' for 2001–2006 (Government of Rwanda and UNICEF Rwanda 2001: 13) indicated that the government's intention was to prioritise juvenile cases before *gacaca* jurisdictions but, as explained in section 5.2.2c, they were not prioritised over all other categories of defendants.

[71] Interview with former UNICEF Rwanda Child Protection Staff Member A, 15 October 2014.

[72] On this, see section 7.6.

[73] Skype interview with former UNICEF Rwanda Child Protection Staff Member B, 19 November 2014. Former UNICEF Rwanda Staff Member B (Skype interview, 20 October 2014) also referred to the government as 'very much in control' of the process.

[74] Cantwell 1997: 91.

consideration of the potential consequences of supporting institutionalisation or of insisting on the release or other treatment of child suspects.

As will be recalled, the CRC provides that a child must not be unlawfully or arbitrarily deprived of liberty, that detention or imprisonment (both pre-trial and post-conviction) of a child is 'a measure of last resort' and must be for the 'shortest appropriate period of time', and that alternatives to institutional care should be available for children to be 'dealt with in a manner appropriate to their well-being and proportionate both to their circumstances and the offence'. Additionally, for children under a state's minimum age of criminal responsibility, the CRC Committee commented, albeit in 2007 and thus some time after the genocide, that 'special protective measures' may be taken if necessary in the child's best interests.

Upon finding minors in detention (including non-responsible children), UNICEF Rwanda considered how best to approach the issue, including whether to advocate for the release and non-pursuance of all children or whether to prioritise the under-14s in discussions with the government. Toole reported that, initially, UNICEF Rwanda had discussed with the government not holding children under 18 criminally responsible, but the discussions 'fell flat'.[75] UNICEF Rwanda therefore focused on ensuring that the existing age categories under Rwandan law were applied in practice (given that the age of criminal responsibility was in compliance with international norms) and on the practical implementation of international standards.

UNICEF Rwanda's conceptual starting point, based on the CRC, was that no minors should be in detention. The initial emphasis was on the removal of the under-14s from prisons and *cachots*, UNICEF Rwanda doing 'a lot of lobbying' with the government for their release.[76] However, the government's response was that they would not be safe. UNICEF Rwanda initially thought the government was 'stalling',[77] but then became cognisant of the 'enormous' risk of revenge attacks against these children[78] and, in the interests of getting the children out of the prisons, agreed

[75] Skype interview with Toole, 16 May 2013.

[76] Ibid.

[77] Ibid.

[78] UNICEF Rwanda 1995c: 6. Former Judicial Defender B (Skype interview, 28 August 2013) commented that, whether or not a child had participated in the genocide, once in prison on suspicion of participating, the child would be labelled a '*génocidaire*' and thus at risk of revenge attacks if simply released.

to placing them in a re-education centre. The study by the SCF-USA corroborated this decision and reinforced UNICEF's approach to institutionalisation. There was also the problem that many of these children did not have a family to return to, family members having been killed, imprisoned or having fled Rwanda. For those that did, they risked rejection.[79] Additionally, as highlighted by the SCF-USA study, it was clear that the release of these children would engender a feeling of impunity. Even though the under-14s could not be held criminally responsible, there was still the view that they would need to be held accountable 'in some way or another' and go through some process, given the nature of the crime and to 'give the community or the survivors the feeling that some justice was done'.[80] The perception was that, unless children were judged and found to be innocent, the victims and broader society would see any release as unjust, 'impunity' being granted to murderers.[81] There was also the perceived need to protect the community from 'additional dangers' that the return of the child might pose,[82] as well as the requirement to provide appropriate educational measures and psychosocial support to rehabilitate the children, given the ideological basis of these crimes and the trauma that they had experienced after being encouraged, pressured or coerced into committing extreme acts of violence.[83]

The decision was thus taken to support the restoration of a re-education centre for the under-14s (Gitagata) and secure the transfer of the children to this facility, where they would receive rehabilitation and support and where steps would be taken (including community sensitisation) to facilitate their reintegration. As for the over-14s, the same challenges were present and, given the deplorable detention conditions, 'UNICEF decided to directly support the rehabilitation of detention facilities – something that

[79] Interview with ASOFERWA Staff Member B, 27 September 2013; UNICEF Rwanda 1997d: 87.

[80] Skype interview with Castrogiovanni, 21 August 2013. Castrogiovanni asserts that, in any jurisdiction where a child under the age of criminal responsibility commits a serious crime, alternative measures must be found to ensure there is some accountability.

[81] UNICEF Rwanda 1995c: 6.

[82] Interviews with Castrogiovanni, 28 November 2013 (Skype); former ASOFERWA Staff Member A, 24 September 2013. A Rwandan Human Rights Lawyer (Skype interview, 29 August 2013) commented that the threat to society was the main argument advanced for the institutionalisation of the under-14s in Gitagata; he did not recall the risk to their security being raised as an argument.

[83] This was the view of former ASOFERWA Staff Member A (interview, 24 September 2013); ASOFERWA Staff Member B (interview, 27 September 2013); Castrogiovanni (Skype interview, 21 August 2013). See also UNICEF Rwanda 1995c: 8; 1997d: 86.

had not been done in the past'.[84] The focus was thus on improving detention conditions by restoring or building minors' wings in existing prisons so as to separate minors as much as possible from adults, providing activities in detention to facilitate reintegration (see below) and accelerating the processing of minors' cases.

Alternatives to institutional care were considered by UNICEF Rwanda but ruled out at that time. Although one of UNICEF Rwanda's objectives in 1995 had been to advocate for community service for juveniles in lieu of detention, given the gravity of the crime, the hostility of the community to these children and the lack of infrastructure, it felt unable to push for such alternatives.[85] Castrogiovanni pointed to the distinction between minor and very serious crimes, commenting that even in a 'normal' context (i.e. not post-genocide) if a child was accused of a very serious crime, it might be difficult to find an alternative to detention, such as a placement in a foster family or in a small 'open' home, as this would require both resources and a receptive community. Whilst hesitant to conclude that institutionalisation can ever be in a child's best interest, she emphasised that alternative measures require a sophisticated social welfare system if 'the best alternative care' is to be provided, but that these services cannot be provided in a 'vacuum', such as was prevailing in Rwanda.[86] Later, UNICEF Rwanda advocated for community work for juveniles in the context of discussions on the *gacaca* jurisdictions, but it does not appear that juveniles were treated any differently than other *génocidaires* in this regard.

Toole spoke of the 'internal churning' coming to the decision not to press for the release of minors. He noted the concern that building facilities could result in more people (including children) being arrested, and that a separate facility might make it easier to justify longer internment and facilitate recruitment of child soldiers if conflict re-ignited. He also stressed that UNICEF Rwanda 'felt and knew' detention was wrong, but that 'we struggled to find the best way forward and did what we could in the very tough context'.[87] A newspaper reporting in 1997 referred to the dilemma faced by UNICEF Rwanda: 'It is a bitter first for humanitarian groups known for feeding and schooling children, not jailing them. But

[84] UNICEF Rwanda 1996c: 29–30.
[85] See e.g. UNICEF Rwanda 1997d: 86 (noting that Rwandan public opinion did not accept the use of re-educative measures given the seriousness of the crimes).
[86] Skype interview with Castrogiovanni, 28 November 2013.
[87] Personal correspondence with Toole, 25 September 2014.

after fierce internal debate, UNICEF officials decided they had no legal or moral grounds to seek blanket amnesty for minors accused of crimes against humanity.'[88]

The Rwandan context necessitated a different approach for minors accused of genocidal acts than for those accused of ordinary crimes, in respect of whom de-institutionalisation would ordinarily be promoted. For most cases involving ordinary crimes, 'deprivation of liberty will not be necessary to secure criminal proceedings, or to protect witnesses or the general public' and, in the absence of state-run facilities other than prisons, it was recommended that juveniles accused of less serious ordinary crimes be released on condition that they were housed in an approved NGO-run centre.[89] In respect of child genocide suspects, however, even though their rights had been clearly violated by their prolonged detention without any arrest warrant or court order, advocating for their immediate release was not an option. This was due to the severity of the crimes as well as the political climate.[90] In such circumstances, UNICEF Rwanda could best fulfil its role under the CRC by separating children from adults such that they could be provided with the programmes and support that would facilitate their prospective reintegration into society, and by providing assistance to the justice system, so as to enhance procedural guarantees and ensure respect for the minimum age of criminal responsibility.[91]

The decision of UNICEF Rwanda to support the institutionalisation of both the under-14s and the 14–18-year-old suspects was not without controversy: within UNICEF, the broader human rights community and Rwandan society. In UNICEF Rwanda, there was 'deep disagreement', some local staff being opposed to helping anyone accused of genocide, including child *génocidaires* whom they found difficult to perceive as still being children.[92] From a more substantive perspective, Torres spoke of UNICEF's general policy not to get involved with detention centres: as a matter of principle, UNICEF considers that it should not participate in the detention of minors (i.e. in terms of reconstructing or providing materials to detention facilities), as this is perceived as 'contributing' to their detention and thus could undermine UNICEF's reputation as a child protection

88 Drogin 1997. See also Matloff 1997.
89 Matthes 1997a: 10–12.
90 See Matthes 1996b: 7.
91 See Chorlton 1996: 42; UNICEF Rwanda 1996c: 29.
92 Skype interview with Toole, 16 May 2013.

agency. The perception was, at least initially, that UNICEF wanted no involvement with detention centres: 'It was completely no-go.'[93] There was also concern that donors would not be supportive.[94] Torres considered, however, that there was a 'moral imperative' to take the position he and others in UNICEF Rwanda adopted. In his view, it is necessary to 'start being pragmatic at some point' and look at something objectively rather than persisting with one organisational policy 'when it results in denying support to children in grave danger to their health, growth and development: it's really about basic human rights'.[95] Castrogiovanni similarly felt that getting involved with improving detention conditions was not 'going in the direction of typical UNICEF work', but given the appalling detention conditions and the impossibility of advocating for outright release of the children back into society, 'something needed to be done'.[96] Indeed, UNICEF Rwanda argued in 1996 that, based on the CRC and other international standards, it had the responsibility 'within its mandate' to contribute to improving detention conditions where immediate release was not viable, whilst remaining cognisant both of the need to reintegrate children as quickly as possible and of not weakening UNICEF's worldwide efforts towards de-institutionalisation. In exceptional circumstances, such as prevailed in Rwanda, failure to take such action was seen as potentially contrary to the best interests of these children, who were at severe risk of abuse, neglect and exploitation. UNICEF Rwanda further, and correctly, asserted that detention is not contrary to the CRC.[97]

Toole, whilst not remembering any specific 'opposition', did recall UNICEF Rwanda's concern that they would face this, and thus took measures to ensure they had 'strong buy-in' from the top. This included, for example, taking high-level visitors from UNICEF headquarters to prisons to see the conditions children were held in, before informing them that UNICEF Rwanda had decided, as a consequence, to construct alternative facilities.[98] Cantwell also referenced the concerns of some in UNICEF that the Rwandan office was taking too much of a micro rather than macro approach in becoming involved with children in prison: 'To

[93] Interview with Torres, 28 September 2013.

[94] See e.g. Drogin 1997 (citing concerns raised by Torres regarding donors' perception of the decision to build minors' wings).

[95] Telephone interview with Torres, 16 April 2013. See also Matloff 1997 (citing similar arguments from Torres at the time).

[96] Skype interview with Castrogiovanni, 28 November 2013.

[97] UNICEF Rwanda 1996d: 20.

[98] Personal correspondence with Toole, 25 September 2014.

this day, there are still murmurs … in some quarters of the agency that … UNICEF was overstepping its mandate and spending undue amounts on a few hundred children.' He commented that, given its inexperience in this area, UNICEF Rwanda could have successfully (and justifiably in the eyes of many) avoided the issue, but this would have constituted an 'unconscionable step backwards'. Instead, UNICEF Rwanda '[t]o its considerable credit … took the plunge with, overall, a probably satisfactory outcome'.[99]

There was also external opposition from NGOs, Torres remembering 'an extremely negative reaction' to what UNICEF Rwanda was trying to do. Only one NGO (Médecins Sans Frontières Belgium) was initially on board and willing to assist with the Gitagata project.[100] Some NGOs were critical of UNICEF for assisting with the reconstruction of Gitagata, seeing it as a prison, and thus considering institutionalisation in Gitagata to be a violation of the best interests of the child.[101] Others were in favour of separating children from adults in prisons but were concerned about the government's view if they were seen to provide support to persons accused of genocide.[102] An expatriate ASF lawyer who visited the Gitagata centre in 1998 questioned what UNICEF was doing, given the conditions that the children were being held in, believing them to have been effectively abandoned and also questioning their 'rehabilitation' which she considered somewhat haphazard.[103] It would appear, however, that even those who were opposed to institutionalisation were not coming up with any concrete alternative proposals.[104]

As regards Rwandan society, the arguments here were not about safeguarding the rights of child *génocidaires* but about respect for victims' (including child victims') rights. As previously noted, some in UNICEF considered that the focus on child *génocidaires* was unjustifiable given their small number. The feeling was much stronger amongst the Rwandan population. There was resentment towards organisations perceived as providing a lot of assistance to *génocidaires* rather than to victims and

[99] Cantwell 1997: 91–92.
[100] Telephone interview with Torres, 16 April 2013.
[101] UNICEF Rwanda 1995c: 6.
[102] Ibid.
[103] Doulliez 1998b: 18.
[104] Confirmed by former UNICEF Rwanda Programme Officer (Skype interview, 31 October 2014).

survivors.[105] Specifically in relation to the under-14s, there was resentment at the attention, funding and support that Gitagata received from donors and international actors, the perception being that the needs of other children, not implicated in the genocide, were being overlooked. Many were against these children being housed in separate installations and having what was perceived as a fairly comfortable lifestyle given that they were considered guilty of genocide and thus deserved to be punished severely.[106] For some, a period spent in Gitagata fell short of dealing adequately with the alleged crimes, it being 'like you did nothing'.[107] Castrogiovanni spoke of the difficulty in devising programmes that would do justice both to children who had allegedly committed genocide-related crimes and to victims.[108] The opening of a school at Gitagata, attended by local children as well as Gitagata residents, was hoped, to some extent, to mitigate the perception of these children being granted preferential treatment as well as promote social reintegration.[109]

Placing the under-14s in re-education centres and improving the detention conditions of the over-14s by building or restoring minors' wings was considered to be the most appropriate way of balancing the different interests, whilst also working within the framework of the CRC, in the particular context. Cantwell's 1997 study of UNICEF Rwanda's approach remains a valuable and, in my view, accurate evaluation. He considered that the decision to send the under-14s to Gitagata was an 'excellent example' of the application of the best interests principle in determining how to implement the rights of a particular group of children. Given the perceived risk to their personal security, as well as the need to 'prepare'

[105] A former Executive Secretary of a Survivors' Organisation (interviews, Kigali, 21 February 2013 and 5 September 2013) spoke of such resentment as did Judge J (interview, 4 October 2013). See also sections 4.2.1 and 4.2.3; LIPRODHOR 1999c: 33. To put this in context, based on a report by MINIJUST and UNICEF Rwanda (1997b: 2–3), approximately 300,000 children were killed during the genocide and 120,000 were orphaned with many more unaccompanied children living in centres, foster families or child-headed households.

[106] See Cantwell 1997: 49; Chorlton 1996: 45; Hackel 1995; Matloff 1997 (reporting that the Gitagata children 'live better than some free Rwandans'). Note that Shepler (2005) reported similar findings in Sierra Leone where some local people expressed annoyance at 'rebel children' receiving food and school fees from the international community whilst many community members struggled to survive without such aid.

[107] Interview with a former Executive Secretary of a Survivors' Organisation, 21 February 2013.

[108] Skype interview with Castrogiovanni, 21 August 2013.

[109] See Chorlton 1996: 44–45; Matthes 1997a: 13.

them for their return to society, 'it was deemed to be in their best interests that their right not to be held criminally responsible be given effect in this manner'.[110] He mooted: 'Whatever the age of criminal responsibility, no country would allow children accused of a serious crime simply to return to the outside world without any form of treatment or follow-up.'[111] The approach was thus also in line with community interests. However, whilst largely supportive, he expressed concerns that the 'full child rights ramifications of the use of "protective custody" for these children have not been thought through in sufficient depth' and raised concerns regarding the publicity Gitagata attracted.[112] As regards the rehabilitation or construction of minors' wings in existing prisons (the aim being to separate those aged 14–18 from adult detainees), Cantwell asserted that, whilst this might at first glance be seen as 'running diametrically counter to the treaty's [CRC's] philosophy', the policy was in fact inspired by the CRC.[113] He suggested that, given that it was likely that many juveniles would later be convicted of genocidal acts and possibly sentenced to long custodial sentences, UNICEF Rwanda's involvement to improve conditions in advance might be considered more reasonable than reacting at that later stage.[114]

The emphasis in the CRC and the related instruments is on alternatives to detention, but the CRC does not prohibit custodial measures being imposed on children:[115] detention should be a measure of last resort. Whilst there were significant problems in the Gitagata centre and also in prisons, UNICEF Rwanda's actions must be considered in light of the prevailing conditions and context of the time. Having gone through the various options open to it, UNICEF Rwanda came to the conclusion that institutionalisation was the best option for these children. In my view, it thus appears that detention was, in effect, the 'last resort' in this case, at least in the first few years after the genocide. Whilst the majority of minors were arrested and detained in violation of procedures (a breach of international and domestic law), UNICEF Rwanda considered that demanding an immediate release was not appropriate; meaningful progress could be

[110] Cantwell 1997: 23.
[111] Ibid.: 48–49.
[112] Ibid.: 49.
[113] Ibid.: 35.
[114] Ibid.: 50. In the event, many minors were kept in detention without trial for many years.
[115] Indeed, various other provisions of the CRC stipulate what treatment should be accorded to children deprived of their liberty, and the Havana Rules that deal specifically with juveniles in detention were adopted after the entry into force of the CRC.

made only incrementally. UNICEF Rwanda came to its decision by the application of the best interests principle: paradoxically, detention was largely being used as a protective measure for these children and to assist with their reintegration (particularly in respect of the under-14s). It is arguable that, over time, some of the challenges diminished. Possibly the greatest challenge facing the government and UNICEF Rwanda was the perceived security risk to the children. The general perception was that, over time, society became more receptive to the releases and the risk of revenge attacks thus declined. It is possible that, at some stage – although it is difficult to pinpoint when – UNICEF Rwanda could have pushed more forcefully for the provisional release of juveniles in prisons,[116] for open facilities, or for alternatives to detention (noting, of course, the resource implications of such facilities and alternatives). This would have been more in line with the emphasis in the CRC on the rehabilitation of juveniles. As outlined earlier, UNICEF Rwanda did advocate for those who had been minors during the genocide to do community service when discussions were taking place on *gacaca*. However, it appears that minors did not benefit from any preferential treatment in this regard. Further, as regards UNICEF Rwanda, it seems that by this time and for whatever reason, other areas of child protection had taken priority.[117]

b Conditions of Detention

Having taken the decision to support institutionalisation, UNICEF Rwanda then sought to improve the conditions within which children were detained. The CRC provides that children must be separated from adults in detention facilities, unless it is considered in the child's best interest not to do so. Also, given the holistic nature of the CRC, children in detention retain other rights, including the right to education and healthcare. These rights are fleshed out in the non-binding instruments, in particular the Havana Rules.

Castrogiovanni, who visited prisons first on behalf of UNHRFOR and then UNICEF Rwanda, commented that it was impossible to move those aged over 14 into separate facilities.[118] It was for this reason that UNICEF Rwanda took the decision to restore or build minors' wings within existing

[116] It seems that children at the Gitagata centre were generally released at the earliest opportunity following an assessment of the child's readiness for release and the receptiveness of the family/community.

[117] On this, see section 7.6.

[118] Skype interview with Castrogiovanni, 21 August 2013.

prisons to house juveniles, which (as discussed above) proved to be contentious. Toole commented that he would 'probably go down in history as the only UNICEF representative to have ever built a child prison' but felt that the only way to protect children, given the horrific prison conditions, was to physically separate them.[119]

As previously discussed, many genocide minors turned 18 whilst in pre-trial detention. Given the particular context – the overwhelming number of prisoners and extremely harsh conditions – UNICEF Rwanda advocated for the continued separation from adults of these detainees on the basis that it would be in their best interests, both in terms of being protected from abuse and harsh conditions and having access to reintegration activities. It remained cognisant, however, of the need to balance the interests of these now adults with the interests of younger children, noting that there could be a need for further separation where resources allowed.[120] This approach was predicated on the Havana Rules and the CRC which allow for the detention of juveniles with those aged over 18 if it is in the formers' best interest. It was suggested that, where keeping the under-18s and those who had turned 18 together was the only alternative to mixing the latter with adults, it was in the interests of the under-18s as they too would benefit from this policy once they reached 18. This approach preceded by some years the CRC Committee's explicit recommendation that, whilst there is no requirement to retain separation for those reaching 18, it should be made possible where it is in that person's best interests and is not contrary to the best interests of the younger children in the facility. As established in Chapter 5, in practice, there was no uniform approach, it largely depending on the prison as to whether separation was maintained for the over-18s. However, it would appear that UNICEF Rwanda's advocacy did leave some impression: participants at a workshop held in 1998 to discuss 'Model Internal Regulations for Minors' Wings based on the United Nations Rules for the Protection of Juveniles Deprived of their Liberty' agreed that genocide minors over 18 should remain with juveniles in separate facilities from adults and suggested that the term 'youth wing' be used instead of 'minors' wing' to reflect this.[121]

As regards other rights of children in detention, UNICEF Rwanda engaged a legal consultant to prepare draft 'Rules and Regulations for

[119] Skype interview with Toole, 16 May 2013.

[120] See Cantwell 1997: 50; Matthes 1997a: 5 and 18–21(who recommended separation of such detainees up to the age of 24). See also HRW 2003a: 35–36.

[121] Referenced in Biseruka 1999: 25.

Children, Juveniles and Adolescents in Rwanda'. In the introduction to his report, the consultant referred to the need to be 'realistic' when considering the implementation of international standards. He added:

> To just put standards in writing that are probably too high given the Rwandan detention reality and the resources available is not to *implement* them. *Implementation* is achieved when standards are actually being applied, which will only be the case if they are somewhat realistic. Thus, without compromising the principles, concessions will have to be made in order to make the feasible possible.[122]

In the preface to his second report that contained the draft standard rules, the consultant noted that, whilst the Havana Rules were used as the foundation, some of the recommendations were not incorporated directly on the basis that 'they did not seem appropriate in the context of the Rwandan detention reality' or because they were too verbose to use as practical rules.[123] Further, many of the standards were adapted to fit the Rwandan context. For example, Rule 38 of the Havana Rules stipulates that education should be provided outside the place of detention wherever possible, but in any event by qualified teachers. The equivalent draft Rule 18 provides that children should receive education from qualified teachers 'where available', and draft Rule 21 refers to the use of qualified detainees from adult facilities where teachers cannot be recruited from outside the prison. As the reader will recall, UNICEF Rwanda supported education projects, in which detainees were often used as teachers. Similar adaptations were made to the rule relating to healthcare.[124] In relation to discipline, Rule 71 of the Havana Rules provides that juveniles should not be responsible for disciplinary functions except in the supervision of specified social, educational or sports activities. Draft Rule 32 adapts this to allow for the selection of a leader within a group of 20–30 detainees who could admonish verbally other detainees. This is to reflect the particular prison structure in Rwanda, in which prisoners themselves play a key role in the day-to-day running of the prison. In some cases, the Havana Rules were expanded. For example, Rule 60 provides for 'regular and frequent visits' from family, but draft Rule 29 specifies that individual visits should not be shorter than 10 minutes and the total length per month should

[122] Matthes 1997a: 1 (original emphasis).

[123] Matthes 1997b: 3.

[124] Rule 49, Havana Rules stipulates that medical care should be provided in the local community where possible; draft Rule 25 refers to medical care 'inside the facility'.

be at least one hour. The draft rule also provides for visits by relatives detained in adult sections of the same facility. This is to reflect the context, in that prison visits were generally extremely brief, and members of the same family were often detained for genocide crimes. As mentioned above, a workshop was held in 1998 on regulations for minors' wings. Although it has not been possible to determine the outcome of this workshop (which was intended to formalise a set of model rules), it nonetheless indicates that UNICEF Rwanda's outputs were shaping discussions amongst key stakeholders.

In drafting the Rules and Regulations, the consultant clearly took note of the particular conditions prevailing in Rwanda, which is in compliance with Rule 16 of the Havana Rules that requires the rules to be implemented in 'the context of the economic, social and cultural conditions prevailing in each Member State'. It was impractical, even impossible, for children to receive education or medical care from outside the prison, partly given the administrative implications, but also given that many professionals had either been targeted during the genocide or were imprisoned themselves. The pragmatic solution was thus to work with the structures in place when drafting the rules.

c Reintegration

An overarching principle of the CRC (and the related non-binding instruments) is the requirement for juvenile justice systems to promote the reintegration of a child who comes into conflict with the law. In addition to the requirement to provide care, treatment and education or vocational training (all of which facilitate a return to society), the Havana Rules expressly stipulate that juveniles should be provided with special services to assist with their return to society and to 'lessen prejudice' against them.[125]

A former coordinator of the MINIJUST/UNICEF Children in Conflict with the Law Project observed that, due to the 'high level of sensitivity' of genocide cases, the reintegration of children accused of participating in the genocide (including those under the age of criminal responsibility) was significantly challenging.[126] UNICEF Rwanda appears to have been involved in the reintegration of the under-14s much more than the over-14s. Most of the former attended the

[125] Rule 80.

[126] Skype interview with former MINJUST/UNICEF Project Coordinator B, 19 February 2014.

Gitagata centre and were either released on an *ad hoc* basis or *en masse* after attending solidarity camps supported by UNICEF Rwanda. Less detailed interventions were undertaken in respect of the over-14s, who again were either released on an *ad hoc* basis or after attending solidarity camps with which UNICEF Rwanda does not appear to have been involved.

Castrogiovanni recalled discussions with NGOs and donors about reintegrating the under-14s, in particular a debate on whether re-education centres should be closed or open centres. The initial approach was to argue in favour of an open centre, in line with detention as a last resort and to facilitate community integration, and of returning the children as soon as possible back to the community. However, she commented: 'Then we realised that none of these things was actually possible in the aftermath of the genocide.'[127] The compromise struck was to support a centre that, although nominally 'open' was in practice 'closed' (in that, although Gitagata was not fenced in, the children were not free to leave) but to open a school that would cater for both Gitagata children and children from the local community to facilitate interaction and subsequent reintegration. Additionally, UNICEF Rwanda supported a reintegration programme in Gitagata that included civic education activities for the children as well as reintegration measures (carried out by ASOFERWA) such as family tracing, mediation between the child and family (and broader community) and community sensitisation. There was then follow-up to evaluate the reintegration.[128]

As regards solidarity camps for the under-14s in 2000 and 2001, it has not been possible to ascertain the extent of UNICEF Rwanda's involvement. HRW reported that UNICEF Rwanda had been informed of the 2001 camp only one week before it took place,[129] and it is thus likely that its support was largely financial. I was unable to find any information on UNICEF Rwanda and the later solidarity camps for minors. For those who remained in prisons and *cachots*, the recommendations and the programmes for education (which would assist with reintegration and subsequent assumption of a 'constructive role in society') were outlined earlier. The project in prisons also provided vocational training and other skills to minors, the aim being to prepare them for life outside, and included sensitisation of communities and follow-up monitoring after

[127] Skype interview with Castrogiovanni, 21 August 2013.

[128] See section 5.3.1 for more details.

[129] HRW 2003a: 30.

reintegration. Given the decision to support institutionalisation, the lack of human resources and the social context, this was considered the most appropriate way of approximating to the requirements of the CRC.

d Child-Specific Procedures and Institutions

Pursuant to Article 40(3) of the CRC, states are required to 'promote the establishment' of juvenile-specific 'laws, procedures, authorities and institutions'. Although not expressly required by the CRC, the CRC Committee recommended (in 2007) that juveniles be tried by specialised courts or, where not immediately possible, by specialised judges.[130]

Before the genocide, there were no juvenile courts or judges in Rwanda. It was one of UNICEF Rwanda's stated objectives to create juvenile courts within the existing judicial system and to introduce special measures compliant with child rights standards into Rwandan law.[131] However given the lack of resources – human, financial and material – as well as a lack of absorptive capacity on the part of the Rwandan government, UNICEF Rwanda had to scale back its designs for a comprehensive juvenile justice system (although see section 7.3). A report from March 1996 referred to the latest draft of the Genocide Law that did not contain any special provisions for minors and suggested that wording be incorporated to provide for juvenile chambers.[132] The report explained that juvenile chambers would only be created if UNICEF Rwanda covered the costs of training judges, their salaries and per diems. It also referred to UNICEF Rwanda's interest in training judges so as to create a 'whole juvenile justice system' that would be capable of dealing with the anticipated rise in juvenile delinquency because of the number of children with social or psychological problems following the genocide. UNICEF Rwanda pushed for separate chambers (and thus implicitly a separate procedure) in discussions with the government, although specifics and practical considerations were not discussed.[133] The result was the inclusion of a provision requiring minors' judges within the Specialised Chambers

[130] CRC Committee 2007a: [93].

[131] Cantwell 1997: 57; UNICEF Rwanda 1995c: 7 (referring to a 'Court of Justice' for minors); UNICEF Rwanda 1995a: 4 and 1996c: 33.

[132] Matthes 1996a. Copies of earlier drafts of the Genocide Law (on file with author) similarly do not have any reference to minors.

[133] Skype interview with Matthes, 28 November 2013.

established to hear genocide cases,[134] which many attribute directly to UNICEF Rwanda's advocacy.[135]

The Genocide Law did not provide for a separate procedure, however, and thus training provided by UNICEF Rwanda to judges and prosecutors focused on providing practical examples of how to apply Rwandan statutory law in accordance with international juvenile justice standards.[136] De Beer, who was involved in providing the training, commented that, although reference was made to international standards, the entry point was very much Rwandan law, given that international standards appeared in many cases unachievable given the context.[137] Nonetheless, judges who took part in the training recalled that, in addition to Rwandan law, the training covered international law (in particular the CRC) and general principles of law relating to minors,[138] and many seemed to internalise some of the main principles, adapting the way in which they approached juvenile trials.[139]

It was thus in this way that UNICEF Rwanda sought to initiate implementation of, and compliance with, this requirement for juvenile-specific institutions and procedures at the trial stage before the formal courts. HRW criticised both UNICEF Rwanda and the government, arguing that the Children in Conflict with the Law Project had failed to 'embark in earnest upon the major task of developing a juvenile justice system', stating that it had launched some initiatives but then suspended them purportedly due to lack of funds but where, allegedly in some cases, MINIJUST had allocated the money to other projects.[140] It further argued that financial resources were not the issue for dealing with minors accused of genocide, citing Gahima in 1996 that '[T]here is plenty of money. People are happy to give money for children.'[141] It has not been possible to substantiate

134 In practice, these benches were operational in some tribunals but not others and did not deal exclusively with juvenile cases. See section 5.2.1b.

135 In addition to UNICEF Rwanda itself claiming that the provision was included as a result of successful lobbying (see e.g. UNICEF Rwanda 1996c: 29 and 1997c: 2), de Beer (interview, 15 October 2014) was also firmly of the view that the provision was included as a result of UNICEF Rwanda's intervention.

136 UNICEF Rwanda 1997b: 2. See section 5.2.1b for further details of the training.

137 Interview with de Beer, 15 October 2014.

138 Interviews with Judge E, 20 September 2013; Judge F, 30 September 2013; Judge G, 1 October 2013; Judge H, 1 October 2013; Judge K, 11 October 2013.

139 See section 5.2.1c and section 7.1.

140 HRW 2003a: 24.

141 Ibid.: 76.

or refute HRW's allegations.[142] However, financial assistance by itself is insufficient: a state's capacity to implement programmes through qualified persons and efficient budgeting is of equal importance. As Torres noted, there was no problem finding funds for children: the problem was finding 'meaningful ways of using these funds' and in short, the government had little capacity to implement projects.[143] Additionally, whilst funding may have been readily available during the emergency phase, once UNICEF Rwanda began to work on medium- and long-term solutions, the funding was scaled down.[144]

Evidently, the legislative provision and subsequent practice falls short of meeting the requirements of the CRC. The criticism can be made that UNICEF Rwanda did not develop or carry through its approach sufficiently, failing to discuss the practical implications of juvenile judges with the government at an early stage and thus failing to secure legal provision for a child-sensitive procedure. And indeed, there were many elements within the trial process itself that contravened fair trial guarantees (including, for example, the right to have the matter heard without delay, the right to privacy and, in some cases, the right to legal assistance). However, given the lack of alternatives available (on the basis that the release of child suspects was considered to be out of the question) and given the significant resource constraints, I would suggest that UNICEF Rwanda at least took some steps towards ensuring implementation of, and compliance with, these international standards for child *génocidaires*. As regards the *gacaca* jurisdictions, UNICEF Rwanda did push for minors to be prioritised before the *gacaca* courts (in addition to advocating for other child rights issues within the *gacaca* process), but there is no evidence to suggest that it recommended a different procedure or different judges, and it does not appear to have been involved in training the *gacaca* judges. However, as argued in section 2.1.2, the position on the applicability of some of the international standards to juveniles who have attained majority by the time of trial is ambiguous. Further, given the experiences of other organisations in Rwanda at this time,[145] it is not clear how much scope UNICEF Rwanda had to engage in the process.

[142] Note that some of UNICEF Rwanda's support did benefit the justice system as a whole, but the underlying aim was to introduce some child-sensitive measures (see section 7.6).

[143] Interview with Torres, 28 September 2013.

[144] Interview with former UNICEF Rwanda Child Protection Staff Member A, 15 October 2014.

[145] See section 4.2.3.

6.3 Conclusion

From an analysis of documents and based on discussions with key stakeholders, it is clear that, whilst many organisations' activities touched on child perpetrators, for most of them this issue was peripheral: child *génocidaires* were just one small category of the many persons under their purview whose rights were at risk. They thus advocated for, and worked on, improving conditions for all those accused of genocide, with children benefiting accordingly.

The CRC Committee, tasked with reviewing compliance with the CRC, raised concerns regarding Rwanda's treatment of child *génocidaires*, but it did not utilise its urgent action procedure and, by the time it came to examine Rwanda's state report in 2004, its recommendations were largely superseded by events. Whilst the HRC did request a special report from Rwanda, the lack of response meant that its observations and recommendations were even longer after the fact than those of the CRC Committee. The role of the UN treaty bodies in realising the rights of child *génocidaires* in the post-conflict context was thus somewhat limited.[146] Other non-operational entities raised (sometimes 'deep') concerns regarding failure to respect international standards and encouraged Rwanda to comply with its commitments. The Special Rapporteur and Special Representative were the most forceful in this regard, pointing to and criticising violations, and it would appear that, at least on one occasion, their advocacy for greater respect of international standards paid off. On the whole, however, their focus was more on raising international awareness of the human rights situation generally and encouraging international assistance.

As for operational actors, given their field presence, they were better able to translate international standards into practice, although as observed, most of their work that pertained to child *génocidaires* was tangential to their overall activities. Those that did engage with the issue frequently relied on the CRC either to support their efforts to improve the situation of child *génocidaires*, or to indicate expressly to the Rwandan government its shortcomings with respect to international standards. The work of ASF, the ICRC, PRI and RCN was frequently acknowledged by research participants as playing a role in Rwanda's response to child

[146] This is in line with O'Flaherty's observation that the value of treaty bodies in post-conflict states exists 'more in potential than in reality'. O'Flaherty 2003: 67.

perpetrators, an NGO staff member commenting that it was through the emphasis by these organisations on 'internationally generally accepted rules' such as the separation of children from adults in prison, that the government began to take measures in prisons.[147]

UNICEF, however, was the main organisation working on child rights generally, and the rights of child *génocidaires* specifically. As referenced earlier, UNICEF's engagement in Rwanda has been described as 'unprecedented', and a local NGO staff member commented that UNICEF Rwanda initially 'did the job themselves' and then worked on building capacity.[148] This type of engagement is not without risk. Cantwell expressed concerns that direct participation in, as opposed to contribution to, the work of the government can create longer term dependency and give external agencies too great an influence.[149] There was also the feeling that UNICEF Rwanda's work was to a large degree substituting initiative that would ideally be the reserve of the government itself or domestic civil society.[150] A further potential risk of significant involvement on the ground in implementing international standards is that it can compromise an organisation's independence as well as the very principles and standards in which its work is grounded. These risks will be revisited in Chapter 8. Given the lack of institutions and groups focusing on juvenile justice in Rwanda, it was considered that there was no real alternative to UNICEF Rwanda's 'direct engagement'.

Having to deal with child genocide suspects in the extreme context of post-genocide Rwanda presented UNICEF with unparalleled challenges. It was the first time in history that children had been accused of genocide. UNICEF Rwanda thus had to grapple with the concept as well as practical implications of criminal and civil responsibility of these children, but also with their 'societal responsibility': these children were perceived by many in the community – not only direct victims – to be culpable of one of humanity's most heinous crimes that had affected the entire country.[151] As Machel would observe in her seminal 1996 report: 'The dilemma of dealing with children who are accused of committing acts of genocide illustrates the complexity of balancing culpability, a community's sense

[147] Interview with NGO Staff Member, 22 February 2013. Former Judicial Defender B (Skype interview, 28 August 2013) made similar comments.

[148] Interview with AJPRODHO Staff Member, 15 February 2013.

[149] Cantwell 1997: 64 and 88.

[150] Matthes 1996b: 3.

[151] UNICEF Rwanda 1996a: 2.

of justice and the "best interests of the child".[152] For UNICEF, it was thus a question of seeking to meet demands (and the need) for social justice whilst remaining within the strictures of child rights law. Further, whilst UNICEF had begun to work on child protection issues in the 1980s, this had not been a priority, and the lack of a clear policy or 'full-fledged organizational stand' meant reliance on 'personal experience and interpretations'.[153] It was against this background that UNICEF Rwanda had to develop its programme, using the CRC as its framework, for child *génocidaires*.

As illustrated in this chapter, UNICEF Rwanda had to adapt its approach to fit the Rwandan context, taking account of perceived risks to personal security, the severity of crimes and the detention reality when operationalising international juvenile justice standards. Additionally, other factors that necessarily had an impact included the Rwandan government's desire to put an end to impunity (which dictated the overall approach to the accountability of child *génocidaires*), society's demands for justice and the lack of resources – financial, material and human. UNICEF Rwanda's approach, in particular its decision to support institutionalisation that then had ramifications for most other aspects of its intervention, was not without criticism, and indeed, as acknowledged, there continued to be significant violations of children's rights. However, it is not clear what alternatives, other than simply releasing the children, could have been advanced, at least in the first few years after the genocide. And, save for the resolutions of the UN General Assembly and Commission on Human Rights (which, by their nature, were not detailed), there is no evidence of other actors calling for the release of child *génocidaires*. In the initial period, the release of the children did not seem an option: UNICEF Rwanda in my view rightly relied upon the best interests principle to assist it in its interpretation of the CRC. Arguably, as time progressed, and UNICEF Rwanda's policy shifted from an emergency response to longer-term considerations, alternatives should have been explored to a greater extent.

As the chapter clearly shows, the decisions UNICEF Rwanda took were not made lightly. Indeed, it was evident from discussions with many people who had worked on juvenile justice that the practical implementation of universal standards presented them with a formidable challenge, both

152 Machel 1996: 250.

153 Cantwell 1997: 77. See also UNICEF Rwanda 1996c: 34.

professionally and personally: they were quite clear what the standards said, but the difficulty was in reconciling these rights with the specific context. Whilst they continued to advocate for the respect of all rights of child perpetrators, it was considered that rights had to be applied contextually. The internal tension was not lost on the Rwandan government, an official who worked closely with UNICEF Rwanda observing its reticence towards institutionalisation of the under-14s but determining that 'it was theoretical reticence that had to give way to the concrete reality. People had to abandon their principles to find solutions to serious problems.'[154] Whether UNICEF Rwanda could be said to have 'abandoned' its principles or compromised the very standards it was seeking to promote, will be addressed in more detail in Chapter 8, which evaluates UNICEF Rwanda's overall approach. However, before that, it is necessary to explore in more detail UNICEF Rwanda's policy and advocacy strategies in seeking to enhance implementation and compliance.

[154] Interview with Nsanzabaganwa, 10 October 2013.

7

UNICEF Rwanda's Policy and Advocacy: A Strategic Approach

In the previous chapter, I provided an account of UNICEF Rwanda's interventions on child *génocidaires*, outlining its general activities before narrowing the analysis to focus on a number of specific areas that illustrate the contextual approach taken. In this chapter, I probe deeper into policy and advocacy approaches, drawing out the strategies and techniques utilised by UNICEF Rwanda when seeking to enhance implementation of, and compliance with, international juvenile justice standards. Drawing on themes that emerged from the empirical data, the strategies and techniques can broadly be categorised as capacity building; sensitising the community; using the existing domestic legal framework; the use of legal and non-legal discourse; capitalising on political will and developing relationships; and offering incentives but making compromises. The first three broadly relate to policy development and implementation, whilst the second three relate more to advocacy approaches (although there is considerable overlap). As I will illustrate, UNICEF Rwanda was very flexible in its approach, adopting a range of strategies and techniques that were considered necessary and appropriate in the given context.

7.1 Capacity Building

The genocide had a devastating impact on all facets of Rwandan society, including the judicial system. Cantwell very accurately describes the Rwandan government, as well as those seeking to assist it (including UNICEF), as having to 'start from zero'.[1] As such, and perhaps to a greater degree than would usually be the case, many of UNICEF Rwanda's activities were directed at developing the capacity of Rwandan institutions and officials to implement and comply with international standards. These focused on overcoming deficiencies in technical knowledge and

[1] Cantwell 1997: 17.

skills, bureaucratic capability, and infrastructural, material and financial resources. UNICEF Rwanda's interventions have been described throughout this book, in particular in Chapter 6, and will not be revisited in detail here; rather, I will highlight some key elements that illustrate capacity-building initiatives.

UNICEF Rwanda provided (or supported the provision of) training programmes on child rights and juvenile justice standards to judges, prosecutors, defence lawyers, law enforcement personnel and prison directors. This included input into the training, coordinating with other actors, identifying experts to deliver the training and providing documentation. A key feature of the training was the practical application of international standards in the domestic context. The immediate objective was to provide Rwandan professionals with the skills and knowledge to deal with child *génocidaires*, although it was also intended that the training would have a longer term, and thus more sustainable, impact on capacity. For example, a stated aim of training judges and court staff was not only for them to work within the Specialised Chambers, but also to invest in the future judicial framework by 'provid[ing] a basis for creating youth courts to ensure the ongoing legal protection of children, not just in penal matters, but for the protection of youth in general'.[2] In practice, some of the minors' judges interviewed for this study who had received the specialised training did continue to be judges (albeit not always in juvenile cases); others however left the judiciary following the extensive judicial reforms of 2004, which introduced new requirements for judges (namely a law degree).[3] Some of those who left did, however, continue to work in the judicial system in another capacity.

In addition to building individual expertise and knowledge, UNICEF Rwanda provided technical advice to key ministries and departments on international standards and law reform (including at the very basic level, copies of relevant treaties and rules). As laid out in Chapter 6, for example, it engaged a legal consultant to provide technical assistance on the formulation of rules for children in prisons. It also assisted the government in establishing a National Commission on Children's and Women's Rights in 1995 (located within the Ministry of the Family and Women's Promotion – MIFAPROFE), which comprised a sub-commission on criminal matters.

[2] UNICEF Rwanda 1997d: 86. See also UNICEF Rwanda 1996d: 14.

[3] Art. 8, Law No. 6 bis/2004 on the Statutes for Judges and Other Judicial Personnel. See also Chapter 4, note 156; Palmer 2015: 92–94.

This sub-commission, composed of government representatives, NGOs, national experts and some UN agencies – including UNICEF – worked on drafting a juvenile justice code that included provision for juvenile courts and special measures for children in conflict with the law.[4] The draft code ultimately was not adopted, and the process stalled. As will be illustrated in section 7.3, although UNICEF Rwanda was advocating for comprehensive legal revision, its focus, particularly in the first few years after the genocide, was on dealing with the emergency situation. However, it is arguable that the process of discussions within ministries on juvenile justice and the various measures that were adopted to deal with children accused of genocide did have a longer-lasting, positive influence on the government's (at least legislative) commitment to children's rights.

UNICEF Rwanda also provided significant financial, logistical and material support after the genocide. This included broad support to re-establish social services and to those working on child rights issues, as well as to institutions involved directly with child *génocidaires*. For example, within the first few weeks of re-establishing its office in Rwanda, UNICEF Rwanda offered financial and material assistance to key ministries for them to restore buildings and obtain basic office supplies and equipment.[5] It also subsequently covered the salary costs of minors' judges as well as Rwandan defence lawyers engaged by the MINIJUST/UNICEF project to provide legal assistance to juveniles before the formal courts. And its involvement in the reconstruction and building of detention facilities has been detailed earlier in this book: in addition to providing funding, UNICEF Rwanda also engaged an architect to oversee the construction process,[6] provided transport for non-responsible minors to the Gitagata Re-education Centre and furnished essential supplies (including food, clothing and beds).[7] In many of these cases, the support provided was unusual and there were concerns of creating dependency. However, given the extreme lack of resources, UNICEF Rwanda considered it essential to

4 Cantwell 1997: 57; UNICEF Rwanda 1996c: 33. Recall comments made in Chapter 6, in text at notes 149 and 150 regarding the risks of direct participation. See Chapter 8 for further discussion.

5 Skype interview with Toole, 16 May 2013. He commented that this was not 'an easy thing' given UNICEF's rules and regulations. See also section 7.6.

6 Seconded by Swiss Disaster Relief (Chorlton 1996: 44; Matthes, Skype interview, 28 November 2013; Perisic, Skype interview, 13 November 2013; Toole, personal correspondence, 25 September 2014).

7 UNICEF Rwanda 1996d: 29–30.

give this assistance, whilst remaining cognisant of the need to create sustainability and national ownership.[8]

Through its engagement with local NGOs, UNICEF Rwanda sought to build the capacity of domestic civil society, as well as create cooperative relationships between the government and such actors. For example, UNICEF Rwanda provided financial assistance and technical support (through SCF)[9] to ASOFERWA, which collaborated with the prison authorities under the 'Protégez-moi' project and with MINITRASO in the Gitagata centre. It also entered into an agreement with CLADHO to undertake trial monitoring. For UNICEF Rwanda, establishing alliances with NGOs and increasing their knowledge of child rights as well as how such rights can be reflected in, and incorporated into, social policies at the local level, was a key means of mobilising local communities to protect against and prevent violations. As Oestreich observes, using the CRC to influence policy does not only happen at the highest levels: efforts are also undertaken at the grassroots level through alliances with NGOs.[10] As illustrated in the next section, a key feature of UNICEF Rwanda's work was community outreach and sensitisation, and it sought to reinforce the work of local NGOs and civil society actors in this process, at the same time as aiming to increase the government's political capacity[11] to implement child-sensitive laws and approaches.

UNICEF Rwanda's approach to capacity building was thus broadly holistic and strategic, in that it sought to encompass those domestic actors, including government institutions, civil society and professionals, who were involved with child *génocidaires*. In many cases, its efforts appear to have had some success: judges and government officials began to use the CRC and other international standards in their work. For example, a judge, who had received training from UNICEF Rwanda on international standards, commented that minors' judges would refer to these standards when coming to a decision on a juvenile's case.[12] Another minors' judge who had also attended the training spoke very enthusiastically about

[8] Ibid.: 15 and 29.

[9] Matthes 1997a: 14–15; UNICEF Rwanda 1997a: 4. In respect of prisons, some of the staff from SCF-USA transferred across to ASOFERWA (e.g. Mukanyangezi, who then went on to work for the National Prisons Service – now the Rwanda Correctional Service).

[10] Oestreich 2007: 52.

[11] Understood in this context as the ability to formulate and implement public policy.

[12] Interview with Judge E, 20 September 2013.

UNICEF Rwanda, reporting that he had felt 'inspired' by the trainings and that, whilst it was difficult to use international law directly, minors' judges tried to implement it 'in spirit' and would always be thinking of the child's best interests.[13] And Murara noted that, as a result of the dissemination of, and training on, the CRC, juvenile judges had started to apply its provisions, referencing a case heard by the Kigali Specialised Chamber in which the judges based their decision on Article 40(3)(a) of the CRC (requiring a minimum age of criminal responsibility) and Article 77 of the Penal Code.[14] Further, documents prepared by ministries included references to child rights and international instruments. For example, the Ministry of Local Government and Social Affairs (MINALOC) expressly referred to the government's concern for respect for child rights and to its efforts, in partnership with UNICEF and ASOFERWA (amongst others), to reintegrate children in the context of the Gitagata and the 'Protégez-moi' projects.[15] And the Ministry of Gender, Family and Social Affairs (MIGEFASO) explicitly acknowledged the importance of the CRC, the Beijing Rules and the Havana Rules in its 'Procedures for Assessment, Care and Release of Children in Gitagata Re-education Centre'.[16]

Whether all of these instances can be attributed to UNICEF Rwanda's capacity building, or indeed the other strategies discussed in this chapter, is difficult to assess. It would appear that the training and technical advice did at least increase awareness of international standards amongst key stakeholders, although the objective of having a longer-term impact on the judiciary was arguably curtailed following the judicial reforms of 2004. As for its financial, material and logistical assistance, the results are more tangible, at least as regards detention facilities, in that many (although not all) juveniles were transferred to newly constructed minors' wings, and non-responsible children were moved to the Gitagata centre. In respect of domestic NGOs, given the relatively few operative NGOs in post-genocide Rwanda, the lack of political space and the difficulties faced by those promoting the rights of alleged *génocidaires*, the targets and thus the scope of influence of UNICEF Rwanda's capacity-building initiatives were somewhat limited.

[13] Interview with Judge F, 30 September 2013.

[14] Murara 2000: 156 (referring to *Ministère Public c/ Maniraguha*).

[15] MINALOC 2001b: 4.

[16] MIGEFASO 1997.

Capacity building is a key tool employed by international agencies as well as NGOs. Indeed, capacity building has long been part of UNICEF's programming approach. In the context of emergencies, it is seen as 'a way of promoting post-emergency rehabilitation and recovery from the first days of an emergency programme', the aim being to move quickly beyond emergency relief activities to more sustainable interventions.[17] The objective of any UNICEF capacity-building activity is to 'enhance self-reliance' and avoid creating dependency. Thus, the emphasis should be on institution building and developing infrastructure, and policies and programmes should be developed not only to deal with current issues, but to lay the foundation for longer-term development.[18]

Capacity building has also been recognised by some theorists as playing a valuable role in enhancing implementation and compliance. Chayes and Chayes, for example, reason that increasing bureaucratic capacity and financial and material resources may improve compliance, where a state is unable to meet its international commitments.[19] And Simmons, recognising that most governments 'operate under administrative and resource constraints' and thus lack the capacity to meet all of their obligations,[20] suggests that the international community can provide assistance.[21] However, this assumes that a government has the political will to comply. Howen (writing on the functions of UN Human Rights Field Operations) contends: 'Where there *is* a minimum level of political will, building the capacity of national institutions like the police, the justice system or ministries can indeed lead to the violations being addressed and leaves a vital long-term impact.'[22] Where political will is lacking, however, there is a risk that capacity building and technical assistance will be used as a smokescreen by the government.[23] As will be explored in more detail in section 7.5, UNICEF Rwanda was of the view that there did exist some political will within the government and sought to target those it considered receptive to its recommendations.

[17] UNICEF 1997c: [15].

[18] UNICEF 1990a: [75].

[19] Chayes and Chayes 1993. See also Börzel and Risse 2013: 82–84.

[20] Simmons 2009: 359. See also Simmons 2013: 371–372 (although her emphasis is on positive rights and she suggests that 'capacity to comply is usually not at stake' for negative rights).

[21] Simmons 2009: 345–346.

[22] Howen 2007: 37.

[23] Ibid. See section 8.1.2a for more discussion on this point.

7.2 Sensitising the Community

As shown throughout this book, societal relations in the aftermath of the genocide were understandably very fragile, and emotions ran high. The study by SCF-USA had highlighted the disconnect between juvenile justice provisions in international and domestic law on the one hand, and the view of ordinary Rwandans towards the culpability of child *génocidaires* on the other. It had also suggested that those with a higher level of education had a different understanding of childhood and culpability, which is supported by the empirical findings of this study. Whilst UNICEF Rwanda felt that the government, or certain individuals within it, provided it with 'space' to give child *génocidaires* a certain level of protection, problems lay in the 'undercurrents' and broader society.[24]

The obstacles that public opinion can create for governments in implementing international juvenile justice standards have been recognised in academic research and were referred to in Chapter 3. Hamilton and Harvey provide an overview of the challenges governments face and how this has an impact on reform.[25] They elucidate that public opinion is 'largely uninformed opinion', with little knowledge about juvenile justice and about developmental psychology of children.[26] A report by MINIJUST and UNICEF Rwanda noted the challenge that public opinion constituted to the longer-term aim of 'launching and administering a thorough system for juvenile justice', stating that without public support for the 'overall objectives' of a juvenile justice system, 'the administration and enforcement of the programs and systems related to it are impossible'.[27] In respect of promoting the rights of child *génocidaires*, the challenges were more fundamental: not only was there a requirement for the public to understand and accept due process of the law, it was also necessary to protect against individual acts of revenge. Both UNICEF Rwanda and the government considered that only 'a significant shift' in public attitudes could 'increase the feasibility of releasing children accused of genocide crimes into their home communities'.[28] UNICEF Rwanda thus considered social mobilisation and awareness-raising to be

[24] Interview with Torres, 28 September 2013.

[25] Hamilton and Harvey 2004.

[26] Ibid.: 380. Note that their focus is on stable, Western countries although they argue that their analysis would also apply to developing countries.

[27] MINIJUST and UNICEF Rwanda 1997b: 29.

[28] Ibid.: 27.

'decisive elements in successfully defending the legitimacy of concepts pertaining to the defence of child rights, in a context where the absolute necessity to provide justice must not undermine the absolute necessity to protect children's rights'.[29]

Aware of the need to sensitise the population on child rights from early on in its involvement with child genocide suspects, UNICEF Rwanda translated the CRC into Kinyarwanda in 1995, after which the text was approved by MINIJUST and subsequently distributed. Informing the public of the contents of the CRC is, in fact, a requirement under Article 42 of the CRC, and the dissemination of the Convention was considered a priority. This reportedly made it the first convention to have an official Kinyarwanda version.[30] But it was also necessary for UNICEF Rwanda to be more targeted in its work with communities if child *génocidaires* were to be released and ultimately accepted back into society. In relation to the under-14s, Toole commented that, although the age division was based on Rwandan law, it was necessary to consider it at the commune level and 'figure out' what process needed to be taken to return these children successfully.[31] Thus taking account of the communities' concerns regarding the reintegration of these children was considered essential. As will be recalled from earlier chapters, UNICEF Rwanda, together with the government and through the domestic NGO, ASOFERWA, undertook comprehensive sensitisation campaigns and outreach activities with the families of the under-14s and local communities. Similar campaigns were conducted under the 'Protégez-moi' project for the over-14s, and there were also other sensitisation campaigns run out of MINIJUST and the prosecutor's office with assistance from international agencies.[32] Further, UNICEF Rwanda worked on producing a guide for bourgmestres (mayors) on protecting child rights, including how to deal with violations such as arrests of non-responsible children accused of genocide and on the rights of minors released from detention.[33] This was part of a broader 'Mayor's Initiative' project that sought to create local-level child rights protection systems, thus decentralising duties and responsibilities and maximising local capacity and potential.

[29] UNICEF Rwanda 1997d: 86.
[30] UNICEF Rwanda 1995c: 7.
[31] Skype interview with Toole, 16 May 2013.
[32] Interview with Mucyo, Kigali, 8 March 2013.
[33] Chorlton 1996: 51; UNICEF Rwanda 1997d: 87.

The sensitisation programmes did not simply involve informing communities of legal standards, be they domestic (existing and in compliance with the CRC, or newly enacted) or international. A former senior Rwandan justice official recalled that explanations relating to differential treatment for children (in particular the under-14s) did not focus on the legal text of the Genocide Law or Penal Code itself: the main explanation given was that minors had been pushed into acting and had not committed genocide willingly; they thus needed to be re-educated and then reintegrated into society.[34] Others involved in the sensitisation programmes commented that, in addition to explaining international and domestic standards requiring age-appropriate punishments and the need to reintegrate children, they would engage in discussions on the lack of children's awareness, the Rwandan culture of obedience, the need for reconciliation and children as the future of Rwanda.[35]

As Hamilton and Harvey note, in addition to disseminating information on the juvenile justice system, research has shown that it is also important to explain the reasons behind, and benefits of, treating children differently from adults.[36] We saw in Chapter 3 that juvenile justice is already a difficult area in which to mobilise public opinion in favour of protection. Given the gravity and ideological nature of genocide crimes, explanations that emphasised the vulnerability of children to adult pressure were crucial to create new 'cognitive frames' through which to view these children and thus bring about a change in public perception.[37] Additionally, these cognitive frames often drew on traditional Rwandan perceptions of childhood from before the genocide. Essential, however, was to avoid 'informing' communities *only* about child rights, which could be seen as imposing Western standards without taking account of local understandings, as well as concerns.[38]

Also important in this process was the medium through which these concepts were imparted. UNICEF Rwanda worked closely with ASOFERWA, a women's association established after the genocide that included *rescapés* amongst its founders and members. ASOFERWA

[34] Skype interview with former Senior Rwandan Justice Official, 24 July 2014.

[35] E.g. Interview with ASOFERWA Staff Member B, 27 September 2013.

[36] Hamilton and Harvey 2004: 384–385.

[37] On the importance of framing where there are 'competing norms and perceptions of interest', see Finnemore and Sikkink 1998: 897.

[38] See also Shepler 2005: 200–201, who describes sensitisation on child rights carried out by NGOs in Sierra Leone, which seemed to work from the premise that Sierra Leoneans were 'ignorant about child rights and simply needed more knowledge'.

worked not only with child *génocidaires*, but also assisted other vulnerable groups. Consequently, it had the legitimacy to act in the local context as well as specific knowledge of Rwandan culture, including, importantly, the emotions in the immediate aftermath of the genocide. As a grassroots organisation, it was also able to remain sensitive to the local context and changing conditions. Further, through the 'Mayor's Initiative', UNICEF Rwanda mobilised local bourgmestres, who had considerable authority in Rwanda, to promote child rights. These local actors could therefore adopt human rights concepts and relay them in language that would 'reach' the local population.

According to the anthropologist, Sally Engle Merry, '[r]ights need to be presented in local cultural terms in order to be persuasive'.[39] Merry argues that it is through a process of 'vernacularisation' that international law can have an impact at the local and domestic levels. In this process, she highlights the important role played by activists, serving as intermediaries, who appropriate the standards, adapt them to the particular context and 'translate' them so as to resonate with the local community.[40] Other scholars have underscored the importance of local 'buy-in' of human rights concepts. According to An-na'im and Hammond, 'externally initiated change is unsustainable except to the extent that it is internalised by the people concerned'.[41] They argue that interventions that promote universal ideas can only be effective at the local level if they are presented 'in local terms, which can best be done by local people'.[42] Twum-Danso, writing on child rights, talks of finding a 'common' or 'middle' ground and of seeking areas of consensus or commonalities between local realities, including local perceptions of children, and international child rights. She argues that the flexibility inherent in human rights standards enables local understandings to be taken into account and facilitates the finding of commonalities.[43] In the Rwandan case, local organisations and local personalities with an intrinsic understanding of Rwandan culture were instrumental in the social mobilisation efforts, as was the reliance on traditional Rwandan concepts of childhood (such as the culture of respect for, and obedience to, elders) as entry points for discussions on, and the promotion of, child rights.

[39] Merry 2006: 5.
[40] See in particular ibid.: 134.
[41] An-na'im and Hammond 2002: 14.
[42] Ibid.: 16.
[43] Twum-Danso 2008 and Twum-Danso Imoh 2011.

As for whether the sensitisation campaigns were successful, there is documentary and empirical data to suggest that there was some change in public opinion from seeking revenge or retribution to forgiveness (or at least tolerance) as well as an understanding of the law. Whilst it is not possible to show a direct causal link, many of those interviewed were of the view that the shift in public opinion was at least in part brought about by the campaigns. As illustrated in Chapter 5, although some problems were registered following the release and reintegration of the under-14s,[44] ASOFERWA considered that, as a result of the sensitisation campaigns, there was an increasing acceptance of the children over time. UNICEF Rwanda commented in 1997 that '[b]y starting a national debate on the question of tolerance, UNICEF showed that through awareness-raising, people's opinions could evolve'. It referred to a public consultation by MIFAPROFE in April 1996 which had revealed that 'public anger was increasingly directed at the responsibility of adults who "educated" and guided children; children were being seen with some forgiveness'.[45] A former senior Rwandan justice official agreed that the campaigns undertaken with the help of UNICEF Rwanda and local administrators at the grassroots level to explain the Genocide Law and the specificity as regards young perpetrators began to have some impact: people gradually came to understand that minors had to be treated differently.[46] In relation to *gacaca* jurisdictions, there are differing narratives: Domitilla Mukantaganzwa, the former Executive Secretary of the NSGC, commented that, by the time the *gacaca* jurisdictions began to operate, the position relating to minors was very clear given the explanations about the law provided during community sensitisation,[47] and a former District Coordinator did not recall receiving any complaints about the sentences passed.[48] However, there are counter-narratives that *rescapés* were unhappy with the gradual reduction of sentences in the Gacaca Laws and that some found it difficult to understand why children under 14 at the time of the genocide could not be punished. Nonetheless, it would appear that, by this time, the desire

[44] In respect of the over-14s, recall that former juvenile detainees interviewed for this study encountered significant difficulties in reintegrating, leading them to leave Rwanda.

[45] UNICEF Rwanda 1997d: 87–88 (suggesting also that the start of criminal trials of adult *génocidaires* had played a role in this shift of opinion). See also UNICEF Rwanda 1996d: 33 (referring to the MIFAPROFE study and asserting the need to continue the sensitisation efforts).

[46] Skype interview with former Senior Rwandan Justice Official, 24 July 2014.

[47] Interview with Mukantaganzwa, 3 September 2013.

[48] Interview with Kisakye, 12 September 2013.

for revenge had decreased and, even if some were unhappy, there was a general understanding of the law and different sentencing provisions for minors.

7.3 Making Use of the Existing Legal Framework

As will be detailed in section 7.4, one of UNICEF Rwanda's advocacy strategies was to reference domestic law on the basis that this would be more persuasive to the Rwandan government. Working within the existing legal framework was itself a strategy used by UNICEF Rwanda to push its agenda for the respect of the rights of child perpetrators. The existing legal framework in Rwanda in 1994 relating to juvenile justice was fairly limited. Whilst the lack of detailed provisions could be considered a hindrance to the implementation of international juvenile justice standards, it arguably provided 'enough space'[49] for organisations like UNICEF to bring about some improvements, if not wholesale reform, to the system.

To take the separation of minors from adults in detention as an example, Article 28 of the Penitentiary Service Statute of 1961 simply provided that male children should be separated from male adults where possible, and women from men, with no further provisions relating to minors. It did, however, allow for more detailed regulations to be drawn up by prison directors and approved by MINIJUST for the internal management of individual prisons.[50] Matthes, the consultant engaged by UNICEF Rwanda to propose a framework for the administration of detention facilities, articulated the view that the best way to introduce rights for minors in prisons would be to advocate for the use of such regulations rather than pushing for an amendment to, or overhaul of, the 1961 Statute.[51] He thus produced a first draft of standard rules and regulations for minors based on the Havana Rules to be considered by MINIJUST.[52] The intention was for MINIJUST to present the regulations to prison directors for discussion, with the aim of agreeing a standard set of regulations which could then be adapted for each prison. The approach adopted (i.e. to use the provision allowing for internal prison guidelines) meant, however, that many of the policy recommendations contained in the Havana

[49] Skype interview with Matthes, 28 November 2013.

[50] Art. 31.

[51] Matthes 1997a: 17.

[52] See section 6.2.2b for details.

Rules (such as restrictions on the use of pre-trial detention and the right to legal representation) could not be incorporated, as these would not be decisions taken by the prison administration.[53] This approach thus narrowed the scope of UNICEF Rwanda's intervention in this area, yet it appears that the decision was taken to try to achieve some small steps for alleged child *génocidaires* utilising existing Rwandan law, rather than attempting to reform the whole juvenile detention policy.

Whilst relying on existing law was considered by some to be the most effective way of enhancing compliance with international juvenile justice standards, by others it was considered the only way, at least in respect of some standards. Regarding the age of criminal responsibility, Toole commented that UNICEF 'didn't have a choice'. As previously noted, he recalled that UNICEF Rwanda's discussions about not holding criminally responsible anyone under the age of 18 'fell flat'; the government argued 'That's not our law'. To have 'any success', UNICEF had to build on Rwanda's existing law. Toole stated that this was true in any country UNICEF works in: 'External standards are internationally signed, but they are implemented through national legislation and the legislation was quite clear and we had to work with that … Now, with many countries behind me, I realise that that's the case everywhere, unless you can manage to change the national legislation.'[54] He added that, in some countries, UNICEF may work hard to change the legislation on the minimum age of criminal responsibility but that would be where the situation was not 'as acute' as the genocide.[55] In any event, the existing minimum age of criminal responsibility at 14 was considered acceptable by many, Matthes commenting that it 'seemed in a good zone'.[56] Indeed, the CRC Committee has previously commended states that have adopted the age of 14.

There were also other existing domestic provisions relating to children in conflict with the law that went some way to meeting UNICEF Rwanda's key concerns. The Penal Code provided for reduced sentences for juveniles aged 14–18 and for the prohibition of the death penalty and life imprisonment. Interventions thus focused on ensuring compliance with these existing provisions, whilst at the same time encouraging the practical application of international juvenile justice standards. In relation to training that UNICEF Rwanda provided to minors' judges in 1997,

53 Matthes 1997b: 3.

54 Skype interview with Toole, 16 May 2013.

55 Ibid.

56 Skype interview with Matthes, 28 November 2013.

the biggest challenge was showing how, in practice, international juvenile justice standards could be incorporated into Rwandan law. For this to be achieved, it was considered that the training had to be delivered by someone familiar with Rwandan law (in particular the Genocide Law) and the legal reality in Rwanda, or through collaboration with such an expert.[57]

The potential advantages of working within the existing legal framework rather than pushing for comprehensive reform have been recognised by UNICEF more broadly. A 2001 paper noted that focusing on wide-reaching reform could be overwhelming, such that resignation might set in. This could be at the cost of the potential inherent in the existing legal framework, institutions and personnel. As such, there should be a detailed analysis of: the penal and criminal procedure codes to consider whether they contain juvenile-specific provisions (such as diversion from legal proceedings and alternatives to deprivation of liberty); existing law enforcement institutions to see whether their rules, regulations and practice contain any flexibility for juveniles; traditional justice mechanisms; and personnel (who can act as agents of change). The paper specifically references UNICEF Rwanda's programme established 'spontaneously' to address child genocide suspects, calling it a 'key event' in UNICEF's involvement in the field of juvenile justice.[58]

Working with existing law has been recognised by others outside UNICEF as sometimes preferential to undertaking wholesale legislative reform. Sloth-Nielsen and Gallinetti reason that 'within existing systems (and without vast injection of fiscal resources), much can be done to implement child justice reform, provided that there are individuals and organisations willing to make a difference'.[59] Petty and Brown comment that law reform may 'not always be possible' and is 'never sufficient', and suggest that it may be more effective to focus on the implementation in practice of existing 'good laws' as well as the CRC.[60] And Flindt Pedersen contends that law reform, whilst necessary to maintain 'the results of improved practices' and further strengthen a juvenile justice system, is not a 'precondition' for improvements, asserting that 'resources, political will and creative use of existing legislation' are what are required.[61]

57 Daniel de Beer, who had been involved in drafting the Genocide Law, moderated and provided the training.
58 UNICEF 2001: 9 and 19–20.
59 Sloth-Nielsen and Gallinetti 2004: 49.
60 Petty and Brown 1998b: 43.
61 Flindt Pedersen 2006: 45.

Indeed, relying on existing provisions is less resource- and time-intensive, on the basis that there is no requirement for legislative debate and approval. As such, it could be a more effective way of enhancing protection for children in a post-conflict society like Rwanda, where resources are severely lacking, and an immediate response is required. Additionally, as explored in the next section, advocating the use of existing law can also be more persuasive to a government. Of course, Rwanda did pass new legislation, namely the Genocide Law of 1996 that enabled prosecutions for genocidal acts. However, this covered acts already sanctioned under the Penal Code of 1977 which, together with the Criminal Procedure Code and other laws, continued to apply to proceedings before the newly constituted Specialised Chambers, save where expressly provided. With respect to minors, the only new provision was the requirement for juvenile benches.[62] Otherwise, the existing age categories continued to apply, and UNICEF Rwanda developed its programmes on this basis.

This is not to say that UNICEF Rwanda abandoned the idea of comprehensive law reform. In 2008, UNICEF articulated that 'crisis situations' can provide opportunities for 'legislative overhaul' of the justice system and that, although post-crisis interventions often focus on the short term, they should form part of a 'broader strategy aimed at establishing a national justice system in line with international standards in the mid to long term'.[63] To some extent, UNICEF Rwanda was adopting this strategy in the 1990s. With Rwanda essentially starting from scratch, and given UNICEF Rwanda's extensive involvement, there was 'a golden opportunity to introduce the CRC at many levels', it being possible to review existing legislation and consider where law reform could lead to implementation of the CRC.[64] The aim, in 1995/6, had been to assist the government in preparing a comprehensive draft juvenile justice code, but given the extreme circumstances, this did not come to fruition. However, UNICEF Rwanda's activities relating to child perpetrators, at least after the initial emergency response, were undertaken with the future of the juvenile justice system in mind. Speaking of establishing a juvenile justice system, MINIJUST and UNICEF Rwanda noted: 'This process is still very much one of transition from a crisis situation to a period of more durable development. Many of the existing structures are temporary responses to immediate problems,

[62] As noted in section 6.2.2d, the view is that this provision was inserted as a result of UNICEF Rwanda's lobbying. See also section 7.5.

[63] UNICEF 2008a: 15. See also UNICEF 2008b: [39]; UNSG 2008: 5.

[64] UNICEF Rwanda 1996c: 33.

while longer-term solutions are actively being debated and prioritized.'[65] A UNICEF Rwanda staff member confirmed that, although the focus was on pushing for realistic measures at the time (such as improvement of detention conditions), UNICEF Rwanda also advocated for longer-term improvements, such as reform of the Penal Code and alternative measures to detention.[66] And, as illustrated in section 7.1, some of the specific measures proposed by UNICEF Rwanda, and subsequently implemented, aimed at laying a foundation for a future juvenile justice system.

In UNICEF's view, this pragmatic approach of working within the existing legal framework does not equate with, and should not be perceived as, lack of support for substantive reforms which may begin to take place at the same time. There are a number of advantages of this approach, including: guaranteeing from the outset, and to the greatest extent possible, the rights of children in conflict with the law; promoting a child rights culture; guaranteeing a sense of 'ownership' over the changes; and stimulating comprehensive reform.[67] Indeed, the situation of child *génocidaires* and the need to take immediate action to enhance their protection brought to light a number of key areas where Rwanda was not compliant with the CRC and was thus seen as an opportunity for more wide-reaching legislative change:

> There is significant political support for the application of the CRC throughout Rwanda; however, there are few laws, practices, or customs that would contribute to its implementation. While the genocide has brought some of the pertinent issues such as issues of detention, trials to the forefront, these do not guarantee a long term acceptance of these children. Legislative reform has to amend provisions that are in outright contradiction with the CRC, as much as it has to seek to incorporate standards set in the CRC into national law prohibiting certain acts and stipulating certain rights.[68]

As we saw in Chapter 4, various legislative changes were made over the years to incorporate juvenile justice standards into domestic law. An analysis of whether these changes have resulted in a comprehensive juvenile justice system (in law and practice) is, however, beyond the scope this book.

[65] MINIJUST and UNICEF Rwanda 1997b: 3.

[66] Skype interview with former UNICEF Rwanda Child Protection Staff Member B, 19 November 2014.

[67] See UNICEF 2001: 20.

[68] MINIJUST and UNICEF Rwanda 1997b: 27.

7.4 The Use of Legal and Non-Legal Discourse

According to Ratner, entities seeking to persuade a party to comply with international standards will not always invoke international law and indeed 'achieving *compliance with law* does not necessitate – or even argue for – a conversation *laden with law.* Legal argumentation might assist the task, but it can equally undermine it.'[69] Pursuant to his theoretical framework on the role of legal argumentation, there is a complex relationship between four factors or 'inputs' that influence the choice to use legal arguments (nature of: the dispute; the target; the persuasive setting; and the persuading entity's identity) and four dimensions of legal argumentation or 'outputs' (publicity, density, directness and tone). The outputs change according to variations in the inputs, and institutions (whilst generally unable to change the nature of their own identity) are constantly adapting their strategies depending on the nature of the dispute, the target and the setting.[70] Whilst this section does not seek to test Ratner's framework in its entirety by application to UNICEF Rwanda's interventions, elements of his model serve as a useful reference for this part of the study.

A review of documentation and interviews conducted with UNICEF Rwanda staff as well as domestic actors who worked on post-genocide juvenile justice issues reveals that UNICEF Rwanda was flexible in framing its policy and advocacy. Sometimes it expressly referred to international standards and other times it used other available discourses, either in lieu of, or as well as, citing international standards. Some of UNICEF Rwanda's interventions were overtly based on international standards: the draft Rules and Regulations for Children, Juveniles and Adolescents in Detention, for example, were drawn up explicitly on the basis of the Havana Rules.[71] In other cases, international law was directly invoked by UNICEF Rwanda to spell out the Rwandan government's obligations. Indeed, Torres commented that he would refer to the CRC 'in every meeting, every discussion'.[72] This was particularly the case for detention issues. UNICEF Rwanda's advocacy for separate minors' wings in central prisons very much drew on the CRC and, according to Cantwell, was seen as being successful.[73] However, whilst the CRC contains basic principles

[69] Ratner 2013: 585 (original emphasis).
[70] See generally Ratner 2013.
[71] Although recall from Chapter 6 that these were adapted to the specific context.
[72] Interview with Torres, 28 September 2013.
[73] Cantwell 1997: 50.

on the treatment of children, Torres considered its provisions on detention not to be very detailed or precise. The CRC was thus useful to show Rwanda that there was an 'international umbrella' providing protection for these children: UNICEF Rwanda would refer to the 'holistic' nature of the CRC and draw the government's attention to other articles that remained applicable to children in detention, such as the right to education or the right to family life.[74] Similar comments were made regarding limitations of the CRC by another UNICEF Rwanda staff member, who found that, in addition to raising other incentives to comply (see below), the non-binding Beijing Rules and Havana Rules were useful advocacy tools.[75]

In the absence of a clear international standard, advocacy could prove difficult. UNICEF Rwanda pushed for separate facilities for detainees under 18 at the time of the genocide but who had reached majority whilst in pre-trial detention. However, the lack of 'explicit guidelines' in international legal documents on this issue made this strand of advocacy more problematic.[76] Further, although it does not appear to have been a conscious process, it is at least arguable that, given the lack of certainty of the applicability of the more procedural rules of the CRC to juveniles who had reached majority, UNICEF Rwanda felt constrained when pushing for child-sensitive measures within the *gacaca* jurisdictions, given that these genocide minors were now in their 20s.

The perception of some government officials as well as domestic NGOs was that UNICEF Rwanda (and other international actors) regularly framed their interventions relating to child genocide suspects by reference to international law. A former Justice Minister stated that 'UNICEF parlait toujours des conventions', stressing that children had to be treated differently from adults,[77] and a prosecutor recalled UNICEF Rwanda citing the CRC and asking Rwanda to 'respect article by article'. He also recalled going through provisions of the CRC with the ICRC, noting that Rwanda could not argue that the CRC did not apply.[78] An NGO staff member asserted that most interventions relating to minors relied on

[74] Interview with Torres, 28 September 2013.

[75] Interview with former UNICEF Rwanda Child Protection Staff Member A, 15 October 2014.

[76] Cantwell 1997: 50. The CRC Committee first offered a recommendation on this in 2007. See the discussion in section 6.2.2b and also section 2.1.4.

[77] [UNICEF was always referring to conventions.] Interview with Mucyo, 13 September 2013.

[78] Interview with Ntete, 27 February 2013.

international conventions, in particular the CRC. Given the lack of a specific domestic law on child rights, the CRC was 'the one law that existed in favour of children' and was thus a guiding document that informed the advocacy of human rights activists, including UNICEF and SCF.[79]

In some cases, UNICEF Rwanda staff avoided arguments based on the CRC or other international standards, but nonetheless remained within the legal realm drawing on existing provisions in Rwandan law. As we have seen, one of UNICEF Rwanda's policy approaches was to work within the existing legal framework. During discussions on the Genocide Law, UNICEF Rwanda's advocacy focused on ensuring that Rwanda's minimum age of criminal responsibility was recognised and ensuring that those aged 14–18 benefited from the reduced sentence structure in the Penal Code. Castrogiovanni noted that UNICEF Rwanda's entry point with the government was to start with those aged under 14, referring not to the Beijing Rules or the CRC but arguing, 'based on *your* [Rwandan] law, these children should not be held criminally accountable'. She considered this to be a good starting point before widening the 'advocacy agenda', and considered that it had had some impact.[80] Other organisations also adopted this strategy, a former judge commenting, for example, that ASF and RCN always looked for a provision in domestic law that was identical to, or the equivalent of, an international standard and then tried to capitalise on this in their advocacy.[81] As Ratner propounds: 'A conversation based on domestic law may prove more successful than one based on international law, as suggested by scholars arguing that prospects for compliance improve when international law is brought home through domestic legislation.'[82]

There were also many interventions where references were made both to international standards and domestic standards. Matthes, who participated in meetings on the Genocide Law, commented that, when pushing for the inclusion of a provision for juvenile chambers, UNICEF Rwanda drew on provisions in Rwandan law as regards the age categories as well as on the CRC.[83] And in a letter to MIGEFASO commenting on draft procedures for the Gitagata centre, UNICEF Rwanda noted that the assessment included questions and references to alleged criminal acts by

79 Interview with AJPRODHO Staff Member, 15 February 2013.
80 Skype interview with Castrogiovanni, 28 November 2013.
81 Interview with Judge J, 4 October 2013.
82 Ratner 2011: 478 (referencing Koh 1998).
83 Skype interview with Matthes, 28 November 2013.

the child. It requested the removal of these points so as to comply with Rwandan law (Article 77 of the Penal Code) and Articles 37, 39 and in particular 40 of the CRC, and stressed the importance of treating these children within the social system rather than judicially.[84]

UNICEF Rwanda, however, also used non-legal discourses, or what Ratner refers to as 'alternatives to law talk',[85] either in isolation, or more often in conjunction with arguments based on international law. As Ratner explains, non-legal arguments may be raised as a reason to comply with a norm or may simply be raised in lieu of a reference to the norm.[86] These non-legal discourses were very much based on issues that were perceived to resonate with the Rwandan government,[87] such as national reconciliation (a key catchphrase of the post-genocide government[88]) and children as the future of Rwanda, the vulnerability of children, international pressure and status, and economic cost.

In a document from 1995 on the Children in Conflict with the Law Project, whilst clear reliance was placed on international standards – one of the key aims being to foster the enforcement of the CRC – several references were also made to the contribution that particular measures would make to national reconciliation. For example, civic education activities and community sensitisation on the rights of the child were promoted with the aim of facilitating reintegration and reconciliation efforts. Further, one of UNICEF Rwanda's objectives was for community service to be an alternative to detention, which it believed would assist with national reconciliation.[89] Indeed, respect of the rights of detained children was described as a 'condition to national reconciliation', the report stressing that failure to comply with procedural guarantees would render reconciliation more challenging.[90] A UNICEF Rwanda child protection staff member listed national reconciliation as a key factor that

[84] Letter from UNICEF Rwanda to MIGEFASO, 9 October 1997 (on file with author).

[85] Ratner 2011: 478 and 2013: 580.

[86] Ratner 2011: 478.

[87] Various scholars have highlighted the importance of using language that resonates in the domestic sphere. See e.g. Goodman and Jinks 2004: 636; Tobin 2011: 84. See also text at notes 39–42.

[88] Note however Sarkin's (2001: 154) assertion that justice was the initial focus for Rwanda: 'It is only recently that "reconciliation" has entered the government's vocabulary.' See also Ingelaere 2016: 18 (reconciliation had 'begun to dominate the ideological framework by the end of the 1990s').

[89] UNICEF Rwanda 1995a: 3.

[90] UNICEF Rwanda 1995a: 2.

would be emphasised in communications with the Rwandan government.[91] And according to Toole, hope for the future rests in young people and the role they can play in rebuilding a torn society.[92] Linking compliance with international standards with national reconciliation and the idea of children as the future was seen as one means of making headway on child rights issues in respect of genocide suspects.

When lobbying the government to ensure that the Rwandan minimum age of criminal responsibility was respected, in addition to calling attention to the requirement under international law to establish and respect a minimum age, and to comply with Rwanda's existing law, Torres also recalled speaking of the manipulation of children by adults, the social and cultural pressure placed on them and the lack of children's discernment. He also stressed to the government that UNICEF was not calling for impunity (the CRC not being 'a Charter of Liberation') and that it accepted that some children needed to be kept from society. However, there had to be a consideration of the children's background and why they became involved, and they needed to be provided with support.[93] Matthes similarly recalled stressing the vulnerability of children, as well as the CRC (and the best interests of the child in particular) when discussing the prioritisation of minors' cases with the government. Whilst everyone in prison was suffering, children were suffering the most.[94] And another UNICEF Rwanda staff member spoke of appealing to the 'human face' of officials, referring to the status of the child as a victim and witness as well as an alleged perpetrator.[95] A judge's reflections on the advocacy calling for the separation of children in prisons confirmed this emphasis on children's nature: it was stressed that the child could be corrupted by adults and absorb a criminal identity; he did not recall any reference to a legal obligation to separate, either under domestic or international law.[96]

External pressure, status or reputation and cost were also prevalent discourses. When advocating for the prioritisation of children's cases and removing them from prisons, Matthes would argue that the resources

91 Interview with former UNICEF Rwanda Child Protection Staff Member A, 15 October 2014.
92 Personal correspondence with Toole, 30 September 2013.
93 Interview with Torres, 28 September 2013.
94 Skype interview with Matthes, 28 November 2013.
95 Interview with former UNICEF Rwanda Child Protection Staff Member A, 15 October 2014.
96 Interview with Judge J, 4 October 2013.

directed towards these objectives, and the achievement of these objectives, would contribute towards reducing the overall caseload, benefiting the justice and penitentiary system in general, and thus help reduce some of the international pressure on the Rwandan government.[97] Torres recalled that UNICEF Rwanda would highlight the importance of respecting international law if Rwanda wished to remain 'part of the concert of nations',[98] and another staff member spoke of highlighting the government's 'popularity', and thus increased legitimacy, if it were to treat the country's children well.[99] In this staff member's opinion, however, cost was the driving factor in Rwanda, and thus the financial burden of keeping children in prisons (as well as the binding obligation under the CRC to use detention as a measure of last resort) was a focal point when communicating with the government.

In many cases these non-legal discourses were used in conjunction with reference to international standards, and thus as leverage to comply with a norm: one clear example being UNICEF Rwanda's insistence that, if Rwanda wished to be a member of the international community in good standing, it had to respect international law. When non-legal discourse was used in lieu of referencing an international standard, for some targets of the advocacy it was nonetheless clear that the underlying basis for the advocated action was an international standard. A government official commented that, whilst UNICEF Rwanda might not have referred to international law specifically in some of its interventions, it was evident to him, and to most 'educated people', that UNICEF would only provide support on the basis of certain values and that such values were founded on international human rights norms: 'It was taken for granted.'[100]

Of particular interest is that UNICEF Rwanda's interventions often refrained from expressly condemning existing violations, underscoring instead the benefits of compliance or identifying measures that could work towards compliance. Indeed, a UNICEF Rwanda staff member reported that, on the rare occasions that a direct condemnatory approach was taken, it 'backfired'.[101] UNICEF's role was seen as assisting governments

97 Skype interview with Matthes, 28 November 2013.

98 Interview with Torres, 28 September 2013.

99 Interview with former UNICEF Rwanda Child Protection Staff Member A, 15 October 2014.

100 Skype interview with Gahima, 5 November 2013.

101 Interview with former UNICEF Rwanda Child Protection Staff Member A, 15 October 2014. This is consistent with Martin's (1998: 11) description of the defensive and sensitive nature of the Rwandan government, it taking 'early exception' to findings that arrests

in establishing effective human rights monitoring systems (thus an emphasis on capacity building) rather than being a 'denunciation organization'.[102] The decision was thus taken not to make public denunciations as it was believed that this would not make a 'positive difference for the children involved'.[103] This is not to say that UNICEF Rwanda did not raise its concerns regarding violations: it would do so 'repeatedly in private meetings' with key government officials.[104] It was thus less adversarial and more constructive in its approach.[105]

Returning now to Ratner's theory of legal argumentation, there are some similarities between his case study, which identifies six 'alternatives to law talk' used by the ICRC,[106] and this study of UNICEF Rwanda. Like the ICRC, UNICEF Rwanda used pragmatic arguments, highlighting the contribution to national reconciliation by granting children due process rights and the benefit to the overall infrastructure by prioritising juvenile cases and removing them from prisons. It also used political arguments, pointing to the potential reduction of international pressure and to compliance as essential for good international standing and legitimacy,[107] and economic arguments, referring to the costs of keeping children in detention. One of the key rhetorical devices used frequently by UNICEF Rwanda was the reference to the vulnerability of children, both in terms of their susceptibility to manipulation during the genocide and their status as a vulnerable group in detention. This is akin to the humanitarian arguments (such as the changed behaviour reducing the 'suffering of

were 'arbitrary' despite clear evidence that most arrests were conducted outside legal procedures.

102 UNICEF Rwanda 1995c: 10.

103 Personal correspondence with Toole, 30 October 2015.

104 Ibid. Former UNICEF Rwanda Child Protection Staff Member A (interview, 15 October 2014) made similar comments.

105 Interestingly, Zimmerman (2017: 201–202), who was examining the translation of the CRC into Guatemalan law, found that UNICEF was initially adversarial in that context (using praising and shaming) and only shifted to a more informal and less public mode of action after facing resistance from the Guatemalan government.

106 Humanitarian, political, economic, pragmatic, moral and customary arguments. Ratner 2011: 478 and 2013: 580.

107 Chayes and Chayes' (1995: 28, 119 and 230) management approach to compliance posits that a state's desire to be a 'member in good standing of the international system' makes the state more likely to comply with international obligations, and thus the approach promotes this type of persuasive argument (together with capacity building to overcome lack of capacity issues). Various other scholars have also argued that reputation and legitimacy can play a central role in a state's compliance with international law (e.g. Finnemore and Sikkink 1998: 903; Guzman 2002; Keohane 1997).

innocent victims') used by the ICRC in Ratner's study, or moral arguments in that this would be the appropriate way of acting given the particularities of children.[108]

Like the ICRC, which relies on the support of the parties to continue its operational presence in conflict zones, UNICEF's work in Rwanda was dependent on maintaining a good working relationship with the Rwandan government. This, as well as the nature of the setting and the nature of the target (the Rwandan government), clearly had an influence on UNICEF Rwanda's approach. UNICEF Rwanda generally avoided outright condemnation of violations, adapting the 'tone' of its interventions to be less confrontational and more constructive. Indeed, one research participant commented that UNICEF Rwanda had to 'mute' its criticisms, for example in relation to public trials, as it was concerned that the Rwandan government would reject the organisation.[109] Similar remarks were made by another participant regarding the general risk to operations in the country: UNICEF Rwanda's management had to keep in mind that pushing too much in areas like juvenile justice could potentially jeopardise UNICEF Rwanda's other programmes. Further, it was careful not to 'annoy the government too much' because of concerns about the potential impact on national staff if it were too critical.[110] On a personal level, it was considered difficult to be highly critical and then switch to discussions about what measures should be taken.[111] And, as noted, it avoided public denunciations: where information was released into the public domain, it was largely factual (such as including information on the number of children in detention and outlining relevant Rwandan legislation) and/or descriptive of the programmatic activities being undertaken by UNICEF Rwanda together with other organisations and the government,

[108] See also Goodale 2007: 146–151 (distinguishing between the connotative power of human rights, where references are made to the 'normative moral universe' brought about by human rights, and the denotative power, where reference is made to specific provisions, and rights are used in a 'legal way').

[109] Interview with former UNICEF Rwanda Child Protection Staff Member A, 15 October 2014.

[110] Skype interview with former UNICEF Rwanda Child Protection Staff Member B, 19 November 2014. Note Howen's (2007: 41) comment that public advocacy can lead to retaliation that can range from refusing to cooperate or provide access to endangering the lives of staff members.

[111] Skype interview with former UNICEF Rwanda Child Protection Staff Member B, 19 November 2014.

rather than containing any statement on compliance with international standards.[112]

Further, the context of post-genocide Rwanda, both in terms of the strong emotions and the lack of resources, influenced the choices made as regards which norms to stress (Ratner's 'density' output) and whether to invoke the international standards directly (referencing only the legal standard), indirectly (using non-legal discourses in conjunction with legal argumentation) or furtively (using only non-legal discourse) (Ratner's 'directness' output).[113] Castrogiovanni, for example, referred to feeling a 'little uncomfortable' simply referring to international standards, the memory of the genocide being too fresh for advocates to 'repeat as a mantra all these provisions and instruments': there had to be a consideration of what was possible in that 'extreme context', with the resources available.[114] Whilst the principles in the CRC and other instruments clearly guided UNICEF Rwanda's actions, and UNICEF Rwanda was pushing for these guarantees, for her the entry point for advocacy with the Rwandan government was domestic law. This was also the feeling of some within other international agencies, such as UNHRFOR, Howland commenting that, whilst the government was very open, it was also pragmatic and thus 'if you are too dogmatic about the principles, then they wouldn't listen to you'. He thus considered that merely citing the requirements under the CRC to, for example, provide separate detention or education whilst in detention was not helpful as there were no means to achieve this.[115]

It was thus considered necessary to adapt the language used, and to use language strategically and instrumentally, in policy and advocacy discourses. To some extent, these empirical findings depart from Tobin's assertion that child rights advocates have generally only referenced the universality and binding nature of child rights[116] or relied upon their

[112] See e.g. UNICEF Rwanda 1995b; 1997b; 1997c. Note that newspaper articles referring to the decisions to build minors' wings and house children in Gitagata evinced the tension and unease felt by UNICEF Rwanda staff members, but highlighted the justifications put forward for the decisions taken (see e.g. Drogin 1997; Hackel 1995; Matloff 1997).

[113] See Ratner 2013: 577–578.

[114] Skype interview with Castrogiovanni, 21 August 2013.

[115] Skype interview with Howland, 7 February 2014.

[116] Cf. Murray and Long 2015: 20–22 and 75–77, who found in their research (not on child rights) that, whilst litigators preferred to reference binding documents in domestic litigation, activists and other lawyers familiar with international and regional standards, including 'softer' documents, would adopt a more 'strategic' or 'imaginative' approach, using whichever document or provision would be helpful in the circumstances.

moral status when framing their claims.[117] He argues that 'these appeals often fail to resonate' with the decision-maker and may result in them having no persuasive force. He suggests that other discourses (such as risk management and economic utility) may have more resonance[118] but notes that using such discourses may result in the rights-based approach being 'reduced to an instrumentalist vision', which may undermine the normative value of rights. He concludes that the challenge is for advocates to combine strategies: using instrumentalist strategies that will resonate with the decision-maker as well as normative or 'intrinsic' strategies founded on legal or moral principles.[119] This challenge is further explored in Chapter 8.

7.5 Capitalising on Political Will and Developing Relationships

As referenced earlier, Sloth-Nielsen and Gallinetti highlight the importance of people 'willing to make a difference' in bringing about improvements in juvenile justice systems. This applies to international actors and also to people within the domestic realm, both in civil society and government. Determining whether a government, or individuals within that government, have the political will to comply with juvenile justice standards is a difficult task. HRW has questioned the Rwandan government's commitment in this regard:

> The government claims to have embraced international standards and has put a partial legal framework for child protection in place. But laws are not enough without adequate enforcement mechanisms. Eight years of promises to protect their rights has meant little for children in practice. The government should take concrete measures to establish a system of juvenile justice in accordance with international standards.[120]

Other observers are a little more positive, Cantwell speaking (albeit much earlier than HRW and also not specifically on juvenile justice) of the will

[117] Tobin 2011: 84. Sharp (2018: 508) comes to a similar conclusion regarding human rights advocates' emphasis on moral and legal dimensions, noting that the 'dominant script of human rights practice has been heavily law-centered', and that '[t]here has been an aversion to basing arguments on utilitarian rather than deontological logics'.

[118] See also Sharp (2018: 518), asserting that engagement with questions of resources and 'hard-tradeoffs of governance' may have more traction than 'simplistic denunciation or policy recommendations ill-suited to … the context'.

[119] Tobin 2011: 84. See also Abramson (2006: 26) who comments that '[h]uman rights advocacy requires a combination of moral, legal and pragmatic arguments'.

[120] HRW 2003a: 2.

of the government to 'make human rights seen to be working'.[121] This included the will to implement the CRC in particular, many interpreting any failure to comply with its provisions as the result of lack of capacity rather than lack of will. He noted, however, that there were some who believed the government was simply paying lip-service to children's rights. UNICEF Rwanda considered that there was 'a great amount of political will in the country to apply the CRC fully', but that there were 'few laws, practices or customs' that could be used as tools.[122] And Howland was of the view that it was practical difficulties and limited infrastructure that narrowed the options available to a government that conceptually saw child perpetrators as victims.[123] In some instances, it was not always possible to decipher the cause behind lack of action, a 1996 document noting that the failure to improve detention conditions and the justice system called into question the government's 'political will and/or capacity' to respect children's rights.[124] A judicial defender considered that, in some cases, the government provided 'legitimate reasons', such as lack of human or financial resources, for failing to respect juvenile justice standards, but in other cases, there was bad faith.[125] And in the view of a former coordinator of the MINIJUST/UNICEF Children in Conflict with the Law Project, there was political will to follow international standards, including the CRC, but it came 'little by little': it was not automatic.[126] It required a balancing of respect for children's rights with the requirement and demands for justice.

From a review of documentation and interviews conducted with Rwandan government officials, it is clear that the Rwandan government (or at least some individuals) recognised the importance of being willing to deal with juvenile justice issues. A paper by MINIJUST and UNICEF Rwanda presented at a global seminar stated that 'willingness' and 'openness are more determinative of the success of different programs within the overall administration of juvenile justice programs than are other factors, such as funding or resources'.[127] Some interviewees expressed a very clear awareness of the importance of child rights and of

[121] Cantwell 1997: 62.
[122] UNICEF Rwanda 1996c: 33.
[123] Skype interview with Howland, 7 February 2014. Former MINJUST/UNICEF Project Coordinator B (Skype interview, 19 February 2014) made similar comments.
[124] UNICEF Rwanda Consultant 1996: 2.
[125] Skype interview with former Judicial Defender B, 28 August 2013.
[126] Interview with former MINJUST/UNICEF Project Coordinator A, 7 October 2013.
[127] MINIJUST and UNICEF Rwanda 1997b: 28.

Rwanda's obligations under the CRC. Gahima, for example, spoke of the debates that took place regarding minors before the enactment of the 1996 Genocide Law. He noted that the decision was taken to prosecute those aged 14–18 in accordance with domestic law, but also to 'find ways to deal with them in humane ways and in accordance with the protection that they have under international law'. He added: 'We knew we had to comply, or at least we knew we were expected to comply with international law', and that this was one of the considerations when determining the approach to take.[128] Similarly, with regard to the separation of juveniles from adults in detention, Gahima referred to it being 'the standard procedure internationally' and being a 'human rights requirement for the protection of children'. In his view, the system suffered not from lack of will 'to live up to our obligations', but lack of capacity.[129] Straton Nsanzabaganwa, who was responsible for developing a policy on vulnerable children (including those in detention) in 1996 and worked on the development of a social protection policy for children from 1999 to 2005, demonstrated an in-depth knowledge of child rights, commenting that he based his work on the CRC, the Beijing Rules and the Havana Rules[130] and asserting that the best interests of the child principle was used in all decisions relating to children.[131] Of course, these individuals were speaking in the context of a research interview conducted many years after they had been dealing with these particular issues, and thus the considerations outlined in Chapter 1 must be recalled.

Whether the political will that did exist was grounded in a genuine commitment to child rights on the part of the government, or at least particular individuals within the government, or was derivative of other concerns is difficult to assess. Some other reasons put forward for child rights initiatives include the need to break with the past (characterised by serious human rights violations and impunity),[132] to reconcile Rwandans and build a future, for which rehabilitation of children was a condition,[133]

[128] Skype interview with Gahima, 5 November 2013. Although see text at note 68, Chapter 5.

[129] Skype interview with Gahima, 5 November 2013.

[130] He had obtained copies of these from an international conference on child rights he had attended in 1998.

[131] Interview with Nsanzabaganwa, 10 October 2013.

[132] Interview with Ntete, 21 February 2013.

[133] A number of interviewees referred to child genocide suspects being treated differently because it was considered essential for them to help rebuild, and be part of the future society of, Rwanda (e.g. AJPRODHO Staff Member, 15 February 2013; former ASOFERWA Staff Member A, 24 September 2013; former MINJUST/UNICEF Project

to increase legitimacy (having taken power by force),[134] to reassure Rwandans both at home and abroad[135] and to secure the support of the international community.[136]

In any event, UNICEF Rwanda sought to capitalise on any political will that did exist, by strategically taking all opportunities to promote child rights, and by identifying and building relationships with key personnel within national institutions who appeared receptive to child rights concepts. Matthes, for example, spoke of attending a workshop on the Genocide Law in early 1996. He recalled that, at this stage, there was openness to suggestions in light of the rising number of detainees and he thus saw this as an 'opportunity to create space for some type of separate dealings' with juveniles. He found the government receptive to proposals for a juvenile-specific trajectory and thus fed this back into UNICEF Rwanda to consider whether they could push for a separate jurisdiction. Ultimately, UNICEF Rwanda advocated for separate juvenile chambers, and the result was minors' benches within the Specialised Chambers. Matthes commented that 'it didn't take a lot of convincing – it just needed someone to make the point'.[137] Toole referred to 'keeping up our advocacy on all fronts', taking the opportunity at an evening cocktail party to raise the issue of education for children in prisons with the Minister of Education, after which, he noted, UNICEF began to provide basic educational materials inside the prisons.[138] And for a UNICEF Rwanda child protection staff member, receptions and dinners gave the opportunity to raise criticisms and concerns informally rather than officially or publicly.[139]

For individuals on the ground, it was clear that good interpersonal professional relationships mattered, and that such relationships were built on mutual trust, an understanding of the concerns of each party and an openness to ideas. As evinced earlier, the view was that certain governmental counterparts provided UNICEF Rwanda with the 'space' to do its work and showed a clear interest in children's

Coordinator A, 7 October 2013; Nsanzabaganwa, 10 October 2013, Ntete, 21 and 27 February 2013).

134 Cantwell 1997: 62.

135 Ibid.

136 Ibid.

137 Skype interview with Matthes, 28 November 2013.

138 Skype interview with Toole, 16 May 2013.

139 Interview with former UNICEF Rwanda Child Protection Staff Member A, 15 October 2014.

rights.[140] Castrogiovanni spoke of having the opportunity to work with 'fantastic people' within MIGEFASO and MINIJUST. She referred to them as being 'definitely very receptive' and was unable to recall any tough negotiations with them: they understood what UNICEF Rwanda wanted to achieve and became 'good allies'.[141] Matthes similarly found senior representatives of MINIJUST, and of the judiciary more broadly, to be 'very open' and 'liberal' in their approach and did not recall encountering 'hardline resistance', but stressed that it was important to remain aware of what was feasible in the context.[142] A national coordinator of the joint MINIJUST/UNICEF Children in Conflict with the Law Project, who straddled the Rwandan government/UNICEF world, spoke of particular individuals in MINIJUST being 'very sensitive about children's rights issues' and noted their 'amount of energy and level of involvement' which facilitated work on the project.[143] And a UNICEF Rwanda child protection staff member spoke of being able to have 'frank discussions' as a result of building up trust and forming alliances with certain officials, and that these individuals acted as 'entry points' into the government.[144] However, where a particularly sensitive issue was involved, UNICEF Rwanda might use 'messengers' to raise the issue with the government. For example, EU member states were requested to pass on concerns about child rights, and external experts were requested to make statements about public trials rather than UNICEF Rwanda doing it directly.[145]

Rwandan officials similarly highlighted the importance of interpersonal relationships. A senior Rwandan justice official spoke of having a productive relationship with UNICEF Rwanda staff members, given that they understood the government's concerns and views as to how to proceed, and that the government likewise understood UNICEF's position and its requirement to uphold certain principles.[146] And Gahima commented that good relationships were generally established with all those Rwanda

[140] Interview with Torres, 28 September 2013. He noted that there were 'undercurrents' in the government who did not share this interest.

[141] Skype interviews with Castrogiovanni, 21 August 2013 and 28 November 2013.

[142] Skype interview with Matthes, 28 November 2013.

[143] Skype interview with former MINJUST/UNICEF Project Coordinator B, 19 February 2014.

[144] Interview with former UNICEF Rwanda Child Protection Staff Member A, 15 October 2014.

[145] Ibid. Keck and Sikkink (1998: 23–24) refer to the use of 'leverage politics' where actors use a more powerful actor, such as another government, to raise issues.

[146] Skype interview with former Senior Rwandan Justice Official, 24 July 2014.

thought were trying to help, but that particularly at the ministerial level, 'personalities' played an important role.[147]

Key to these relationships was the goodwill established between the government and UNICEF Rwanda, as well as the latter's legitimacy. Research participants referred to UNICEF Rwanda assisting the government with child *génocidaires* from the very beginning.[148] And financial and logistical support provided to various government sectors was not only 'valuable in itself, but [it] also had the apparently unplanned effect of putting UNICEF in good stead with the authorities', which, given the general feeling towards UN agencies, was extremely useful for subsequent collaboration on child rights issues.[149] Further, UNICEF had a long-term field presence in Rwanda, which was felt to facilitate its work with the government (even in the very difficult circumstances after the genocide).[150] It was also the authoritative agency for child protection. These factors enhanced its legitimacy, important for its continued presence in Rwanda as well as the regard paid to its advice. It was nonetheless important for UNICEF Rwanda staff members to reaffirm this legitimacy and integrity in their interactions with government counterparts.

These strategies used by UNICEF Rwanda are not unique: in his analysis of human rights field operations, Howen lists a number of strategies developed by field officers to influence authorities and those who have influence on the decision-makers. These include 'persuasive human rights diplomacy' that involves 'exploiting the myriad day-to-day conversations and communications', and 'encouragement' through which field operations use their presence to support others, including 'reformers in the government', in bringing about change.[151] UNICEF itself recognises the role that nationals within institutions and systems that directly deal with child offenders can play and stresses the importance of forging links and cultivating relationships with such individuals, so as to create national ownership. These individuals can be agents of change: it is thus essential to work with them to build their capacity and provide them with the necessary means to bring about change.[152]

[147] Skype interview with Gahima, 5 November 2013.
[148] E.g. former Senior Rwandan Justice Official, Skype interview, 24 July 2014.
[149] Cantwell 1997: 77.
[150] Skype interview with Castrogiovanni, 28 November 2013.
[151] Howen 2007: 41.
[152] UNICEF 2001: 20–21.

UNICEF Rwanda's efforts to build capacity were discussed in detail earlier in this chapter. By accessing, and building relationships with, key personnel inside relevant national institutions, and by drawing attention to applicable juvenile justice standards, UNICEF Rwanda sought to provide these individuals with a relevant framework on which to base policies and the support to pursue these within their respective institutions. It was considered essential to create a sense of national ownership over the process of promoting and protecting child rights within the Rwandan justice system. Further, as many individuals moved from one institution to another, they took with them their previous experiences and outlook. In this respect, a coordinator of the joint MINIJUST/UNICEF project posited that, by the time discussions were taking place on the Gacaca Law 2001, some judicial personnel were already 'child-friendly', having been exposed to child rights in their earlier roles through interaction with UNICEF Rwanda.[153] UNICEF Rwanda was thus arguably able to have a longer-term influence through establishing good relationships from the outset. Of course, it might be that these officials were already sensitive to child rights and that UNICEF Rwanda's interventions did no more than coincide with their views, or indeed that they gave the impression of being committed to child rights, but took decisions based on other factors. However, an alternative explanation is that UNICEF Rwanda's interventions influenced or at the very least reinforced these sensitivities and thus to some extent brought about the acceptance by these individuals of child rights as authoritative.

7.6 Offering Incentives but Making Compromises

Although some individuals within the Rwandan government were seen as very open to child rights concepts, the perception was that the government, as a whole, did not see child perpetrators as the priority; rather the main concerns were the high-profile perpetrators and managing the overall caseload. UNICEF Rwanda thus sought to use its support in other areas as leverage to make some progress on child rights. This strategy was adopted from the very beginning of UNICEF Rwanda's involvement with the post-genocide government, even though it required a very pragmatic and flexible approach to the mandate. As outlined in the discussion

[153] Skype interview with former MINJUST/UNICEF Project Coordinator B, 19 February 2014.

on capacity building, soon after re-establishing the office in Rwanda, UNICEF Rwanda provided financial and material assistance to main government departments working on child rights. Toole stated that, although 'it wasn't an easy thing by our rules and regulations, it was one of the smartest things we ever did', as it enabled the ministries to begin work and was also 'a gesture of trust, support and flexibility'.[154] As noted earlier, the provision of this assistance had a positive impact on the government's view of UNICEF and arguably facilitated its work on more sensitive issues. In terms of advancing child rights, it gave UNICEF Rwanda the opportunity to link this support to specific initiatives: for example, discussions relating to child soldiers with the Ministry of Defence.[155]

In addition to its 'child protection' programme, UNICEF Rwanda was very active in other areas, with programmes on education, water, sanitation and hygiene, health and psychosocial assistance. Within the 'child protection' programme itself (of which children in conflict with the law was just one subset), one of the main projects focused on tracing and reunifying unaccompanied children. Thus there were many interventions that were targeting *all* children, or victims in particular, which in Castrogiovanni's view, meant there was a 'balance' and resulted in the government being more open to UNICEF Rwanda's involvement with child perpetrators.[156] However, whilst this arguably enabled UNICEF Rwanda to make some headway, there were limitations. Given the various different programmes and the significant challenges in post-genocide Rwanda, UNICEF Rwanda had to prioritise. In the view of some, this resulted in the rights of other children being given precedence over those of child *génocidaires*. A child protection staff member considered that child-headed households were the priority for the 'child protection' programme and suggested that this was one reason for UNICEF Rwanda not being so involved with the *gacaca* jurisdictions.[157] And another considered that programmes for orphans and for child soldier demobilisation sometimes took priority over juvenile justice issues. However, in this staff member's view, there was no deliberate decision to 'demote' juvenile justice: the

154 Skype interview with Toole, 16 May 2013.

155 Ibid. Demobilisation of child soldiers is not addressed in this book but would be an interesting area for further research.

156 Skype interview with Castrogiovanni, 28 November 2013. Former UNICEF Rwanda Child Protection Staff Member A (interview, 15 October 2014) made similar observations.

157 Interview with former UNICEF Rwanda Child Protection Staff Member A, 15 October 2014. As may be recalled, it was also this participant's view that child protection in general was not a priority for UNICEF.

approach taken was generally to focus on areas where UNICEF Rwanda thought it could make a tangible difference for a large number of children rather than those where it considered it was likely to see very little progress. The approach was also partially driven by funding and, after the initial flurry of support for children in detention, donor interest shifted to orphans and child soldier demobilisation.[158]

To a large extent, improving the lot of child genocide suspects was contingent on getting the overall machinery working. This was recognised by those working for UNICEF Rwanda, Matthes noting that it was not politically feasible to divert resources away from the general system. For example, it was not possible to have IPJs (investigators within the public prosecution) from the very beginning working solely on minors' cases, as the resources were simply too scarce. He commented that UNICEF had to be realistic as, at that time, children represented less than 3 per cent of the prison population.[159] In Matthes' view, there was no hard-line resistance to special treatment for children: rather it was more a question of what was feasible 'within the bigger scheme of things'.[160] At the programme level, some in UNICEF Rwanda thus took the view that one way of advancing the rights of child suspects would be to provide support that benefited child *génocidaires* to some extent, but that at the same time also benefited the system as a whole. It was considered that the Rwandan government would be more receptive to child-focused initiatives if this approach were adopted, Matthes referring to feedback from the Ministry of Justice that there would be no obstacles if extra personnel trained to deal with children's cases could subsequently be used for adults' cases.[161] Accordingly, UNICEF Rwanda provided support in the form of training and salaries for IPJs designated to work on minors' cases. However, whilst these IPJs were appointed to deal exclusively with minors' cases initially, in practice they were sometimes assigned to cases involving adults.[162] A former senior Rwandan justice official confirmed that this did occur (although asserted that it was rare), and that it sometimes gave rise to complaints from UNICEF Rwanda, but there was no significant conflict.[163] As previously documented, within the penitentiary

[158] Skype interview with former UNICEF Rwanda Child Protection Staff Member B, 19 November 2014.

[159] Matthes 1996b: 8.

[160] Skype interview with Matthes, 28 November 2013.

[161] Matthes 1996b: 8.

[162] See ASF 1999b: 40; HRW 2003a: 22–23.

[163] Skype interview with former Senior Rwandan Justice Official, 24 July 2014.

system UNICEF Rwanda provided support for the rehabilitation or building of minors' wings that resulted in many, but not all, juveniles being separated from adults. The government had expressed its intention to use these wings for adult prisoners after the child *génocidaires* had grown up, whereas UNICEF Rwanda had envisaged them being used for juveniles who had committed ordinary crimes. In practice, some of these minors' blocks were subsequently transformed into adult prisons. A former senior Rwandan justice official did not know whether UNICEF Rwanda was 'happy about this',[164] but it did not appear that any conditions had been imposed by UNICEF Rwanda on the future use of such facilities.

In respect of this strategy, and with reference to both the training of personnel and rehabilitation of minors' wings, it was noted that, although benefiting children in the short term, UNICEF Rwanda's assistance would ultimately strengthen the overall adult penitentiary and justice system. It was suggested that this could be an acceptable approach for UNICEF – not least to counterbalance the significant donor funding earmarked for children – but it was asserted that UNICEF should make a 'conscious decision' on this.[165] It has not been possible to ascertain whether any 'conscious decision' was made officially, although it would appear that this use of incentives – which also involved a degree of compromise both in the short and longer term – continued to be used as a strategy by UNICEF Rwanda to make some progress on issues concerning child *génocidaires*.[166] This approach led to some criticism from organisations such as HRW, which claimed that UNICEF Rwanda had 'failed to require demonstrable progress' in the implementation of its joint project with MINIJUST on Children in Conflict with the Law, referring to the diversion of resources from child-specific measures to the other projects and the justice system generally.[167]

UNICEF Rwanda also had to compromise, by accepting that some international standards could not be implemented or complied with immediately. In Toole's view, whilst all the rights in the CRC are indivisible and interdependent, and whilst UNICEF would constantly lobby

[164] Ibid.

[165] UNICEF Rwanda Consultant 1996: 2.

[166] Confirmed by former UNICEF Rwanda Child Protection Staff Member A, interview, 15 October 2014 (noting that there remains no clear global UNICEF policy on – and indeed that UNICEF is split on the issue of – investing in child-sensitive measures which will also benefit the wider system).

[167] HRW 2003a: 23–24.

for the respect of all rights, it is nonetheless necessary to acknowledge that things take time. In these circumstances, UNICEF Rwanda would focus on what *was* achievable in a given context, whilst working on broader efforts. For example, UNICEF Rwanda looked at the 'current rights' of children in detention, in terms of protection, education and health and sought to actualise these rights, whilst also working towards the removal of these children from prisons.[168] Another UNICEF Rwanda staff member insisted that, when faced with a factual situation of children in detention (as in Rwanda), the focus must be on ensuring a minimum set of humane conditions for these children. This is not to say that other rights and standards are neglected: advocacy on these standards, such as on alternatives to detention and legislative reform, can be done in parallel.[169]

The use of incentives, such as providing rewards (a positive incentive) or imposing sanctions (a negative incentive) has been recognised by some theorists as a means of enhancing compliance with human rights and is considered most useful where a state is materially or socially vulnerable.[170] Whether a conscious decision or not, UNICEF Rwanda appears to have been linking progress on the rights of child perpetrators with cooperation in other areas or with material support to the broader judicial system. From the perspective of those in government, it was clear that UNICEF Rwanda's support, whilst benefiting the overall machinery, did not come without reciprocal obligations. As mentioned earlier, Gahima recognised that UNICEF's assistance was predicated on child rights, and it was clear to a former Justice Minister that UNICEF would not provide financial assistance if Rwanda was acting in violation of the CRC: 'Comment est-ce qu'on peut travailler avec UNICEF si on n'est pas en accord avec ces conventions?'[171] Of course, there did continue to be violations in practice, and UNICEF Rwanda had to compromise and prioritise rights according to what it considered achievable. However, as Nolan and van Heerden

168 Skype interview (16 May 2013) and personal correspondence (30 September 2014) with Toole.

169 Skype interview with former UNICEF Rwanda Child Protection Staff Member B, 19 November 2014.

170 See e.g. Risse and Ropp 2013: 14 (who identify 'changing incentives' amongst four mechanisms that they consider enhance human rights compliance, the other three being coercion, persuasion and capacity-building). See also Keohane 1997 who argues that incentives (such as the use of sanctions or risk to reputation) can lead to compliance.

171 [How could we work with UNICEF if we did not act in accordance with these conventions?] Interview with Mucyo, 8 March 2013.

note in respect of their work on the Fair Labor Association which adopted a similar method of human rights promotion:

> The fact that such a process is likely to be incremental (accepting that achieving something, even if not perfect, is preferable to achieving nothing) and may involve prioritising (or some might argue compromising) some rights over others are valid limitations and criticism of the process, but not necessarily fatal flaws.[172]

7.7 Conclusion

As illustrated in this chapter, UNICEF Rwanda adopted a variety of strategies when seeking to enhance the implementation of, and compliance with, international standards relating to child *génocidaires*. The strategies were very much dependent on, and adapted to, the Rwandan context and, in many cases, spotlighted the 'domestic' or 'local'. Given the significant resource deficiencies, emphasis was placed on capacity-building initiatives aimed at responding to the immediate crisis of children being detained on suspicion of genocide but also, at least to some extent, with an eye on the future, the objective being to create sustainable self-reliance. The lack of resources, as well as the need for an emergency response, also influenced the decision to defer to national law and use the existing legal framework: although UNICEF Rwanda did advocate for wider reform, it focused on ensuring that domestic provisions already compliant with international law were respected and on incorporating international standards into domestic practice where feasible. The other major challenge that had a discernible influence on UNICEF Rwanda's policy approach was the social context. Although juvenile justice is often a polemic issue, in post-genocide Rwanda there was evidence of extreme societal pressure for retribution. Given fears that child *génocidaires* could become the target of revenge attacks, a key feature of UNICEF Rwanda's overall policy strategy was community sensitisation. As illustrated, both the form this took (in terms of the explanations provided to the community in the campaigns) as well as the medium through which it was delivered (by a local NGO and mayors) were of importance: UNICEF Rwanda relied on local concepts of childhood and on local organisations and personalities as entry points.

[172] Nolan and van Heerden 2013: 159.

The context also had an impact on UNICEF Rwanda's advocacy techniques. Given the post-genocide challenges, but also the relationship between Rwanda and the UN, UNICEF Rwanda staff considered that simply reciting international standards to the government and highlighting violations would be unproductive. It thus utilised a range of discourses, both legal (referencing international law and domestic law) and non-legal (relying on language that would resonate with the Rwandan government), to promote the rights of child *génocidaires*. Staff members also focused on developing relationships with individuals in key government institutions who were considered receptive to child rights. Establishing these relationships was considered intrinsic to successful advocacy and enabled UNICEF Rwanda to raise concerns on a more informal and frank basis and thus push its agenda on this sensitive issue. It was also considered essential in the sense of creating national ownership over changes to the juvenile justice approach. UNICEF Rwanda staff members were able to form these alliances partly due to UNICEF's pedigree and long-term field presence in Rwanda, but also due to the trust established as a result of the organisation's flexibility and pragmatism immediately after the genocide. Given UNICEF's broad remit on children generally, the Rwandan office was also able to take advantage of its work in other areas to have access to the government on the issue of child perpetrators. It was thus, to use James Grant's words, using its 'favoured partnership relationship' to support its work as a 'critical partner' on this sensitive issue. However, as noted, there were some limitations, UNICEF Rwanda having to prioritise between competing objectives. This was also evident to some extent at the project level, in terms of what UNICEF Rwanda could achieve and how it could best persuade the government to take steps towards protecting the rights of child *génocidaires*. It thus encouraged the government to take some child-friendly measures through investing in the wider judicial system, accepting that these measures would only partially benefit children.

This combination of strategies and techniques suggests that UNICEF Rwanda took a broadly collaborative and pragmatic approach to implementation and compliance. The following, and final, substantive chapter will seek to evaluate this approach, noting if and how it appears to have had a positive influence, and also drawing out the risks, criticisms and limitations of such an approach to operationalising international standards.

8

Evaluating UNICEF Rwanda's Approach: A Case of Principled Pragmatism?

The previous chapters illustrated that UNICEF Rwanda was pragmatic in its approach to enhancing the implementation of, and compliance with, international standards on child *génocidaires*. As Sharp sums up: 'The essence of human rights pragmatism involves weighing the costs and benefits of a particular vocabulary and set of strategies against alternatives in a particular context.'[1] In UNICEF Rwanda's case, this included interpreting the provisions in a non-restrictive way to fit the Rwandan context, accepting that many of the standards could not be realised immediately and thus working towards implementation and compliance, and prioritising some rights over others. It also included utilising a range of strategies and techniques to enhance implementation and compliance that can broadly be categorised as collaborative rather than coercive, and that were tailored to the Rwandan context. This chapter seeks to evaluate that approach. It begins by examining the risks, criticisms and limitations of this approach, before it turns to address the perceived results. It then looks at the factors that influenced UNICEF Rwanda so as to situate its approach in the broader context and to consider whether the findings from this research might have wider application. It is argued that UNICEF Rwanda's approach, which was pragmatic yet remained true to child rights principles, was overall appropriate and achieved some positive results, although there were shortcomings.

8.1 Criticisms, Risks and Limitations

Criticisms, risks and limitations of UNICEF Rwanda's approach have been alluded to throughout this book. Here, some of those negative evaluations will be revisited. Broadly, it could be argued, first, that UNICEF Rwanda was giving too much weight to the local context; and second, that UNICEF

[1] Sharp 2018: 502.

Rwanda risked being instrumentalised or co-opted by the Rwandan government and resorted too much to collaborative efforts, failing to condemn serious violations. In both cases, there is a suggestion that UNICEF Rwanda could have been weakening the normative content of the very international standards it was seeking to promote.

8.1.1 Contextual Application or Weakening the Standards?

In 'The Dark Sides of Virtue', Kennedy notes that humanitarian work (which includes human rights activism) often requires '*strategizing* about the law'.[2] This includes considering whether rules should be strictly or flexibly interpreted and whether the neutrality of norms should be stressed in preference to an accent on 'their pragmatic link to political realities'.[3] Kennedy asserts that, in the work of UNHCR (his case study), such strategising has not always resulted in 'imaginative pragmatism in response to refugee flows', decisions being based on 'fealty to coherence of the doctrinal structure' as opposed to responding to the needs of refugees.[4] In another work, Kennedy again criticises human rights organisations, contending that 'to maintain the claim to universality and neutrality, the human rights movement practices a systematic lack of attention to background sociological and political conditions that will determine the meaning a right has in particular contexts, rendering the evenhanded pursuit of "rights" vulnerable to all sorts of distorted, and distinctly non-neutral outcomes'.[5]

In stark contrast to Kennedy's assertions, and to his analysis of UNHCR,[6] UNICEF Rwanda was very pragmatic and strategic in its approach to operationalising international standards, taking into account the context and the realities of post-genocide Rwanda. As will be recalled from Chapter 6, a Rwandan official suggested that people had to 'abandon their principles' when faced with the challenges in post-genocide Rwanda, and UNICEF Rwanda's approach could be criticised for giving too much weight to the local context. This contextual orientation arguably gave rise to risks of diluting the normative content, or even accepting the violation,

[2] Kennedy 2004: 199 (original emphasis).

[3] Ibid.

[4] Ibid.: 229 and 233.

[5] Kennedy 2002: 110.

[6] Cf. Verdirame and Harrell-Bond's analysis of UNHCR which comes to a very different conclusion – see section 8.1.2a.

of the international standards that were being operationalised. However, as I argue below, there is an element of flexibility inherent in the CRC (in particular the best interests principle) that permits a contextual approach and, to the extent that this argument does not stand up, I suggest that there are strong policy arguments in favour of the approach adopted by UNICEF Rwanda.

a Legal Flexibility

The non-binding instruments that address children in conflict with the law allow for context and resources to be taken into account in respect of all standards, whilst the CRC allows for consideration of resources only in respect of economic, social and cultural rights, and there is only a fleeting reference to culture in the preamble. However, the CRC contains various provisions that are considered to be indeterminate,[7] and it is reasoned here that this lack of precision allows for local conditions to be taken into account.

If we take as an example UNICEF Rwanda's support for institutionalisation, which was determinative of its overall approach, the relevant provision in the CRC provides the flexibility required when seeking to apply the text to a concrete situation. The CRC provides that detention or imprisonment 'shall be used only as a measure of last resort and for the shortest appropriate period of time'. As noted in Chapter 6, having explored alternative actions, UNICEF Rwanda concluded that detention was, at that time, the only option for genocide minors (although it was also working towards their release through other activities). It is clear from the wording that detention *can* be used as a last resort, and the use of the word 'appropriate' allows for some flexibility in terms of duration (although long-term pre-trial detention likely exceeds any such inherent flexibility and would also conflict with other provisions, such as the presumption of innocence). Similar modifying words and phrases are found in the CRC's other juvenile justice provisions. For example, diversion should be used 'whenever appropriate and desirable',[8] alternative measures to institutionalisation should be available to ensure the juvenile is treated in a manner 'appropriate' to the juvenile's well-being and 'proportionate' to the juvenile's circumstances and the offence,[9] and states shall 'seek to promote' juvenile-specific laws and institutions.[10] As

[7] See section 3.1.3.
[8] Art. 40(3)(b).
[9] Art. 40(4).
[10] Art. 40(3).

Price Cohen explains: 'The purpose of the modifying phrase is to make allowances for local conditions.'[11] UNICEF itself has identified this type of phrase as recognition of differences between societies.[12]

Further, as illustrated in Chapter 6, UNICEF Rwanda clearly drew on the best interests principle when interpreting the requirements of the CRC. Indeed, the issue of how UNICEF Rwanda could and should defend the best interests of child genocide suspects dominated discussions both within UNICEF and between UNICEF and its governmental and civil society partners. The best interests principle was consequently used as a 'master' principle that could, if circumstances required it, even allow for making exceptions from apparently strict and exception-less requirements. A case in point is the decision to support the institutionalisation of minors despite them having been arrested and detained in breach of arrest and detention procedures. In contrast to the provision requiring detention to be a measure of last resort, the prohibition on unlawful or arbitrary detention is precise, allowing for no variation. Had UNICEF Rwanda followed a strict interpretation of this provision, it should arguably have insisted on the release of child suspects from detention, irrespective of the possible consequences.[13] However, it chose not to pursue this course of action, relying on the best interests principle to support its approach. The best interests principle should not be used to justify a violation of a CRC provision, but it is a substantive right in itself and can also be used to resolve conflicts between rights. In this particular example, given the perceived risk to the safety of children accused of genocide, it appears that UNICEF Rwanda was giving effect to the best interests principle and also giving precedence to the right to life[14] and the protection of the child from all forms of physical or mental violence[15] over the right not to be arbitrarily or unlawfully detained. In my view, it is therefore legally sound. In any event, there are strong policy reasons to support this approach, at least in the first few years after the genocide when the risk of revenge attacks appeared more acute. Insistence on compliance with this one provision could have led, to borrow Kennedy's term,

[11] Price Cohen 1987: 81.

[12] UNICEF 1999c: 12.

[13] It is worth recalling that there is no evidence of other international actors (including those most critical of the Rwandan government) calling for the release of children on these grounds.

[14] Art. 6, CRC (one of the CRC's key general principles).

[15] Art. 19, CRC.

to a 'distorted' outcome. Further, in coming to the decision to support institutionalisation and in the development of subsequent programmes, UNICEF Rwanda took account of the severity of the crime and the need to rehabilitate and reintegrate the children, and the interests of others in society (including child victims), all of which are valid factors.

UNICEF Rwanda further relied on the best interests principle to argue that all those who were under 18 at the time of the offence should continue to be separated from adults in detention facilities. It also asserted that it had a responsibility under its mandate as well as the CRC and related standards to improve the physical conditions of children in detention, contending that failure to do so would be contrary to the best interests of these children. It could be argued, however, that UNICEF Rwanda's support, particularly of the construction of minors' wings, is at variance with the CRC. UNICEF's global policy set out in its Toolkit on Diversion and Alternatives to Detention[16] states that UNICEF should 'limit as much as possible direct assistance in the improvement of physical conditions in closed institutions, and refrain from contributing to the building of new ones'. It adds that the focus should be on diversion and alternative measures, rather than solely or mainly on 'isolated initiatives' to improve detention conditions and suggests that 'other partners' may be able to address detention conditions.[17] Clearly this would be the preferred approach in a normalised situation. However, as discussed in previous chapters, given the resource constraints, the social context and the lack of a social welfare system,[18] alternatives to detention and diversion were not feasible. Further, whilst the ICRC and some other actors were targeting detention conditions and did make significant contributions to the protection of children in detention, their focus was on all detainees (rather than minors specifically). It must also be recalled that, in addition to the restrictions on the use of detention, the CRC contains various other provisions relevant to detained children (including the requirement for separation from adults and to treat children in detention with humanity and respect, and the rights to education, health and an adequate standard of living). UNICEF Rwanda was thus seeking to enhance implementation of, and compliance with, these rights, and relied on the best interests principle to support its overall approach to detention conditions. This

[16] UNICEF (undated).

[17] Ibid.

[18] See comments in section 8.1.1b regarding consideration of resources and other factors in the implementation of civil and political rights.

would seem legitimate, although there is an argument that prioritisation of rights is not envisaged under the CRC (see next section).

The best interests of the child must be a factor in all decisions relating to children, but other interests (such as interests of justice and the broader society) can also be taken into account. Indeed, as Cantwell propounds, using the best interests principle as 'a kind of general trump card … that eliminates the need to take account of external factors' is a 'misreading' of the CRC.[19] And Alston comments that the use of the indefinite article in Article 3 of the CRC – the bests interests of the child shall be '*a* primary consideration' – was to 'ensure that there is sufficient flexibility, at least in certain extreme cases, to enable the interests of those other than the child to prevail'.[20] It is possible that the application of the principle could unjustly allow for other interests to be prioritised over those of the child or may permit cultural considerations to be foregrounded at the expense of the substantive rights. The best interests principle, however, provides the elasticity to allow local conditions to be taken into account when implementing the substantive provisions and, in my view, was used appropriately in the Rwandan context. Although other factors were taken into account by UNICEF Rwanda, it appears that concern for the safety of the children was, in practice, the prevailing consideration. It is also worth recalling Cantwell's comments that the CRC as a whole should be seen as a 'living document' that is able to adapt to new issues not in the contemplation of the drafters at the time:[21] serious violent crimes, and crimes of atrocity in particular, were perhaps unlikely to have been at the forefront of minds.

The CRC thus contains language that allows for contextual application of the standards. Various scholars have identified the inherent flexibility within human rights treaties and argue that this enables practical application.[22] For example, Charlesworth asserts that human rights treaties 'have strong elements of pragmatism … allow[ing] considerable leeway in national translation of their standards'.[23] And Galligan and Sandler argue that human rights standards are often 'open-ended', with the result

[19] Cantwell 2011: 49 (he also stresses that using it to 'override rights' considered dispensable is a misreading of the CRC).

[20] Alston 1994: 12–13 (although he notes that the onus is on those seeking to promote other interests to show that there were no other 'feasible and acceptable alternatives').

[21] Cantwell 2011: 52–53.

[22] Cf. Chayes and Chayes, Franck and Shelton's view that textual determinacy is important for compliance (see Chapter 3, note 20).

[23] Charlesworth 2002: 130.

that the state has discretion as to their interpretation as well as how to implement them.[24] States are thus able to 'tailor abstract human rights standards to local values, social structures and institutional capacities'.[25] Galligan and Sandler aver that this flexibility to decide how international standards apply in the domestic context is 'fundamental' to the human rights regime and that this 'is the compromise between the universalist claims of human rights and the imperatives of local culture'.[26] However, whilst they accept that some variation is perhaps necessary during implementation, they reject the idea that standards are 'wholly subject to local interpretation' and consider that differences are not so much based on normative incompatibility but rather on issues that arise between 'universal standards and particular conditions' during implementation.[27]

This last point raises the issue of whether contextualisation amounts to relativity, calling into question the universality[28] of human rights. Veale asserts that 'there are inevitable tensions between an international tool that aims to make universal claims on behalf of all children, and such a tool being sufficiently meaningful to the localised experiences of children across the globe'.[29] In my view, this does not, however, call into question the universality of child rights, and more specifically juvenile justice standards. Rather, the issue is one of enforcement and universal implementation.[30] I would thus agree with Donnelly that '[t]he moral universality of human rights, which has been codified in a strong set of authoritative international norms, must be in the end realized through the particularities of national action'.[31] He speaks of the 'relative universality' of human rights, where there is space to take account of local

[24] Galligan and Sandler 2004: 27–28. Although Galligan and Sandler are speaking of a state's implementation, the same considerations can be applied to international agencies seeking to enhance implementation by the state.

[25] Ibid.: 32.

[26] Ibid.: 27–28. See also Twum-Danso 2008, who argues that the CRC provides the flexibility for governments to take account of social and cultural factors when domesticating the Convention and that some of its terms leave room for local interpretation.

[27] Galligan and Sandler 2004: 32.

[28] Note the distinction between universalism, defined as 'the attempt to eliminate particularity and achieve uniformity at global level', and universality, which is 'the attempt to bring out and develop the global resonance of particular ideas' and which accepts limitations (Marks and Clapham 2005: 398).

[29] Veale 1999: 106.

[30] See also Grover 2007: 432–433 (commenting that child protection rights are universal conceptually and morally, even if they are not universally enforced), but cf. Bentley 2005.

[31] Donnelly 2013: 210.

particularities, and proposes that 'universal human rights not only may but should be implemented in different ways at different times and in different places'.[32] In his view, interpreting and implementing rights 'within the range of variation consistent with the overarching concept' is a 'matter of legitimate variation'.[33]

b Policy Considerations

Whilst a number of UNICEF Rwanda's interventions can be said to fall within the range of variation permitted by the CRC, some of its approaches could be seen as technically incompatible with the CRC's express wording or overall nature. As illustrated in the previous two chapters, UNICEF Rwanda accepted that some rights could not be achieved immediately, choosing to focus on those rights where it considered it could have more immediate, positive influence. It thus prioritised some rights over others. For example, it focused on enhancing the rights to education, health and humane conditions for children in detention, and their separation from adults, accepting that alternatives to detention were not feasible at that point, although it did continue to advocate for, and work towards, the removal of minors from prisons.

As previously indicated, the CRC does not allow resources to be a factor in the implementation of civil and political rights. It also contains no derogation provision. This suggests that such rights can be implemented in full, immediately, in any situation. Additionally, the CRC is considered to be holistic, with all rights being indivisible and interdependent. As Tobin explains, however, interpreting indivisibility to mean that there is no hierarchy of rights could result in a standstill if there is no prioritisation when decisions are being made regarding the allocation of scarce resources. He thus asserts that the concept of indivisibility was 'never intended to prohibit the prioritisation of individual human rights within particular jurisdictions and contexts', rather it was introduced to 'level up the playing field' between the two sets of rights (civil and political, and economic, social and cultural).[34] Indeed, UNICEF recognised in its 1998 guidelines for human rights-based programming that the 'principle of indivisibility … does not prevent UNICEF from deciding with national partners on priorities for action, based on a combination of situation assessment, problem analysis, and available resources'.[35] Such prioritisation does not

[32] Ibid.: 105. See also Twum-Danso 2008 and Twum-Danso Imoh 2011.
[33] Donnelly 2013: 103.
[34] Tobin 2011: 80.
[35] UNICEF 1998d.

imply that other rights are not of concern to UNICEF; simply that it is not feasible for UNICEF to take immediate action in all situations where there is a threat to children's rights.[36] In a post-conflict situation like Rwanda, where all types of resources (financial, human, material and organisational) are deficient, the prospects for full implementation of, and compliance with, either set of rights are slim. As Tully asserts, 'there is little difference between protecting civil and political rights and protecting economic and social rights in that they both require countries with limited resources to enact positive law and to expend limited resources'.[37] Indeed, White and Klaasen perceptively comment: 'In the practical world, claiming that all rights are immediately applicable in a post-conflict situation may well result in none being adequately protected.'[38]

There is thus a strong policy argument for the prioritisation of rights in practice and for working towards implementation and compliance. This means that international actors may have to accept that some rights (including civil and political) cannot be realised immediately and adapt their policy development and advocacy accordingly. Howen states:

> Human rights field officers will often face difficult trade-offs between insisting that the best global human rights safeguards must be put in place, and encouraging or acquiescing in a step that is short of the human rights standards, to achieve at least a modicum of protection. What compromises are acceptable? … Response will require a complex balancing of principle and pragmatism, understanding the human rights 'bottom line' and in some cases encouraging immediate achievable action while working for the ultimate human rights goal.[39]

A former UNICEF Rwanda staff member commented that, although the CRC establishes minimum standards, in a certain context 'that minimum can be an ideal that is still very far away'. The staff member referred to the numerous juvenile justice standards in the Convention, noting that, in a post-genocide situation, it is 'simply not possible' to ask the government to comply with all the standards overnight: attention should be drawn to the standards, but it must be accepted that they can be implemented only incrementally. This does not mean that the principles and standards in the CRC should be modified: rather, it is a question of 'how' UNICEF approaches their realisation in a given context, and this may require

[36] See UNICEF 1991a: [20] and UNICEF 2007a: 9.
[37] Tully 2003: 387.
[38] White and Klaasen 2005: 3.
[39] Howen 2007: 43.

emphasising some rights over others.[40] Note that this does not equate to a 'salami' approach, which was identified by Abramson as a reason for the marginalisation of juvenile justice:[41] rather, it is adopting a holistic and comprehensive approach, considering all the applicable rights and determining what can realistically be achieved at the relevant point in time. Todd Howland, the former Head of the Legal and Human Rights Promotion Unit of UNHRFOR, asserted that, whilst the use of a progressive realisation discourse is less usual in the context of civil and political rights, it was what was required in a situation of mass violations. For him, the most useful approach was to use the standards as the starting point for discussions and consider how to move 'in the direction' of these standards. The 'pragmatic path' was not to point to violations and insist that 'from today to tomorrow' the government must create whole systems; rather partnerships must be created to work towards standards over a longer period.[42] This approach is supported by Himes, who asserts that organisations seeking to assist with progressive realisation of rights should aim to assist states to improve compliance over time rather than only highlighting violations or shortcomings.[43] Indeed, establishing achievable goals is essential in difficult contexts, particularly where there is instability. As noted by Nyi Nyi, it is 'easier to generate political will if leaders can expect results during their political lives in office' (noting that in many developing countries, 'political life spans are short'). Thus, programmes need to be 'doable with results and measurable impact in the not too distant future'.[44] In Rwanda, the same party has been in power now since the genocide. However, this was not a foregone conclusion in the years after the genocide, and it will certainly not always be the case in other countries.

Arguably, engaging with the domestic authorities to achieve some progress that falls short of the CRC standards, but which nonetheless improves the child's human rights situation, is preferable to insisting on full compliance and risk making no progress. As Pedersen notes, in 'the most difficult contexts, the alternative to incremental change will often be no change at all'.[45] Oestreich's review of UNICEF's position on child

[40] Skype interview with former UNICEF Rwanda Child Protection Staff Member B, 19 November 2014.

[41] See section 3.2.

[42] Skype interview with Howland, 7 February 2014.

[43] Himes 1993: 13.

[44] Nyi Nyi 2001: 72.

[45] Pedersen 2013: 32.

labour suggests that UNICEF has taken this approach in other areas. UNICEF 'implicitly accepted' that the elimination of child labour could only be achieved progressively, 'despite the requirements of the CRC'. This context-sensitive orientation was considered 'an asset rather than a liability in pursuing human rights goals'.[46] Of course, as time went on and some of the challenges diminished, UNICEF Rwanda could conceivably have insisted on greater compliance. HRW was of the view that arguments by 'international experts' that 'major weaknesses of the justice system as a whole' had to be addressed before it was possible to focus on juvenile justice were 'more persuasive in the years immediately following the genocide'.[47] This is a valid criticism although it is difficult to pinpoint when the emergency situation evolved into a more stable situation.

Some scholars have suggested that progressive implementation should be extended to all human rights or that a limited human rights framework could be applied to post-conflict situations. Brems, for example, sees 'little danger' in making civil and political rights subject to progressive realisation, as the concept does not allow governments to rely on lack of resources 'as a total excuse'.[48] Even where rights are subject to progressive realisation, states are under an immediate obligation to undertake measures 'to move as expeditiously and effectively as possible towards the full realization', and ensure a minimal level, of each right ('minimum core obligations').[49] White and Odello suggest that the legal framework of state of emergency could be used to guide post-conflict situations (although they note the two situations may differ), allowing states and international actors to prioritise rights, focusing on those requiring immediate protection, with positive measures to protect other rights being taken 'after the core is secured'.[50] An analysis of these approaches, and what 'core obligations' might be in the context of child rights, is beyond the scope of this book, but these could be interesting areas for further research. However, I do submit that the concepts of progressive realisation and of a limited human rights framework can justifiably inform the approach of international actors that are seeking to enhance a state's implementation

[46] Oestreich 1998: 189.

[47] HRW 2003a: 76.

[48] Brems 2001: 356.

[49] CRC Committee 2007b: [46–48]. See also Himes 1995: 25, noting that it is essential to have targets, programmes and strategies from the beginning to ensure 'some minimal essential level' and then monitor progress towards full realisation.

[50] White and Odello 2007: 61–63. They stress, however, that the state or other actors should not violate other rights by adopting this approach.

of, and compliance with, international standards in a post-conflict situation.[51]

In summary, I consider a contextual approach to be not only useful in operationalising international standards, but necessary. Failing to take account of the context and specific challenges when designing a policy approach could result in more harm than good. White, who is stressing the importance of local acceptance of human rights values, comments:

> If universal standards are merely transposed into the context of post-conflict situations, with broken state structures and economies, and little or non-existent justice, education or health systems, then they are unlikely to have any positive sustainable effect. It should be recognised that such interventions can be harmful or counterproductive. The UN must ensure that in its actions it goes beyond the rhetoric of human rights. The UN ought to translate human rights standards into the local context in its operations.[52]

This inevitably means considering what can realistically be achieved in light of the prevailing conditions and tailoring the norms set out in the CRC to the particular society.[53] The challenge then for international actors is to seek to enhance implementation and compliance in a manner that remains true to principles and standards, whilst also remaining cognisant of, and sensitive to, the context. I would argue that, although UNICEF Rwanda's approach was not a panacea and there remained serious violations of the rights of child perpetrators, on the whole, UNICEF Rwanda met that challenge.

8.1.2 Collaborative or Compromised?

UNICEF Rwanda utilised multifarious strategies when seeking to enhance the rights of child perpetrators in the particular context of post-genocide Rwanda. There are differing views on the best way to enhance compliance with human rights standards. This is often presented as a tension between the coercion or enforcement model and the persuasion or management

[51] See also Hannum 2006: 56, who, referring to the OHCHR's operations, argues that the concept of temporary derogation should guide technical assistance and capacity-building projects in post-conflict situations.

[52] White 2005: 473 (references omitted).

[53] See also Parry Williams 1998: 29 (noting that although the CRC standards 'represent universal values, their realisation requires a pragmatic approach').

model.[54] The coercion or enforcement model is confrontational in nature. It focuses on demanding compliance and may punish governments that violate human rights standards. Coercion or enforcement may take the form of humanitarian intervention or the imposition or threat of various types of sanctions (military or economic), but it can also include rewarding good behaviour (through positive incentives).[55] The alternative perspective is non-confrontational and facilitative in nature, and encourages compliance through dialogue and a process of socialisation, which emphasises the legitimacy or value of the norm and seeks the internalisation of the norm by the target state. Capacity building is often incorporated within the broader concept of persuasion or management, although it can also be considered an approach to human rights promotion in itself. Whilst an overall strategy will generally be grounded in one of the main approaches, an actor may use techniques from across the spectrum, and indeed there is some overlap between the main approaches. Further, some techniques are difficult to categorise: 'naming and shaming', for example, which involves documenting and then publicising or condemning violations could be considered a form of persuasion,[56] or conversely could serve a coercive function.[57] This book does not propose to evaluate the strengths and weaknesses of these strategies, or indeed the theoretical perspectives underlying them, but it is worth keeping them in mind when evaluating

[54] See e.g. Goodman and Jinks 2004 and 2013 (who also refer to a third way of promoting human rights – not considered in this book – namely acculturation, which emphasises cognitive and social pressures to conform); Hafner-Burton 2013: 62–65. The management approach is most associated with the work of Chayes and Chayes (1993 and 1995). The promotion strategies are grounded in the underlying theoretical perspective (and related assumptions) on whether and why states comply with international norms. Some theorists argue that, where states are in compliance, this is due to coercion or coincidence of interests (e.g. Goldsmith and Posner 2005); some highlight the importance of interests and changing incentives, such as the use of sanctions or risk to reputation (e.g. Guzman 2002; Keohane 1997); and others focus on the content of the norm itself (e.g. Franck 1988, propounding that the legitimacy of norms results in a 'compliance-pull') and/or the importance of interactions of states within institutions or with transnational actors (e.g. Chayes and Chayes 1993 and 1995; Koh 1997). For a comprehensive overview of compliance literature, see Hathaway 2002; Koh 1997; Raustiala and Slaughter 2002.

[55] Zimmerman (2017: 17–18 and 60) refers to the use of sanctions and incentives as 'conditionality-oriented' modes of interaction.

[56] Risse and Ropp (2013: 14–16) include naming and shaming under 'persuasion', contrasting coercion as the use of force or legal enforcement and identifying capacity building and incentives as two additional mechanisms to induce compliance.

[57] On the basis that it is adversarial in nature, it is in effect seeking to hold a state accountable, it constitutes a sanction and it could result in a change to material interests. See Montoya 2013: 42.

UNICEF Rwanda's multipronged but broadly collaborative approach to implementation and compliance.

a The Risk of Usurpation or Co-option

As illustrated in Chapters 6 and 7, a key element of UNICEF Rwanda's collaborative approach was the provision of support to, and capacity building of, Rwanda's institutions. Capacity building has been identified by some theorists as key to enhancing compliance with international law where a state lacks the ability (as opposed to political will) to meet its obligations. However, it has been suggested that, in some instances, UNICEF Rwanda went beyond providing assistance and took on the role itself of implementing programmes and policies relating to child *génocidaires*. In some cases, it directly participated in legal and policy development, for example being part of the government commission discussing criminal law reform. It was also directly involved in the building or reconstruction of minors' wings in detention facilities and in the provision of various forms of support to institutions involved with child *génocidaires*.

Putnam argues that, in a post-conflict society, '[a]chieving anything approaching immediate compliance with international human rights standards in the sphere of policing, judicial operations, or the distribution of economic and social resources is feasible only if outside implementers assume responsibility for day-to-day operations in these areas'. As she notes, however, this '"takeover" method hinders the development of a domestic capacity to protect human rights'.[58] The risk of creating dependency and of substituting initiatives that should come from the government and/or domestic civil society was recognised by UNICEF Rwanda at the time (as well as by commentators).[59] UNICEF Rwanda's involvement in government commissions was unusual, and it is arguable that it exceeded its mandate of providing technical 'assistance' which Cantwell explains should be more a role of informing decisions rather than 'securing decisive influence on outcomes'.[60] As regards its direct involvement in reconstruction and the provision of support, these could, in effect, be seen as 'implementing' programmes, rather than assisting the government with implementation and, again, going beyond its mandate. However, it is important to note that the government retained responsibility over all decisions relating to

[58] Putnam 2002: 249.
[59] See e.g. text at notes 149–150, Chapter 6 and at note 8, Chapter 7.
[60] Cantwell 1997: 88.

child *génocidaires* and over all relevant facilities. Given the extreme circumstances, in particular the devastation of Rwanda's infrastructure and the lack of other actors (including domestic NGOs) working on the rights of child perpetrators, I would agree with Matthes' comment that there was no alternative to this 'direct engagement',[61] at least during the first few years after the genocide. Further, as detailed in Chapter 7, UNICEF Rwanda was seeking to build capacity of the authorities and local organisations at the same time as this direct engagement, so as to create sustainability and local ownership.

A different approach may be required by international actors when providing technical or other assistance in a post-conflict or post-disaster scenario when compared to a normal, stable situation. UNICEF itself has identified that different situations require unique strategies. This includes situations at opposite ends of the scale: a situation where a national government is 'willing and able' to care and protect children will mean that no assistance is required from UNICEF; but in 'exceptional circumstances when government systems collapse or fragment so completely', it may be necessary for UNICEF (or other external actors) to 'assume temporarily a more central role in the delivery of assistance to children than would otherwise be the case'.[62] Whilst UNICEF may usually assume a 'facilitative role' that aims to 'enhance rather than displace local efforts', in emergency situations its approach may need to be more direct.[63]

A further issue regarding capacity building as a strategy is that it is not always possible to determine whether the issue is one of lack of will or lack of capacity (or a combination of the two). Where there is an element of lack of will, there is a risk that the provision of technical assistance and other capacity-building activities will become a smokescreen: a government may request assistance from international actors to shield it from greater scrutiny and avoid international accountability.[64] Indeed, as Oestreich opines: 'A conciliatory approach to implementing human rights standards could conceivably weaken standards in the name of cooperation. Making a show of cooperating with intergovernmental organizations might be used cynically by states to divert real pressure; or it might be manipulated as public relations "damage control." '[65] This

[61] Matthes 1996b: 3.

[62] UNICEF 1995c: [24].

[63] Ibid.: [25].

[64] Howen 2007: 37.

[65] Oestreich 1998: 196–197.

risk can be reduced where protection activities (involving monitoring, documenting, analysing and reporting on violations) are undertaken and inform the capacity-building projects by providing baseline data and benchmarks.[66] Monitoring is of course essential to identify areas where material and financial assistance, legal reform and training are needed and is also essential for evaluating the effectiveness of technical assistance and capacity-building activities.[67] There is evidence that UNICEF Rwanda did undertake monitoring, although this was perhaps directed more often at the formulation of policies rather than evaluating results. As will be discussed in greater detail below, monitoring and reporting (in particular public reporting) can lead to conflict with the government, whilst capacity building may lead to monitoring and reporting being relegated in order to maintain good relations with the government. It is thus essential for organisations to strike a balance between the two: something that was particularly difficult in Rwanda given the sensitivity of the government to criticism and the difficult relationship between the government and the UN.[68]

The risk of being instrumentalised by a government is greater where an organisation is more deeply involved in policy and programme development. Referring to the experiences of the ICRC and UNHCR, Oestreich comments that, where an international institution takes on the role of implementing standards, 'political controversy inevitably results'. Both the ICRC and UNHCR have been accused of 'backing away too quickly from controversy rather than standing on an ethical point'.[69] Not only might an organisation lose its objectivity, but it may also be used by the government to legitimise ongoing violations and, in some cases, may even participate in those violations itself: thus the very opposite of promoting international standards and principles. One way of minimising the risk of legitimising 'bad governments' is by criticising human rights violations where appropriate.[70]

[66] Howen 2007: 37–38.

[67] Ibid.: 38.

[68] Recall that UNHRFOR ceased to operate in Rwanda after the Rwandan government had wished to remove the monitoring function from its mandate (see note 33, Chapter 6).

[69] Oestreich 1998: 194.

[70] Pedersen 2013: 31. Pedersen is writing on repressive states, but his comments regarding criticisms can also be applied to post-conflict states which may lack the will to implement and comply with international standards.

Verdirame and Harrell-Bond explore the risk of co-option and compromising principles in their seminal work on UNHCR.[71] They argue that UNHCR's protective function and its supervision of compliance with refugee law were compromised once it assumed control over refugee policy.[72] They point to various violations of rights perpetrated by the government or other actors under UNHCR's watch (or on some occasions even by UNHCR staff themselves) in refugee camps. UNHCR sometimes admitted that the violations were occurring but relied on 'implausible arguments to justify their conduct' or more frequently denied the violations.[73] The authors thus argue that UNHCR either acquiesced in, or was directly responsible for, violations in refugee camps over which it exercised powers of administration. In Verdirame and Harrell-Bond's assessment:

> UNHCR staff and programmes had become almost impervious to arguments based on the law. As explained by Goodwin-Gill, 'that portion of UNHCR protection work that was rooted in international law, standards and principles, has been eclipsed by so-called pragmatic approaches to refugee problems, in which everything seems to be negotiable'. The belief that 'in extreme cases, principles and standards can seem almost academic in deciding action' pervaded the work of the organisation.[74]

Verdirame and Harrell-Bond's account highlights the risk of pragmatism prevailing over principles, particularly where an organisation is closely involved with the government, or even steps into the government's shoes.

It is clear that UNICEF Rwanda played a significant role with regard to child perpetrators, particularly in terms of its support of institutionalisation and related assistance. However, in contrast to UNHCR, UNICEF Rwanda did not occupy a position of power (administrative or otherwise) over institutions. Its greatest involvement was perhaps with the Gitagata Re-education Centre, but even then, the government retained full responsibility for the administration and the decisions taken. Further, UNICEF Rwanda was very much conscious of the risks. Whilst it recognised its

[71] Verdirame and Harrell-Bond 2005. Note that UNHCR's role differs from that of UNICEF, UNHCR having an express duty to supervise the application of the 1951 Refugee Convention, whereas the CRC Committee has this role in respect of child rights.

[72] This took the form of providing significant material, financial and technical assistance, running camps directly and determining refugee status. Verdirame and Bond (ibid.: 273) comment that it was not clear why UNHCR assumed this role: whether it pushed for it or whether it was reluctant.

[73] Ibid.: 120. See 120–213 for illustrations of civil and political rights violations.

[74] Ibid.: 290 (references omitted).

primary role in the Gitagata process, it affirmed that it was imperative that the government retain control over re-education centres and other places of detention, not only for accountability reasons, but also for longer-term sustainability and for reintegration efforts. Perceptions also had to match reality: in addition to actual control being in the hands of the government, UNICEF Rwanda saw it as essential that re-education centres were not seen as 'UNICEF centres'.[75] White, addressing pragmatism versus principles in the context of UN humanitarian programmes and human rights protection, comments that where activities are under UN control – such as refugee camps run by UNHCR – the 'principled approach' must prevail. In other situations, provided that 'the UN insists on gradual improvement of human rights by the state', a pragmatic approach (which in White's analysis entails providing humanitarian assistance whilst tolerating human rights violations) can take precedence.[76] I would suggest that his arguments remain valid for the case study in this book.

In any event, as argued earlier, I do not consider that UNICEF Rwanda abandoned its principles. Although violations of the rights of child perpetrators did occur, UNICEF Rwanda did not ignore them or deny they were occurring; rather it argued that some international standards could not be met immediately given the particular context and outlined measures it was taking, or for which it was advocating, to improve the situation. It is true that UNICEF Rwanda sought to justify its approach, but it is also clear from explanations provided in documents, to the media and during this research that the tension was there and that UNICEF Rwanda was aware of potential criticisms: ultimately, UNICEF Rwanda staff considered that the measures (particularly relating to institutionalisation) were required both legally and morally.

b Condemnation versus Cooperation

A key criticism of UNHCR by Verdirame and Harrell-Bond was that it failed to denounce serious violations, even though it knew that they were taking place. HRW made similar criticisms of UNICEF Rwanda. Whilst it acknowledged that the collaborative approach adopted by UNICEF Rwanda (and donors) was 'often useful', it argued that there should also have been 'open criticism when it fail[ed] to achieve progress if the abuses

[75] UNICEF Rwanda 1996d: 21.

[76] White 2005: 466–467 (note that White is referring to UN activities in the period prior to a stable post-conflict stage, but it would be difficult to establish at what point in time such a post-conflict stage was reached in Rwanda).

in question [were] serious and ongoing'.[77] It considered that the international community as a whole 'largely muted its criticism', choosing instead to praise Rwanda's progress in juvenile justice 'despite its failure to follow through on its commitments'.[78] HRW's criticism is valid to some extent: an international actor that seeks to enhance compliance with international standards cannot ignore, or even worse be complicit in, violations. The issue is achieving a balance between criticism and cooperation.

UNICEF Rwanda did not make public denunciations of violations and was reticent about using condemnatory language when dealing with the government. Arguably, it did err on the side of caution, and it could have been more critical in its interventions with the government and possibly publicly, but it is at least understandable that a condemnatory approach was considered inappropriate and potentially counter-productive to making progress on international standards. There is evidence that where UNICEF Rwanda did denounce violations this backfired, and other commentators have referred to the sensitivity of the Rwandan government to criticisms, particularly when such criticisms came from UN institutions.[79] UNICEF Rwanda was also concerned that criticism and condemnation could have resulted in the Rwandan government withdrawing its cooperation, not only in juvenile justice matters (just one subset of its child protection programme) but also in UNICEF Rwanda's other programmes, or even put its staff at risk. As Pedersen asserts, coercive strategies (including condemnation) can limit opportunities to use other non-coercive strategies such as engaging with reformers in government and providing assistance in areas where there is lack of capacity rather than lack of political will.[80] Additionally, it is by no means conclusive that denouncing violations in general is more effective at enhancing protection of rights: addressing them diplomatically and privately could, in practice, result in greater progress being made.[81]

There was also very much the feeling that highlighting violations without offering assistance would not lead to greater implementation

[77] HRW 2003a: 76.

[78] Ibid.: 75–76.

[79] See e.g. O'Neill 2007: 129. See also note 68.

[80] Pedersen 2013: 20–21. See also Putnam 2002: 252 ('[T]he adversarial ethos that underpins the enforcement approach sets IHRO [international human rights organisations] advocates in formal opposition to suspected violators, which in turn limits severely the level of constructive engagement IHROs can undertake with violator institutions and governments.').

[81] See also O'Donnell 1992: 35.

and compliance. As Howland argues: 'The objective for human rights interventionists is to improve the situations they encounter, rather than simply denouncing them.'[82] Indeed, UNICEF Rwanda seems to have largely eschewed an enforcement approach, using the CRC more as a policy tool to shape law, policy and practice rather than a legal tool to evaluate (and subsequently punish non-) compliance.[83] One option could have been for UNICEF Rwanda to insist on compliance with juvenile justice standards and refuse to provide assistance until Rwanda met its obligations. However, as one UNICEF Rwanda staff member noted, this is not the way UNICEF works.[84] Further, as Davidson argues, the CRC is 'not a criminal enforcement statute'; its value is in providing 'an important legal framework that legislators and reformers can and should use, and have used, to advocate for domestic legislation, policies, and practices that enforce those rights within their own countries'.[85] Davidson's comments can be extended to international actors seeking to enhance implementation and compliance, particularly in difficult contexts.

In a post-conflict situation, it is essential to identify shortcomings, but also to offer realistic, context-specific solutions. Martin, in his evaluation of UNHRFOR, concurs: 'Certainly in a situation where institutions have been destroyed or have never existed, to point to human rights violations while offering no linkage to assistance would have been to invite dismissal, and to pursue technical co-operation while ignoring serious ongoing violations would have been naive and unacceptable.'[86] And, as Putnam comments in relation to post-conflict situations, human rights organisations must 'choose their tactics according to the conditions actually prevailing in those situations, and not according to an abstract ideal'. She adds that this will involve going beyond 'traditional international human rights enforcement roles and methods' and adopting 'more flexible, consultative approaches to human rights protection that focus on

[82] Howland 2007: 329.

[83] Tobin (2011: 66–67) refers to this type of approach as 'rights-based', in which rights are used to shape policies to achieve human rights protection. He contrasts this with the 'traditional compliance model' of human rights, which involves a determination as to whether a standard has been violated or protected.

[84] Skype interview with former UNICEF Rwanda Child Protection Staff Member B, 19 November 2014.

[85] Davidson 2014: 522–523.

[86] Martin 1998: 19. See also Henkin 2000, an edited volume on UN human rights field operations in which numerous authors refer to the tension between monitoring/reporting and institution building.

building and enabling institutions'. By adopting such an approach, she argues, it is possible to have a direct influence on human rights implementation.[87] Cole makes a similar argument regarding the necessity to build capacity along with monitoring shortcomings. He adds: 'Weak countries cannot be shamed into compliance any more than they can be coerced to comply.'[88] Specifically speaking of the implementation of child rights, Cantwell asserts that organisations frequently lack 'realism', one reason for which is a '"jurist-purist" approach that sticks, come what may, to a principle and refuses to take a more pragmatic view of the issue at hand'. Thus advocates may demand change but fail themselves to identify, and suggest, constructive ways for the state to bring about this change. Citing Tomasevski who said, 'No government can be legally obliged to do the impossible', Cantwell lists a number of factors that may render change impossible, including lack of resources and opposition from society. He suggests that advocates 'might usefully take this into account' when devising strategies to enhance child rights.[89]

UNICEF Rwanda appears to have adopted an approach that is contrary to Cantwell's general observation that child rights advocates lack realism, very much taking into account the various factors hindering progress in Rwanda. Through monitoring the situation, it focused on identifying areas for improvement and locating a strategic entry point, and then used its assistance strategically to obtain some progress towards the realisation of the rights of child *génocidaires*. And although it does not appear to have expressly condemned violations of international standards, it did raise concerns and made its values and perspectives, firmly grounded in the CRC and related instruments, very clear to the Rwandan government in areas that were considered especially difficult and politically sensitive.

UNICEF Rwanda frequently drew attention to Rwanda's obligations under the CRC, but, on some occasions, it referenced domestic law and/or non-binding international instruments or deployed non-legal arguments. An argument could be made that this approach undermines the normative value, or the binding nature, of CRC rights, perhaps suggesting that UNICEF Rwanda did not perceive the standards set out in the CRC as binding law, but more as an aspirational set of values. However, this is not supported by the empirical data. Although UNICEF Rwanda staff members did not *always* invoke Rwanda's legal obligations, it was clear

[87] Putnam 2002: 255 and 260.
[88] Cole 2015: 436.
[89] Cantwell 2011: 51–52.

that they viewed the CRC as binding law, and that they saw value in its binding nature. Staff members spoke of the 'authority' or 'legitimacy' that the CRC provides because it is binding on those states that have ratified it.[90] The question was 'how' to communicate with the government to work towards compliance. In some cases, a deliberate decision was taken to refer to domestic law as it was considered that this would resonate more with the Rwandan government[91] and thus provide an inroad into compliance. It was also necessary to refer to non-binding instruments where these expanded on the CRC rights, provided interpretative guidance, or where the CRC was considered to have limitations.[92] And non-legal arguments were deployed (as noted, often in addition to a reference to a legal standard) either to provide a more detailed explanation of the reasons behind a standard or to offer Rwanda an incentive to comply with a standard, relying once again on language that would resonate in the domestic sphere. Where non-legal discourses were used in lieu of a standard, the ultimate objective was nonetheless compliance with the CRC. The argument that such an approach might undermine the normative value is based on the assumption that internalisation of the norm is required for effective implementation,[93] whereas compliance (behaviour that conforms to a standard) is arguably sufficient. As illustrated, it would in any event appear that most of the advocacy targets were well aware that the CRC was the underlying framework, seeing UNICEF Rwanda as synonymous with the CRC.

It must also be recalled that, although UNICEF Rwanda avoided condemnation, this was just one strand of its overall approach. It also utilised

[90] E.g. former UNICEF Rwanda Child Protection Staff Member A, interview, 15 October 2014 (who also commented that the fact the CRC has been so widely ratified further enhances its legitimacy). Note Donnelly's (2013: 95) assertion that 'international legal universality', in the form of binding treaties, 'may be the most important *practical* legacy of international action on behalf of human rights'. Cf. Hafner-Burton, LeVeck and Victor (2016: 176) who found that non-binding law was 'just as powerful a tool' for human rights activists as binding treaty law, except when it came to litigation.

[91] This, together with using non-legal language that would resonate in the domestic sphere, brings to mind Twum-Danso's supplication to search for a 'middle' or 'common' ground: whilst Twum-Danso's attention is directed at facilitating dialogue on child rights with local communities, we can also see the importance of using local frames of reference with government officials.

[92] Murray and Long (2015: 20–22) speak of the 'strategic' or 'imaginative' approach adopted by some advocates, who use soft-law instruments to strengthen their argument, broaden the understanding of an issue, expand on a particular treaty obligation or clarify an issue.

[93] See also note 115. Koh (1997: 2600–2601, note 3) refers to this as 'obedience' to law.

various other strategies and techniques to enhance compliance, all tailored to the context. These included capacity building (as evaluated earlier), the use of incentives for Rwanda to adopt measures that would, at least partially, benefit child *génocidaires*, sensitising the community to facilitate the respect of child rights (and thus attenuate one of the reasons put forward by Rwanda for non-compliance), the use of existing legal provisions to push for compliance, and capitalising on political will by building relationships with persons receptive to child rights and raising child rights issues at every opportunity. Its approach was predicated on collaboration, but this enabled it to have access to decision-makers, and it was thus able to exert influence on the Rwandan government. Compromise and diplomacy were necessary, but this did not equate with lack of progress. As referenced earlier, Pedersen argues that avoiding coercive measures opens up the use of other 'influence mechanisms': this does not remove pressure; rather pressure is still exerted but in 'more context-specific ways'.[94] This is one element of Pedersen and Kinley's 'principled engagement', a strategy for human rights promotion which straddles two extremes of 'Ostracism' (in which states or international institutions shun a country that is violating human rights or vociferously condemn it) and 'Business as Usual' (where states/international institutions continue to trade, invest in and provide aid to violators).[95]

UNICEF Rwanda's approach to improving respect of the rights of child *génocidaires* was thus to establish a collaborative partnership with the Rwandan government whilst seeking to retain independence. It was not the only international actor to pursue this form of engagement. Chakravarty's research into the politics of engagement of NGOs with the *gacaca* courts reveals a split in the NGO community: some, such as HRW and Amnesty International, harshly criticised *gacaca* (she calls this the

94 Pedersen 2013: 29. See also Chayes and Chayes 1995: 230, who note that whilst the management approach is non-adversarial and relies mainly on persuasion rather than coercion, it may nonetheless exert pressure (such as through the use of material sanctions or the threat of naming and shaming).

95 Pedersen and Kinley 2013. Much of their emphasis is placed on the decision as to whether or not to 'engage' with recalcitrant states or non-state actors and, in most of the contributions, the theoretical framework is applied to governmental approaches to violating states (e.g. donor governments) and to broad human rights concerns. Further, the focus is on repressive states rather than states emerging from conflict (which they expressly exclude from their analysis). Nonetheless, elements of this theoretical framework resonate with what was observed in Rwanda and has assisted with the development of what I call 'principled pragmatism'.

'confrontational model of engagement'), whilst others, such as ASF, RCN and PRI, cooperated with the government without ceding independence (she calls this the 'critical partnership approach').[96] Gready, examining the work of NGOs in post-genocide Rwanda, asserts that their '[e]ffectiveness is predicated on the ability to continue to engage with a complex state, without being co-opted by it'.[97] Key to this type of engagement is balancing criticism with cooperation and using a variety of strategies, which inevitably must be adapted to the particular context.[98] Of course, UNICEF is not an NGO and it thus has different institutional considerations; arguably its need to avoid fallout is greater. I would conclude that, in the circumstances, UNICEF Rwanda did broadly achieve an appropriate balance between criticism and cooperation and, by using a multifaceted approach in terms of strategies and techniques, did have some influence, albeit perhaps limited, on Rwanda's responses in law, policy and practice to child *génocidaires*. It is to that influence that this chapter now turns.

8.2 Perceived Results

Having highlighted the risks associated with the approach taken by UNICEF Rwanda, the next stage is to consider whether its approach had any success: in other words, whether Rwanda took actions, adopted policies or implemented legislative changes that moved closer to implementing, or complying with, international standards on child *génocidaires* and that can be linked back to UNICEF Rwanda's activities. In previous chapters, I indicated where UNICEF Rwanda appeared to have had an influence on Rwanda's law, policy and practice. This section draws on some of those instances but does not purport to provide a comprehensive list of perceived successes. In any event, as will be evident from previous chapters, there are few examples of concrete changes in law, policy or practice, and the section thus presents other less tangible influences that are suggested by the empirical data. It therefore relies on examples of legal change, recognising that practice did not always follow the law, as well as

[96] Chakravarty 2006: 142. She refers to two other models of engagement: failed activism (where NGOs lose independence) and dominant initiative (where NGOs effectively act as 'shadow states'). See also Demay et al. 2005: 55–56, noting that ASF considered it better to be engaged in Rwanda, even though there were problems of governmental legitimacy, than to pull out and leave Rwandans to their own devices.

[97] Gready 2011: 97.

[98] Gready (ibid.) talks of 'role combination' (balancing advocacy and partnership) and 'shifting register' (moving between different strategies and different interlocutors).

changes in practice, without accompanying legal reform. Further, partial compliance with an international standard, very limited improvements in practice or even a change in perception or focus are taken as indicative of a positive influence. As Forsythe explains: 'In dealing with the sometimes elusive notion of success or achievement, sometimes it help[s] to distinguish among the following: success in getting an item or subject on the agenda for discussion, success in achieving serious discussion, success in getting procedural or institutional change, and finally success in achieving substantive policy change that clearly ameliorated or limited the problem.'[99]

As may be obvious, there could be various explanations for why Rwanda decided to take a particular approach. In the absence of direct acknowledgement by the Rwandan government of the influence of an intervention, establishing a causal link between an intervention and a measure is extremely difficult, if not impossible.[100] Using a process-tracing method that seeks to identify why particular measures or approaches were adopted, I have tried to mitigate this issue. It is acknowledged, however, that in this particular research, this method has limitations given the necessity to rely significantly on interviews and the related methodological issues (in particular the possibility that interviewees may exaggerate their own influence or downplay another's).[101] One final point is that influence was not assessed purely on the basis of whether, or how often, international standards or UNICEF were referenced; rather, the nature of the measure or approach and how it was arrived at were taken into account to determine whether they indicate implicitly any recognition or influence of international standards and whether this can be linked to UNICEF Rwanda's activities.

The previous chapters provided some fairly clear, unequivocal examples of where UNICEF Rwanda's direct interventions had positive outcomes for some children accused of genocide. The provision of education for, and the separation from adults of, children in detention, legal representation before the formal courts and efforts to prioritise juvenile cases (for

99 Forsythe 2012: 255–256.

100 See Murray and Long 2015: 28–30 regarding causation and their commentary on 'effectiveness' and 'influence'.

101 UNICEF Rwanda staff members, for example, may have overemphasised the influence of their interventions and Rwandan government officials may have overstated their role/vision and downplayed UNICEF Rwanda's influence, particularly given Rwanda's aspiration to be self-reliant and maintain control over judicial developments.

conditional release or trial) can all be linked to UNICEF Rwanda's work (and in some instances also the work of other organisations) with the Rwandan government.

The empirical data strongly support a conclusion that UNICEF Rwanda was instrumental in the recognition of these rights through its provision of support (technical, logistical, material and financial) and through its advocacy, although there are also some other factors that were noted as influential. For example, a judicial defender commented that the Rwandan government began to separate minors from adults after pressure from international organisations (in particular UNICEF and the ICRC) which were relying on international law,[102] and a former detainee commented that both the ICRC and UNICEF Rwanda's monitoring, and then highlighting, of the problem of the under-14s in detention led to the relocation of these minors to Gitagata.[103] Indeed many interviewees stressed the important role played by UNICEF Rwanda in the Gitagata initiative in particular, highlighting the support received from UNICEF Rwanda as well as its advocacy on behalf of the under-14s.[104] A Rwandan NGO worker referred to UNICEF Rwanda 'making a lot of noise' about children in detention and was of the view that minors were released as a result of this advocacy,[105] and a former juvenile detainee also considered that pressure applied by UNICEF Rwanda and other organisations resulted in releases.[106] Other participants referred to the overcrowding of prisons (and thus financial implications as well as the risk of criminal contamination) as well as the need to rebuild Rwanda (youth being key to the future) as important factors behind the release of minors, although some of these also mentioned international pressure.[107] A public prosecutor referred to UNICEF Rwanda's strong advocacy for the prioritisation of juvenile cases

[102] Interview with former Judicial Defender C, 17 September 2013. Lawyer B (interview, 15 February 2013) made the same comment.

[103] Interview with former Detainee of KCP, 30 September 2013.

[104] E.g. Interviews with AJPRODHO Staff Member, 15 February 2013; former Prosecutor F, 9 October 2013; former Detainee of KCP, 30 September 2013 (Skype); Gahima, 5 November 2013 (Skype). See also UNICEF Rwanda 1995c: 9 (commenting that UNICEF Rwanda had advocated for and then facilitated the transfers of children to Gitagata); UNICEF 2002: 121–122 (noting that UNICEF was 'instrumental' in securing the separation of minors from adults and the rehabilitation of the under-14s).

[105] Interview with NGO Staff Member, 22 February 2013.

[106] Skype interview with Gahunde, 19 August 2013.

[107] Interviews with AJPRODHO Staff Member, 15 February 2013; former Executive Secretary of a Survivors' Organisation, 21 February 2013; former RCN Staff Member, Kigali, 18 February 2013.

(pushing for conditional release) and suggested that the government had responded to this advocacy. He argued that it was not the 'pressure' applied by UNICEF Rwanda but rather the reminder about international child rights that had convinced the government that these minors should be released, and that this was in line with the government's desire to reconstruct Rwanda.[108] A former senior Rwandan justice official made similar comments, noting that the initiative for expediting juvenile trials came from UNICEF, but that this tallied with the government's thinking at that time regarding the risk of criminal contamination and the need to rebuild Rwandan society.[109] As should be recalled, these rights were not respected in full, and not all children benefited from these interventions. Efforts to prioritise minors' cases, for example, had very limited success, leading one research participant to conclude that UNICEF Rwanda's advocacy on this point had failed.[110] Nonetheless, without UNICEF Rwanda's interventions (and of course those of other organisations where applicable), it seems clear that those children who did benefit would have seen their rights violated to a greater extent.

Another cogent example of UNICEF Rwanda's influence was the inclusion of the provision in the Genocide Law requiring minors' benches to be established in the Specialised Chambers. As discussed in previous chapters, this provision appears to be attributable primarily to UNICEF Rwanda's advocacy. This is supported by a review of archival documents, in particular various drafts of the Genocide Law, which indicates that the provision was first introduced after UNICEF Rwanda had noted the absence of any special treatment for minors in the law and made specific recommendations to the Rwandan government. It finds further support in the account provided by UNICEF Rwanda in contemporaneous documents (referring to the provision being included as a result of 'successful lobbying')[111] and by staff members interviewed for this research.[112] And it was also the view of an expert involved in the drafting of the Genocide Law that the inclusion of the provision was directly

108 Interview with Ntete, 27 February 2013. Former IPJ/Prosecutor (interview, 26 September 2013) made similar comments.

109 Skype interview with former Senior Rwandan Justice Official, 24 July 2014.

110 Skype interview with former Judicial Defender B, 28 August 2013.

111 UNICEF Rwanda 1997b: 2. See also UNICEF Rwanda 1996c: 29 ('UNICEF successfully advocated' for the provision); UNICEF Rwanda 1997a: 3 (minors' benches were 'introduced upon UNICEF intervention').

112 E.g. Skype interview with Matthes, 28 November 2013.

attributable to UNICEF Rwanda's advocacy.[113] As previously documented, the provision appears to have been implemented in some, but not all, courts.

As regards less tangible influence, there is some evidence that UNICEF Rwanda's advocacy on the Genocide Law, as well as its involvement in governmental commissions, put child offenders on the agenda as regards post-genocide legislation. As will be recalled, the later Gacaca Laws contained more precise provisions regarding the accountability and sentencing of genocide minors, and various legislative changes were made over the years that incorporated juvenile justice standards into domestic law. Whilst it cannot be concluded that all of this can be ascribed to UNICEF Rwanda, it is reasonable to believe that UNICEF Rwanda contributed to the process, stimulating debate on the rights of child perpetrators and increasing the focus on these individuals. Further, UNICEF Rwanda identified shortcomings in Rwandan law and practice in relation to international standards, which were slowly addressed in the coming years.

The empirical data also support the conclusion that UNICEF Rwanda's activities increased awareness of international standards amongst key stakeholders in juvenile justice as well as the broader community. Promoting awareness of child rights and sensitising public opinion on the different treatment for child offenders constituted a key objective and strategy for UNICEF Rwanda. There is empirical evidence that these efforts paid off, many participants in the research specifically referring to sensitisation campaigns as key to a perceived shift in public opinion. However, increased tolerance could also be attributed to the passage of time rather than any increased understanding and acceptance of the law, and there are also counter-narratives that some parts of Rwandan society continued to fail to understand why those who had been children at the time of the genocide were treated more leniently than adults. In any event, it seems fair to say that UNICEF Rwanda exerted at least an indirect influence by creating a more child rights-sensitive environment, and that its monitoring of public opinion (through organisations such as ASOFERWA) facilitated the reintegration of child *génocidaires*, a key aim of the juvenile justice framework.

As regards key stakeholders, the contribution made by UNICEF Rwanda through training provided to judicial and law enforcement

[113] Interview with de Beer, 15 October 2014.

personnel was detailed in Chapter 7. There is strong empirical evidence that knowledge of international standards, but also their application in practice by these personnel, was enhanced by the training. In particular, judges interviewed for this research appeared to have internalised many of the underlying juvenile justice principles and sought to apply those in practice. As Finnemore and Sikkink aver: 'Professional training does more than simply transfer technical knowledge; it actively socializes people to value certain things above others.'[114] UNICEF Rwanda's interactions with government officials and other stakeholders, either through daily interactions or through workshops, also raised awareness of the standards and arguably contributed to there being greater sensitivity to child rights in policy decisions. Certain government officials were clear that they saw international standards as authoritative and, in some cases, demonstrated a commitment to these standards that appeared to be personal and cognitive, as opposed to purely professional.[115] They sought to give greater effect to these standards in their domestic system through their professional roles, which, as noted, often changed over the years. It is of course very plausible that these officials were already aware of, and committed to, the standards,[116] and it would be highly speculative to conclude that UNICEF Rwanda was the key determinant in shaping these views. However, it is reasonable to infer that UNICEF Rwanda at least reinforced child-sensitive attitudes and values, bolstered the personal commitment of these individuals and provided them with the support to advance child-sensitive policies in the domestic arena. Several government officials spoke very positively of the significant support provided by UNICEF Rwanda.[117] Gahima commented that he would 'forever be grateful' for UNICEF Rwanda's support and, when asked whether Rwanda would have come to the same decisions regarding children if UNICEF had not been there, concluded: 'Maybe not, for want of the technical expertise

[114] Finnemore and Sikkink 1998: 905.

[115] According to Galligan and Sandler (2004: 29) implementation is successful where standards are 'accepted as authoritative by national institutions and officials in such manner that their practical actions and decisions are in compliance with them … The ideal position is the internalisation of standards by officials so that they become central to their cognitive and normative understandings.'

[116] Some participants spoke of lack of capacity as opposed to understanding or will being the impediment to compliance (e.g. Skype interviews with Gahima, 5 November 2013; former Senior Rwandan Justice Official, 24 July 2014). See also section 7.5.

[117] E.g. Interviews with Nsanzabaganwa, 8 and 19 October 2013; Ntete, 27 February 2013; former Senior Rwandan Justice Official, 24 July 2014 (Skype).

that UNICEF brought to this process. So would we have come to the same decisions without UNICEF? Maybe not.'[118]

It is possible that measures were taken by the Rwandan government, not because of commitment to the standards, but for other reasons. However, as indicated above, even where measures were attributed to other factors, some participants identified the pressure applied by UNICEF Rwanda as contributive to decision-making. Further examples are a Rwandan NGO staff member suggesting that the government had taken measures to be in the international community's 'good books', after pressure was applied by UNICEF Rwanda regarding child perpetrators,[119] and a public prosecutor stating that juvenile cases were accelerated after UNICEF Rwanda made demands, as Rwanda wanted to 'show good governance'.[120] As illustrated in Chapter 7, UNICEF Rwanda's advocacy frequently had recourse to non-legal discourse, including references to reputation and good standing, on the supposition that this would encourage compliance.

One further way in which UNICEF Rwanda appears to have exerted a positive influence on the respect of child rights is through its visibility and presence in Rwanda. Howen argues that international presence can have a dissuasive effect on human rights violations.[121] As noted in Chapter 5, there were few irregularities in juvenile trials before the Specialised Chambers, arguably because judges were aware that they were being observed by UNICEF Rwanda (or someone monitoring the trial on its behalf). It is also possible that the presence of UNICEF Rwanda and other organisations that visited prisons, in particular the ICRC, had a restraining influence on potential violations. This was the view of Tertsakian who found that ill-treatment and killings decreased considerably after the ICRC became involved.[122] The interviews conducted for this study do not corroborate (nor do they refute) any conclusion that violations in the form of physical abuse abated as a result of UNICEF Rwanda's (or other organisations') presence, but there is evidence that conditions of detention improved: this

[118] Skype interview with Gahima, 5 November 2013. Note that NGO Staff Member (interview, 22 February 2013) commented that UNICEF had 'a lot of influence'.

[119] Interview with NGO Staff Member, 22 February 2013.

[120] Interview with former Prosecutor E, 27 September 2013. See also Reuters 2000, reporting that the Rwandan government had confirmed it would prioritise juvenile trials 'in response to an international outcry' – referring to criticism from the United Nations and human rights groups.

[121] See e.g. Howen 2007: 41.

[122] Tertsakian 2008: 48.

could be a result of visibility in prisons but also a result of pressure being applied or assistance provided to the authorities.[123]

To sum up, there are strong indicators that it was through UNICEF Rwanda's support and/or advocacy that Rwanda adopted measures and practices that moved towards implementation of, or compliance with, international standards, and that there was an increasing acceptance of the validity of the rights of child perpetrators. Interviewees referred to the key role of UNICEF Rwanda (and sometimes other organisations) both in drawing attention to Rwanda's international obligations under the CRC and providing support to the government to comply with these obligations.[124] However, there are also narratives that Rwanda adopted particular measures either independently of UNICEF Rwanda's interventions, or more frequently where UNICEF Rwanda's approach coincided with the government's thinking.[125] It is difficult to extricate whether an intervention was the sole reason for Rwanda taking a particular positive action (the likelihood being that there were various factors that led to a decision), but the evidence does point to UNICEF Rwanda's approach having some positive influence on the Rwandan government's responses to child *génocidaires*. As van Krieken asserted specifically in relation to juvenile justice in Rwanda: '[I]t can not be denied that Unicef has been able to bring about important changes, has had added value, and has been able to put the issue of children and children rights high on the Agenda.'[126]

8.3 Factors Influencing the Approach

As discussed above, UNICEF Rwanda's interventions, which I have identified as contextual and largely collaborative, led to increased implementation of, and compliance with, international standards relating to child *génocidaires* (although it is acknowledged that there continued to be many violations). This section considers briefly why UNICEF Rwanda adopted its particular approach and thus whether these findings have

[123] Former Judicial Defender B (Skype interview, 28 August 2013) spoke of UNICEF both supplying material assistance to prisons and asserting pressure on the government.

[124] UNICEF staff members, perhaps predictably, referred to the contribution made by UNICEF Rwanda to enhancing the rights of child perpetrators, but as indicated throughout this chapter, a significant number of other participants, including government officials, judges, lawyers and NGO workers attested to the important role played by UNICEF Rwanda.

[125] This provides support for Goldsmith and Posner's (2005) 'coincidence of interests' theory.

[126] van Krieken 2000: 29.

broader application. It first considers whether Rwanda was unique (also touching briefly on specific post-conflict challenges), then whether the CRC predisposes a particular approach, and finally whether the institutional nature of UNICEF makes it different from other organisations.

8.3.1 Rwanda: A Unique Situation?

Chapter 4 of this book provided the context of the case study and highlighted the challenges facing both the Rwandan government and international organisations in operationalising international standards relating to child *génocidaires*. As submitted in the current chapter, context-specific interpretation and application of rights is essential if international actors are to make progress in enhancing implementation and compliance. But the context also very much constrains the approach of international actors. In some respects, Rwanda could be considered unique. However, some challenges and contextual elements will be common to other situations.

Perhaps the most unique factor in Rwanda was that children were accused of genocidal crimes. The Rwandan genocide was notable for its mass public participation and its large number of victims, as well as the primitive methods used to inflict injury and death. The gravity of the crimes, the number of perpetrators and society's perception of *génocidaires* influenced and constrained the way in which UNICEF Rwanda approached the issue of child perpetrators and thus how it sought to secure the respect of their rights. In a non-genocidal context, a different approach could potentially be adopted: depending on the nature of crimes committed, it might be possible, for example, to promote diversion and alternatives to detention as emotions are less acute and the relationship between victims and perpetrators is more remote (assuming the necessary institutions and systems are functioning). Further, victims and the broader community may be prioritising other aspects of transitional justice over criminal prosecutions. This is more likely to be the case where the crimes committed are non-violent or minor. Alternative approaches may also be more feasible where crimes are unconnected to a conflict, not only because society may be less hostile, but also because international institutions themselves may feel less conflicted where the relevant crime is not one that is suppressed by international law.

Another key factor in Rwanda, but one that will be common to other post-conflict (and possibly post-disaster) states, was the lack of resources, including functioning institutions. As illustrated, this may require a different approach to rights, accepting prioritisation and incremental application. As Tully affirms, 'the application of international standards must be based on the possible – but not unrealistic – ideals in countries like Rwanda, which are actively engaged in post-conflict reconstruction and reconciliation'.[127] But it may also demand strategies that would not ordinarily be deployed. For example, UNICEF Rwanda felt compelled to provide various types of assistance to improve detention conditions and to take on a greater role more generally than would perhaps usually be the case. Although, as a general policy, UNICEF does not advocate such assistance, arguably in extreme cases it is necessary to deviate from usual practice to avoid greater violations of children's rights. Indeed, UNICEF recognised the special circumstances in Rwanda, commenting in 2002, 'Save in exceptional circumstances such as Rwanda, UNICEF will … not support the creating or refurbishing of separate detention facilities for children.'[128] And as one UNICEF Rwanda staff member noted, emergencies may require different approaches than 'normal' situations.[129] Further, in such situations, there may need to be a greater emphasis on capacity building and the provision of technical assistance as a pathway towards increased compliance with rights. As Risse and Ropp comment, where the issue is lack of political and administrative capacity, capacity building should take precedence, as other mechanisms 'will not do the trick'.[130] Clearly, where lack of political will is a factor, capacity building could be used, as indicated earlier, as a smokescreen, and sanctions or incentives may be more appropriate. The difficulty is, of course, identifying the root cause for non-compliance (particularly in an autocratic but weak state),[131] and it is thus necessary for international actors to adapt their strategies, and combine different approaches, according to what they perceive to be the prevailing reason for non-compliance.

Additionally, as illustrated, UNICEF Rwanda generally avoided 'naming and shaming' as a strategy.[132] A key reason for this was the need to retain a

127 Tully 2003: 387.

128 UNICEF 2002: 121.

129 Skype interview with former UNICEF Rwanda Child Protection Staff Member B, 19 November 2014.

130 Risse and Ropp 2013: 15–16. See also Chayes and Chayes 1993.

131 Simmons (2009: 397) classifies Rwanda as 'never democratic' in her coding of regimes. Note that some scholars (Hafner-Burton 2013; Simmons 2009) argue that human rights laws are most likely to have an influence in emerging democracies, rather than in states where human rights are most at risk (such as a state that lacks functioning institutions, political space and a strong civil society).

132 For an evaluation of naming and shaming, see Hafner-Burton 2008.

good relationship with the Rwandan government (essential for UNICEF's work), which was particularly difficult given the lack of trust towards the UN (which may be specific to the Rwandan situation). But it was also considered that naming and shaming would not lead to increased protection for child *génocidaires*, partly because UNICEF Rwanda saw lack of capacity as being a major factor, but also because broader society was, on the whole, hostile to *génocidaires*. Public condemnation may have greater influence where there is a domestic audience that is receptive to, and supportive of, the relevant rights. As explained in Chapter 3, it is difficult to mobilise support for accused criminals (even children) and, in Rwanda, there was also a lack of operative NGOs taking up this issue.[133] Where children are not accused of serious, conflict-related crimes, domestic civil society may be easier to mobilise, particularly in societies where NGOs are functioning and are not under tight governmental control.

Whilst not relying on denunciation of violations, UNICEF Rwanda did refer to Rwanda's international reputation when advocating for rights protection and there is some evidence that this paid off. Numerous participants in this research referred to Rwanda's concern about its international reputation, its wish to gain legitimacy given that the government had taken power by force, and its desire to show that it was putting an end to impunity and establishing rule of law.[134] It was thus seen as being susceptible to pressure based on reputation, and this was utilised by UNICEF Rwanda in its advocacy. Various scholars have referred to human rights providing international legitimacy to regimes, particularly new regimes following a conflict.[135] This advocacy strategy could thus have influence in post-conflict or other transitional states, where a government is seeking to enhance its international standing.

[133] Note Gready's (2011: 92) comment that some models of compliance, such as Keck and Sikkink's 'boomerang' model (1998) (whereby domestic NGOs use international actors to assert pressure) did not work in Rwanda. He asserts that this was because states and international actors were generally supportive of the Rwandan government, but I would add that the lack of domestic NGOs was also relevant. See also Jetschke and Liese 2013 and Simmons 2009 who emphasise the importance of domestic civil society in asserting pressure on governments.

[134] E.g. Judge A (interview, 18 February 2013); Lawyer B (interview, 15 February 2013); NGO Staff Member (interview, 22 February 2013); former Prosecutor E (interview, 27 September 2013); Rwandan Academic (interview, Kigali, 4 March 2013); former UNICEF Rwanda Child Protection Staff Member A (interview, 15 October 2014).

[135] See Bell 2000 generally, and in particular 297–298 (referring to human rights language and mechanisms as internationally recognised 'chic language', which when used in peace agreements can provide international legitimacy); Donnelly 2013: 62.

What seems clear is that the approach to implementation and compliance in a post-conflict society must differ from that in a normal, stable situation. Putnam argues that many human rights organisations fail to recognise this and continue to rely on the enforcement model, in which international attention is drawn to violations through monitoring and reporting. She asserts that this approach is more likely to 'detract from the goals of substantive human rights protection' than lead to their achievement.[136] My research reveals that this was not the approach adopted by UNICEF Rwanda: staff members utilised a variety of strategies, often simultaneously, to seek to enhance implementation of, and compliance with, international standards on child *génocidaires*. In a complex situation like Rwanda, being flexible in the choice of strategies appears essential.

8.3.2 The CRC: A Different Approach?

As will be recalled, the CRC and the non-binding instruments differ in terms of their wording regarding the conditions that may be taken into account during implementation, but various provisions of the CRC, in particular the best interests principle, contain flexibility and do permit a contextual approach. It could also be argued that the CRC suggests a particular approach as regards how best to secure the implementation of, and compliance with, its provisions.

In Chapter 3, it was shown that the CRC favours constructive over confrontational methods of implementation. The CRC Committee's practice has generally been in line with this overall approach and, as illustrated in this book, UNICEF Rwanda similarly avoided confrontational strategies, seeking to assist, rather than coerce, Rwanda to move towards implementation and compliance. In relation to human rights treaties generally, Galligan and Sandler note the lack of enforcement capacity at the international level and suggest that the 'international order's contribution to implementation then necessarily depends primarily on the weaker processes of encouraging, facilitating, and cajoling, with rare cases of direct intervention'.[137] Raustiala and Slaughter, commenting on the UN HRC (as an example of human rights institutions), note that the approach adopted is 'largely non-confrontational and forward-looking' and that these institutions 'engage in the collective supervision and facilitation of

[136] Putnam 2002: 237–238.

[137] Galligan and Sandler 2004: 27.

performance that lies at the heart of managerial theory'.[138] The view then appears to be that the promotion of human rights generally (as opposed to child rights specifically) has been grounded in the persuasion or management model as opposed to the coercion or enforcement model. Given the emphasis on international cooperation, in particular technical assistance, in the CRC and the explicit assignation of a role to UN agencies (including UNICEF) to provide such technical assistance, as well as the lack of an individual complaints mechanism until very recently,[139] the CRC arguably endorses a managerial approach to a greater extent than other human rights treaties.[140] Davidson suggests that, whilst international treaties are generally seen as hard law, 'the CRC did *not include* a traditional enforcement mechanism, such as a right of action in an international tribunal or the threat of sanctions. Therefore, perhaps the CRC's influence is most deeply felt in the not-easily-quantifiable area of soft law, as its very existence prompts norm-influencing discussions.'[141] As previously evinced, UNICEF Rwanda did perceive the CRC as binding law and considered that its binding nature was useful in its advocacy with the Rwandan government. However, the way in which the CRC envisages its implementation arguably influenced how UNICEF Rwanda sought to enhance Rwanda's implementation of, and compliance with, CRC provisions.

A further factor that influenced the approach is the sensitivity of juvenile justice. As discussed in Chapter 3, although child rights are often considered to be less controversial when compared to other human rights, juvenile justice standards have proven difficult to implement given that they relate to alleged criminals. Inevitably, the social context must be given serious consideration as this influences measures that can be taken to reintegrate children and, as seen in the Rwandan context, may restrict the use of diversion and alternative measures to detention. It may also

[138] Raustiala and Slaughter 2002: 549.

[139] An individual complaints mechanism was introduced through an optional protocol to the CRC that came into force in 2014.

[140] Note that the International Labour Organization (ILO) has a similar technical assistance procedure in place ('direct contacts') which aims to complement the work of treaty-monitoring bodies through direct dialogue with governments on complex or controversial issues identified by such bodies. See O'Donnell 1992: 35–36.

[141] Davidson 2014: 512 (original emphasis). Murray and Long (2015: 16–18) discuss the more conciliatory mechanisms of compliance (such as 'constructive dialogue' or 'promotional tools') in the case of soft law (their focus is the non-binding decisions of quasi-judicial bodies) as opposed to binding treaties, and argue that these mechanisms can have an impact on implementation and compliance.

require emphasis to be placed on sensitisation programmes that not only impart awareness of child rights standards (domestic and international) but also provide explanations for differential treatment for children generally, and in that specific context. Further, juvenile justice may require more constructive, and less confrontational, approaches with the relevant government, as advocates may be seen as sympathisers with alleged criminals;[142] taking a condemnatory approach could simply result in the entrenchment of government positions.

It thus appears that organisations with a specific role under the CRC, and possibly to a greater extent in the area of juvenile justice, are more likely to pursue collaboration over condemnation in accordance with the principle of international cooperation, although more confrontational strategies should not be ruled out. As regards standards in other human rights treaties, whilst there is not the same accent on technical assistance in most treaties,[143] the overall approach that appears to be favoured is persuasion and management.

8.3.3 UNICEF: Institutional Particularities

As explored in Chapter 3, UNICEF is an intergovernmental organisation and is dependent on a government's consent to operate in a particular country. It must also be recalled that UNICEF has a significant field presence and is an operational organisation in the sense that it seeks to *assist* with the implementation of projects.[144] As such, there are certain constraints on UNICEF's activities.

There is some evidence that the direction of UNICEF Rwanda's work was steered by funding considerations (see section 7.6 for an example) and it should now be clear that UNICEF Rwanda was cautious in its interactions with the Rwandan government. Retaining a good relationship with the government was especially difficult given hostility towards the international community and UN institutions in particular. However, as also illustrated, UNICEF Rwanda did not limit itself in

142 As will be recalled, lawyers were reluctant to act for alleged *génocidaires* for this reason and activists were sometimes perceived as putting the rights of *génocidaires* before the rights of victims.

143 Only three of the major human rights treaties (the CRC, ICESCR and the Convention on the Rights of Persons with Disabilities) refer expressly to technical assistance or advice in the context of fostering implementation.

144 Recall also that UNICEF's role is not to monitor and enforce the CRC: that is the role of the CRC Committee.

terms of strategies: it made use of more instrumental strategies such as incentives, although it chose not to make assistance contingent on full and immediate respect of the rights of child *génocidaires* and broadly avoided coercive or enforcement methods. As we have seen, there was some criticism of UNICEF Rwanda's collaborative approach, but I would stress again that UNICEF differs from international, in particular non-operational, NGOs. Whilst UNICEF Rwanda staff members did, in some cases, consider that they were 'stretching' UNICEF's mandate, they were inevitably constrained by UNICEF's institutional and operational nature and thus the need for government consent. This cautious approach is not unusual for UNICEF. Oestreich (writing in 2007) observes that UNICEF staff members 'remain wary' of adopting policies that 'appear to violate the sovereignty of states or that risk so angering states that they will curtail cooperation with UNICEF'.[145] As I have shown, the potential risk of the government withdrawing its cooperation in other programme areas was one key concern. As staff of a UN agency, UNICEF Rwanda staff members had to appreciate the political context in which they were working and build alliances with the government. This should not, however, be seen as a shortcoming. As Galligan and Sandler comment:

> [I]nternational institutions are able to utilise informal administrative authority and discretions, and to develop relationships with states and their officials, within which processes, mechanisms, and structures are created to facilitate a continuing internalisation of international standards and norms … They have the quiet capacity to work with national officials and institutions to create extensive networks of governmental and non-governmental officials to foster conditions within society for the positive adoption of international norms and standards.[146]

In UNICEF's case, developing relationships with the Rwandan government was facilitated by its institutional legitimacy and its long-term field presence in Rwanda.

In contrast, international NGOs such as HRW and Amnesty International are more likely, and more able, to be confrontational. They have one agenda[147] – their mission being to highlight and raise awareness of violations of human rights through targeted advocacy – and are thus 'unburdened by the need to build working relationships

[145] Oestreich 2007: 42.
[146] Galligan and Sandler 2004: 46–47.
[147] Chakravarty (2006: 141) refers to them as 'single-sector' NGOs.

with governments'.[148] However, these organisations also play an essential role. UNICEF Rwanda staff members spoke of the importance of these organisations. One commented that, 'if you want to send a strong message, then you use existing mechanisms like Amnesty International and Human Rights Watch – not intergovernmental organisations'.[149] And another stressed that the work of Amnesty International and HRW in denouncing violations is a 'very important tool' for organisations like UNICEF which have to work with the government in the relevant country.[150] The different approaches to enhancing the rights of child perpetrators should therefore be considered mutually reinforcing, but they do not have to come from within the same organisation.

One further aspect of UNICEF's institutional nature that played a key role in UNICEF Rwanda's approach to implementation and compliance is its decentralised structure. UNICEF field offices operate generally with little interference from the New York headquarters, and, as will be recalled, UNICEF's work during the 1990s on CEDC was predominantly the reserve of the field offices. As such, UNICEF Rwanda staff members felt able to take positions that they considered difficult from a UNICEF global policy perspective but necessary in the context, and that they considered would build trust with the Rwandan government and thus lead to greater influence.[151] This included the approach to institutionalisation and the provision of financial, material and logistical support to governmental institutions including prison authorities. The decentralised mode of operation thus enabled a context-specific approach both in terms of how international standards were applied and in terms of strategies and techniques used to enhance implementation and compliance. Oestreich, referring to the programmatic independence of local field offices, observes that, whilst UNICEF headquarters creates strategy documents, the field offices can 'implement the convention in a culturally sensitive way'. He posits that this approach 'decentraliz[es] the interpretation of these standards and suggest[s] that their terms will be seen through the lens of local culture and experience' which may encourage states to respect

148 Ibid.

149 Interview with former UNICEF Rwanda Child Protection Staff Member A, 15 October 2014.

150 Skype interview with former UNICEF Rwanda Child Protection Staff Member B, 19 November 2014.

151 Note that the lack of technology at that time may also have contributed to the independence of field offices given reduced contact between the field and headquarters.

the standards.[152] It should also be recalled that UNICEF engages not only international but also local staff who have an understanding of local culture and sensitivities.

This decentralised structure, together with continuous country-level presence, enables UNICEF to respond quickly and flexibly to changing conditions and demands. UNICEF considers decentralisation to be integral to its success 'because it operates around the world and recognizes the need to adapt to local conditions, customs, political climates, and the like'.[153] Indeed, a UNICEF Rwanda staff member expressly referred to decentralisation as one of UNICEF's 'advantages' as an organisation, as it allows considerable flexibility to adapt to the realities of the relevant country.[154] Such a decentralised structure leaves a lot to individual initiative and this certainly appears to have been the case in Rwanda. Indeed, one participant referred to individuals as having 'free reign'.[155] Oestreich suggests that intergovernmental organisations should thus be seen as more than 'unitary actors' as it can be difficult to say that an *organisation* did something when it was actually the 'programmatic division' that acted with 'minimal direction from the headquarters staff'.[156]

A potential drawback of this structure that relies on individual initiative is the lack of institutional guidance and supervision. A comprehensive review of this particular aspect is beyond the scope of this book, but it is worth noting that a UNICEF staff member referred to the lack of institutional memory when it came to child protection, feeling that it was not possible to draw on experiences from other contexts.[157] Although child *génocidaires* was a new issue for UNICEF, and juvenile justice more generally was a relatively nascent area in the mid-1990s, there may have been other juvenile justice experiences that could have assisted UNICEF Rwanda staff in developing their programmes and approaches. Certainly,

[152] Oestreich 2007: 188. Black (1996: xii) similarly speaks of the decentralised and flexible nature of UNICEF, 'whose strength is in the field and grounded in local realities'. See also Beigbeder 2001: 91; Quesnel 2002: 17.

[153] Oestreich 2007: 47.

[154] Skype interview with former UNICEF Rwanda Child Protection Staff Member B, 19 November 2014.

[155] Interview with former UNICEF Rwanda Child Protection Staff Member A, 15 October 2014.

[156] Oestreich 2007: 166. Indeed, he comments that, in some cases, 'units' of organisations have 'acted in ways actively opposed to the official rights policy set in headquarters'.

[157] Former UNICEF Rwanda Child Protection Staff Member A, interview, 15 October 2014 (also commenting on the lack of records within the Rwandan office itself).

by 1997, there would have been opportunities for knowledge exchange.[158] O'Donnell had lamented in 1992 that, whilst some country offices had made 'valuable efforts' in the area of CEDC, 'many of those experiences are poorly known, even within UNICEF itself' and recommended a survey be conducted both to evaluate progress made and to 'yield many valuable ideas and experiences'.[159] In 1997, Cantwell, noting that UNICEF Rwanda had often had to rely on 'individual intuition' (and short-term consultants), affirmed the need for an 'accessible, proactive and systematically fed institutional memory or knowledge-bank'.[160]

It had been suggested during an Executive Board meeting in 1996 that UNICEF's Innocenti Research Centre become UNICEF's 'institutional memory', 'draw[ing] more upon information from UNICEF field experiences and translat[ing] that information into useful research products'.[161] It is clear that, over the years, the Innocenti Research Centre has played an active role in researching juvenile justice, including in post-conflict situations, with the aim of disseminating results to facilitate policy development. It has conducted workshops and seminars on these issues, in which lessons learned from countries including Rwanda were shared.[162] Further, at least at the headquarters level, country programme experiences have been reviewed for the purposes of building UNICEF's knowledge base on child protection.[163]

The extent to which country programme documents, evaluations and resource materials have been made easily accessible to field staff is, however, unclear. A number of UNICEF documents I reviewed mentioned various initiatives aimed at information sharing, including: a global evaluation database; UNICEF's Intranet (established in 1998) which contains a document repository and manuals; global technical support networks; and the appointment of regional child protection advisers to facilitate intercountry information exchange.[164] Whether the database and intranet materials contain(ed) detailed reviews of UNICEF's work in specific

158 By 1997, various country offices had worked on juvenile justice issues. See UNICEF 1997a: [47–49].

159 O'Donnell 1992: 30–31.

160 Cantwell 1997: 78 (see also 86). See also UNICEF 1996b: [60], referring to the need for an information network for systematic intercountry exchanges of experience.

161 UNICEF 1996e: [543].

162 See UNICEF 1998c: [14] and UNICEF 2002: 121.

163 See e.g. UNICEF 1998c: [3–5] which refers to a review of 75 country annual reports used to identify global action priorities.

164 See e.g. UNICEF 1996d: [43]; UNICEF 1997a: [51]; UNICEF 1999b: [121].

sectors and guidance on tangible policy or programming approaches, particularly in the area of post-conflict juvenile justice, is unknown. We must also keep in mind the state of technology at the relevant time: in the mid- to late 1990s, many field offices would not have had access to the Internet. Today, technology has significantly advanced and one would hope that this would facilitate intercountry exchange of expertise. However, according to some UNICEF staff consulted during this research, there has been no development of an institutional memory.[165] I am unable to confirm or refute this: not only was this not a focus of my research, but I have also been unable to access the centralised UNICEF archives and, as an external researcher, I do not have access to any internal UNICEF Intranet or databases. However, what I can say is that, from my own attempts to retrieve documentation on the Rwandan experience, it appears that there has been no systematic archiving of policy documents[166] or comprehensive evaluation of UNICEF Rwanda's activities in this particular area.[167] If such records do exist, it would seem that UNICEF staff members in the field at least are often not aware of them. Clearly, each context is unique and requires tailored responses, but having previous experiences as a reference point and learning from them is nonetheless useful, particularly in the complex programming environments of conflict or post-conflict situations, where there is frequently a high turnover of staff.[168] Otherwise, the only cross-fertilisation that may occur would arise from individuals sharing their personal experiences or moving from one field station to another.

[165] Note that a 2005 evaluation of UNICEF's learning strategy underscored the need for more systematic documentation of experiences so as to avoid reliance on intuition particularly in the area of child protection in emergencies. UNICEF 2005a: 41–44.

[166] As will be recalled, a UNICEF Rwanda employee informed me that all documents are destroyed after five years, and, as I was unable to access centralised UNICEF archives in New York, it is not known what documents may be available there.

[167] Note that some broader evaluations of UNICEF's field operations in emergency and crisis situations have drawn on experiences in Rwanda, but these have been at a much more general level rather than reviewing child protection programmes in any detail. I have not found any exhaustive coverage of UNICEF Rwanda's interventions in respect of child *génocidaires*. Indeed, a key objective of this book is to fill that gap in knowledge.

[168] The view of Castrogiovanni (Skype interview, 28 November 2013) was that in such environments, it is essential to 'institutionalise the learning'. Note that high turnover of staff can impede the development of relationships, local knowledge and continuity of programmes, but on the other hand enables staff to transfer knowledge and skills from one context to another.

8.4 Conclusion

Oestreich argues that '[p]rogress in the enforcement and implementation of human rights standards will depend on progress in reconciling [two] contradictory trends: intrusiveness versus respect for sovereignty, and universalism versus particularism'. He asserts that UNICEF has achieved this in its approach to implementing the CRC.[169] This case study provides empirical evidence in support of this assertion. By adopting a contextual and pragmatic approach, UNICEF Rwanda was, to some extent, able to move from 'universal idealism' to 'practical implementation'[170] of key principles of child rights in the difficult context of post-genocide Rwanda. Whilst there was a risk of weakening the normative content in the desire to operationalise the standards in a socially sensitive and context-specific way, I submit that this risk was not borne out. UNICEF Rwanda's interpretation and application of CRC provisions on the whole fell within the range of variation permitted by the inherent flexibility of the CRC and, to the extent that this was not the case, there are strong policy arguments to support UNICEF Rwanda's contextual approach.

UNICEF Rwanda adopted a broadly collaborative approach, providing significant practical assistance to the Rwandan government. It is acknowledged that, on occasion, this went beyond the provision of technical assistance, but this engagement was justifiably considered necessary given the context, and ultimately UNICEF Rwanda did not step into the state's shoes: the Rwandan government retained responsibility and accountability for all measures that were adopted. This factor also mitigated the risk of UNICEF Rwanda's capacity building being used as a smokescreen and the risk of UNICEF Rwanda being instrumentalised by the government. It is true that UNICEF Rwanda did not highlight, and denounce, violations. Indeed, in its efforts to enhance implementation and compliance, it largely avoided explicit statements on compliance (although it did identify shortcomings), focusing instead on using the CRC to shape law, policy and practice. It is arguable that it could have been more critical, and in certain contexts it may be appropriate for UNICEF to denounce violations, but UNICEF Rwanda was very much constrained by the Rwandan context. The relationship between Rwanda and UN institutions inevitably informed the extent to which

[169] Oestreich 1998: 184.

[170] To borrow de Berry's (2001: 102) terms (de Berry is arguing in favour of a contextual approach to the implementation of the CRC).

UNICEF Rwanda felt able to criticise. Further, staff members were aware of limitations in terms of resources and the hostility of public opinion and thus considered that offering assistance to overcome these challenges was crucial. By offering such assistance, and by combining it with other strategies and techniques – which I argue enabled UNICEF Rwanda to retain independence and remain true to its principles yet collaborate with the government – UNICEF Rwanda was able to have some influence on measures adopted, and this led to small steps being taken in the right direction towards compliance. This book does not seek to justify non-compliance with international standards on the basis of lack of resources or social sensitivity, and, as will be clear from earlier chapters, child *génocidaires* continued to see their rights violated. However, I would argue that pragmatism as to what can be realistically achieved, together with flexibility in terms of strategies and techniques to overcome obstacles and build alliances through which to exert pressure, was a valid approach for UNICEF Rwanda to adopt when seeking to enhance implementation and compliance in post-genocide Rwanda.

It is evident that UNICEF Rwanda was constrained as an actor by the wider factual conditions in which it was operating, by its institutional status and also arguably by the CRC which assigns it a specific role. Whilst the Rwandan situation may be unique (and indeed the issue of child *génocidaires* was a first for UNICEF), many of the challenges that faced UNICEF Rwanda are likely to arise in other post-conflict situations where children are accused of international crimes. What seems clear is that the approach adopted in a post-conflict, or post-emergency, situation should be different from a 'business as usual' approach in a normalised context, and it would be useful for UNICEF to create a comprehensive database (if indeed this does not exist) to enable field offices to have access to lessons learned from other situations. Given its institutional status, UNICEF – and other UN agencies – will always have to collaborate with the host government: the question will be where UNICEF (or another agency) situates itself on the cooperation versus criticism spectrum, which will, to a large extent, be determined by the context and existing relationships. For other international actors, such as NGOs, their approach is likely to be influenced by whether they are operational or, in Chakravarty's words, 'single-sector' NGOs. In any event, whatever overall perspective to implementation and compliance is adopted, contextualisation will still be necessary. As this study has indicated, even the most critical NGOs still acknowledged the extreme challenges in Rwanda.

Finally, as noted earlier, the specific role assigned to UNICEF and other agencies by the CRC suggests that a constructive approach to implementation, based on persuasion and management as opposed to coercion or enforcement, is favoured. Oestreich argues that this role, as well as UNICEF's approach to implementation and the response of states, 'is significant and suggests a new model for future human rights instruments'.[171] Whilst most existing human rights treaties do not place the same emphasis on technical assistance, I would suggest that, given the lack of international enforcement capacity, persuasion and management (in particular capacity building in cases where non-compliance is due to lack of capacity) may more likely lead to progress towards implementation and compliance.

171 Oestreich 1998: 184–185.

9

Child Perpetrators and Child Rights: Rwanda and Beyond

This book set out to investigate how international standards on child perpetrators of atrocities can be operationalised in a post-conflict society. Adopting a multidisciplinary approach, the book has provided an empirical and systematic account of Rwanda's treatment in law, policy and practice of child *génocidaires* in light of its international obligations, and has critically appraised international actors', in particular UNICEF Rwanda's, interventions to enhance the rights of these child perpetrators. This concluding chapter synthesises the main findings of the study, drawing insights for advances in theories on human rights promotion in post-conflict societies, before outlining the implications and further questions raised by the research.

9.1 Key Findings and Theoretical Insights

After the 1994 genocide, Rwanda took the decision to criminally prosecute all those who participated, including children. As clearly evinced in Chapter 2, child perpetrators of atrocities *can* be prosecuted at the domestic level for international or ordinary crimes. However, there are a significant number of international juvenile justice standards, found mainly in the CRC but supplemented by best practice instruments, that apply. These standards emphasise age-appropriate treatment of children who come into conflict with the law at all stages of the judicial or administrative process. The relevant age, at least for determining penal accountability and certain sanctions, but also possibly for the enjoyment of all procedural rights, is the age at the time of the alleged commission of the crime. For states, like Rwanda, that have ratified the CRC, the standards apply in full, irrespective of the prevailing context in which they are to be implemented. Many of the standards, whilst categorised as 'negative' civil and political rights, require significant resources and action on the part of the state. Additionally, juvenile justice has been identified as a particularly contentious area of child rights, with public opinion often unsympathetic to the rights of the child offender. This can limit a state's political capacity to implement and comply with international standards. Whilst all states face these economic and social challenges to a greater or lesser degree, for states emerging from conflict, these challenges can be of such magnitude that implementing and complying with international juvenile justice standards appears an almost insurmountable task. And this, of course, assumes that the state, in the first place, has the political will to respect international law.

This book has clearly illustrated the obstacles to the domestic realisation of the rights of child perpetrators in post-genocide Rwanda. Chapter 4 set out in detail the significant resource and institutional limitations confronting Rwanda, in particular the lack of a functioning judicial system. Despite these extreme constraints, in an effort to combat impunity the Rwandan government took a maximalist approach to accountability. This included the prosecution of juveniles – initially before Specialised Chambers within the formal courts and later before the *gacaca* jurisdictions – who had participated in the whole range of acts committed during the genocide. The resource limitations, together with hostility from a society whose perception of child offenders had, like all other facets of Rwandan life, been ruptured by the genocide, rendered the application of international juvenile justice standards extremely difficult and significantly impeded efforts to put in place child-sensitive laws and policies in respect of child *génocidaires*. Of course, the treatment of all perpetrators – not just children – fell short of meeting international standards, but arguably, where maximal accountability is pursued with minimal resources, the interests of the child should prevail.

The in-depth appraisal of Rwanda's responses to child perpetrators in Chapter 5 revealed that Rwanda did, to some degree, prioritise those who had been minors at the time of the genocide. Minors did benefit from special treatment on account of their age, but there were many violations of their rights. Efforts were made to ensure that existing domestic provisions that were compliant with international law (including reduced sentences for juveniles, separation from adults in prisons and an implicit minimum age of criminal responsibility of 14) were respected in practice. Some provisions and policies that aimed at moving the system towards greater respect for the rights of child *génocidaires* were also introduced. These included juvenile justice training for law enforcement and judicial personnel, minors' judges and legal representation (in some cases) for juveniles appearing before the Specialised Chambers, and more explicit provisions on minority status and on reduced sentences for those aged 14–18 at the time of the genocide in the Gacaca Laws. The extreme challenges that faced Rwanda, however, hampered these efforts and narrowed the options available. To take a prime example, societal demands for all children to be held accountable as well as the gravity of the alleged crimes ruled out the outright release of children under 14. The Rwandan authorities (and UNICEF Rwanda) considered it to be in the best interests of these children in terms of personal security, as well as rehabilitation and reintegration, to place them in re-education centres. Whether these placements constituted a social welfare measure, or as some allege a punitive response, remains open to debate. And as regards separation in prisons, the sheer number of suspects as well as the lack of detention facilities delayed segregation. The result was that many juveniles continued to be held with adults,[1] often for many years in pre-trial detention (contrary to international standards) given the lack of personnel and the slow rate of case processing. Further, although some juvenile-specific provisions and measures were introduced, trials were held in public and there was no diversion from criminal proceedings or alternatives to detention (save that community service and suspended sentences were later introduced for all detainees). Additionally, little emphasis was placed on measures to reintegrate children, particularly those aged over 14 at the time of the genocide. Of course, as reiterated throughout this book, given the time lag between the genocide and the processing of cases, many 'children' would have been over 18 by the time of their trial (particularly before the *gacaca* courts) and thus it is not certain that all juvenile-specific safeguards would apply.[2] However, all international standards were applicable in respect of those minors under 18, both at the time of the genocide and at the time of trial – a category that encompasses many of those appearing before the formal courts. In short, although Rwanda complied with some international juvenile justice standards to some degree, child *génocidaires* were not granted the full protection envisaged under the CRC.

However, whilst the state has primary responsibility for meeting its international obligations, as Chapter 3 illustrated, there are various mechanisms at the international level that have a role in promoting child rights, or human rights (including child rights) more generally.

[1] Recall that some of these individuals would have reached adulthood whilst in detention, and that there is no requirement under international law to retain separation once an individual reaches 18.

[2] Although recall the CRC Committee's view that the rules of juvenile justice should apply to all those aged under 18 at the time of the alleged offence.

Chapters 6–8 explored the approach and contribution of these various bodies to the rights of child *génocidaires*, focusing on UNICEF given that it was the lead organisation on this issue in Rwanda and in view of its designated role under the CRC to provide technical assistance to states.

The comprehensive exploration and evaluation of UNICEF Rwanda's work in this book showed that UNICEF Rwanda was pragmatic yet principled in operationalising international juvenile justice standards. Its interpretation of CRC requirements was highly contextual and non-restrictivist, with frequent reliance on the best interests of the child principle. Clear examples are its support of the institutionalisation of the under-14s in re-education centres in light of the social context and its involvement in the building of minors' wings in prisons given the large number of detainees and resource limitations. UNICEF Rwanda made compromises from the 'ideal' application of the standards, prioritised some rights over others and accepted that some standards could only be implemented over time, but considered this necessary to make any progress in enhancing the rights of child *génocidaires*. As argued in Chapter 8, whilst the CRC does not expressly allow for consideration of local conditions, in many provisions the wording provides the flexibility for a contextual interpretation, and where not, it is contended that reliance on the best interests of the child principle to avoid a 'distorted' outcome is justifiable. Additionally, whilst prioritisation of rights and progressive realisation of civil and political rights are not expressly permitted by the CRC, approaching rights in this way is defensible from a policy perspective. This argument is consistent with scholars writing on human rights in post-conflict situations, who suggest that progressive realisation and a limited human rights framework could guide interventions in such contexts.

The empirical findings also indicate that UNICEF Rwanda was pragmatic in its use of strategies and techniques in policy development and advocacy. Whilst UNICEF Rwanda did not eschew more instrumentalist measures, such as offering incentives and using non-legal discourse as leverage to comply with a particular standard, the main thrust of the approach was collaborative and constructive. UNICEF Rwanda identified obstacles to implementation and compliance and sought to diminish them through, in particular, capacity building and community-sensitisation campaigns. It further identified when it was preferable to defer to existing domestic law rather than pushing for comprehensive law reform. And it ascertained where and how it could assert influence, focusing on developing relationships with Rwandan officials receptive to child rights and using all opportunities to raise rights. It also adapted its advocacy in light of the difficult relationship between the UN and Rwanda and the sensitivity of the subject area, generally avoiding overt condemnation of existing violations. Again, context moulded the interventions and an emphasis was placed on the domestic or local: whilst UNICEF Rwanda's engagement in some instances was direct (such as its involvement in the construction of minors' wings), this was accompanied by efforts to create sustainable local ownership, and UNICEF Rwanda frequently invoked local laws, local concepts and local individuals when seeking to influence approaches to child perpetrators.

Each of the strategies and techniques used by UNICEF Rwanda has been recognised by other scholars from various disciplines as a useful tool in encouraging compliance. However, as argued in Chapter 8, in a post-conflict situation there may need to be greater emphasis on the provision of support and collaboration. There are risks associated with this approach: too much involvement in a state's law and policy development could create dependency or lead to instrumentalisation by a state. However, although UNICEF Rwanda's involvement was significant, given the lack of government capacity as well as domestic NGOs working on juvenile justice, I believe that this was the only option if UNICEF Rwanda was to engage meaningfully with the issue of child *génocidaires*. It must be asked, what was the alternative? Some may argue that, in such circumstances, it would be preferable for an organisation to withdraw (or be sufficiently obstructive to be expelled), asserting the importance of maintaining credibility and fealty to principles. Others would suggest that withdrawing (or being expelled) would achieve nothing: maintaining some kind of presence that enables some kind of influence and dialogue is better than no presence at all. I find myself in the second camp: at least where operational organisations are concerned. Collaboration, rather than criticism, was considered key to having any influence over law, policy and practice on child perpetrators: such collaboration did not involve compromising independence or principles, and as evinced, did have some positive results. It must also be recalled that UNICEF's engagement did not extend into assuming control over Rwanda's treatment of child *génocidaires*, thus minimising the risk of being instrumentalised by the Rwandan government. Finding a middle ground where some compromises are made but principles are not abandoned is in my view better than simply exiting in the sure knowledge that significant violations will occur. By this, I do not intend to downplay the role that may be played by NGOs or indeed other limbs of the UN in criticising and condemning human rights violations by an incumbent government: I consider this watchdog role to be absolutely crucial for the promotion and protection of human rights, including in post-conflict societies. I simply suggest that there are mutually reinforcing roles that can be played by different actors and that, for operational organisations, a collaborative approach may enable incremental progress in enhancing human rights.

Whilst each post-conflict context is unique and there can be no one-size-fits-all approach, a contextual, constructive and collaborative approach to implementation and compliance could be an appropriate and valid means of operationalising juvenile justice standards, and possibly human rights standards more generally, in a post-conflict society. Overall then, based on the empirical findings here, this book makes the case for principled pragmatism as an approach to human rights promotion in post-conflict societies.

9.2 Implications and Further Questions

Dealing with child *génocidaires* was a first for Rwanda, for UNICEF and for the international community as a whole. Unfortunately, the issue of child perpetrators of atrocities is not likely to go away: in the course of researching and writing this book, reports of vast numbers of children being trained by ISIS in Syria to commit atrocities have come to light. Given the mass destruction of Syrian society and institutions, it is not beyond the realms of possibility that any future Syrian government may face challenges similar to those faced by the post-genocide Rwandan government. Of course, some may argue that child perpetrators involved in more recent or current armed conflicts, like that in Syria, are 'different' from Rwandan child *génocidaires*, or indeed from child perpetrators associated with armed groups in previous conflicts. These children, associated with armed groups designated as 'terrorist' groups, are frequently portrayed as a security threat, with a resulting 'punitive shift' in how they are perceived and treated.[3] I do not engage with the extensive debate here, but I would suggest that there is a thin line between the child 'terrorist' and other child perpetrators of atrocities. International juvenile justice standards apply to child 'terrorists' just as they do to child *génocidaires*. And whilst each conflict or post-conflict context will

[3] See Drumbl and Rona 2018 (identifying a shift towards punishment both inside and outside conflict contexts – where for example children are suspected of travelling to join 'terrorist' groups).

be unique with its own specific challenges, commonalities exist. What, then – other than what has already been discussed as regards approaches to implementation and compliance – can be learned from the Rwandan experience?

Perhaps an initial conceptual issue raised by my research relates to the impact of children's participation in violent conflict on the perception of childhood. As touched on in this book, childhood is a social and cultural construct and, as such, varies through time as well as geographical space. We saw in Rwanda how society's view of the capacities of children was upended by the violent acts committed during the genocide, such that child perpetrators were no longer seen as children, but as adults, deserving of the harshest punishment. This had an impact not only on the treatment of child perpetrators but also on the strategies and techniques adopted by UNICEF Rwanda. Considering community 'buy-in' to be essential for the reintegration of children suspected, or indeed convicted, of genocide crimes, UNICEF Rwanda made community sensitisation a pivotal strand of its overall approach. This relied to some extent on traditional Rwandan understandings of childhood from before the genocide (including the culture of respect for, and obedience to, elders), but that were considered to still have resonance with society, as well as other concepts that would 'reach' the local population. Sociologists and anthropologists have highlighted the importance of finding language that resonates at the local level when seeking to promote human rights, and my findings support this. What my findings also suggest is that, where the construction of childhood has been thrown into disarray by violent conflict, it may be necessary to search for meanings given to childhood from before the conflict, particularly where these meanings can be used as a potential explanation for children's conduct during the conflict.

A further issue raised by my research is whether pursuing individual criminal prosecutions of juveniles in the circumstances that prevailed in Rwanda was preferable to simply leaving these children in society. As expressly noted in the introduction to this book, my intention was not to consider whether children should or should not be prosecuted for atrocities – and I do not propose to enter into this contentious debate here. It was also not my intention to assess whether Rwanda's decision to prosecute children was justifiable. However, my research has clearly demonstrated that it was evident from the outset that violations of international juvenile justice standards were unavoidable (and indeed were already being committed when the Rwandan government took the decision to pursue a maximalist approach to accountability that would include children).

There was no existing juvenile justice system and thus no history of special treatment for children, there was a lack of functioning institutions, financial and material resources and trained personnel, and there was a huge number of suspects, all factors which meant that juveniles were held in deplorable conditions of detention for years awaiting trial. Inevitably, that raises the question as to whether the criminal trial approach for juveniles was appropriate.

This could be viewed from various perspectives: those of the victims and broader society and those of the alleged child perpetrators to name two. As I did not set out to examine the impact of Rwanda's transitional justice policy on victims and society in general, I have collated only limited data on this point and, to some extent, can only speculate as to whether criminal prosecutions of juveniles were seen as valuable. Based on the perception of child *génocidaires* as revealed by the SCF-USA study, as well as interviews conducted for this research, in the first few years after the genocide it appears that anything short of criminal prosecutions would have been rejected by society. And the comments made by research participants regarding victims' views on the *gacaca* jurisdictions suggest that victims considered the sentences passed by *gacaca* to be too lenient (in general – rather than specific to juveniles) but did not question the criminal justice approach. Indeed, it would appear that some were still of the view that children under 14 (at the time of the genocide) should have been punished for their involvement in genocidal acts. On balance, I would thus conclude that the criminal prosecution of juveniles, for victims and broader society, was rightly considered, at least at the time, to be the only appropriate mechanism.

As for child genocide suspects themselves, the choice was made to institutionalise children (and subsequently prosecute those over the age of 14 at the time of the genocide) even though it was clear that there would be violations of their rights. This was primarily on the basis that institutionalisation and accountability were necessary to maintain their personal safety. On the face of it, this approach appears defensible: it would be unreasonable to suggest that the Rwandan government should have released all child suspects into a society that a study (by a well-known and respected NGO) had revealed was demanding severe punishment for children, up to and including the death penalty. Over time, it is possible that the risks diminished, and it is certainly arguable that alternatives should have been considered already in the late 1990s, particularly given the slow processing of cases. Whilst the approach to institutionalisation might have been defensible (at least in the first few years after the genocide), the result was that many children – including some who were innocent and had been incarcerated on the basis of false denunciation – were held in pre-trial detention, and thus in limbo, for many years, which would inevitably have a profoundly detrimental impact not only on their lives during detention but also on their future. Indeed, the experiences of some individuals who had been minors at the time of the genocide and who had spent time in prison and then attended *ingando* were related in Chapter 5: the prolonged period of detention – in some cases ten years – had been extremely damaging and made it difficult to reintegrate into society, and two of the participants in my research (one of whom was subsequently acquitted by *gacaca* in absentia) had left Rwanda as a result. The limitations of this research in terms of time and scope, and also methodological challenges relating to interviews, in particular issues of access and trust, did not allow for extensive interviewing with former child *génocidaires*. Unfortunately, I was unable to speak with any child suspects who had personally gone through a full trial before the Specialised Chambers or the *gacaca* jurisdictions, or who had spent time in the Gitagata Re-education Centre. Further research by a scholar with greater connections with, and access to, Rwandans (in Rwanda and/or the diaspora) on, for example, the trial process and reintegration as experienced by child *génocidaires*, and indeed the administrative measures such as the Gitagata centre, would thus be valuable in taking the results of my research further. In particular, it would be useful to hear whether these individuals themselves felt that their personal security would have been at risk had they been left in society rather than detained. It would also be valuable to learn whether they felt that, despite the violations of their rights, the process they went through ultimately facilitated their reintegration into society, or whether they were never accepted and felt irreparably harmed by their experiences.

The next questions relate more directly to UNICEF. Whilst UNICEF has worked in various conflict and post-conflict contexts since its experiences in Rwanda, based on conversations with some current UNICEF staff, it appears that there have been few opportunities to learn from previous country programmes and approaches. It was not an aim of this book to provide policy recommendations, but I nonetheless hope that my findings will provide a reference point for future interventions (whether by UNICEF or other international actors) and broaden the debate on responses to child perpetrators.

As highlighted in Chapter 6, UNICEF first got involved with the issue of child *génocidaires* after being alerted to the presence of children in Rwandan prisons. As such, its response was somewhat reactive, and there was a suggestion that, given that children in detention had not come within the original agreement entered into between UNICEF and the Rwandan government, UNICEF could have taken the decision not to have engaged at all. This may have been justifiable owing to the vast numbers of child victims, child refugees and unaccompanied children requiring assistance from UNICEF Rwanda's child protection team. It may also have been understandable given that juvenile justice was a nascent area for UNICEF at that time. Notwithstanding, UNICEF Rwanda did take up the issue. The question thus arises as to whether UNICEF Rwanda made the right decision: for the organisation itself and for child perpetrators, the intended beneficiaries of its interventions.

As regards UNICEF as an institution, the Rwandan experience drew it into contention with other human rights advocates and even caused some tension within UNICEF itself. However, there do not seem to have been broader negative ramifications, for example, on its reputation as a child protection agency. And UNICEF's relationship with the Rwandan government appears to remain strong. From discussions with some UNICEF Rwanda staff working on the child *génocidaire* issue, my impression was that they would take the same decisions again: both in terms of initial involvement and the subsequent policy direction. However, as noted, there appears to have been little institutional learning. Indeed, one participant in the research suggested that global UNICEF wants to 'forget' what happened in Rwanda, not seeing its work there in a positive light. This, I suggest, would be a mistake. The involvement in Rwanda, with its negatives and positives, should be considered useful from both a policy and strategy perspective. Evidently, policies will always have to be tailored to the context, but it would be useful to have an institutional resource that provides details of previous engagements and also to provide examples, such as from Rwanda, where it may be necessary to deviate from the preferred approach (e.g. getting involved in improving detention conditions when the ideal would be focusing on diversion and alternatives to detention), whilst clearly setting out the extraordinary circumstances and reasons for that deviation. If such a resource already exists, its existence needs to be communicated more clearly to staff members, particularly those working in the field. Finally, although UNICEF will always be constrained by its institutional status and the nature of its relationship with the relevant government, it can make use of various strategies and techniques in its interventions as identified in this research.

In relation to child perpetrators, I have suggested that, although there were violations of their rights, there were some steps towards compliance, and that some of these can be traced directly, or indirectly, to UNICEF Rwanda's interventions. For those individuals who benefited from, for example, education in detention facilities, legal representation or a modified approach from a minors' judge, the involvement of UNICEF appears unequivocally positive: whilst it is not possible to state definitively what would have occurred had UNICEF Rwanda not intervened, given the decision by the Rwandan government to proceed with accountability measures for minors, it seems to me indisputable that UNICEF Rwanda's involvement was valuable. I outlined the limitations of this research earlier in terms of interviewing former child suspects: further research on their perception of UNICEF Rwanda's work – and indeed whether child suspects even came into contact with UNICEF Rwanda – would be a useful contribution to my findings. Looking more broadly, it would be interesting to explore more recent changes to Rwanda's juvenile justice laws, policy and practice: as noted in this book, there is evidence that UNICEF Rwanda's engagement with child *génocidaires* put the issue of juvenile justice on the agenda for future legislative reform.

A final question raised by my research is: what approaches should UNICEF be promoting when it is seeking to protect the rights of child perpetrators? Should it support a state in its chosen approach to accountability? As the reader will recall, it has been asserted that UNICEF should not engage in an 'ideological' campaign on children's rights, and I suggested that this may include the decision on whether or not to hold minors accountable. Whilst I maintain that this is a correct approach – i.e. that it is a matter for the state to decide on accountability – it is nonetheless open to, and arguably imperative for, UNICEF (and other actors) to explore and, if considered appropriate, advocate for the use of other accountability mechanisms, where an accountability process is seen as crucial for delivering social justice and for the reintegration of child perpetrators.

Such accountability measures could come within a TRC established specifically to deal with past atrocities[4] or take the form of community-based programmes, such as tradition-based justice and reconciliation mechanisms. Any such measures would still have to respect children's rights. Thus far, however, TRCs that have allowed for the participation of child perpetrators (in Sierra Leone and Liberia) have downplayed

[4] See Teitel 2000: 89–90 on the 'pseudo-punishment' function that can be served by TRCs. Note that the truth commission mechanism was rejected in Rwanda (see Clark 2011: 56; Palmer 2015: 96).

children's personal culpability for atrocities, and in Sierra Leone it was decided as matter of policy to treat all children coming before the TRC equally as witnesses, irrespective of whether they had perpetrated violations.[5] A TRC in which child perpetrators participate as 'offenders' and thus provide an account and reasons for their actions, accept responsibility for these actions and their consequences, and acknowledge the harm caused (possibly accompanied by reparations – which may be non-monetary – for victims) could potentially, however, be one way of dealing with children's participation in atrocities. How the process would unfold would necessarily be context dependent.

'Traditional' or indigenous mechanisms, which may focus on purification and/or forgiveness, may include elements of restorative justice and aim at the successful reintegration of child perpetrators, have been used following conflicts in various African countries.[6] In Mozambique, purification ceremonies were used to cleanse the child of 'the contamination from war and death', protect against harmful spirits, acknowledge atrocities committed and absolve the child from sin and guilt.[7] Honwana comments that these rituals are 'a fundamental condition for individual and collective healing and protection' as well as 'important means of conflict resolution, reconciliation, and social reintegration of war-affected persons'.[8] In northern Uganda, the *mato oput* justice mechanism was mooted as a potential means of holding child perpetrators accountable and 'generating acknowledgement and long-term reconciliation'.[9] Central to this process, which uses mediation to restore relationships after a killing within a family or clan, are confession to, and apology for, the crime, collective responsibility and compensation. However, as I have discussed elsewhere,[10] *mato oput* appears to have been used to a much lesser degree for returning former child soldiers than other rituals, in particular the 'stepping on the egg ceremony'. This latter ritual, used to cleanse and welcome home a person

[5] TRC 2004: [17]. See also Drumbl 2012: 180–188; Fisher 2013: 160–163; Steinl 2017: 51–68 (also 341–346 for further discussion of TRCs).

[6] See UNICEF and OSRSG-CAAC 2009: 72.

[7] See Honwana 2006: 110 (she notes similar rituals in Angola); Thompson 1999: 199.

[8] Honwana 2006: 106.

[9] Acirokop 2010: 268. See also Veale and Stavrou 2003: 46–47 (on *mato oput* and other rituals in Northern Uganda); Fisher 2013: 153–159 (discussing *mato oput* as a mediation process and suggesting that a community-based process of 'modified mediation' that incorporates retribution and/or restitution elements could be a useful accountability mechanism for child perpetrators).

[10] Barrett 2019.

returning after a long period of absence, cannot really be said to serve an accountability function but, to the extent that it facilitates reconciliation, could be viewed as a form of socio-cultural justice or at least a complementary instrument in the transitional justice toolbox. The purported advantage of indigenous mechanisms is that they are rooted in local traditional practices and beliefs and may thus be an acceptable means of meeting societal demands for accountability of child perpetrators (where such demands exist and are considered a primary consideration in determining the appropriate transitional justice approach and in facilitating reintegration). However, their use is not unproblematic. Traditional justice mechanisms have been described as 'ethnojustice': projects that are donor- and state-sponsored that seek to re-establish the traditional social order (on the assumption that it reflects community consensus), and that may often recreate the very power imbalances that caused the conflict.[11] Additionally, their use is often founded on romanticised views, and misguided notions, of local justice as restorative rather than retributive, and as being grounded in forgiveness.[12] And ultimately, they are all very context specific – the values and belief systems underlying the processes may be limited to just one community or geographical region – and whether they constitute an appropriate replacement for criminal proceedings will likely depend on the magnitude and nature of the alleged crimes and the conflict more generally.

In the context of Rwanda, having first become involved *after* children had already been arrested and detained and then becoming aware of public opinion's hostility towards these children, UNICEF Rwanda seems to have felt constrained to support the government's prosecutorial approach. Initially, this took the form of trials before Specialised Chambers in the formal courts, but later Rwanda introduced the *gacaca* jurisdictions, which could perhaps best be described as a 'tradition-inspired' justice mechanism. As illustrated in this book, UNICEF Rwanda had fairly limited involvement in the *gacaca* process and it has not been possible to determine why this was the case: whether UNICEF Rwanda had other pressing priorities; whether it was due to the passage of time and the fact that these 'minors' were now adults; whether the Rwandan government's tight control over the process left little scope for outside

[11] See Branch 2014. Such mechanisms may reflect gendered or age-based hierarchies that are no longer relevant after (or were the cause of) the conflict.

[12] See e.g. Allen 2008: 47–48; Allen and Schomerus 2006: 17.

involvement; or for some other reason. There is some evidence that, during discussions on *gacaca*, UNICEF Rwanda advocated for the prioritisation of juveniles before these jurisdictions and for juveniles to do community service instead of serving prison sentences, but had the *gacaca* process been introduced earlier, UNICEF Rwanda could have pushed for greater adaptation of the process to accommodate child-sensitive approaches. Indeed, UNICEF Rwanda could have advocated for a separate track based on the traditional *gacaca* model of dispute resolution[13] for juveniles after first discovering children in prisons. This does not appear to have been considered by UNICEF Rwanda – the reason for this remains a matter of conjecture: perhaps UNICEF Rwanda was not familiar with the traditional *gacaca* process, did not consider it appropriate for genocide crimes or did not feel able to raise it as a possibility given that *gacaca* had been rejected as an accountability measure for serious genocide-related crimes during initial discussions on how to deal with the past.[14] It is also possible that, since this was UNICEF's first real involvement with juvenile justice issues on a large scale and/or given the lack of institutional guidance from UNICEF's involvement in other post-conflict jurisdictions, UNICEF Rwanda simply did not have examples of alternative accountability mechanisms to hand.

Of course, ultimately the choice of whether to pursue minors for atrocity crimes, and indeed the form of any accountability, rests with the state, as does responsibility for the implementation of, and compliance with, international standards. As is clear from this book, post-conflict challenges can be so great as to render the full realisation of rights impossible. Whilst UNICEF can advocate for alternatives and push for compliance, a post-conflict situation will always require an element of pragmatism, realism and flexibility, and any evaluation of UNICEF's efforts must similarly be firmly grounded in realism. After all, if states cannot be required or coerced into achieving the impossible, UNICEF should not be held to unreasonable expectations of influence or impact.

[13] For details of traditional *gacaca* (which generally did not deal with more serious crimes), see Bornkamm 2012: 31–35; Clark 2011: 52–54; Ingelaere 2008: 32–35; Karekezi, Nshimiyimana and Mutamba 2004: 73–74; OHCHR 1996c: 10–15.

[14] See Clark 2011: 55; Digneffe and Fierens 2003: 77. It was recommended that *gacaca* serve as a sort of 'truth commission' separating the guilty from the innocent to assist the formal courts, or at most deal with minor crimes – on this see Ingelaere 2008: 35–37 and 2016: 20–22; Office of the President 1995: 23; OHCHR 1996a and 1996c: 10.

Annex 1

List of Archives/Institutions Consulted

Note: this list does not reference institutions that were approached, but that did not provide access to documents.

ASF (ASF-Rwanda's archives were passed on to RCN in Rwanda)
ASOFERWA, Kigali, Rwanda
CCM (Centre for Conflict Management), Butare and Kigali, Rwanda
CLADHO, Kigali, Rwanda
Coopération Technique Belge, Kigali, Rwanda
Danish Centre/Institute for Human Rights (by correspondence)
Human Rights Watch, Kigali, Rwanda
ICRC, Kigali, Rwanda
Judicial Defenders Corps, Kigali, Rwanda
Legal Aid Forum, Kigali, Rwanda
LGDL, Kigali, Rwanda
LIPRODHOR, Kigali, Rwanda
Ministry of Justice, Kigali, Rwanda
National Commission for the Fight against Genocide (CNLG), Kigali, Rwanda
National Public Prosecution Authority, Kigali, Rwanda
National Unity and Reconciliation Commission, Kigali, Rwanda
National University of Rwanda, Butare, Rwanda
Parliament, Kigali, Rwanda
PRI, Kigali, Rwanda and London, UK
RCN Justice et Democratie, Kigali, Rwanda and Brussels, Belgium
Rwanda Correctional Service, Kigali, Rwanda
Rwandan Bar Association, Kigali, Rwanda
Rwandan Demobilisation and Reintegration Commission, Kigali, Rwanda
UNDP, Kigali, Rwanda
UNICEF (located at One UN Rwanda), Kigali, Rwanda; and Innocenti Research Centre, Florence, Italy (by correspondence)

Annex 2

Sentencing under the Genocide Law 1996

	Category 1 Planners; perpetrators in position of authority; notorious killers; perpetrators of sexual torture		Category 2 Intentional acts causing death		Category 3 Other serious acts against persons		Category 4 Offences against property
	Adults	Minors	Adults	Minors	Adults	Minors	
Confession *before* prosecution	Re-classification to Cat. 2	Re-classification to Cat. 2	7–11 years	3½–5½ years	Third of sentence in Penal Code	Max. ⅙ of adult sentence	Civil damages as agreed between parties, failing which – suspended sentence
Confession *after* prosecution	Not eligible (Art. 5)	Not eligible (Art. 5)	12–15 years	6–7½ years	Half of sentence in Penal Code	Max. ¼ of adult sentence	
Sentence without valid confession	Death	10–20 years	Life	10–20 years	According to Penal Code	Max. ½ of adult sentence	
Accessory sanctions	Permanent withdrawal of all civic rights: (1) removal/expulsion from public office/employment (2) deprivation of all electoral and political rights including right to vote (3) inability to act as expert witness (4) inability to be family council member or court-appointed guardian (5) deprivation of right to bear arms and to serve in armed forces or police, or in teaching (6) deprivation of right to hold driving licence		Permanent withdrawal of selected civic rights (2), (3) and (5) (see Cat. 1)		Withdrawal of rights as set out in Penal Code		

Annex 3

Sentencing under the Gacaca Laws

Gacaca Law 2001

	Category 1		**Category 2**		**Category 3**		**Category 4**
	Planners; perpetrators in position of authority; notorious killers; perpetrators of sexual torture/rape		Intentional acts causing death or serious assault with intent to kill		Serious attacks without intent to kill		Property crimes
	Adults	Minors	Adults	Minors	Adults	Minors	
Confession *before* list	25 years to life imprisonment	10–20 years or half the adult sentence? *	7–12 years (½ in TIG)	Half the adult sentence	1–3 years (½ in TIG)	Half the adult sentence	Civil reparation of damages only (no special provisions for juveniles)
Confession *after* list	Death or life imprisonment	10–20 years? *	12–15 years (½ in TIG)		3–5 years (½ in TIG)		
Sentence without confession	Death or life imprisonment	10–20 years	25 years to life		5–7 years (½ in TIG)		
Accessory sanctions	Permanent withdrawal of all civic rights (see Annex 2 for list)		Permanent withdrawal of selected rights (2), (3) and (5) (see Annex 2)				

* Article 74 simply provides that juveniles convicted of category 1 offences will be sentenced to 10–20 years' imprisonment: no reference is made to the confession procedure.

Gacaca Law 2004

	Category 1		**Category 2 (1) & (2)**		**Category 2 (3)**		**Category 3**
	Planners; perpetrators in position of authority; notorious killers; perpetrators of torture, rape, dehumanizing acts on dead body		Intentional acts causing death; serious assault with intent to kill		Offences without intent to kill		Property crimes
	Adults	Minors	Adults	Minors	Adults	Minors	
Confession *before* list	25–30 years	8–10 years	7–12 years (½ in TIG)	3.5–6 years (½ in TIG)	1–3 years (½ in TIG)	6 months–1.5 years (½ in TIG)	Civil reparation of damages only (no special provisions for juveniles)
Confession *after* list	Death or life imprisonment	10–20 years? *	12–15 years (½ in TIG)	6–7.5 years (½ in TIG)	3–5 years (½ in TIG)	1.5–2.5 years (½ in TIG)	
Sentence without confession	Death or life imprisonment	10–20 years	25–30 years	8–10 years	5–7 years (½ in TIG)	2.5–3.5 years (½ in TIG)	
Accessory sanctions	Permanent withdrawal of all civic rights (see Annex 2) & inclusion on public notice		Permanent withdrawal of selected rights (2), (3) and (5) (plus deprivation of right to be medical staff) (see Annex 2) & inclusion on public notice		Inclusion on public notice		

* Article 78 provides that juveniles convicted of category 1 offences will be sentenced to 10–20 years if they have not made a valid confession or to 8–10 years if they have confessed in accordance with Article 60. Article 60 refers to the process for accepting confessions but makes no reference to timing. No reference is made to Article 55 which provides that category 1 offenders benefit from the confession procedure if their confession is made before their names appear on the list drawn up by the cell-level *gacaca* court.

Gacaca Law 2007

	Category 1		Category 2 (1), (2) & (3)		Category 2 (4) & (5)		Category 2 (6)		Category 3
	Planners; perpetrators in position of authority; perpetrators of rape or sexual torture		Notorious killer; perpetrators of torture not resulting in death, dehumanizing acts on dead body		Acts causing death; serious assault with intent to kill		Offences without intent to kill		Property crimes
	Adults	Minors	Adults	Minors	Adults	Minors	Adults	Minors	
Confession *before* list	20–24 years	6.5–7.5 years	20–24 years (⅓ in custody; ½ in TIG; ⅙ suspended)	6–7 years (⅙ in custody; ½ in TIG; ⅓ suspended)	8–11 years (⅓ in custody; ½ in TIG; ⅙ suspended)	2.5–3.5 years (⅙ in custody; ½ in TIG; ⅓ suspended)	1–2 years (⅙ in custody; ½ in TIG; ⅓ suspended)	6 months–1.5 years (⅙ in custody; ½ in TIG; ⅓ suspended)	Civil reparation of damages only (no special provisions for juveniles)
Confession *after* list	25–30 years	8–9 years	25–29 years (⅓ in custody; ½ in TIG; ⅙ suspended)	6.5–7.5 years (⅓ in custody; ½ in TIG; ⅙ suspended)	12–14 (⅓ in custody; ½ in TIG; ⅙ suspended)	4–5 years (⅓ in custody; ½ in TIG; ⅙ suspended)	3–4 years (⅓ in custody; ½ in TIG; ⅙ suspended)	1.5–2.5 years (⅓ in custody; ½ in TIG; ⅙ suspended)	
Sentence without valid confession	Death/life imprisonment*	10–20 years	30 years or life imprisonment	10–15 years	15–19 years	4.5–5.5 years	5–7 years (⅓ in custody; ½ in TIG; ⅙ suspended)	2.5–3.5 years (½ in TIG)**	
Accessory sanction	Permanent withdrawal of rights to be elected, serve in armed forces and police, be teacher, medical staff, magistrate, public prosecutor or judicial counsel & inclusion on public notice		No confession: Permanent withdrawal of selected rights (see Cat. 1) Confession: Withdrawal of selected rights (see Cat. 1) during principal sentence Both: inclusion on public notice		Withdrawal of selected rights (see Cat. 1) during principal sentence & inclusion on public notice		Withdrawal of selected rights (see Cat. 1) during principal sentence & inclusion on public notice		

* The death penalty was abolished in 2007. Article 17 of Gacaca Law 2008 provided for a maximum sentence of life imprisonment with special provisions.

** Article 20 of Gacaca Law 2008 provided that the sentence of 2.5–3.5 years could be served ⅓ in custody, ½ in TIG and ⅙ suspended.

BIBLIOGRAPHY

Judicial Proceedings

East Timor Special Panel for Serious Crimes

Prosecutor v. *X*, Case No. 04/2002, Judgment, Special Panel for Serious Crimes – ETPA Dili District Court, 2 December 2002

War Crimes Chamber in the Court of Bosnia and Herzegovina

Prosecutor v. *Elvir Jakupović*, Case No. X-KR-10/906, Verdict, Section I for War Crimes, Court of Bosna and Herzegovina, Sarajevo, 23 August 2010

Second World War Military Court/Tribunals

Bommer Trial: Trial of Alois and Anna Bommer and their Daughters, Case No. 50, Permanent Military Tribunal at Metz, France, 19 February 1947, in Vol. IX of United Nations War Crimes Commission, *Law Reports of Trials of War Criminals* (London: 1949)

Oenning Trial: Trial of Johannes Oenning And Emil Nix, Case No. 67, British Military Court, Borken, Germany, 21 and 22 December 1945, in Vol. XI of United Nations War Crimes Commission, *Law Reports of Trials of War Criminals* (London: 1949)

African Commission on Human and People's Rights

Groupe de Travail sur les Dossiers Judiciaires Stratégiques v. *Democratic Republic of Congo*, Communication 259/2002, July 2013

Rwandan Jurisdictions

Formal Courts

Auditorat Militaire c/Pte Habimana Vincent, RP/GEN/0005/TM, Tribunal Militaire Gatagara/Butare, 15 May 2005, in ASF Recueil de Jurisprudence Contentieux du Génocide, Tome VII, 267

Ministère Public c/ Banzi Wellars et consorts, RP 35/1/99, CS TPI Gisenyi, 25 May 2001, in ASF Recueil de Jurisprudence Contentieux du Génocide, Tome VI, 71

Ministère Public c/ Kabirigi Anastase et consorts, RP 005/01/97, CS TPI Kibuye, 10 December 1998, in ASF Recueil de Jurisprudence Contentieux du Génocide, Tome II, 119

Ministère Public c/ Karangwa Théogène et consorts, RP 037/R1/99, CS TPI Ruhengeri, 11 April 2000, in ASF Recueil de Jurisprudence Contentieux du Génocide, Tome IV, 205

Ministère Public c/ Maniraguha, RP 125/CS, CS TPI Kigali, 4 June 1999, referenced in Murara 2000: 156

Ministère Public c/ Minani François, RP 007/GIT/CH.S/97, CS TPI Gitarama, 23 September 1997, in ASF Recueil de Jurisprudence Contentieux du Génocide, Tome II, 87

Ministère Public c/Mudaheranwa, RP 004/EX/R1/98/KGO, CS TPI Kibungo, 20 January 1999

Ministère Public c/ Niyoniringiye Félix et consorts, RP 128/R2/2000, CS TPI Gisenyi, 27 October 2000, in ASF Recueil de Jurisprudence Contentieux du Génocide, Tome V, 91

Ministère Public c/ Niyonsenga Jean Bosco, RP 116/EX/R2/99/KGO, CS TPI Kibungo, 14 October 1999, in ASF Recueil de Jurisprudence Contentieux du Génocide, Tome II, 111

Ministère Public c/ Nsabamungu Jean de Dieu, RP 0124/EX/R2/99/KGO, CS TPI Kibungo, 16 November 1999, in ASF Recueil de Jurisprudence Contentieux du Génocide, Tome I, 55

Ministère Public c/ Nsabimana Célestin et consorts, RP 0115/EX/R2/99/KGO, CS TPI Kibungo, 3 February 2000, in ASF Recueil de Jurisprudence Contentieux du Génocide, Tome V, 139

Ministère Public c/ Ntahondi Ildéphonse alias Bizimana, RP 049/R1/2000, CS TPI Ruhengeri, 12 December 2000, in ASF Recueil de Jurisprudence Contentieux du Génocide, Tome III, 231

Ministère Public c/ Nzabonimpa J. Bosco, RP 88/R1/98, CS TPI Gisenyi, 28 December 1998, in ASF Recueil de Jurisprudence Contentieux du Génocide, Tome IV, 111

Ministère Public c/ Rwagakiga et consorts, RP 027/R1/98, CS TPI Ruhengeri, 25 March 1999, in ASF Recueil de Jurisprudence Contentieux du Génocide, Tome V, 221

Mugabo c/ Ministère Public, RPA 25/97/R1/Kig., Kigali Appeal Court, 30 November 1998 referenced in Murara 2000: 157

Gacaca Jurisdictions

Habyarimana, ASF Observations des juridictions gacaca dans l'ex-province de Byumba, December 2006

Havugimana, ASF Observations des juridictions gacaca dans l'ex-province de Cyangugu, August 2007

Jean Baptiste N. Nyamata, Kigali Ngali, June 2007 (Sector Court) and July 2007 (Appeal Court)

Joseph M. Butare Ville, March 2009 (Sector Court), May 2009 (Appeal Court) and March 2010 (Appeal Court)

Kanyamugara, ASF Observations des juridictions gacaca dans l'ex-province de Kibuye, November 2006

Mutabazi alias Gitarama, ASF Observations des juridictions gacaca dans l'ex-province de Kibungo, February 2007

Mutabazi C., ASF Observations des juridictions gacaca, Kigali Ngali, May 2005

Mwenedata, ASF Observations des juridictions gacaca dans l'ex-province de Gitarama, May 2007

Ngabonzima, ASF Observations des juridictions gacaca dans l'ex-province de Butare et Gikongoro, November 2007

Ntihabose and Ugeziwe, ASF Observations des juridictions gacaca, Kigali Ville, October 2006

Nyirimbabazi, ASF Observations des juridictions gacaca dans l'ex-province de Gikongoro et Butare, June 2007

Twagirayezu, Habyarimana and Ndahayo, ASF Observations des juridictions gacaca dans l'ex-province de Kibuye, August 2006

Other National Courts

Roper v. *Simmons*, 543 US 551 (2005)

T v. *United Kingdom*, No. 24724/94 and *V* v. *United Kingdom*, No. 24888/94, 30 EHRR 121 (2000)

Treaties and Other International Instruments

1924 Geneva Declaration of the Rights of the child (26 September 1924)

1948 Convention on the Prevention and Punishment of the Crime of Genocide (adopted 9 December 1948, entered into force 12 January 1951) 78 UNTS 277

1948 Universal Declaration of Human Rights, UNGA Resolution 217A(III) (10 December 1948)

1949 Geneva Convention Relative to the Protection of Civilian Persons in Time of War (12 August 1949) 75 UNTS 287 (Geneva Convention IV)

1951 Convention relating to the Status of Refugees (adopted 28 July 1951, entered into force 22 April 1954) 189 UNTS 137

1959 United Nations Declaration of the Rights of the Child, UNGA Resolution 1386 (XIV) (20 November 1959)

1966 International Covenant on Civil and Political Rights (adopted 16 December 1966, entered into force 23 March 1976) 999 UNTS 171

1966 International Covenant on Economic, Social and Cultural Rights (adopted 16 December 1966, entered into force 3 January 1976) 993 UNTS 3

1977 Protocol Additional to the Geneva Conventions of 12 August 1949 and Relating to the Protection of Victims of International Armed Conflicts (adopted 8 June 1977, entered into force 7 December 1979) 1125 UNTS 3 (Protocol I)

1977 Protocol Additional to the Geneva Conventions of 12 August 1949 and Relating to the Protection of Victims of Non-International Armed Conflicts (adopted 8 June 1977, entered into force 7 December 1978) 1125 UNTS 609 (Protocol II)

1981 African Charter on Human and People's Rights (adopted 27 June 1981, entered into force 21 October 1986) 1520 UNTS 217

1985 United Nations Standard Minimum Rules for the Administration of Juvenile Justice (The Beijing Rules), UNGA Resolution 40/33, annex (29 November 1985)

1988 Body of Principles for the Protection of All Persons under Any Form of Detention or Imprisonment, UNGA Resolution 43/173, annex (9 December 1988)

1989 Convention on the Rights of the Child (adopted 20 November 1989, entered into force 2 September 1990) 1577 UNTS 3

1990 African Charter on the Rights and Welfare of the Child (adopted 1990, entered into force 29 November 1999) OAU Doc. CAB/LEG/24.9/49

1990 United Nations Standard Minimum Rules for Non-custodial Measures (The Tokyo Rules), UNGA Resolution 45/110, annex (14 December 1990)

1990 Basic Principles for the Treatment of Prisoners, UNGA Resolution 45/111, annex (14 December 1990)

1990 United Nations Guidelines for the Prevention of Juvenile Delinquency (The Riyadh Guidelines), UNGA Resolution 45/112, annex (14 December 1990)

1990 United Nations Rules for the Protection of Juveniles Deprived of their Liberty (The Havana Rules), UNGA Resolution 45/113, annex (14 December 1990)

1997 The Cape Town Principles and Best Practice on the Prevention of Recruitment of Children into the Armed Forces and Demobilization and Social Reintegration of Child Soldiers in Africa (April 1997)

1997 Guidelines for Action on Children in the Criminal Justice System (The Vienna Guidelines), recommended by ECOSOC Resolution 1997/30 (21 July 1997)

1998 Rome Statute of the International Criminal Court (adopted 17 July 1998, entered into force 1 July 2002) 2187 UNTS 90

2000 Optional Protocol to the Convention on the Rights of the Child on the Sale of Children, Child Prostitution and Child Pornography (adopted 25 May 2000, entered into force 18 January 2002) 2171 UNTS 227 (First Optional Protocol)

2000 Optional Protocol to the Convention on the Rights of the Child on the Involvement of Children in Armed Conflict (adopted 25 May 2000, entered into force 12 February 2002) 2173 UNTS 222 (Second Optional Protocol)

2000 United Nations Transitional Administration in East Timor (UNTAET) Regulation No. 2000/30 on the Transitional Rules of Criminal Procedure (25 September 2000) as amended by Regulation 2001/25 (14 September 2001)

2002 Basic Principles on the Use of Restorative Justice Programmes in Criminal Matters, ECOSOC Resolution 2002/12 (24 July 2002)

2002 Statute of the Special Court for Sierra Leone, annexed to the Agreement between the United Nations and the Government of Sierra Leone on the Establishment of the Special Court for Sierra Leone (16 January 2002) 2178 UNTS 137

2006 Convention on the Rights of Persons with Disabilities (adopted 13 December 2006, entered into force 3 May 2008) 2515 UNTS 3

2007 The Paris Commitments to Protect Children from Unlawful Recruitment or Use by Armed Forces or Armed Groups (February 2007)

2007 The Paris Principles: Principles and Guidelines on Children Associated with Armed Forces or Armed Groups (February 2007)

2009 Lima Declaration on Restorative Juvenile Justice (7 November 2009)

2011 Optional Protocol to the Convention on the Rights of the Child on a Communications Procedure (adopted 19 December 2011, entered into force 14 April 2014) (UN Doc. A/RES/66/138) (Third Optional Protocol)

2015 United Nations Basic Principles and Guidelines on Remedies and Procedures on the Right of Anyone Deprived of Their Liberty to Bring Proceedings Before a Court (adopted by the Working Group on Arbitrary Detention, 20–29 April 2015) (UN doc A/HRC/30/37, annex)

2015 United Nations Standard Minimum Rules for the Treatment of Prisoners (The Nelson Mandela Rules), UNGA Resolution 70/175 (17 December 2015)

Rwandan Legislation

1888 Décret du 30 juillet 1888 relatif aux contrats ou obligations conventionnelles, code civil, Bulletin Officiel, 1888, p. 109 (Book III, Civil Code)

1896 Décret du roi-souverain du 23 mai 1896 sur le vagabondage et la mendicité

1961 Ordonnance No. 111/127 du 30 mai 1961 organisant le service pénitentiaire du Ruanda-Urundi

1963 Loi du 23 février 1963 portant Code de Procédure Pénale, modifiée par Décret-loi No. 07/1982 du 7 janvier 1982

1975 Arrête Présidentiel No. 234/06 du 21 octobre 1975 portant création de centres de rééducation et de production

1975 Décret-loi No. 08/75 du 12 février 1975 approuvant et ratifiant diverses Conventions Internationales relatives aux droits de l'homme, au désarmement, à la prévention et à la répression de certains actes susceptibles de mettre en danger la paix entre les hommes et les nations

1977 Décret-loi No. 21/77 du 18 août 1977 instituant le Code Pénal au Rwanda

1988 Loi No. 42/1988 du 27 octobre 1988 portant création du titre préliminaire et livre premier du code civil (Book I, Civil Code)

1991 Constitution de la République Rwandaise du 10 juin 1991

1993 Peace Agreement between the Government of the Republic of Rwanda and the Rwandese Patriotic Front of 4 August 1993 (Arusha Peace Agreement)

1994 Déclaration du FPR du 17 juillet 1994 relative à la mise en place des Institutions (RPF Declaration of 17 July 1994)

1996 Organic Law No. 08/96 of 30 August 1996 on the Organisation of Prosecutions for Offences Constituting the Crime of Genocide or Crimes against Humanity Committed since 1 October 1990

1996 Law No. 09/96 of 8 September 1996 Relating to Provisional Modifications to the Criminal Procedure Code

1997 Law No. 16/97 of 26 December 1997 Modifying the Law No. 09/96 of 8 September 1996 Relating to Provisional Modifications to the Criminal Procedure Code

1997 Organic Law No. 03/97 of 19 March 1997 Establishing a Bar Association in Rwanda

2000 Loi No. 20/2000 du 26 juillet 2000 relative aux associations sans but lucratif

2001 Organic Law No. 40/2000 of 26 January 2001 Setting Up 'Gacaca Jurisdictions' and Organising Prosecutions for Offences Constituting the Crime of Genocide or Crimes against Humanity Committed between 1 October 1990 and 31 December 1994

2001 Law No. 27/2001 of 28 April 2001 Relating to the Rights and Protection of the Child Against Violence

2001 Presidential Order No. 26/01 of 10 December 2001 Relating to the Substitution of the Penalty of Imprisonment for Community Service

2003 Constitution of the Republic of Rwanda of 4 June 2003

2004 Law No. 6 bis/2004 of 14 April 2004 on the Statutes for Judges and Other Judicial Personnel

2004 Organic Law No. 07/2004 of 25 April 2004 Determining the Organisation, Functioning and Jurisdiction of Courts

2004 Law No. 13/2004 of 17 May 2004 Relating to the Code of Criminal Procedure

2004 Organic Law No. 16/2004 of 19 June 2004 Establishing the Organisation, Competence and Functioning of the Gacaca Courts Charged with Prosecuting and Trying the Perpetrators of the Crime of Genocide and Other Crimes against Humanity Committed between 1 October 1990 and 31 December 1994

2005 Presidential Order No. 10/01 of 7 March 2005 Determining the Modalities of Implementation of Community Service as Alternative Penalty to Imprisonment

2005 Presidential Order No. 50/01 of 16 October 2005 Modifying and Complementing Presidential Order No. 10/01 of 7 March 2005 Determining the Modalities of Implementation of Community Service as Alternative Penalty to Imprisonment

2006 Law No. 38/2006 of 25 September 2006 on the Establishment and Organisation of the National Prisons Service

2007 Organic Law No. 10/2007 of 1 March 2007 Modifying and Complementing Organic Law No.16/2004 of 19 June 2004 Establishing the Organisation, Competence and Functioning of the Gacaca Courts Charged with Prosecuting and Trying the Perpetrators of the Crime of Genocide and Other Crimes against Humanity Committed between 1 October 1990 and 31 December 1994

2008 Organic Law No. 51/2008 of 9 September 2008 Determining the Organisation, Functioning and Jurisdiction of Courts

2008 Organic Law No. 13/2008 of 19 May 2008 Modifying and Complementing Organic Law No. 16/2004 of 19 June 2004 Establishing the Organisation, Competence and Functioning of the Gacaca Courts Charged with Prosecuting and Trying the Perpetrators of the Crime of Genocide and Other Crimes against Humanity Committed between 1 October 1990 and 31 December 1994

2010 Law No. 34/2010 of 12 November 2010 on the Establishment, Functioning and Organisation of Rwanda Correctional Service (RCS)

2011 Law No. 54/2011 of 14 December 2011 Relating to the Rights and the Protection of the Child

2011 Law No. 22/2011 of 28 June 2011 Establishing the National Commission for Children and Determining its Mission, Organisation and Functioning

2012 Organic Law No. 01/2012 of 2 May 2012 Instituting the Penal Code

2013 Law No. 30/2013 of 24 May 2013 Relating to the Code of Criminal Procedure

2017 Law No. 19bis/2017 of 28 April 2017 Modifying and Complementing Law No. 34/2010 of 12 November 2010 on the Establishment, Functioning and Organisation of Rwanda Correctional Service (RCS)

2018 Law No. 68/2018 of 30 August 2018 Determining Offences and Penalties in General

2018 Law No. 71/2018 of 31 August 2018 Relating to the Protection of the Child

Literature and Documents from International Organisations

Note: copies of unpublished documents are on file with author

Abramson, B. 2006. 'Juvenile Justice: The "Unwanted Child": Why the Potential of the Convention on the Rights of the Child is Not Being Realized, and What We Can Do About It', in E.L. Jensen and J. Jepsen (eds.), *Juvenile Law Violators, Human Rights, and the Development of New Juvenile Justice Systems* (Oxford; Portland, OR.: Hart Publishing) 15

Acirokop, P. 2010. 'The Potential and Limits of *Mato Oput* as a Tool for Reconciliation and Justice', in S. Parmar, M.J. Roseman, S. Siegrist and T. Sowa (eds.), *Children and Transitional Justice: Truth-Telling, Accountability and Reconciliation* (Cambridge, MA: UNICEF; Harvard Law School) 267

African Rights 1995a. *Rwanda: Death, Despair and Defiance*, Revised Edition (London: African Rights)

1995b. *Rwanda: Not So Innocent – When Women Become Killers* (Kigali: African Rights)

2000. *Confessing to Genocide: Responses to Rwanda's Genocide Law* (London: African Rights)

2003. *Gacaca Justice: A Shared Responsibility* (Kigali: African Rights)

Allen, T. 2008. 'Ritual (Ab)Use? Problems with Traditional Justice in Northern Uganda', in N. Waddell and P. Clark (eds.), *Courting Conflict? Justice, Peace and the ICC in Africa* (London: Royal African Society)

Allen, T. and Schomerus, M. 2006. 'A Hard Homecoming: Lessons Learned from the Reception Center Process in Northern Uganda: An Independent Study' (Washington, DC: Management Systems International)

Alston, P. 1994. 'The Best Interests Principle: Towards a Reconciliation of Culture and Human Rights', in P. Alston (ed.), *The Best Interests of the Child: Reconciling Culture and Human Rights* (Oxford: Clarendon Press) 1

1997. 'The Purposes of Reporting', in OHCHR, UN Institute for Training and Research and UN Staff College Project, *Manual on Human Rights Reporting: Under Six Major International Human Rights Instruments* (Geneva: UN) 19

Alston, P. and Gilmour-Walsh, B. 1996. *The Best Interests of the Child: Towards a Synthesis of Children's Rights and Cultural Values* (Florence: UNICEF)

Amann, D.M. 2001. 'Calling Children to Account: The Proposal for a Juvenile Chamber in the Special Court for Sierra Leone' 29 *Pepperdine Law Review* 167

Amnesty International 1995a. 'Rwanda: Crying Out for Justice', AI Index: AFR 47/05/95 (6 April)

1995b. 'Rwanda and Burundi: A Call for Action by the International Community', AI Index: AFR 02/24/95 (31 August)

1997a. 'Rwanda – Unfair Trials: Justice Denied', AI Index: AFR 47/08/97 (8 April)

1997b. 'Rwanda: Ending the Silence', AI Index: AFR 47/32/97 (25 September)

2000a. 'Rwanda: The Troubled Course of Justice', AI Index: AFR 47/10/00 (April)

2000b. 'Sierra Leone: Childhood – a Casualty of Conflict', AI Index: AFR 51/69/00 (31 August)

2000c. 'Sierra Leone: Recommendations on the Draft Statute of the Special Court', AI Index: AFR 51/83/00 (14 November)

2000d. 'Child Soldiers: Criminals or Victims?', AI Index: IOR 50/02/00 (December)

2002. 'Rwanda – Gacaca: A Question of Justice', AI Index: AFR 47/007/2002 (December)

An-na'im, A.A. and Hammond, J. 2002. 'Cultural Transformation and Human Rights in African Societies', in A.A. An-na'im (ed.), *Cultural Transformation and Human Rights in Africa* (London; New York: Zed Books) 13

Aptel, C. 2010. 'Children and Accountability for International Crimes: The Contribution of International Criminal Court', Innocenti Working Paper No. 2010–20 (Florence: UNICEF Innocenti Research Centre)

Arts, K. and Popovski, V. (eds.) 2006. *International Criminal Accountability and the Rights of Children* (The Hague: Hague Academic Press)

Arzoumanian, N. and Pizzutelli, F. 2003. 'Victimes et bourreaux: questions de responsabilité liées à la problématique des enfants-soldats en Afrique' 85 *International Review of the Red Cross* 827

ASF [Avocats Sans Frontières] 1996. 'Justice pour tous au Rwanda' (October)

1997a. 'Projet Justice pour tous au Rwanda avec le soutien de l'Union Européenne: Protocole de Collaboration' (draft) (7 February)

1997b. 'Projet Justice pour tous au Rwanda, Rapport Annuel 1997'

1998a. 'Project Justice pour tous au Rwanda, Rapport 1° semestre 1998'

1998b. 'Justice for All in Rwanda, Annual Report 1998'

1999a. 'Justice pour tous au Rwanda, Rapport d'activités: 1er Janvier – 30 Juin 1999'

1999b. 'Justice pour tous au Rwanda, Rapport Annuel 1999'

2000a. 'Justice pour tous au Rwanda, Rapport Semestriel 2000, Janvier – Juin 2000'

2000b. 'Justice pour tous au Rwanda, Rapport d'activités 2000'

2004a. *Vade-Mecum: Le crime de génocide et les crimes contre l'humanité devant les juridictions ordinaire du Rwanda* (Kigali and Brussels: ASF)

2004b. 'Rapport: Formation des Formateurs des Juges Gacaca Phase de Jugement Organisée pars Avocats Sans Frontières en Collaboration avec le Service National des Juridictions Gacaca du 02 au 12 Novembre 2004'

2005a. 'Rapport: Formation des Inyangamugayo des Juridictions Gacaca de Secteur et d'Appel du 29 Novembre 2004 au 7 Janvier 2005'

2005b. 'Monitoring des Juridictions Gacaca, Phase de Jugement, Rapport Analytique, Mars – Septembre 2005'

2007a. 'Monitoring des Juridictions Gacaca, Phase de Jugement, Rapport Analytique No. 2, Octobre 2005 – Septembre 2006'

2007b. 'Monitoring des Juridictions Gacaca, Phase de Jugement, Rapport Analytique No. 3, Octobre 2006 – April 2007'

2010. 'Recueil de jurisprudence relative au contentieux des mineurs' (July)

ASOFERWA [Association de Solidarité des Femmes Rwandaises] 1998a. 'Rapport Annuel 1997: Projet Gitagata'

1998b. 'Rapport Mensuel: Project Gitagata, Juin 1998'

1998c. 'Rapport Mensuel: Projet Protégez-moi, Septembre'

1998d. 'Rapport Mensuel: Projet Protégez-moi, Octobre'

1998e. 'Rapport Mensuel: Projet Protégez-moi, Novembre'

1998f. 'Rapport Mensuel: Projet Protégez-moi, Décembre'

1999a. 'Rapport semestriel pour le projet: La réintégration des mineurs rééduqués au CRP Gitagata, Janvier – Juin'

1999b. 'Activités réalisées par ASOFERWA ASBL dans la réintégration des mineurs ayant participé dans le génocide'

1999c. 'Rapport d'activité pour le projet: Réintégration des mineurs rééduqués au CRP Gitagata'

2000. 'Projet d'accélération de la réintégration social des jeunes du CRP Gitagata' (July)

2001. 'Rapport d'activité du projet: Réintégration des mineurs présumés coupables en ayant moins de 14 ans, Année 2000' (February)

2002a. 'Rapport Trimestriel Janvier – Mars 2002: Projet Protégez-moi' (March)

2002b. 'Rapport Bimestriel Avril et Mai 2002: Projet Protégez-moi' (June)

2002c. 'Rapport Bimestriel Juin et Juillet 2002: Projet Protégez-moi' (July)

2002d. 'Rapport Trimestriel Août à Octobre 2002: Projet Protégez-moi' (December)

2003a. 'Rapport Bimestriel Novembre et Décembre 2002: Projet Protégez-moi' (January)

2003b. 'Rapport Mensuel Janvier 2003: Projet Protégez-moi' (February)

2003c. 'Rapport Mensuel Février 2003: Projet Protégez-moi' (March)

2003d. 'Rapport Mensuel Mars 2003: Projet Protégez-moi' (April)

2003e. 'Rapport Bimestriel Avril – Mai 2003: Projet Protégez-moi' (July)

Bakker, C. 2010. 'Prosecuting International Crimes against Children: the Legal Framework', Innocenti Working Paper No. 2010–13 (Florence: UNICEF Innocenti Research Centre)

Balton, D.A. 1990. 'The Convention on the Rights of the Child: Prospects for International Enforcement' 12 *Human Rights Quarterly* 120

Barrett, J.C. 2019. 'Navigating the Mystical: Child Soldiers and Reintegration Rituals in Northern Uganda', in M.A. Drumbl and J.C. Barrett (eds.), *Research Handbook on Child Soldiers* (Cheltenham: Edward Elgar Publishing), 409

Beigbeder, Y. 2001. *New Challenges for UNICEF: Children, Women and Human Rights* (New York; London: Palgrave Macmillan)

Bell, C. 2000. *Peace Agreements and Human Rights* (Oxford: Oxford University Press)

Bentley, K.A. 2005. 'Can There Be Any Universal Children's Rights?' 9 *International Journal of Human Rights* 107

Biseruka, F. 1999. 'A Socio-Legal Analysis of Juvenile Justice in Post-Genocide Rwanda' (unpublished BA thesis, Faculty of Law, National University of Rwanda, Butare)

Black, M. 1996. *Children First: The Story of UNICEF, Past and Present* (Oxford: Oxford University Press for UNICEF)

Bloom, M. 2019. 'Weaponizing the Weak: The Role of Children in Terrorist Groups', in M.A. Drumbl and J.C. Barrett (eds.), *Research Handbook on Child Soldiers* (Cheltenham: Edward Elgar Publishing), 195

Bornkamm, P.C. 2012. *Rwanda's Gacaca Courts: Between Retribution and Reparation* (Oxford: Oxford University Press)

Börzel, T.A. and Risse, T. 2013. 'Human Rights in Areas of Limited Statehood: The New Agenda', in T. Risse, S.C. Ropp and K. Sikkink (eds.), *The Persistent Power of Human Rights: From Commitment to Compliance* (Cambridge: Cambridge University Press) 63

Boyle, A.E. 1999. 'Some Reflections on the Relationship of Treaties and Soft Law' 48 *International and Comparative Law Quarterly* 901

Branch, A. 2014. 'The Violence of Peace: Ethnojustice in Northern Uganda' 45 *Development and Change* 608

Brazilian Delegation 1978. 'Amendments to Draft Additional Protocol I and Annex: Article 68 – Protection of Children: Brazil' (CDDH/III/325), 30 April 1976, reprinted in Vol. III of 'Official Records of the Diplomatic Conference on the Reaffirmation and Development of International Humanitarian Law applicable in Armed Conflicts, Geneva, 1974–1977' 301

Brems, E. 2001. *Human Rights: Universality and Diversity* (The Hague: Martinus Nijhoff Publishers)

Briggs, J. 2005. *Innocents Lost: When Child Soldiers Go to War* (New York: Basic Books)

Cacioppo, C. 2005. 'Report on Education and Reintegration of Former Prisoners in Rwanda' (Kigali, Rwanda: LDGL)

Cantwell, N. 1997. *Starting from Zero: The Promotion and Protection of Children's Rights in Post-Genocide Rwanda: July 1994–December 1996* (Florence: UNICEF)

2011. 'Are Children's Rights Still Human?', in A. Invernizzi and J. Williams (eds.), *The Human Rights of Children: From Visions to Implementation* (Farnham: Ashgate) 37

Cappelaere, G., Grandjean, A. and Naqvi, Y. 2005. *Children Deprived of Liberty: Rights and Realities* (Liège, Belgium: Éditions Jeunesse et droit)

Casey-Maslen, S. 2019. 'Children Associated with Boko Haram: Disassociation, Protection, Accountability and Reintegration', in M.A. Drumbl and J.C. Barrett (eds.), *Research Handbook on Child Soldiers* (Cheltenham: Edward Elgar Publishing), 452

Cassese, A. 2008. *International Criminal Law* (Oxford: Oxford University Press)

Chakravarty, A. 2006. 'Gacaca Courts in Rwanda: Explaining Divisions within the Human Rights Community' 1 *Yale Journal of International Affairs* 132

Charlesworth, H. 2002. 'Author! Author!: A Response to David Kennedy' 15 *Harvard Human Rights Journal* 127

Chayes, A. and Chayes, A.H. 1993. 'On Compliance' 47 *International Organization* 175

1995. *The New Sovereignty: Compliance with International Regulatory Agreements* (Cambridge, MA; London: Harvard University Press)

Chorlton, R. 1996. 'Retrieving Childhood: A Report of the Children in Especially Difficult Circumstances (CEDC) Programme in Rwanda 1994–1996' (draft) (October)

Cipriani, D. 2009. *Children's Rights and the Minimum Age of Criminal Responsibility* (Farnham: Ashgate)

CLADHO 1995. 'Rapport d'activités du CLADHO 1993–1994' (Kigali, April)

1997. 'Project: « Programme de Suivi de la Situation des Mineurs Accusés de Génocide (PSMAG) » Rapport du mois de novembre' (Kigali, December)

1998. 'Project: « Programme de Suivi de la Situation des Mineurs Accusés de Génocide (PSMAG) » Rapport du mois de décembre' (draft) (Kigali, January)

(undated). 'Renforcement des capacités des juges inyangamugayo: Formation juridique pratique Ville de Kigali, District Gikondo, Secteurs Kigarama et Gatenga, Rapport Final'

Clark, P. 2011. *The Gacaca Courts, Post-Genocide Justice and Reconciliation in Rwanda: Justice without Lawyers* (Cambridge: Cambridge University Press)

2012. 'Creeks of Justice: Debating Post-Atrocity Accountability and Amnesty in Rwanda and Uganda', in F. Lessa and L.A. Payne (eds.), *Amnesty in the Age of Human Rights Accountability – Comparative and International Perspectives* (Cambridge: Cambridge University Press) 210

Clark, P. and Kaufman Z. (eds.) 2008. *After Genocide: Transitional Justice, Post-Conflict Reconstruction and Reconciliation in Rwanda and Beyond* (London: Hurst & Company)

2012. 'Rwanda: Recent History', in I. Frame (ed.), *Africa South of the Sahara 2013* (London: Routledge) 984

Clark, R. and Triffterer, O. 2008. 'Article 26, Exclusion of Jurisdiction over Persons under Eighteen', in O. Triffterer (ed.), *Commentary on the Rome Statute of the International Criminal Court: Observer's Notes, Article by Article* (Munich; Oxford; Baden-Baden: Beck; Hart; Nomos) 771

Coalition to Stop the Use of Child Soldiers 2004. *Child Soldiers Global Report 2004*

2008. *Child Soldiers Global Report 2008*

Cohn, I. 1991. 'The Convention on the Rights of the Child: What it Means for Children in War' 3 *International Journal of Refugee Law* 100

1999. 'The Protection of Children in Peacemaking and Peacekeeping Processes' 12 *Harvard Human Rights Journal* 129

2001. 'The Protection of Children and the Quest for Truth and Justice in Sierra Leone' 55 *Journal of International Affairs* 1

Cohn, I. and Goodwin-Gill, G.S. 1994. *Child Soldiers: The Role of Children in Armed Conflict* (Oxford: Oxford University Press)

Cole, W. 2015. 'Mind the Gap: State Capacity and the Implementation of Human Rights Treaties' 69 *International Organization* 405

Commission of Experts 1994. 'Final Report of the Commission of Experts Established Pursuant to Security Council Resolution 935' (UN Doc. S/1994/1405, annex)

Committee III 1978a. 'Summary record of the Forth-Fifth Meeting of Committee III' (CDDH/III/SR.45), 5 May 1976, reprinted in Vol. XV of the 'Official Records of the

Diplomatic Conference on the Reaffirmation and Development of International Humanitarian Law applicable in Armed Conflicts, Geneva, 1974–1977' 63

1978b. 'Report of the Fourth Session of Committee III' (CDDH/407/Rev.1), 17 March–10 June 1977, reprinted in Vol. XV of the 'Official Records of the Diplomatic Conference on the Reaffirmation and Development of International Humanitarian Law applicable in Armed Conflicts, Geneva, 1974–1977' 445

Committee of the Whole 1998. 'Summary Record of the 2nd Meeting of the Committee of the Whole' (UN Doc. A/CONF.183/C.1/SR.2), 16 June 1998, reprinted in Vol. II of the 'Official Records of the United Nations Diplomatic Conference of Plenipotentiaries on the Establishment of an International Criminal Court, Rome, 15 June–17 July 1998' 138

Coomaraswamy, R. 1998. 'Report of the Special Rapporteur on Violence against Women, its Causes and the Consequences: Report of the mission to Rwandan on the Issue of Violence against Women in Situations of Armed Conflict' (UN Doc. E.CN.4/1998/54.Add.1) (4 February)

2006. 'Promotion and Protection of the Rights of Children: Report of the Special Representative of the Secretary-General for Children and Armed Conflict' (UN Doc. A/61/275) (17 August)

2007. 'Promotion and Protection of the Rights of Children: Report of the Special Representative of the Secretary-General for Children and Armed Conflict' (UN Doc. A/62/228) (13 August)

2008. 'Promotion and Protection of the Rights of Children: Report of the Special Representative of the Secretary-General for Children and Armed Conflict' (UN Doc. A/63/227) (6 August)

2009a. 'Promotion and Protection of all Human Rights, Civil, Political, Economic, Social and Cultural Rights, including the Right to Development: Annual Report of the Special Representative of the Secretary-General for Children and Armed Conflict' (UN Doc. A/HRC/12/49) (30 July)

2009b. 'Promotion and Protection of the Rights of Children: Report of the Special Representative of the Secretary-General for Children and Armed Conflict' (UN Doc. A/64/254) (6 August)

2010a. 'Promotion and Protection of the Rights of Children: Report of the Special Representative of the Secretary-General for Children and Armed Conflict' (UN Doc. A/65/219) (4 August)

2010b. 'Promotion and Protection of all Human Rights, Civil, Political, Economic, Social and Cultural Rights, including the Right to Development: Annual Report of the Special Representative of the Secretary-General for Children and Armed Conflict' (UN Doc. A/HRC/15/58) (3 September)

2011a. 'Promotion and Protection of all Human Rights, Civil, Political, Economic, Social and Cultural Rights, including the Right to Development: Annual Report of the Special Representative of the Secretary-General for Children and Armed Conflict' (UN Doc. A/HRC/18/38) (21 July)

2011b. 'Promotion and Protection of the Rights of Children: Report of the Special Representative of the Secretary-General for Children and Armed Conflict' (UN Doc. A/66/256) (3 August)

2012a. 'Promotion and Protection of all Human Rights, Civil, Political, Economic, Social and Cultural Rights, including the Right to Development: Annual Report of the Special Representative of the Secretary-General for Children and Armed Conflict' (UN Doc. A/HRC/21/38) (28 June)

2012b. 'Promotion and Protection of the Rights of Children: Report of the Special Representative of the Secretary-General for Children and Armed Conflict' (UN Doc. A/67/256) (6 August)

Coopération Belge 1999. 'Compte rendu de la « Réunion informelle sur la Justice » a la GTZ' (Kigali, 18 March)

Corbin, J. and Strauss, A. 2008. *Basics of Qualitative Research: Techniques and Procedures for Developing Grounded Theory* (London: SAGE Publications)

Crawford, J. 2000. 'The UN Human Rights Treaty System: A System in Crisis?', in P. Alston and J. Crawford (eds.), *The Future of UN Human Rights Treaty Monitoring* (Cambridge: Cambridge University Press) 1

CRC Committee [Committee on the Rights of the Child] 1992a, 'Initial Report of Rwanda' (UN Doc. CRC/C/8/Add.1) (12 October)

1992b. 'Urgent Action Procedure', in 'Report on the Second Session, Geneva, 28 September–9 October' (UN Doc. CRC/C/10) (19 October) 18

1992c. 'General Discussion on Children in Armed Conflict', in 'Report on the Second Session, Geneva, 28 September–9 October' (UN Doc. CRC/C/10) (19 October) 20

1993a. 'Consideration of Report of Rwanda, Summary Record of the Second Part (public) of the 98th Meeting held at the Palais des Nations, Geneva on Tuesday, 5 October 1993, at 3 p.m.' (UN Doc. CRC/C/SR.98/Add.1) (11 October)

1993b. 'Preliminary Observations of the Committee on the Rights of the Child: Rwanda' (UN Doc. CRC/C/15/Add.12) (18 October)

1993c. 'Written Replies by the Government of Rwanda to the List of Issues (UN Doc. CRC/C/3/WP.4) Addressed to it by the Committee in Connection with the Initial Report of Rwanda' (25 November)

1994. 'Summary Record of the 97th Meeting held at the Palais des Nations, Geneva on Tuesday, 5 October 1993, at 10 a.m.' (UN Doc. CRC/C/SR.97) (4 November)

1996. 'General Guidelines Regarding the Form and Contents of Periodic Reports to be Submitted by States Parties under Article 44, paragraph 1(b) of the Convention' (UN Doc. CRC/C/58) (20 November)

1999. 'Commemoration of the Tenth Anniversary of the Convention', in 'Report on the Twenty-Second Session, Geneva, 20 September–8 October 1999' (UN Doc. CRC/C/90) (7 December) 59

2002. 'Methods of Work of the Committee' (UN Doc. CRC/C/40/Rev.21) (2 April)

2003a. 'Second Periodic Report of Rwanda' (UN Doc. CRC/C/70/Add.22) (8 October)

2003b. 'General Comment No.5: General Measures of Implementation of the Convention on the Rights of the Child (Arts. 4, 42 and 44, para. 6)' (UN Doc. CRC/GC/2003/5) (27 November)

2004a. 'Written Replies by the Government of Rwanda Concerning the List of Issues (UN Doc. CRC/C/Q/RWA/2) Received by the Committee on the Rights of the Child Relating to the Consideration of the Second Periodic Report of Rwanda' (UN Doc. CRC/C/RESP/57) (22 April)

2004b. 'Summary Record of the 954th Meeting Held at the Palais Wilson, Geneva on Friday, 21 May 2004, at 3 p.m.' (UN Doc. CRC/C/SR.954) (3 June)

2004c. 'Compte rendu analytique de la 953e Séance tenue au Palais Wilson, à Genève, le vendredi 21 mai 2004, à 10 heures' (UN Doc. CRC/C/SR.953) (8 June)

2004d. 'Concluding Observations: Rwanda' (UN Doc. CRC/C/15/Add. 234) (1 July)

2007a. 'General Comment No. 10: Children's Rights in Juvenile Justice' (UN Doc. CRC/C/GC/10) (25 April)

2007b. 'Day of General Discussion on "Resources for the Rights of Children – Responsibility of States" Held on 21 September 2007: Recommendations' (5 October)

2012. 'Consolidated Third and Fourth Periodic Reports of Rwanda' (UN Doc. CRC/C/RWA/3–4) (1 March)

2013a. 'General Comment No. 14 on the Right of the Child to Have His or Her Best Interests Taken as a Primary Consideration (art. 3, para.1)' (UN Doc. CRC/C/GC/14) (29 May)

2013b. 'Concluding Observations on the Third and Fourth Periodic Reports of Rwanda' (UN Doc. CRC/C/RWA/CO/3–4) (8 July)

2015a. 'Treaty-Specific Guidelines Regarding the Form and Content of Periodic Reports to be Submitted by States Parties under Article 44, paragraph 1(b) of the Convention on the Rights of the Child' (UN Doc. CRC/C/58/Rev.3) (3 March)

2015b. 'Rules of Procedure' (UN Doc. CRC/C/4/Rev. 4) (18 March)

2018. 'General Comment No. 24 (201x), replacing General Comment No. 10 (2007) on Children's Rights in Juvenile Justice' (UN Doc. CRC/C/GC/24) (draft) [www.ohchr.org/EN/HRBodies/CRC/Pages/DraftGC10.aspx (accessed 17 December 2018)]

Cryer, R., Friman, H., Robinson, D. and Wilmshurst, E. 2010. *An Introduction to International Criminal Law and Procedure* (Cambridge: Cambridge University Press)

Dallaire, R. 2004. *Shake Hands with the Devil: The Failure of Humanity in Rwanda* (London: Arrow Books)

2011. *They Fight Like Soldiers, They Die Like Children* (London: Arrow Books)

Davidson, H. 2014. 'Does the UN Convention on the Rights of the Child Make a Difference?' 22 *Michigan State International Law Review* 497

DCHR [The Danish Centre for Human Rights] 1999. 'Rapport d'activités de l'équipe des cinq (candidats) défenseurs judiciaires chargés des dossiers des mineurs' (1 December)

de Beer, D. 1997a. 'La justice rwandaise: la défense des personnes suspectées d'avoir trempé dans le génocide et les massacres ou "la défense de la défense?"' (February)

1997b. *Loi Organique du 30 août 1996 sur l'organisation des poursuites des infractions constitutives du crime de génocide ou de crime contre l'humanité: Commentaire* (Alter Egaux Editions)

1999. *Commentaire et jurisprudence de la loi rwandaise du 30 août 1996 sur l'organisation des poursuites des infractions constitutives du crime de génocide ou de crime contre l'humanité* (Alter Egaux Editions)

de Berry, J. 2001. 'Child Soldiers and the Convention on the Rights of the Child' 575 *Annals of the American Academy of Political and Social Science* 92

de Brouwer, A-M. and Ruvebana, E. 2013. 'The Legacy of the *Gacaca* Courts in Rwanda: Survivors' Views' 13 *International Criminal Law Review* 937

Degni-Ségui, R. 1994a. 'Report on the Situation of Human Rights in Rwanda Submitted by the Special Rapporteur of the Commission on Human Rights under Paragraph 20 of Resolution S-3/1 of 25 May 1994' (UN Doc. E/CN.4/1995/7) (28 June)

1994b. 'Report on the Situation of Human Rights in Rwanda Submitted by the Special Rapporteur of the Commission on Human Rights under Paragraph 20 of Resolution S-3/1 of 25 May 1994' (UN Doc. E/CN.4/1995/70) (11 November)

1995a. 'Report on the Situation of Human Rights in Rwanda Submitted by the Special Rapporteur of the Commission on Human Rights under Paragraph 20 of Resolution S-3/1 of 25 May 1994' (UN Doc. E/CN.4/1995/71) (17 January)

1995b. 'Report on the Situation of Human Rights in Rwanda Submitted by the Special Rapporteur of the Commission on Human Rights under Paragraph 20 of Resolution S-3/1 of 25 May 1994' (UN Doc. E/CN.4/1996/7) (28 June)

1996. 'Report on the Situation of Human Rights in Rwanda Submitted by the Special Rapporteur of the Commission on Human Rights under Paragraph 20 of Resolution S-3/1 of 25 May 1994' (UN Doc. E/CN.4/1996/68) (29 January)

1997. 'Report on the Situation of Human Rights in Rwanda Submitted by the Special Rapporteur of the Commission on Human Rights under Paragraph 20 of Resolution S-3/1 of 25 May 1994' (UN Doc. E/CN.4/1997/61) (20 January)

Demay, S., Reyntjens, F., Rombouts, H. and Vandeginste, S. 2005. 'Evaluation du programme 2001–2003 d'Avocats sans Frontières en Afrique Centrale' (Institut de Politique et de Gestion du Développement, Université d'Anvers) (February)

Département des Juridictions Gacaca (Cour Suprême) 2001. 'Manuel Explicatif sur la Loi Organique portant création des juridictions gacaca' (Kigali)

Derluyn, I., Mels, C., Parmentier S. and Vandenhole W. (eds.) 2012. *Re-Member: Rehabilitation, Reintegration and Reconciliation of War-Affected Children* (Cambridge: Intersentia)

De Schutter, O. 2014. *International Human Rights Law: Cases, Materials, Commentary* (Cambridge: Cambridge University Press)

Des Forges, A. 1999. *'Leave None to Tell the Story': Genocide in Rwanda* (New York: Human Rights Watch; FIDH)

Des Forges, A. and Longman, T. 2004. 'Legal Responses to Genocide in Rwanda', in E. Stover and H.M. Weinstein (eds.), *My Neighbour, My Enemy: Justice and Community in the Aftermath of Mass Atrocity* (Cambridge: Cambridge University Press) 49

Destexhe, A. 1995. *Rwanda and Genocide in the Twentieth Century* (London; East Haven, CT: Pluto Press)

Detrick, S. 1999. *A Commentary on the United Nations Convention on the Rights of the Child* (The Hague: Martinus Nijhoff Publishers)

Digneffe, F. and Fierens, J. (eds.) 2003. *Justice et Gacaca: L'expérience rwandaise et le génocide* (Namur, Belgique: Presses universitaires de Namur)

Doek, J.E. 2012. 'Foreword – A Children's Rights Approach to Recovery and Reintegration: An Agenda for Action', in I. Derluyn, C. Mels, S. Parmentier and W. Vandenhole (eds.), *Re-Member: Rehabilitation, Reintegration and Reconciliation of War-Affected Children* (Cambridge: Intersentia) ix

Doná, G. 2011. 'Researching Children and Violence in Evolving Socio-Political Contexts', in C. Cramer, L. Hammond and J. Pottier (eds.), *Researching Violence in Africa: Ethical and Methodological Challenges* (Leiden: Brill) 39

Donnelly, J. 2006. 'The Virtues of Legalization', in S. Meckled-García and B. Çali (eds.), *The Legalization of Human Rights: Multidisciplinary Perspectives on Human Rights and Human Rights Law* (Abingdon, Oxon; New York: Routledge) 67

2013. *Universal Human Rights in Theory and Practice* (Ithaca; London: Cornell University Press)

Doulliez, V. 1998a. 'Les mineurs d'âge accusés de génocide et de crimes contre l'humanité au Rwanda', *Droit de l'enfant international (supplément au JDJ n°176)* (June)

1998b. 'Rapport de Mission, 27 juin 1998–1 août 1998'

1999. 'Rapport de Mission, 6 mars 1999–10 avril 1999'

Drogin, B. 1997. 'Children Accused of Genocide', *Sun Sentinel* (25 February)

Drumbl, M. 1998. 'Rule of Law amid Lawlessness: Counseling the Accused in Rwanda's Domestic Genocide Trials' 29 *Columbia Human Rights Law Review* 545

2000. 'Punishment, Postgenocide: From Guilt to Shame to *Civis* in Rwanda' 75 *New York University Law Review* 1221

2007. *Atrocity, Punishment, and International Law* (Cambridge: Cambridge University Press)

2012. *Reimagining Child Soldiers in International Law and Policy* (Oxford: Oxford University Press)

Drumbl, M. and Rona, G. 2018. 'Navigating Challenges in Child Protection and the Reintegration of Children Associated with Armed Groups', in S. O'Neil and K. Van Broeckhoven (eds.), *Cradled by Conflict: Child Involvement with Armed Groups in Contemporary Conflict* (United Nations University)

Dyregrov, A., Gupta, L., Gjestad, R. and Mukanoheli, E. 2000. 'Trauma Exposure and Psychological Reactions to Genocide Among Rwandan Children' 13 *Journal of Traumatic Stress* 3

Eltringham, N. 2004. *Accounting for Horror: Post-Genocide Debates in Rwanda* (London: Pluto Press)

Eser, A. 2008. 'Article 31 – Grounds for Excluding Criminal Responsibility', in O. Triffterer (ed.), *Commentary on the Rome Statute of the International Criminal Court: Observer's Notes, Article by Article* (Munich; Oxford; Baden-Baden: Beck; Hart; Nomos) 863

Feld, B. 2006. 'The Inherent Tension of Social Welfare and Criminal Social Control: Policy Lessons from the American Juvenile Court Experience', in E.L. Jensen and J. Jepsen (eds.), *Juvenile Law Violators, Human Rights, and the Development of New Juvenile Justice Systems* (Oxford; Portland, OR: Hart Publishing) 407

Finnemore, M. and Sikkink, K. 1998. 'International Norm Dynamics and Political Change' 52 *International Organization* 887

Fisher, K.J. 2013. *Transitional Justice for Child Soldiers: Accountability and Social Reconstruction in Post-Conflict Contexts* (Basingstoke; New York: Palgrave Macmillan)

Fitzpatrick, J. 1994. *Human Rights in Crisis: The International System for Protecting Rights During States of Emergency* (Philadelphia: University of Pennsylvania Press)

Flindt Pedersen, C. 2006. 'Support for the Implementation of Humane Responses to Children in Conflict with the Law in DIHR Partner Countries', in E.L. Jensen and J. Jepsen (eds.), *Juvenile Law Violators, Human Rights, and the Development of New Juvenile Justice Systems* (Oxford; Portland, OR.: Hart Publishing) 39

Forsythe, D.P. 2012. *Human Rights in International Relations* (Cambridge: Cambridge University Press)

Fottrell, D. 2000. 'One Step Forward or Two Steps Sideways? Assessing the First Decade of the United Nations Convention on the Rights of the Child', in D. Fottrell (ed.), *Revisiting Children's Rights:10 years of the UN Convention on the Rights of the Child* (The Hague; London: Kluwer Law International) 1

Franck, T. 1988. 'Legitimacy in the International System' 82 *American Journal of International Law* 705

Freeland, S. 2008. 'Mere Children or Weapons of War – Child Soldiers and International Law' 29 *University of La Verne Law Review* 19

Frulli, M. 2002. 'Jurisdiction Ratione Personae', in A. Cassese, P. Gaeta and J.R.W.D. Jones (eds.), *The Rome Statute of the International Criminal Court: A Commentary* (Oxford: Oxford University Press) 527

Gahima, G. 2013. *Transitional Justice in Rwanda: Accountability for Atrocity* (Abingdon, Oxon: Routledge)

Gallagher, A. 2000. 'Making Human Rights Treaty Obligations a Reality: Working With New Actors and Partners', in P. Alston and J. Crawford (eds.), *The Future of UN Human Rights Treaty Monitoring* (Cambridge: Cambridge University Press) 201

Galligan, D. and Sandler, D. 2004. 'Implementing Human Rights', in S. Halliday and P. Schmidt (eds.), *Human Rights Brought Home: Socio-Legal Perspectives on Human Rights in the National Context* (Oxford: Hart Publishing) 23

Gamba, V. 2017. 'Promotion and Protection of the Rights of Children: Report of the Special Representative of the Secretary-General for Children and Armed Conflict' (UN Doc. A/72/276) (2 August)

2018. 'Promotion and Protection of all Human Rights, Civil, Political, Economic, Social and Cultural Rights, Including the Right to Development: Annual Report of the Special Representative of the Secretary-General for Children and Armed Conflict' (UN Doc. A/HRC/37/47) (8 January)

George, A.L. and Bennett, A. 2005. *Case Studies and Theory Development in the Social Sciences* (Cambridge, MA; London: MIT Press)

Giacca, G. 2014. *Economic, Social, and Cultural Rights in Armed Conflict* (Oxford: Oxford University Press)

Gibson, B. and Hartman, J. 2014. *Rediscovering Grounded Theory* (London: SAGE Publications)

Goldsmith, J.L. and Posner, E.A. 2005. *The Limits of International Law* (Oxford: Oxford University Press)

Goodale, M. 2007. 'The Power of Right(s): Tracking Empires of Law and New Modes of Social Resistance in Bolivia (and Elsewhere)', in M. Goodale and S.E. Merry (eds.), *The Practice of Human Rights: Tracking Law between the Global and the Local* (Cambridge: Cambridge University Press) 130

Goodale, M. and Merry, S.E. (eds.) 2007. *The Practice of Human Rights: Tracking Law between the Global and the Local* (Cambridge: Cambridge University Press)

Goodman, R. and Jinks, D. 2004. 'How to Influence States: Socialisation and International Human Rights Law' 54 *Duke Law Journal* 621

2013. *Socializing States: Promoting Human Rights through International Law* (Oxford University Press)

Goonesekere, S. 2007. 'Introduction and Overview', in UNICEF (ed.), *Protecting the World's Children: Impact of the Convention on the Rights of the Child in Diverse Legal Systems* (Cambridge: Cambridge University Press) 1

Gourevitch, P. 2000. *We Wish to Inform You That Tomorrow We Will Be Killed with Our Families* (London: Picador) (Originally published: New York: Farrar, Straus & Giroux, 1998)

Government of Rwanda and UNICEF Rwanda 2001. 'Master Plan of Operations 2001–2006: A Programme of Cooperation between the Government of Rwanda and UNICEF'

Gready, P. 2011. 'Beyond "You're with Us or Against Us": Civil Society and Policymaking in Post-Genocide Rwanda', in S. Straus and L. Waldorf (eds.), *Remaking Rwanda: State Building and Human Rights after Mass Violence* (Madison, WI: The University of Wisconsin Press) 87

Gross, O. and Ní Aoláin, F. 2006. *Law in Times of Crisis: Emergency Powers in Theory and Practice* (Cambridge: Cambridge University Press)

Grossman, N. 2007. 'Rehabilitation or Revenge: Prosecuting Child Soldiers for Human Rights Violations' 38 *Georgetown Journal of International Law* 323

Grover, S. 2007. 'A Response to K.A. Bentley's "Can There Be Any Universal Children's Rights?"' 11 *The International Journal of Human Rights* 429

2012. *Child Soldier Victims of Genocidal Forcible Transfer: Exonerating Child Soldiers Charged with Grave Conflict-Related International Crimes* (Heidelberg: Springer)

Guzman, A. 2002. 'A Compliance-Based Theory of International Law' 90 *California Law Review* 1823

Habimana, A. 1997. 'Séminaire sur les procès des mineurs: Rapport réalisé par Aloys Habimana de l'Equipe d'observation du CLADHO'

Hackel, J. 1995. 'When Kids Commit Genocide', *Christian Science Monitor* (5 December)

Hafner-Burton, E.M. 2008. 'Naming and Shaming the Human Rights Enforcement Problem' 62 *International Organization* 689

2013. *Making Human Rights a Reality* (Princeton, NJ: Princeton University Press)

Hafner-Burton, E.M., LeVeck, B.L. and Victor, D.G. 2016. 'How Activists Perceive the Utility of International Law' 78 *Journal of Politics* 167

Halliday, S. and Schmidt, P. (eds.) 2004. *Human Rights Brought Home: Socio-Legal Perspectives on Human Rights in the National Context* (Oxford; Portland, OR: Hart Publishing)

Hamilton, C. and Harvey, R. 2004. 'The Role of Public Opinion in the Implementation of International Juvenile Justice Standards' 11 *The International Journal of Children's Rights* 369

Hammarberg, T. 1994. 'Innovative Procedures' 2 *The International Journal of Children's Rights* 83

Hannum, H. 2006. 'Human Rights in Conflict Resolution: The Role of the Office of the High Commissioner for Human Rights in UN Peacemaking and Peacebuilding' 28 *Human Rights Quarterly* 1

Happold, M. 2005. *Child Soldiers in International Law* (Manchester: Manchester University Press)

2006. 'The Age of Criminal Responsibility for International Crimes under International Law', in K. Arts and V. Popovski (eds.), *International Criminal*

Accountability and the Rights of Children (The Hague: Hague Academic Press) 69

Hathaway, O. 2002. 'Do Human Rights Treaties Make a Difference?' 111 *Yale Law Journal* 1935

Hatzfeld, J. 2008. *A Time for Machetes: The Rwandan Genocide – The Killers Speak* (London: Serpent's Tail)

Henkin, A. (ed.) 2000. *Honoring Human Rights* (The Hague; London: Kluwer Law International)

Himes, J.R. 1993. 'The United Nations Convention on the Rights of the Child: Three Essays on the Challenges of Implementation', *Innocenti Essays No. 5* (Florence: UNICEF)

1995. 'Introduction', in J.R. Himes (ed.), *Implementing the Convention on the Rights of the Child: Resource Mobilization in Low-Income Countries* (The Hague: Martinus Nijhoff Publishers) 1

Hodgkin, R. and Newell, P. 2007. *Implementation Handbook for the Convention on the Rights of the Child* (Geneva: UNICEF)

Honwana, A. 2006. *Child Soldiers in Africa* (Philadelphia: University of Pennsylvania Press)

Howen, N. 2007. 'The Fundamental Protection Function of the Human Rights Field Operation', in M. O'Flaherty (ed.), *The Human Rights Field Operation: Law, Theory and Practice* (Aldershot: Ashgate) 31

Howland, T. 2007. 'Case Study: The United Nations Human Rights Field Operation in Angola', in M. O'Flaherty (ed.), *The Human Rights Field Operation: Law, Theory and Practice* (Aldershot: Ashgate) 317

HRC [Human Rights Committee] 1992. 'General Comment No. 21: Article 10 (Humane Treatment of Persons Deprived of their Liberty)', replacing General Comment No. 9 (10 April)

1994. 'General Comment No. 24: Issues Relating to Reservations' (UN Doc. CCPR/C/ 21/Rev.1/Add.6) (2 November)

1995. 'Report of the Human Rights Committee' (UN Doc. A/50/40) (3 October)

2001. 'General Comment No. 29: States of Emergency (Article 4)' (UN Doc. CCPR/C/21/ Rev.1/Add.11) (24 July)

2007. 'Third Periodic Report: Rwanda' (UN Doc. CCPR/C/RWA/3) (27 November)

2008. 'Replies of the Government of Rwanda to the List of Issues to be Taken Up in Connection with the Consideration of the Third Periodic Report of Rwanda' (UN Doc. CCPR/C/RWA/Q/3/Rev.1/Add.1) (9 March)

2009a. 'Concluding Observations of the Human Rights Committee: Rwanda' (UN Doc. CCPR/C/RWA/CO/3) (7 May)

2009b. 'Report of the Human Rights Committee Volume I', General Assembly Official Reports, Sixty-fourth Session, Supplement No. 40 (UN Doc. A/64/40)

2010. 'Written Answers to the Concluding Observations Issued by the Human Rights Committee after the Presentation of the Rwandan Third Periodic Report on the Implementation of the ICCPR' (December)

HRW [Human Rights Watch] 1994. 'The Aftermath of the Genocide in Rwanda: Absence of Prosecution, Continued Killings' (September) [http://speakingout.msf.org/en/node/608 (accessed 17 December 2018)]

1996. 'Children in Combat', Human Rights Watch Children's Rights Project (Vol. 8, No. 1(G), January) [www.hrw.org/sites/default/files/reports/general961.pdf (accessed 17 December 2018)]

1999. 'Sierra Leone: Getting Away with Murder, Mutilation, Rape – New Testimony from Sierra Leone' (Vol. 11, No. 3(A), July)

2003a. 'Rwanda – Lasting Wounds: Consequences of Genocide and War for Rwanda's Children' (Vol. 15, No. 6(A), March)

2003b. 'Uganda: Drop Treason Charges against Child Abductees' (press release) (4 March)

2003c. ' "You'll Learn Not to Cry": Child Combatants in Colombia' (September)

2008. 'Law and Reality: Progress in Judicial Reform in Rwanda' (July)

2009. 'Uganda: Drop Treason Charges against Abducted Child' (press release) (6 January)

2011. 'Justice Compromised: The Legacy of Rwanda's Community-Based Gacaca Courts' (May)

ILC 1994. 'Report of the International Law Commission on the Work of its Forty-Sixth Session, 2 May–22 July 1994', UN GAOR 49th Sess, Spp. No. 10 (UN Doc. A/49/10)

Ingelaere, B. 2008. 'The Gacaca Courts in Rwanda', in L. Huyse and M. Salter (eds.), *Traditional Justice and Reconciliation after Violent Conflict: Learning from African Experiences* (Stockholm: International Institute for Democracy and Electoral Assistance (IDEA)) 25

2016. *Inside Rwanda's Gacaca Courts: Seeking Justice after Genocide* (Madison, WI; London: The University of Wisconsin Press)

IRIN [Integrated Regional Information Networks] 2002. 'Sierra Leone: Special Court Will Not Indict Children – Prosecutor' (4 November)

2007. 'In-Depth: Youth in Crisis: Coming of Age in the 21st Century, RWANDA: Twelve Years On: The Post-Genocide Youth' (23 February)

Jenks, C. 2005. *Childhood: Second Edition* (London; New York: Routledge)

Jensen, E.L. and Jepsen, J. 2006. 'Conclusions: Themes, Trends, and Challenges', in E.L. Jensen and J. Jepsen (eds.), *Juvenile Law Violators, Human Rights, and the Development of New Juvenile Justice Systems* (Oxford; Portland, OR: Hart Publishing) 443

Jetschke, A. and Liese, A. 2013. 'The Power of Human Rights a Decade After: From Euphoria to Contestation?', in T. Risse, S.C. Ropp and K. Sikkink (eds.), *The Persistent Power of Human Rights: From Commitment to Compliance* (Cambridge: Cambridge University Press) 26

Jolly, R. 2014. *UNICEF (United Nations Children's Fund): Global Governance That Works* (Abington, Oxon: Routledge)

Karekezi, U.A., Nshimiyimana, A. and Mutamba, B. 2004. 'Localizing Justice: Gacaca Courts in Post-Genocide Rwanda', in E. Stover and H.M Weinstein (eds.), *My Neighbour, My Enemy: Justice and Community in the Aftermath of Mass Atrocity* (Cambridge: Cambridge University Press) 69

Keck, M.E. and Sikkink, K. 1998. *Activists beyond Borders: Advocacy Networks in International Politics* (Ithaca, NY: Cornell University Press)

Kelsall, T. 2009. *Culture under Cross-Examination: International Justice and the Special Court for Sierra Leone* (Cambridge: Cambridge University Press)

Kennedy D. 2002. 'The International Human Rights Movement: Part of the Problem?' 15 *Harvard Human Rights Journal* 101

2004. *The Dark Sides of Virtue* (Princeton, NJ; Oxford: Princeton University Press)

Keohane, R.O. 1997. 'International Relations and International Law: Two Optics' 38 *Harvard International Law Journal* 487

Kilkelly, U. 2011. 'Using the Convention on the Rights of the Child in Law and Policy: Two Ways to Improve Compliance', in A. Invernizzi and J. Williams (eds.), *The Human Rights of Children: From Visions to Implementation* (Farnham: Ashgate) 179

Kimonyo, J-P, Twagiramungu, N. and Kayumba, C. 2004. 'Supporting the Post-Genocide Transition in Rwanda: The Role of the International Community', Conflict Research Unit Working Paper 32 (The Hague: Netherlands Institute of International Relations 'Clingendael') (December)

Koh, H.H. 1997. 'Why Do Nations Obey International Law?' 106 *Yale Law Journal* 2599

1998. 'The 1998 Frankel Lecture: Bringing International Law Home' 35 *Houston Law Review* 623

Konge, P. 2010. 'International Crimes and Child Soldiers' 16 *Southwestern Journal of International Law* 41

Kuperman, A.J. 2001. *The Limits of Humanitarian Intervention: Genocide in Rwanda* (Washington DC: Brookings Institution Press)

Landgren, K. 2007. 'Protection: The United Nations Children's Fund Experience', in M. O'Flaherty (ed.), *The Human Rights Field Operation: Law, Theory and Practice* (Aldershot: Ashgate) 183

Lansdown, G. 2000. 'The Reporting Process under the Convention on the Rights of the Child', in P. Alston and J. Crawford (eds.), *The Future of UN Human Rights Treaty Monitoring* (Cambridge: Cambridge University Press) 113

LDGL 2006. 'Etat des lieux de la libération de certains détenus, suite au communiqué de la Présidence de la République du Rwanda du 1er janvier 2003' (Kigali, October)

LeBlanc, L.J. 1995. *The Convention on the Rights of the Child: United Nations Lawmaking on Human Rights* (Lincoln, NE; London: University of Nebraska Press)

Linden, I. 1999. 'The Role of Non-African NGOs in African Conflicts: The Case of Rwanda', in A. Adedeji (ed.), *Comprehending and Mastering African*

Conflicts: The Search for Sustainable Peace and Good Governance (London: Zed Books) 282

LIPRODHOR 1998a. 'Le Génocide devant les tribunaux: Rapport de la LIPRODHOR-CPIDG sur la situation des procès de génocide au Rwanda du 27 décembre 1996 au 27 décembre 1997' (Kigali, January)

1998b. 'Le Génocide devant les tribunaux: Situation des procès de génocide au Rwanda: Période janvier – août 1998' (Kigali, October)

1999a. 'Procès de génocide au Rwanda: Deux ans après (Dec. 96–Dec. 98)'

1999b. 'Situation des accusés de génocide rwandais mis en liberté. Période: 15 décembre 1998–15 mars 1999' (Kigali, 15 March)

1999c. 'Rapport d'activités de fin de 1ère phase du projet de suivi des accusés de génocide mis en liberté (PSAG): Problématique des libérations des accusés de génocide rwandais' (Kigali, July)

1999d. 'Regard rétrospectif sur les procès de génocide au Rwanda (Période: dec. 96–juin 99)'

2001a. 'Quatre ans de procès de génocide: quelle base pour les « juridictions gacaca »?' (Centre CDIPG) (July)

2001b. *Le Verdict*, No. 29 (August)

2003a. 'Situation des droits de la personne au Rwanda en 2002' (June)

2003b. 'Juridictions Gacaca: Potentialités et Lacunes Révélées par les Débuts' (Kigali, July)

2005. 'Situation des droits de la personne au Rwanda: Rapport 2003–2004' (December)

2007. 'Situation des droits de la personne au Rwanda: Rapport 2006' (September)

Lubell, N. 2012. 'Human Rights Obligations in Military Occupation' 94 *International Review of the Red Cross* 317

Machel, G. 1996. 'Impact of Armed Conflict on Children: Report of the Expert of the Secretary-General Submitted Pursuant to General Assembly Resolution 48/157' (UN Doc. A/51/306) (26 August)

Mamdani, M. 2001. *When Victims Become Killers: Colonialism, Nativism, and the Genocide in Rwanda* (Princeton, NJ: Princeton University Press)

Marks, S. and Clapham, A. 2005. *International Human Rights Lexicon* (Oxford: Oxford University Press)

Martin, I. 1998. *After Genocide: The United Nations Human Rights Field Operation in Rwanda* (Colchester: Human Rights Centre, University of Essex)

Matloff, J. 1997. 'Rwanda's Bind: Trying Children for Genocide', *The Christian Science Monitor* (28 January)

Matthes, J. 1996a. 'Proposal for the Creation of Specialized Juvenile Chambers for Genocide Cases'

1996b. 'Consultancy Report: 20 April–25 May 1996' (May)

1997a. 'Consultancy on Rules and Regulations for Children, Juveniles and Adolescents in Rwanda – First Report: General Assessment of Present

Conditions of and Legal Framework for Detention; Propositions for Basing Regulations in Rwandan Statutory Law; Propositions for the Process of Drafting, Implementation and Follow-Up' (17 December)

1997b. 'Consultancy on Rules and Regulations for Children, Juveniles and Young Adults in Detention in Rwanda – Second Report: Draft Standard Rules for Juveniles, Adolescents and Young Adults in Detention – Against the Background of the UN Rules for the Protection of Juveniles Deprived of their Liberty (JDLs)' (17 December)

Melvern, L. 2000. *A People Betrayed: The Role of the West in Rwanda's Genocide* (London; New York: Zed Books)

2008. 'The Past is Prologue: Planning the 1994 Rwandan Genocide', in P. Clark and Z. Kaufman (eds.), *After Genocide: Transitional Justice, Post-Conflict Reconstruction and Reconciliation in Rwanda and Beyond* (London: Hurst & Company) 21

Merry, S.E. 2006. *Human Rights and Gender Violence: Translating International Law into Local Justice* (Chicago: University of Chicago Press)

Mezmur, B. 2008. 'Children at Both Ends of the Gun: Child Soldiers in Africa', in J. Sloth-Nielsen (ed.), *Children's Rights in Africa: A Legal Perspective* (Aldershot: Ashgate) 199

Mgbako, C. 2005. '*Ingando* Solidarity Camps: Reconciliation and Political Indoctrination in Post-Genocide Rwanda' 18 *Harvard Human Rights Journal* 201

MIGEFASO [Ministry of Gender, Family and Social Affairs] 1997. 'Procedures for Assessment, Care and Release of Children in Gitagata Re-education Centre' (29 September)

MINALOC [Ministry of Local Government and Social Affairs] 2001a. 'Dénombrement des victimes du génocide' (Kigali, March)

2001b. 'Projet d'encadrement psycho-social des enfants ex-combattants infiltrés transférés au Centre de Gitagata' (August)

2003. 'National Policy for Orphans and Other Vulnerable Children'

MINIJUST [Ministry of Justice/Ministère de la Justice et des Relations Institutionnelles] 2001. 'Le Kit Gacaca' (Kigali, May)

2004. 'Justice Sector Strategy 2005–2007' (Kigali, December)

MINIJUST and UNICEF Rwanda 1997a. 'POA: Legal Assistance to Children in Conflict with the Law'

1997b. 'Juvenile Justice in Rwanda: A Case Study Presented to 1997 Innocenti Global Seminar on Children Involved with the System of Juvenile Justice'

Montoya, C. 2013. *From Global to Grassroots: The European Union, Transnational Advocacy, and Combating Violence Against Women* (Oxford: Oxford University Press)

Morrill, C. 2004. 'Reconciliation and the *Gacaca*: The Perceptions and Peace-Building Potential of Rwandan Youth Detainees' 6 *The Online Journal of Peace and Conflict Management* 1

2005. 'Perpetrators Only: The "Role" of Accused Youth in Rwanda's "Modern" Gacaca', in UNICEF, 'Expert Discussion on Transitional Justice and Children, 10–12 November 2005: Background Documents' (Florence: UNICEF Innocenti Research Centre) 103

Moussalli, M. 1997. 'Report of the Special Representative of the Commission on Human Rights on the Situation of Human Rights in Rwanda' (UN Doc. A/52/522) (22 October)

1998a. 'Report on the Situation of Human Rights in Rwanda Submitted by the Special Representative Pursuant to Resolution 1997/66' (UN Doc. E.CN.4/1998/60) (19 February)

1998b. 'Report on the Situation of Human Rights in Rwanda Prepared by the Special Representative Pursuant to Economic and Social Council Decision 1998/266 of 30 July 1998' (UN Doc. A/53/402) (18 September)

1999a. 'Report on the Situation of Human Rights in Rwanda Submitted by the Special Representative Pursuant to Resolution 1998/69' (UN Doc. E/CN.4/1999/33) (8 February)

1999b. 'Report of the Situation of Human Rights in Rwanda Prepared by the Special Representative of the Commission on Human Rights Pursuant to Economic and Social Council Decision 1999/288 of 30 July 1999' (UN Doc. A/54/359) (17 September)

2000a. 'Report on the Situation of Human Rights in Rwanda Submitted by the Special Representative Pursuant to Commission Resolution 1999/20' (UN Doc. E/CN.4/2000/41) (25 February)

2000b. 'Report of the Special Representative of the Commission on Human Rights on the Situation of Human Rights in Rwanda' (UN Doc. A/55/269) (4 August)

2001. 'Question of the Violation of Human Rights and Fundamental Freedoms in Any Part of the World: Situation of Human Rights in Rwanda' (UN Doc. E/CN.4/2001/45/Add.1) (21 March)

Mugenzi, L-M. 1995. 'Éléments de Droit Pénal / Iby'ingenzi mu mategeko ahana' (MINIJUST)

Murara, O. 2000. 'Genocide Committed by Minors', in United Nations, *Bringing International Human Rights Law Home: Judicial Colloquium on the Domestic Application of the Convention on the Elimination of All Forms of Discrimination against Women and the Convention on the Rights of the Child* (New York: United Nations) 154

Murray, C. 2010. 'Children's Rights in Rwanda: A Hierarchical or Parallel Model of Implementation?' 18 *International Journal of Children's Rights* 387

Murray, R. and Long, D. 2015. *The Implementation of the Findings of the African Commission on Human and People's Rights* (Cambridge: Cambridge University Press)

Mutagwera, F. 1996. 'Détentions et poursuites judiciaires au Rwanda', in J-F. Dupaquier (ed.), *La justice internationale face au drame rwandais* (Paris: Karthala) 17

NHRC [National Human Rights Commission/Commission Nationale des Droits de la Personne] 2001. 'Annual Report 2000' (Kigali, March)

2005a. 'Rapport d'Observation des Juridictions Gacaca, Janvier–Mars 2005' (Kigali, September)

2005b. 'Rapport d'Observation des Juridictions Gacaca, Avril–Juin 2005' (Kigali, October)

Nolan, J. and van Heerden, A. 2013. 'Engaging Business in the Business of Human Rights', in M.B. Pedersen and D. Kinley (eds.), *Principled Engagement: Negotiating Human Rights in Repressive States* (Farnham: Ashgate) 153

No Peace Without Justice and UNICEF Innocenti Research Centre 2002. 'International Criminal Justice and Children' (September)

NSGC [National Service of Gacaca Courts] 2004. 'Process of Collecting Information Required in Gacaca Courts' (November)

2005. 'Trial Procedure in Gacaca Courts' (January)

2012. 'Gacaca Courts in Rwanda' (June)

NURC [National Unity and Reconciliation Commission] 2000. 'Rapport annuel des activités de la Commission Nationale pour l'Unité et la Réconciliation, période allant de mars 1999 à juin 2000' (Kigali)

2002. 'Annual Report 2001' (Kigali, May)

Nyi Nyi 2001. 'Building Foundations for the Castles in the Air', in R. Jolly (ed.), *Jim Grant UNICEF Visionary* (Florence: UNICEF Innocenti Research Centre)

Odongo, G.O. 2005. 'The Domestication of International Law Standards on the Rights of the Child with Specific Reference to Juvenile Justice in the African Context' (unpublished PhD thesis, University of the Western Cape, South Africa)

O'Donnell, D. 1992. 'The Convention on the Rights of the Child: A Challenge for UNICEF', 'The Rights of the Child' 91 *Bulletin of Human Rights* 25

Oestreich, J.E. 1998. 'UNICEF and the Implementation of the Convention on the Rights of the Child' 4 *Global Governance* 183

2007. *Power and Principle: Human Rights Programming in International Organizations* (Bristol: Georgetown University Press)

Office of the President, Republic of Rwanda 1995. 'Recommendations of the Conference Held in Kigali from November 1st to 5th 1995 on: "Genocide, Impunity and Accountability: Dialogue for a National and International Response"' (Kigali, December)

1999. 'Report on the Reflection Meetings Held in the Office of the President of the Republic from May 1998 to March 1999' (Kigali, August)

Office of the Resident Co-ordinator 1996. 'United Nations Situation Report for Rwanda Covering the Month of December 1995' (Kigali, 15 January)

O'Flaherty, M. 2002. *Human Rights and the UN: Practice Before the Treaty Bodies* (The Hague: Martinus Nijhoff Publishers)

2003. 'Future Protection of Human Rights in Post-Conflict Societies: The Role of the United Nations' 3 *Human Rights Law Review* 53

(ed.) 2007. *The Human Rights Field Operation: Law, Theory and Practice* (Aldershot: Ashgate)

OHCHR [Office of the United Nations High Commissioner for Human Rights] 1995. 'Report of the United Nations High Commissioner for Human Rights on the Human Rights Field Operation in Rwanda' (UN Doc. A/50/743) (13 November)

1996a. 'Gacaca: Le droit coutumier au Rwanda: Rapport final de la première phase d'enquête sur le terrain' (31 January)

1996b. 'Report of the United Nations High Commissioner for Human Rights on the Human Rights Field Operation in Rwanda' (UN Doc. E.CN.4/1996/111) (2 April)

1996c. 'Gacaca: Le droit coutumier au Rwanda: Rapport final de la deuxième phase d'enquête sur le terrain' (30 June)

1996d. 'Report of the United Nations High Commissioner for Human Rights on the Human Rights Field Operation in Rwanda' (UN Doc. A/51/478) (10 October)

1997a. 'Report of the High Commissioner for Human Rights on the Activities of the Human Rights Field Operation in Rwanda' (UN Doc. E/CN.4/1997/52) (17 March)

1997b. 'Report of the United Nations High Commissioner for Human Rights on the Human Rights Field Operation in Rwanda' (UN Doc. A/52/486) (16 October)

1997c. 'Addendum to the report of the United Nations High Commissioner for Human Rights on the Human Rights Field Operation in Rwanda' (UN Doc. A/52/486.Add.1/Rev.1) (12 November)

1998a. 'Report of the United Nations High Commissioner for Human Rights on the Human Rights Field Operation in Rwanda' (UN Doc. E/CN.4/1998/61) (19 February)

1998b. 'Report of the United Nations High Commissioner for Human Rights on the Human Rights Field Operation in Rwanda' (UN Doc. A/53/367) (11 September)

2007a. 'Legislative History of the Convention on the Rights of the Child: Volume 1' (New York and Geneva)

2007b. 'Legislative History of the Convention on the Rights of the Child: Volume 2' (New York and Geneva)

O'Neill, W.G. 2007. 'The Human Rights Field Operation in Partnership for Security', in M. O'Flaherty (ed.), *The Human Rights Field Operation: Law, Theory and Practice* (Aldershot: Ashgate) 125

Oomen, B. 2005. 'Donor-Driven Justice and its Discontents: The Case of Rwanda' 36 *Development and Change* 887

Oosterveld, V. 2019. 'The Construction of Gender in Child Soldiering in the Special Court for Sierra Leone', in M.A. Drumbl and J.C. Barrett (eds.), *Research Handbook on Child Soldiers* (Cheltenham: Edward Elgar Publishing), 74

Orentlicher, D.F. 1991. 'Settling Accounts: The Duty to Prosecute Human Rights Violations of a Prior Regime' 100 *The Yale Law Journal* 2537

Orr, D. 1995. 'Children of the Machete', *The Independent* (23 August)

Otunnu, O.A. 1998a. 'Interim Report of the Special Representative of the Secretary-General' (UN Doc. E/CN.4/1998/119) (12 March)

1998b. 'Protection of Children Affected by Armed Conflict: Report of the Special Representative of the Secretary-General for Children and Armed Conflict' (UN Doc. A/54/482) (12 October)

1999. 'Protection of Children Affected by Armed Conflict: Report of the Special Representative of the Secretary-General for Children and Armed Conflict' (UN Doc. A/54/430) (1 October)

2000a. 'Rights of the Child: Additional Report of the Special Representative of the Secretary-General for Children and Armed Conflict' (UN Doc. E/CN.4/2000/71) (9 February)

2000b. 'Protection of Children Affected by Armed Conflict: Report of the Special Representative of the Secretary-General for Children and Armed Conflict' (UN Doc. A/55/442) (3 October)

2001. 'Protection of children Affected by Armed Conflict: Report of the Special Representative of the Secretary-General for Children and Armed Conflict' (UN Doc. A/56/453) (9 October)

2002. 'Protection of Children Affected by Armed Conflict: Report of the Special Representative of the Secretary-General for Children and Armed Conflict' (UN Doc. A/57/402) (25 September)

2003. 'Protection of Children Affected by Armed Conflict: Report of the Special Representative of the Secretary-General for Children and Armed Conflict' (UN Doc. A/58/328) (29 August)

2004. 'Promotion and Protection of the Rights of Children: Report of the Special Representative of the Secretary-General for Children and Armed Conflict' (UN Doc. A/59/426) (8 October)

2005. 'Promotion and Protection of the Rights of Children: Report of the Special Representative of the Secretary-General for Children and Armed Conflict' (UN Doc. A/60/335) (7 September)

PAPG [Projet d'Appui de la Société Civile au Processus Gacaca au Rwanda] 2003. 'Compte rendu de la journée de communication et d'échanges sur l'état d'avancement des travaux des juridictions gacaca' (Kigali, August)

Palmer, N. 2015. *Courts in Conflict: Interpreting the Layers of Justice in Post-Genocide Rwanda* (Cambridge: Cambridge University Press)

Parmar, S., Roseman, M.J., Siegrist, S. and Sowa, T. (eds.) 2010. *Children and Transitional Justice: Truth-Telling, Accountability and Reconciliation* (Cambridge, MA: UNICEF; Harvard Law School)

Parquet Général 2003. 'Instruction concernant l'exécution du Communiqué Présidentiel du 01 janvier 2003 venant de la Présidence de la République qui concerne la libération provisoire des détenus des différentes catégories' (9 January)

Parry Williams, J. 1998. 'The Process of Child Law Reform', in C. Petty and M. Brown (eds.), *Justice for Children: Challenges for Policy and Practice in Sub-Saharan Africa* (London: Save the Children) 26

Pedersen, M.B. 2013. 'The Theoretical Case for Principled Engagement', in M.B. Pedersen and D. Kinley (eds.), *Principled Engagement: Negotiating Human Rights in Repressive States* (Farnham: Ashgate) 13

Pedersen, M.B. and Kinley, D. (eds.) 2013. *Principled Engagement: Negotiating Human Rights in Repressive States* (Farnham: Ashgate)

Peter, C. and Kibalama, E. 2006. *Searching for Sense and Humanity: Civil Society and the Struggle for a Better Rwanda: A Report of the Fact-finding Mission to Rwanda Organised under the Auspices of Kituo Cha Katiba, July, 2004–February, 2006* (Kampala: Fountain Publishers)

Petty, C. and Brown, M. 1998a. 'Juvenile Justice: The Great Debate', in C. Petty and M. Brown (eds.), *Justice for Children: Challenges for Policy and Practice in Sub-Saharan Africa* (London: Save the Children) 5

(eds.) 1998b. *Justice for Children: Challenges for Policy and Practice in Sub-Saharan Africa* (London: Save the Children)

Pottier, J. 2002. *Re-Imagining Rwanda: Conflict, Survival, and Disinformation in the Late Twentieth Century* (Cambridge: Cambridge University Press)

Preparatory Committee 1998. 'Report of the Preparatory Committee on the Establishment of an International Criminal Court' (UN Doc. A/CONF.183/2/Add.1) (14 April)

President of the Security Council 2000. 'Letter from the President of the Security Council Addressed to the Secretary-General' (UN Doc. S/2000/1234) (22 December)

2001. 'Letter from the President of the Security Council Addressed to the Secretary-General' (UN Doc. S/2001/95) (31 January)

PRI 2000. 'Rwanda Country Programme: Annual Report'

2002a. 'PRI Research on Gacaca report, Rapport I: "Gacaca Jurisdictions and its Preparations" July–December 2001' (January)

2002b. 'PRI Research on Gacaca report, Rapport III, April–June 2002'

2003a. 'PRI Research on Gacaca report, Report IV: "The Guilty Plea Procedure, Cornerstone of the Rwandan Justice System"' (January)

2003b. 'PRI Research on the Gacaca, Report V' (September)

2003c. 'Rwanda Country Programme: Annual Report 2003'

2004a. 'Research Report on the Gacaca, Report VI: From Camp to Hill, the Reintegration of Released Prisoners' (May)

2004b. 'Research Report on Gacaca Courts: Gacaca and Reconciliation – Kibuye Case Study' (May)

2005. 'Integrated Report on Gacaca Research and Monitoring: Pilot Phase January 2002–December 2004' (December)

2006. 'Monitoring and Research report on the Gacaca: Information-Gathering during the National Phase' (June)

2007. 'Monitoring and Research Report on the Gacaca: Community Service (TIG) – Areas of Reflection' (March)

2008. 'Monitoring and Research Report on the Gacaca: Testimonies and Evidence in the Gacaca Courts' (August)

2010. 'Final Monitoring and Research Report on the Gacaca Process: The Contribution of the Gacaca Jurisdictions to Resolving Cases Arising From the Genocide – Contributions, Limitations and Expectations of the Post-Gacaca Phase'

Price Cohen, C. 1987. 'Elasticity of Obligation and the Drafting of the Convention on the Rights of the Child' 3 *Connecticut Journal of International Law* 71

Prunier, G. 1995. *The Rwanda Crisis: History of a Genocide* (New York: Columbia University Press)

Purdekova, A. 2011. 'Rwanda's Ingando Camps: Liminality and the Reproduction of Power', University of Oxford Refugee Studies Centre Working Paper Series No. 80 (September)

Putnam, T. 2002. 'Human Rights and Sustainable Peace', in S.J. Stedman, D. Rothchild and E.M. Cousens (eds.), *Ending Civil Wars: The Implementation of Peace Agreements* (London; Boulder, CO: Lynne Rienner Publishers, Inc.) 237

Quesnel, J. 2002. 'End-Decade Review of Strategic Lessons Learned from UNICEF's Experience: An Ad Hoc Effort to Access Institutional Memory', Working Paper Series (New York: UNICEF) (December)

Racelis, M. 2001. 'Controversy and Continuity: Programming for Women in Jim Grant's UNICEF', in R. Jolly (ed.) *Jim Grant: UNICEF Visionary* (Florence: UNICEF) 111

Racine, S. 1998. 'Etude portant sur les moyens d'accélérer les procès des mineurs accusés de crimes de génocide: Etude réalisée pour l'UNICEF-Rwanda' (Kigali, January)

Ratner, S.R. 2011. 'Law Promotion Beyond Law Talk: The Red Cross, Persuasion, and the Laws of War' 22 *EJIL* 459

2013. 'Persuading to Comply: On the Deployment and Avoidance of Legal Argumentation', in J.L. Dunoff and M.A. Pollack (eds.), *Interdisciplinary Perspectives on International Law and International Relations: The State of the Art* (Cambridge: Cambridge University Press) 568

Raustiala, K. and Slaughter, A-M. 2002. 'International Law, International Relations and Compliance', in W. Carlsnaes, T. Risse and B.A. Simmons (eds.), *Handbook of International Relations* (London: SAGE Publications) 538

RCN 1995. 'La Reconstruction d'un Système Judiciaire Démocratique: Programmes d'Assistance Technique, octobre 1994–mars 1995 – Compilation'

1996. 'Situation des Parquets au Rwanda', in J-F. Dupaquier (ed.), *La justice internationale face au drame rwandais* (Paris: Karthala) 37

2000. 'Justice rwandaise liée au génocide et aux massacres – Programme d'appuis urgents aux aveux et aux procédures: Rapport d'activités couvrant la période d'avril 1999 à juillet 2000'

2001. 'Appui urgent aux procédures judiciaires liées au contentieux du génocide: Rapport d'activités 1er juin 2001 au 30 novembre 2001'

2002a. 'Appui urgent aux procédures judiciaires liées au contentieux du génocide: Rapport d'activités 1er janvier 2001 au 31 décembre 2001'

2002b. 'Programme d'aide à la justice classique (AJC) – "Appui urgent aux procédures judiciaires liées au contentieux du génocide rwandais": Rapport d'activités Décembre 2001/Mai 2002'

2002c. 'Programme d'aide à la justice classique (AJC) – "Appui urgent aux procédures judiciaires liées au contentieux du génocide rwandais": Rapport d'activités Juin 2001/Mai 2002; Juin 2001/Septembre 2002'

2002d. 'Appui urgent aux procédures judiciaires liées au contentieux du génocide: Rapport d'activités 1er janvier 2002 au 30 septembre 2002'

2003a. 'Programme Rwanda – "Appui urgent aux procédures judiciaires liées au contentieux du génocide": Rapport d'activités pour la période du 1er janvier au 31 mars 2003'

2003b. 'Programme Rwanda – "Appui urgent aux procédures judiciaires liées au contentieux du génocide": Rapport d'activités pour la période du 1er juillet au 30 septembre 2003'

2003c. '"Aide urgente aux procédures judiciaires relatives au génocide" 1er décembre 2001 au 31 mars 2003: Rapport d'activités pour l'Union Européenne'

2004a. 'Programme Rwanda – "Appui urgent aux procédures judiciaires liées au contentieux du génocide et aux massacres": Rapport d'activités pour la période du 1er janvier 2004 au 30 juin 2004'

2004b. 'Programme Rwanda – "Appui urgent aux procédures judiciaires liées au contentieux du génocide et aux massacres": Rapport d'activités du 1er janvier 2003 au 30 septembre 2004'

2004c. 'Programme Rwanda – "Appui urgent aux procédures judiciaires liées au contentieux du génocide et aux massacres": Rapport d'activités pour la période du 1er juillet 2004 au 30 septembre 2004'

2004d. 'Rapport d'activité 2004 – "Appui urgent aux procédures judiciaires liées au contentieux du génocide et aux massacres", République du Rwanda'

2004e. 'Programme Rwanda – Synthèse des activités pour la période de 1994 à 2004'

2005. 'République du Rwanda – "Programme d'appui au règlement du contentieux du génocide et à la justice de proximité": Projet 2005'

Reis, C. 1997. 'Trying the Future: Avenging the Past: The Implications of Prosecuting Children for Participation in Internal Armed Conflict' 28 *Columbia Human Rights Law Review* 629

Rettig, M. 2011. 'The Sovu Trials: The Impact of Genocide Justice on One Community', in S. Straus and L. Waldorf (eds.), *Remaking Rwanda: State*

Building and Human Rights after Mass Violence (Madison, WI: The University of Wisconsin Press) 194

Reuters 2000. 'Rwanda Vows to Speed Trials of Minors: 4,000 Youths Held in 1994 Massacres' (13 August)

Reyntjens, F. 2004. 'Rwanda, Ten Years On: From Genocide to Dictatorship' 103 *African Affairs* 177

Reyntjens, F. and Vandeginste, S. 2005. 'Rwanda: An Atypical Transition', in E. Skaar, S. Gloppen and A. Suhrke (eds.), *Roads to Reconciliation* (Lanham, MD: Lexington Books) 101

Risse, T. and Ropp, S.C. 2013. 'Introduction and Overview', in T. Risse, S.C. Ropp and K. Sikkink (eds.), *The Persistent Power of Human Rights: From Commitment to Compliance* (Cambridge: Cambridge University Press) 3

Risse, T. Ropp, S.C. and Sikkink, K. (eds.) 2013. *The Persistent Power of Human Rights: From Commitment to Compliance* (Cambridge: Cambridge University Press)

Rosen, D.M. 2019. 'Child Soldiers in Historical and Comparative Perspective: Creating a Space for Data-Driven Analysis', in M.A. Drumbl and J.C. Barrett (eds.), *Research Handbook on Child Soldiers* (Cheltenham: Edward Elgar Publishing), 150

Rutazana, A. 1998. 'La Répression des Mineurs Auteurs du Crime de Génocide ou des Crimes Contre l'Humanité en Droit Rwandais' (unpublished BA thesis, Faculty of Law, National University of Rwanda, Butare)

Sandoz, Y. Swinarski C. and Zimmermann, B. (eds.) 1987. *Commentary on the Additional Protocols of 8 June 1977 to the Geneva Conventions of 12 August 1949* (Geneva: ICRC; Martinus Nijhoff Publishers)

Santos País, M. 1997. 'The Convention on the Rights of the Child', in OHCHR, UN Institute for Training and Research and UN Staff College Project, *Manual on Human Rights Reporting: Under Six Major International Human Rights Instruments* (Geneva: UN) 393

Sarkin, J. 2001. 'The Tension between Justice and Reconciliation in Rwanda: Politics, Human Rights, Due Process and the Role of the *Gacaca* Courts in Dealing with the Genocide' 45 *Journal of African Law* 143

SCF Rwanda 1998. 'Post-Genocide Reform of Children's Law in Rwanda', in C. Petty and M. Brown (eds.), *Justice for Children: Challenges for Policy and Practice in Sub-Saharan Africa* (London: Save the Children) 112

SCF-USA 1996. 'Children, Genocide and Justice: Rwandan Perspectives on Culpability and Punishment for Children Convicted of Crimes Associated with Genocide' (Save the Children Federation USA)

Schabas, W.A. 1996. 'Justice, Democracy, and Impunity in Post-Genocide Rwanda: Searching for Solutions to Impossible Problems' 7 *Criminal Law Forum* 523

2005. 'Genocide Trials and *Gacaca* Courts' 3 *Journal of International Criminal Justice* 879

2008a. 'Article 37, Prohibition of Torture, Prohibition of Death Penalty and Life Imprisonment and the Deprivation of Liberty', in W.A. Schabas, *War Crimes and Human Rights: Essays on the Death Penalty, Justice and Accountability* (London: Cameron May) 161

2008b. 'The Rwanda Case: Sometimes It's Impossible', in W.A. Schabas, *War Crimes and Human Rights: Essays on the Death Penalty, Justice and Accountability* (London: Cameron May) 531

2008c. 'Post-Genocide Justice in Rwanda: A Spectrum of Options', in P. Clark and Z. Kaufman (eds.), *After Genocide: Transitional Justice, Post-Conflict Reconstruction and Reconciliation in Rwanda and Beyond* (London: Hurst & Company) 207

Schabas, W.A. and Imbleau, M. 1997. *Introduction to Rwandan Law* (Cowansville, Canada: Les Editions Yvon Blais)

Schotsmans, M. 2011. '"But We Also Support Monitoring": INGO Monitoring and Donor Support to *Gacaca* Justice in Rwanda' 5 *The International Journal of Transitional Justice* 390

SCSL [Special Court for Sierra Leone] 2002. 'Special Court Prosecutor Says He Will Not Prosecute Children' (press release, Public Affairs Office) (2 November)

Shaffer, G. and Ginsburg, T. 2012. 'The Empirical Turn in International Legal Scholarship' 106 *American Journal of International Law* 1

Sharp, D.N. 2018. 'Pragmatism and Multidimensionality in Human Rights Advocacy' 40 *Human Rights Quarterly* 499

Shelton, D. 2000. 'Introduction: Law, Non-Law and the Problem of Soft Law', in D. Shelton (ed.), *Commitment and Compliance: The Role of Non-Binding Norms in the International Legal System* (Oxford: Oxford University Press) 1

Shepler, S. 2005. 'The Rites of the Child: Global Discourses of Youth and Reintegrating Child Soldiers in Sierra Leone' 4 *Journal of Human Rights* 197

2014. *Childhood Deployed: Remaking Child Soldiers in Sierra Leone* (New York; London: New York University Press)

Simmons, B.A. 2009. *Mobilizing for Human Rights: International Law in Domestic Politics* (Cambridge: Cambridge University Press)

2013. 'International Law', in W. Carlsnaes, T. Risse and B.A. Simmons (eds.), *Handbook of International Relations* (London: SAGE Publications) 352

Sloth-Nielsen, J. and Gallinetti, J. 2004. *Child Justice in Africa: A Guide to Good Practice* (Bellville, South Africa: Community Law Centre, University of Western Cape)

Smith, L. 2009. 'Monitoring the CRC', in G. Alfredsson, J. Grimheden, B.G. Ramcharan, and A. de Zayas (eds.), *International Human Rights Monitoring Mechanisms: Essays in Honour of Jakob Th. Möller* (Leiden; Boston: Martinus Nijhoff Publishers) 109

Steinl, L. 2017. *Child Soldiers as Agents of War and Peace: A Restorative Transitional Justice Approach to Accountability for Crimes Under International Law* (The Hague: TMC Asser Press)

Straus, S. 2004. 'How Many Perpetrators Were There in the Rwandan Genocide? An Estimate' 6 *Journal of Genocide Research* 85

2006. *The Order of Genocide: Race, Power, and War in Rwanda* (Ithaca, NY: Cornell University Press)

Sullo, P. 2012. 'When Hurbinek Survives – Transitional Justice and Children's Rights: Lessons Learnt from Rwanda', in I. Derluyn, C. Mels, S. Parmentier and W. Vandenhole (eds.), *Re-Member: Rehabilitation, Reintegration and Reconciliation of War-Affected Children* (Cambridge: Intersentia) 127

Teitel, R.G. 2000. *Transitional Justice* (Oxford: Oxford University Press)

Tertsakian, C. 2008. *Le Château: The Lives of Prisoners in Rwanda* (London: Arves Books)

2011. '"All Rwandans Are Afraid of Being Arrested One Day": Prisoners Past, Present and Future', in S. Straus and L. Waldorf (eds.), *Remaking Rwanda: State Building and Human Rights after Mass Violence* (Madison, WI: The University of Wisconsin Press) 210

Thompson, C. 1999. 'Beyond Civil Society: Child Soldiers as Citizens in Mozambique' 26 *Review of African Political Economy* 191

Thomson, S. 2011. 'Reeducation for Reconciliation: Participant Observations on *Ingando*', in S. Straus and L. Waldorf (eds.), *Remaking Rwanda: State Building and Human Rights after Mass Violence* (Madison, WI: The University of Wisconsin Press) 331

Tobin, J. 2011. 'Understanding a Human Rights Based Approach to Matters Involving Children: Conceptual Foundations and Strategic Considerations', in A. Invernizzi and J. Williams (eds.), *The Human Rights of Children: From Visions to Implementation* (Farnham: Ashgate) 61

Tomuschat, C. 2008. *Human Rights: Between Idealism and Realism* (Oxford: Oxford University Press)

TRC [Truth and Reconciliation Commission] 2004: *Witness to Truth: Report of the Sierra Leone Truth & Reconciliation Commission*, Vol. 3B, Ch. 4

Tully, L.D. 2003. 'Human Rights Compliance and the Gacaca Jurisdictions in Rwanda' 26 *Boston College International and Comparative Law Review* 385

Türkelli, G.E. and Vandenhole, W. 2012. 'The Convention on the Rights of the Child: Repertoires of NGO Participation' 12 *Human Rights Law Review* 33

Twum-Danso, A. 2008. 'A Cultural Bridge, Not an Imposition: Legitimizing Children's Rights in the Eyes of Local Communities' 3 *The Journal of the History of Childhood and Youth* 391

Twum-Danso Imoh, A. 2011. 'Searching for a Middle Ground in Children's Rights in Ghana' 10 *Journal of Human Rights* 376

UN Commission on Human Rights. Resolution S-3/1 on the Situation of Human Rights in Rwanda (UN Doc. E/CN.4/S-3/1) (25 May 1994)

Resolution 1995/91 on the Situation of Human Rights in Rwanda (UN Doc. E/CN.4/RES/ 1995/176) (8 March 1995)

Resolution 1996/76 on the Situation of Human Rights in Rwanda (UN Doc. E/CN.4/1996/ 76) (23 April 1996)

Resolution 1997/66 on the Situation of Human Rights in Rwanda (UN Doc. E/CN.4/1997 /66) (16 April 1997)

Resolution 1998/69 on the Situation of Human Rights in Rwanda (UN Doc. E/CN.4/RES/ 1998/69) (21 April 1998)

Resolution 1999/20 on the Situation of Human Rights in Rwanda (UN Doc. E/CN.4/RES/ 1999/20) (23 April 1999)

Resolution 2000/21 on the Situation of Human Rights in Rwanda (UN Doc. E/CN.4/2000/ 21) (18 April 2000)

Resolution 2001/23 on the Situation of Human Rights in Rwanda (UN Doc. E/CN.4/2001/ 23) (20 April 2001)

UNDG [United Nations Development Group] 2000a. 'Common Country Assessment 1999–2000, Paper 6: Governance, Justice, Human Rights and National Reconciliation'

2000b. 'Common Country Assessment 1999–2000, Paper 11: Child Protection'

UNDP [United Nations Development Programme] 1999. 'Rwanda: 1999 Human Development Report' (October)

2005. 'Annual Report 2004'

2006. 'Annual Report 2005'

2007. 'Annual Report 2006'

2008. 'Annual Report 2007'

2009. 'Annual Report 2008'

UNGA [United Nations General Assembly] Resolution 57(1) on Establishment of an International Children's Fund (11 December 1946)

Resolution 417(V) on Continuing Needs of Children: United Nations International Children's Emergency Fund (1 December 1950)

Resolution 802(VIII) on United Nations Children's Fund (UNICEF) (6 October 1953)

Resolution 49/23 on Emergency International Assistance for a Solution to the Problem of Refugees, the Restoration of Total Peace, Reconstruction and Socio-Economic Development in War-Stricken Rwanda (UN Doc. A/RES/49/ 23) (22 December 1994)

Resolution 49/206 on the Situation of Human Rights in Rwanda (UN Doc. A/ RES/49/206) (6 March 1995)

Resolution 51/77 on The Rights of the Child (UN Doc. A/RES/51/77) (12 December 1996)

Resolution 50/200 on the Situation of Human Rights in Rwanda (UN Doc. A/ RES/50/200) (11 March 1996)

Resolution 51/114 on the Situation of Human Rights in Rwanda (UN Doc. A/ RES/51/114) (7 March 1997)

Resolution 52/146 on the Situation of Human Rights in Rwanda (UN Doc. A/ RES/52/146) (9 March 1998)

Resolution 53/156 on the Situation of Human Rights in Rwanda (UN Doc. A/RES/53/156) (9 February 1999)

Resolution 54/188 on the Situation of Human Rights in Rwanda (UN Doc. A/RES/54/188) (29 February 2000)

UNHRFOR [United Nations Human Rights Field Operation in Rwanda] 1996a. 'Update on the Human Rights Situation during April 1996'

1996b. 'The Administration of Justice in Post-Genocide Rwanda' (June)

1997a. 'Legal Unit: Structure, Priorities and Action Programme for 1997' (February)

1997b. 'Genocide Trials to 30 June 1997: Status Report as of 15 July 1997'

1997c. 'Procès de Génocide au 31 octobre 1997: Rapport de situation du 19 décembre 1997'

UNICEF 1953. 'A Special Report of the Executive Board', Economic and Social Council Official Records: Sixteenth Session, Supplement No. 6A (UN Doc. E/ICEF/226) (25 March)

1980. 'Report of the Executive Board', Economic and Social Council Official Records: Supplement No. 11 (UN Doc. E/ICEF/673) (19–30 May)

1986a. 'Policy Review: Children in Especially Difficult Circumstances' (UN Doc. E/ICEF/1986/L.3) (27 February)

1986b 'Policy Review – Overview: Children in Especially Difficult Circumstances' (UN Doc. E/ICEF/1986/L.6) (28 February)

1986c Executive Board Decision 1986/12 on Children in Especially Difficult Circumstances (25 April) in 'Report of the Executive Board', Economic and Social Council Official Records, Supplement No. 8 (UN Doc. E/1986/L.29) (14–26 April) 44

1990a. 'Development Goals and Strategies for Children: Priorities for UNICEF Action in the 1990s' (UN Doc E/ICEF/1990/L.5) (13 February)

1990b. 'Plan of Action for Implementing the World Declaration on the Survival, Protection and Development of Children in the 1990s' (UN Doc. A/45/625, Annex) (18 October)

1991a. 'The Role of UNICEF in the Implementation of the Convention on the Rights of the Child' (UN Doc. E/ICEF/1991/L.7) (6 February)

1991b. *The Convention: Child Rights and UNICEF Experience at the Country Level* (Florence: UNICEF)

1992. 'Executive Directive: Role of UNICEF in the Implementation of the Convention on the Rights of the Child' (2 July)

1993a. 'Comments of the Executive Director on the Evaluation of UNICEF' (UN Doc. E/ICEF/1993/CRP.8) (24 February)

1993b. 'Statement by Mr James P Grant, Executive Director of the United Nations Children's Fund (UNICEF) at the close of the General Debate of the 1993 Executive Board' (UN Doc. E/ICEF/1993/CRP.17) (29 April)

1995a. 'Report of the Executive Director' (UN Doc. E/ICEF1995/14 (Part II)) (20 April)

1995b. 'Management Review: Issues Concerning the UNICEF Mission' (UN Doc. E/ICEF/1995/AB/L.11) (25 April)

1995c. 'UNICEF Emergency Services: Mission and Strategy' (UN Doc. E/ICEF/1996/4) (24 November)

1995d. 'UNICEF Emergency Operations' (UN Doc. E/ICEF/1996/7) (1 December)

1995e. 'Annual Report – 1 January to 31 December 1995'

1996a. 'UNICEF Mission Statement' (UN Doc. E/ICEF/1996/12) (Part I, decision 1996/1) (January)

1996b. 'A Review of UNICEF Policies and Strategies on Child Protection' (UN Doc. E/ICEF/1996/14) (8 April)

1996c. 'Report of the Executive Director' (UN Doc. E/ICEF/1996/10) (17 April)

1996d. 'Annual Report of the United Nations Children's Fund to the Economic and Social Council' (UN Doc. E/1996/69) (12 June)

1996e. 'Executive Board of the United Nations Children's Fund: Report on the First, Second and Third Regular Sessions and Annual Session of 1996', Economic and Social Council Official Records, Supplement No. 12 (UN Doc. E/ICEF/1996/12/Rev.1)

1996f. 'Letter from Carol Bellamy, UNICEF Executive Director, to the UN Secretary General' (14 November) Folder S-1083-0035-05

1997a. 'Children in Need of Special Protection Measures: Report on Steps for Policy Implementation' (UN Doc. E/ICEF/1997/16) (25 March)

1997b. 'Executive Board of the United Nations Children's Fund: Report on the First, Second and Third Regular Sessions and Annual Session of 1997', Economic and Social Council Official Records, Supplement No. 12 (UN Doc. E/ICEF/1997/12/Rev.1)

1997c. 'Children and Women in Emergencies: Strategic Priorities and Operational Concerns for UNICEF' (UN Doc. E/ICEF/1997/7) (11 November)

1998a. 'Innocenti Digest No.3: Juvenile Justice' (Florence: UNICEF) (January)

1998b. 'Statement by Carol Bellamy, Executive Director of the United Nations Children's Fund, at the Opening of the First Regular Session of the UNICEF Executive Board New York, 26 January 1998' (UN Doc. E/ICEF/1998/CRP.2) (26 January)

1998c. 'Implementation of the UNICEF Policy on Children in Need of Special Protection Measures' (UN Doc. E/ICEF/1998/CRP.11) (20 March)

1998d. 'Guidelines for Human Rights-Based Programming Approach. A Human Rights Approach for Children and Women: What It Is, and Some Changes It Will Bring' (CF/EXD/1998–04) (21 April)

1999a. 'Programme Cooperation for Children and Women from a Human Rights Perspective' (UN Doc. E/ICEF/1999/11) (5 April)

1999b. 'Report of the Executive Director: Progress and Achievements against the Medium-Term Plan' (UN Doc. E/ICEF/1994/4 (Part II)) (22 April)

1999c. *Human Rights for Children and Women: How UNICEF Helps Make them a Reality* (New York: UNICEF) (June)

2000. 'Report of the Executive Director: Progress and Achievements against the Medium-Term Plan' (UN Doc. E/ICEF/2000/4 (Part II)) (12 April)

2001. 'UNICEF and Juvenile Justice: A Proposed Policy and Action Framework for UNICEF's Activities for Children in Conflict with the Law, Discussion Paper' (draft) (February)

2002. *Children Affected by Armed Conflict: UNICEF Actions* (New York: UNICEF)

2005a. 'Evaluation of UNICEF Learning Strategy to Strengthen Staff Competencies for Humanitarian Response 2000–2004', Evaluation Report (June)

2005b. 'Expert Discussion on Transitional Justice and Children, 10–12 November 2005: Background Documents' (Florence: UNICEF Innocenti Research Centre)

2005c. 'Expert Discussion on Transitional Justice and Children, 10–12 November 2005: Outcome Document' (Florence: UNICEF Innocenti Research Centre)

2007a. *Programme Policy and Procedure Manual: Programme Operations Revised February 2007* (New York: UNICEF)

2007b. *Protecting the World's Children: Impact of the Convention on the Rights of the Child in Diverse Legal Systems* (Cambridge: Cambridge University Press)

2008a. 'UN Common Approach to Justice for Children' (March)

2008b. 'UNICEF Child Protection Strategy' (UN Doc. E/ICEF/2008/5/Rev.1) (20 May)

2010. 'Key Principles for Children and Transitional Justice: Involvement of Children and Consideration of Children's Rights in Truth, Justice and Reconciliation Processes: Outcome of Children and Transitional Justice Conference, Harvard Law School, Cambridge, Massachusetts, 27–29 April 2009', in S. Parmar, M.J. Roseman, S. Siegrist and T. Sowa (eds.), *Children and Transitional Justice: Truth-Telling, Accountability and Reconciliation* (Cambridge, MA: UNICEF; Harvard Law School), Annex, 403

(undated) 'Toolkit on Diversion and Alternatives to Detention: Why does UNICEF Promote Diversion and Alternatives?' [www.unicef.org/tdad/index_55676.html (accessed 17 December 2018)]

UNICEF and OSRSG-CAAC [Office of the Special Representative of the Secretary-General for Children and Armed Conflict] 2009. 'Machel Study 10-Year Strategic Review: Children and Conflict in a Changing World' (April)

UNICEF Rwanda 1995a. 'Protection of Children in Conflict with the Law Project 1995' (Project Report)

1995b. 'Children in Prison' (May) (press release)

1995c. 'The Protection and Best Interests of Children in Conflict with the Law in Rwanda: CEDC Focal Points Meeting, Kigali, 5–6 November'

1996a. 'Children in Conflict with the Law, and Women with Children in Prison: Penitentiary, Reeducation and Production Centers – Project Submitted to the Dutch Government' (February)

1996b. 'Rwanda Emergency Programme: Progress Report 2, April '95 to January '96' (February)

1996c. 'Rwanda Emergency Programme: Progress Report 3, January to December 1996' (November)

1996d. 'Protection and Rights of the Child Unit: Policies and Strategies – Draft proposal for Discussion and Comments' (CEDC Section)

1997a. 'Fact Sheet: Trials of Minors Accused of Genocide' (July)

1997b. 'Fact Sheet: Child Trials and Children in Detention in Rwanda' (September)

1997c. 'Child Protection Survey'

1997d. 'Children and Women of Rwanda: A Situation Analysis of Social Sectors' (Kigali, Rwanda)

2000. 'UNICEF Country Programme in Rwanda: Progress Report 6, January to December 1999' (July)

2002. 'UNICEF Rwanda 2002 Annual Report' (December)

UNICEF Rwanda Consultant 1996. 'Report on Children and Women with Infants in Detention'

UN Independent Inquiry 1999. 'Report of the Independent Inquiry into the Actions of the United Nations during the 1994 Genocide in Rwanda' (UN Doc. S/1999/1257) (15 December)

UNSC [UN Security Council] Resolution 912 (UN Doc. S/RES/912) (21 April 1994)

Resolution 1612 (UN Doc. S/RES/1612) (26 July 2005)

UNSG [UN Secretary-General] 1994. 'Report of the Secretary-General on the Situation in Rwanda' (UN Doc. S/ 1994/640) (31 May)

1997. 'Report of the Secretary-General on International Assistance to Rwanda for the Reintegration of Returning Refugees, the Restoration of Total Peace, Reconstruction and Socio-Economic Development' (UN Doc. A/52/568) (5 November)

1998. 'Coordination of the Policies and Activities of the Specialized Agencies and Other Bodies of the United Nations System Related to the Coordinated Follow-Up to and Implementation of the Vienna Declaration and Programme of Action, Report of the Secretary-General' (UN Doc. E/1998/60) (1 June)

2000a. 'Report of the Secretary-General on Children and Armed Conflict' (UN Doc. A/55/ 163-S/2000/712) (19 July)

2000b. 'Report of the Secretary-General on the Establishment of a Special Court for Sierra Leone' (UN Doc. S/2000/915) (4 October)

2001a. 'Letter from the Secretary-General Addressed to the President of the Security Council' (UN Doc S/2001/40) (12 January)

2001b. 'Report of the Secretary-General on Children and Armed Conflict' (UN Doc. A/56/ 342-S/2001/852) (7 September)

2002. 'Report of the Secretary-General on Children and Armed Conflict' (UN Doc. S/ 2002/1299) (26 November)

2003. 'Report of the Secretary-General on Children and Armed Conflict' (UN Doc. A/58/ 546-S/2003/1053) (10 November)

2004. 'Report of the Secretary-General on the Rule of Law and Transitional Justice in Conflict and Post-Conflict Societies' (UN Doc. S/2004/616) (23 August)

2005. 'Report of the Secretary-General on Children and Armed Conflict' (UN Doc. A/59/ 695-S/2005/72) (9 February)

2006. 'Report of the Secretary-General on Children and Armed Conflict' (UN Doc. A/61/ 529-S/2006/826) (26 October)

2007. 'Report of the Secretary-General on Children and Armed Conflict' (UN Doc. A/62/ 609-S/2007/757) (21 December)

2008. 'Guidance Note of the Secretary-General: UN Approach to Justice for Children' (September)

2009. 'Report of the Secretary-General on Children and Armed Conflict' (UN Doc. A/63/ 785-S/2009/158) (26 March)

2010. 'Report of the Secretary-General on Children and Armed Conflict' (UN Doc. A/64/ 742-S/2010/181) (13 April)

2011. 'Report of the Secretary-General on Children and Armed Conflict' (UN Doc. A/65 /820-S/2011/250) (23 April)

2012. 'Report of the Secretary-General on Children and Armed Conflict' (UN Doc. A/66/ 782-S/2012/261) (26 April)

2013. 'Report of the Secretary-General on Children and Armed Conflict' (UN Doc. A/67/ 845-S/2013/245) (15 May)

2014. 'Report of the Secretary-General on Children and Armed Conflict' (UN Doc. A/68/ 878-S/2014/339) (15 May)

2015. 'Report of the Secretary-General on Children and Armed Conflict' (UN Doc. A/69/ 926-S/2015/409) (5 June)

2016. 'Report of the Secretary-General on Children and Armed Conflict' (UN Doc. A/70/836-S/2016/360) (20 April)

2017. 'Report of the Secretary-General on Children and Armed Conflict' (UN Doc. A/72/361-S/2017/821)

2018. 'Report of the Secretary-General on Children and Armed Conflict' (UN Doc. A/72/865-S/2018/465) (16 May)

US Department of Defense 2010. 'DOD Announces Sentence for Detainee Omar Khadr' (press release) (31 October)

Uvin, P. and Mironko, C. 2003. 'Western and Local Approaches to Justice in Rwanda' 9 *Global Governance* 219

Van Bueren, G. 1998. *The International Law on the Rights of the Child* (The Hague: Martinus Nijhoff Publishers)

2011. 'Acknowledging Children as International Citizens: A Child-Sensitive Communication Mechanism for the Convention on the Rights of the Child', in A. Invernizzi and J. Williams (eds.), *The Human Rights of Children: From Visions to Implementation* (Farnham: Ashgate) 117

van Krieken, P. 2000. 'Rwanda: Children in Conflict with the Law – A Case Study' (The Hague: Röling Foundation) (September/October)

Veale, A. 1999. 'War, Conflict, Rehabilitation and Children's Rights in Rwanda' *Trocaire Development Review* 105

2006. 'The Criminal Responsibility of Former Child Soldiers: Contributions from Psychology', in K. Arts and V. Popovski (eds.), *International Criminal Accountability and the Rights of Children* (The Hague: Hague Academic Press) 97

Veale, A. and Stavrou, A. 2003. *Violence, Reconciliation and Identity: The Reintegration of the Lord's Resistance Army Child Abductees in Northern Uganda* (Pretoria: Institute for Security Studies)

Veerman, P. and Waldman, A. 1996. 'When Can Children and Adolescents be Detained Separately from Adults?' 4 *The International Journal of Children's Rights* 147

Verdirame, G. and Harrell-Bond, B. 2005. *Rights in Exile: Janus-Faced Humanitarianism* (New York; Oxford: Berghahn Books)

Waldorf, L. 2006. 'Mass Justice for Mass Atrocity: Rethinking Local Justice as Transitional Justice' 79 *Temple Law Review* 1

2009a. 'Revisiting *Hotel Rwanda*: Genocide Ideology, Reconciliation and Rescuers' 11 *Journal of Genocide Research* 101

2009b. 'Transitional Justice and DDR: The Case of Rwanda' (International Center for Transitional Justice) (June)

Waschefort, G. 2014. *International Law and Child Soldiers* (Oxford: Hart Publishing)

Wessells, M. 2009. *Child Soldiers: From Violence to Protection* (London: Harvard University Press)

West, K. 2001. *Agents of Altruism: The Expansion of Humanitarian NGOs in Rwanda and Afghanistan* (Aldershot: Ashgate)

White, N.D. 2005. 'Towards a Strategy for Human Rights Protection in Post-Conflict Situations', in N.D. White and D. Klaasen (eds.), *The UN, Human Rights and Post-Conflict Situations* (New York; Manchester: Manchester University Press) 463

White, N.D. and Klaasen, D. 2005. 'An Emerging Legal Regime?', in N.D. White and D. Klaasen (eds.), *The UN, Human Rights and Post-Conflict Situations* (New York; Manchester: Manchester University Press) 1

White, N.D. and Odello, M. 2007. 'The Legal Base for Human Rights Field Operations', in M. O'Flaherty (ed.), *The Human Rights Field Operation: Law, Theory and Practice* (Aldershot: Ashgate) 47

Working Group to the Commission on Human Rights 1988: 'Question of a Convention on the Rights of the Child: Report of the Working Group on a Draft Convention on the Rights of the Child' (UN Doc. E/CN.4/1988/28) (6 April)

1989: 'Question of a Convention on the Rights of the Child: Report of the Working Group on a Draft Convention on the Rights of the Child' (UN Doc. E/CN.4/1989/48) (2 March)

Zermatten, J. 2010. 'The Best Interests of the Child Principle: Literal Analysis and Function' 18 *International Journal of Children's Rights* 483

Zerrougui, L. 2013a. 'Promotion and Protection of the Rights of Children: Report of the Special Representative of the Secretary-General for Children and Armed Conflict' (UN Doc. A/68/267) (5 August)

2013b. 'Promotion and Protection of all Human Rights, Civil, Political, Economic, Social and Cultural Rights, Including the Right to Development: Annual Report of the Special Representative of the Secretary-General for Children and Armed Conflict' (UN Doc. A/HRC/25/46) (26 December)

2014a. 'Promotion and Protection of the Rights of Children: Report of the Special Representative of the Secretary-General for Children and Armed Conflict' (UN Doc. A/69/212) (31 July 2014)

2014b. 'Promotion and Protection of all Human Rights, Civil, Political, Economic, Social and Cultural Rights, Including the Right to Development: Annual Report of the Special Representative of the Secretary-General for Children and Armed Conflict' (UN Doc. A/HRC/28/54) (29 December)

2015a. 'Promotion and Protection of the Rights of Children: Report of the Special Representative of the Secretary-General for Children and Armed Conflict' (UN Doc. A/69/926) (5 June)

2015b. 'Promotion and Protection of the Rights of Children: Report of the Special Representative of the Secretary-General for Children and Armed Conflict' (UN Doc. A/70/162) (20 July)

2015c. 'Promotion and Protection of all Human Rights, Civil, Political, Economic, Social and Cultural Rights, Including the Right to Development: Annual Report of the Special Representative of the Secretary-General for Children and Armed Conflict' (UN Doc. A/HRC/31/19) (28 December)

2016a. 'Promotion and Protection of the Rights of Children: Report of the Special Representative of the Secretary-General for Children and Armed Conflict' (UN Doc. A/71/205) (25 July)

2016b. 'Promotion and Protection of all Human Rights, Civil, Political, Economic, Social and Cultural Rights, Including the Right to Development: Annual Report of the Special Representative of the Secretary-General for Children and Armed Conflict' (UN Doc. A/HRC/34/44) (22 December)

Zimmerman, L. 2017. *Global Norms with a Local Face: Rule-of-Law Promotion and Norm Translation* (Cambridge: Cambridge University Press)

Zorbas, E. 2011. 'Aid Dependence and Policy Independence: Explaining the Rwandan Paradox', in S. Straus and L. Waldorf (eds.), *Remaking Rwanda: State Building and Human Rights after Mass Violence* (Madison, WI: The University of Wisconsin Press) 103

INDEX

For EU product safety concerns, contact us at Calle de José Abascal, 56–1°, 28003 Madrid, Spain or eugpsr@cambridge.org.

www.ingramcontent.com/pod-product-compliance
Lightning Source LLC
LaVergne TN
LVHW011529200926
848484LV00001B/200

* 9 7 8 1 1 0 8 4 9 6 5 5 1 *